Sadlier

WE·BELIEVE

We Live Our Faith

As Members of the Church

Volume II

Sadlier

A Division of William H. Sadlier, Inc.

The Ad Hoc Committee to Oversee the Use of the Catechism, United States Conference of Catholic Bishops, has found this catechetical series, copyright 2007, to be in conformity with the *Catechism of the Catholic Church.*

Nihil Obstat

✠ Most Reverend Robert C. Morlino

Imprimatur

✠ Most Reverend Robert C. Morlino
Bishop of Madison
October 3, 2006

The *Nihil Obstat* and *Imprimatur* are official declarations that a book or pamphlet is free of doctrinal or moral error. No implication is contained therein that those who have granted the *Nihil Obstat* and *Imprimatur* agree with the contents, opinions, or statements expressed.

Acknowledgments

Scripture excerpts are taken from the *New American Bible with Revised New Testament and Psalms* Copyright © 1991, 1986, 1970 Confraternity of Christian Doctrine, Inc., Washington, DC. Used with permission. All rights reserved. No part of the *New American Bible* may be reproduced by any means without permission in writing from the copyright owner.

Excerpts from the English translation of *The Roman Missal* © 1973, International Committee on English in the Liturgy, Inc. (ICEL); excerpts from the English translation of *Rite of Baptism for Children* © 1969, ICEL; excerpts from the English translation of *Rite of Penance* © 1974, ICEL; excerpts from the English translation of *Book of Blessings* © 1988, ICEL. All rights reserved.

Excerpts from *Catholic Household Blessings and Prayers* © 1988 United States Catholic Conference, Inc. Washington, D.C. Used with permission. All rights reserved.

Excerpts from *Sharing Catholic Social Teaching: Challenges and Directions* © 1998, United States Conference of Catholic Bishops, Inc. Washington, D.C. (USCCB). Used with permission. All rights reserved.

English translation of the Glory to the Father, Lord's Prayer, and Apostles' Creed by the International Consultation on English Texts (ICET).

Excerpts from the documents of Vatican II on pages 24, 91, 121, 194, 209, 219, 231, 249, and 261 are as reprinted in *The Documents of Vatican II*, Walter M. Abbott, General Editor, copyright © 1966 America Press.

Excerpt on page 185 from the Vatican II document *Nostra Aetate (Declaration on the Relation of the Church to Non-Christian Religions)* copyright © Libreria Editrice Vaticana.

Excerpts from the encyclical *Pacem in terris (Peace on Earth)*, by Pope John XXIII, April 11, 1963, and the encyclical *Sollicitudo rei socialis (On the Social Concern of the Church)*, by Pope John Paul II, December 30, 1987 copyright © Libreria Editrice Vaticana.

Excerpt from the document *Instruction on Respect for Human Life in Its Origin*, by the Congregation for the Doctrine of the Faith, February 22, 1987, copyright © Libreria Editrice Vaticana.

Excerpts from Pope Benedict XVI's homily on May 7, 2005, and his World Youth Day addresses on August 20 and 21, 2005, copyright © Libreria Editrice Vaticana.

Excerpt from "Prayer in Preparation for World Youth Day, 2005" copyright © Libreria Editrice Vaticana.

Excerpt from *General Directory for Catechesis* copyright © 1997 Libreria Editrice Vaticana. Published in the United States in 1998 by the United States Conference of Catholic Bishops (USCCB), Washington, DC. All rights reserved.

Excerpts from the documents *The Challenge of Peace* (copyright © 1983); *Economic Justice for All* (copyright © 1986); *Living the Gospel of Life* (copyright © 1998); *Pastoral Plan for Pro-Life Activities* (copyright © 2001); *A Matter of the Heart* (copyright © 2002) all copyright © United States Conference of Catholic Bishops (USCCB), Washington, DC. All rights reserved.

Excerpt from Pope John Paul II, *Crossing the Threshold of Hope*, a Borzoi Book, published by Alfred A. Knopf, Inc. Copyright © 1994 by Arnoldo Mondadori Editore. Translation copyright © 1994 by Alfred A. Knopf, Inc.

Excerpt from June Sochen, *Movers and Shakers: American Women Thinkers and Activists, 1900–1970*, Quadrangle Books, New York, 1973. Copyright © 1973.

Excerpt from Thomas McNally, CSC, and William George Storey, DMS, Editors, *Day by Day: The Notre Dame Prayer Book for Students*, Ave Maria Press, Notre Dame, IN, 1975. Copyright © 1975 by Ave Maria Press.

Excerpt from Anne Frank *The Diary of a Young Girl—The Definitive Edition*, edited by Otto H. Frank and Mirjam Pressler. Copyright © 1991 by the Anne Frank-Fonds, Basel, Switzerland; English translation copyright © 1995 by Doubleday, a division of Random House, Inc.

Excerpts from Robert Frost, "Mending Wall" (1914) and "The Road Not Taken" (1920), in *The Poetry of Robert Frost: The Collected Poems, Complete and Unabridged*, Henry Holt and Company, Inc., New York.

Excerpt from Phyllis McGinley, *The Province of the Heart* copyright © 1959.

Excerpt from Rosa Parks' interview with NBC-TV, December 1, 1985, copyright © 1985.

Excerpt from "Interview with Mario Primicerio, the Mayor of Florence" copyright © 1996, *Florence ART News*, Florence, Italy.

English translation of excerpt from Gianni Cardinale, "Il conclave de Papa Luciani: Il signore sceglie la nostra povertà," *30 Giorni*, N. 8, 2003, copyright © 2003.

Excerpt from Maya Lin's design submission for the Vietnam Veterans Memorial competition copyright © 1981.

Excerpt from Marge Kennedy, *Peterson's 100 Things You Can do to Keep Your Family Together . . . When It Sometimes Seems Like the Whole World Is Trying to Pull It Apart* copyright © 1994, Peterson's, the Thomson Company, Lawrenceville, NJ.

Excerpt from Ernst Fischer, *The Necessity of Art: A Marxist Approach*, 1959; English translation by Anna Bostock, 1963. Peregrine/Puffin Books, New York, 1978. Copyright © 1978.

Excerpt from J. R. R. Tolkien, *The Fellowship of the Ring*, Houghton Mifflin Company, New York, 1954. Copyright © 1954, 1965, 1966 by J. R. R. Tolkien. 1954 edition copyright © renewed 1982 by Christopher R. Tolkien, Michael H. R. Tolkien, John F. P. Tolkien, and Priscilla M. A. R. Tolkien. 1965/1966 editions copyright © renewed 1993, 1994 by Christopher R. Tolkien, John F. P. Tolkien, and Priscilla M. A. R. Tolkien.

Excerpt from Virginia Satir, *Friends Can Be Good Medicine*, Avanta, the Virginia Satir Network, Burien WA, 1981. Copyright © 1981.

Excerpt from Max Frisch, *Sketchbook 1946–1949*, translated by Geoffrey Skelton, Harcourt Brace Jovanovich, New York, 1977. Copyright © 1977.

Excerpt from C. S. Lewis, *Letters to Malcolm: Chiefly on Prayer*, Harvest Books, Harcourt, Inc., Orlando, FL. Copyright © 1964, 1963 by C. S. Lewis PTE Limited. Copyright renewed 1992, 1991 by Arthur Owen Barfield.

Excerpt from Dr. Seuss (Theodor Geisel), *Oh, the Places You'll Go!* Random House, New York. Copyright © 1990 by Dr. Seuss Enterprises L.P.

Quotation from Mary Lou Retton copyright © Mary Lou Retton.

Quotations from Mohandas K. Gandhi copyright © Navjeevan Trust, Ahmedabad, India.

Quotations from The Christophers copyright © The Christophers, New York.

Quotation from Dale Carnegie copyright © Dale Carnegie & Associates, Inc., New York.

Quotation from César Chávez copyright © César E. Chávez Foundation, Glendale, CA.

Quotation from Christa McAuliffe copyright © estate of Christa McAuliffe.

Quotation from George Burns copyright © Roger Richman Agency, Inc., Beverly Hills, CA.

Quotation from Casey Stengel copyright © estate of Casey Stengel.

Quotation from Mae West copyright © Roger Richman Agency, Inc., Beverly Hills, CA.

Quotation from Mother Teresa of Calcutta copyright © Missionaries of Charity, Calcutta, India.

Quotations from Albert Einstein copyright © Albert Einstein Archives, The Jewish National & University Library, The Hebrew University, Jerusalem, Israel.

Quotation from President Lyndon B. Johnson, speech delivered August 29, 1965.

Excerpts from John Henry Newman, *Meditations and Devotions* (Part III), Longmans, Green, and Company, New York, 1907.

Excerpt from Ralph Waldo Emerson, *Nature*, 1836.

Excerpt from Henry Wadsworth Longfellow, *Hyperion*, 1882.

"Prepare the Way," copyright © 1991 Christopher Walker. Published by OCP Publications, 5536 NE Hassalo, Portland, OR 97213. All rights reserved.

"We Are Yours, O Lord," copyright © 1996 Janet Vogt. Published by OCP Publications, 5536 NE Hassalo, Portland, OR 97213. All rights reserved.

"Christ, Be Our Light," copyright © 1993, 2000, Bernadette Farrell. Published by OCP Publications, 5536 NE Hassalo, Portland, OR 97213. All rights reserved.

"Holy Spirit, Come into Our Lives" copyright © 1998 Ken Canedo. Published by OCP Publications, 5536 NE Hassalo, Portland, OR 97213. All rights reserved.

"Psalm 98: All the Ends of the Earth," music copyright © 1999, 2000, Barbara Bridge. Published by OCP Publications, 5536 NE Hassalo, Portland, OR 97213. All rights reserved. Refrain copyright © 1969, International Committee on English in the Liturgy, Inc. (ICEL). Verse copyright © 1970, CCD. All rights reserved. The English translation of Psalm 98 response from *Lectionary for Mass* copyright © 1969, 1981, 1997, ICEL. All rights reserved.

"Praise to Our God, Creation's Lord," Michael Kwatera, OSB. Copyright © 1991, The Order of Saint Benedict, Inc., Collegeville, MN. All rights reserved.

William H. Sadlier, Inc.
9 Pine Street
New York, NY 10005-1002

ISBN: 978-0-8215-5678-8
89 / 11 10

The Sadlier *We Live Our Faith* Program was developed by nationally recognized experts in catechesis, curriculum, and adolescent development:

Catechetical and Liturgical Consultants

Dr. Gerard F. Baumbach
Director, Center for Catechetical Initiatives
Concurrent Professor of Theology
University of Notre Dame
Notre Dame, Indiana

Carole M. Eipers, D.Min.
Vice President, Executive Director of Catechetics
William H. Sadlier, Inc.

Curriculum and Adolescent Catechesis Consultants

Sr. Carol Cimino, SSJ, Ed.D.
National Consultant

Joyce A. Crider
Associate Director
National Conference of Catechetical Leadership
Washington, D.C.

Kenneth Gleason
Director of Religious Education
Cincinnati, Ohio

Saundra Kennedy, Ed.D.
National Religion Consultant
William H. Sadlier, Inc.

Mark Markuly, Ph.D.
Director, Loyola Institute for Ministry
New Orleans, Louisiana

Kevin O'Connor, CSP
Institute of Pastoral Studies
Loyola University Chicago
Long Grove, Illinois

Gini Shimabukuro, Ed.D.
Associate Professor
Institute for Catholic Education Leadership
School of Education, University of San Francisco

Scriptural Consultant

Reverend Donald Senior, CP, Ph.D., S.T.D.
Member, Pontifical Biblical Commission
President, The Catholic Theological Union
Chicago, Illinois

Media/Technology Consultant

Sister Jane Keegan, RDC
Senior Internet Editor
William H. Sadlier, Inc.

Catholic Social Teaching Consultants

John Carr
Secretary, Department of Social Development and World Peace
United States Conference of Catholic Bishops
Washington, D.C.

Joan Rosenhauer
Coordinator, Special Projects, Department of
Social Development and World Peace
United States Conference of Catholic Bishops
Washington, D.C.

Sadlier Consulting Team

Michaela Burke Barry
Director of Consultant Services

Kenneth Doran
National Religion Consultant

Inculturation Consultants

Reverend Allan Figueroa Deck, SJ, Ph.D.
Executive Director
Loyola Institute for Spirituality
Orange, California

Kirk P. Gaddy, Ed.D.
Principal
St. Katharine School
Baltimore, Maryland

Dulce M. Jiménez-Abreu
Director of Spanish Programs
William H. Sadlier, Inc.

Theological Consultants

Most Reverend Edward K. Braxton, Ph.D., S.T.D.
Official Theological Consultant
Bishop of Belleville, Illinois

Reverend Joseph A. Komonchak, Ph.D.
Professor, School of Theology and Religious Studies
The Catholic University of America
Washington, D.C.

Most Reverend Richard J. Malone, Th.D.
Bishop of Portland, Maine

Writing/Development Team

Rosemary K. Calicchio
Vice President, Publications

Blake Bergen
Editorial Director

Melissa D. Gibbons
Director of Research and Development

Joanne McDonald
Senior Editor, Project Director

Mary Ann Trevaskiss, Supervising Editor
Maureen Gallo, Senior Editor
William Beebe, Ph.D.
Kerri Anne Burke
Joanna Dailey
William M. Ippolito
Allison Johnston
Mary Ellen Kelly
Regina Kelly
Daniel Sherman

Publishing Operations Team

Deborah Jones
Vice President, Publishing Operations

Vince Gallo
Creative Director

Francesca O'Malley
Associate Art Director

Jim Saylor
Photography Manager

Design Staff

Debrah Kaiser, Sasha Khorovsky, Maria Pia Marella

Production Staff

Diane Ali, Brent Burket, Robin D'Amato, Tresse DeLorenzo, Maria Jimenez, Joe Justus, Vincent McDonough, Yolanda Miley, Maureen Morgan, Jovito Pagkalinawan, Julie Riley, Gavin Smith, Martin Smith, Sommer Zakrzewski

Contents

We Live Our Faith!

Welcome to the *We Live Our Faith* program! Each chapter will help us to grow as Jesus' disciples and members of the Church by:

GATHERING . . . BELIEVING . . . and RESPONDING

We Live Our Faith As Members of the Church presents the Church, from her beginning at the Pentecost event through her history, encompassing her teachings and Tradition. It presents the mission of the Church, entrusted to her by Jesus, as the responsibility of all baptized Catholics.

Hi! My name is Megan. Come with me as I walk through a chapter of *We Live Our Faith.*

Let's start with the **GATHERING** section.

Prayer helps me to focus my energy and to reflect on God's presence in my life.

I do a survey, quiz, puzzle, or game with my friends and classmates.

I check with other students my age at **www.weliveourfaith.com**.

I respond to a Big Question about life.

The goals help me to see how this chapter will engage my mind, my heart, and my actions in living my faith.

There is always an interesting story, profile, current event, or report, plus an activity in this section.

GATHERING...

2
We Make Moral Choices

"The aim . . . is love from a pure heart, a good conscience, and a sincere faith."
(1 Timothy 1:5)

✛ **Leader:** Lord, our lives are filled with important choices that we can make in response to your great love. We ask you to guide us through these many important decisions as we pray together.

All: I praise you as my constant helper and call on you as my loving protector.
Guide me by your wisdom, correct me with your justice, comfort me with your mercy, protect me with your power.

I want to do what you ask of me:
In the way you ask,
for as long as you ask it,
because you ask it.

Lord, I believe in you: increase my faith.
I trust in you: strengthen my trust.
I love you: let me love you more and more.
Amen.

(from the "Universal Prayer," attributed to Pope Clement XI)

Visit www.weliveourfaith.com to find appropriate music and songs.

GATHERING...

Discover how everyday decisions can be affected by fear. The list below names some fears that people may have of everyday situations and objects. These fears are called phobias. A phobia is a persistent, irrational fear of a specific object, activity, or situation. Identify the phobia by choosing a name from the box and writing it on the line.

The BiG Question
How do I make decisions?

atrophobia   pyrophobia
claustrophobia   phonophobia
felinophobia   aquaphobia
triskaidekaphobia

1 fear of speaking aloud _____
2 fear of water _____
3 fear of the number 13 _____
4 fear of fire _____
5 fear of heights _____
6 fear of closed spaces _____
7 fear of cats _____

The fear of making a decision is called *decidophobia.* Making a decision can be difficult, overwhelming, and even downright scary at times. Think about some decisions that seem overwhelming to you.

In this chapter we learn more about the process of moral decision making that is essential to our lives as Jesus' disciples. Through this chapter, we hope

☐ **to know** that our conscience is our moral compass, directing us in our moral decision-making

☐ **to care** for our conscience by forming it well and also by doing what is right

☐ **to follow** Jesus not only by making good personal decisions but also by working to end unjust behaviors and conditions in society.

Arianna was really upset. Her so-called best friend Nicole was spreading rumors about her. Arianna could not figure out why Nicole would do something like that. She called Nicole to talk about it, but things only got worse. Soon Arianna was getting really hateful text messages from students she didn't even know! She didn't know what to do to make them stop.

Paula was also friendly with Arianna and Nicole. She heard the rumors about Arianna and knew that they were false, but Nicole was pressuring her to "join the fight against Arianna." Nicole even wanted her to post lies about Arianna on a Web site. Paula was afraid that if she didn't do what Nicole wanted, she would be Nicole's next target.

Paula had a decision to make.

Activity What decision does Paula have to make? What do you think she should do? Finish the story.

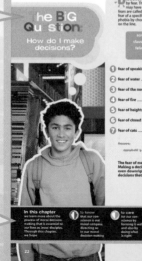

"We all must try to be the best person we can: by making the best choices, by making the most of the talents we've been given, by treating others as we would like to be treated," said Mary Lou Retton (1968–), Olympic gold medalist in gymnastics.

22   23

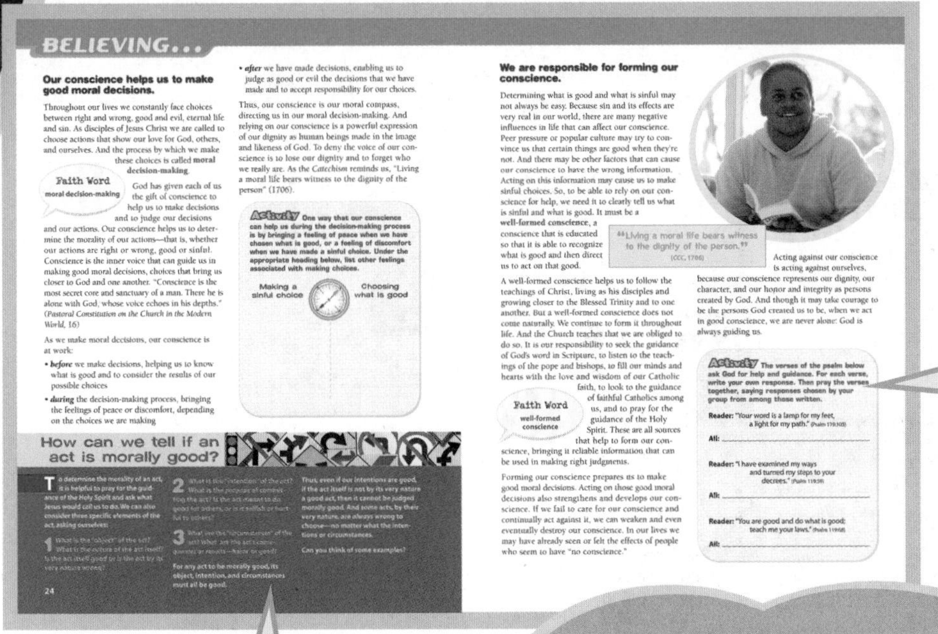

BELIEVING...

Our conscience helps us to make good moral decisions.

Throughout our lives we constantly face choices between right and wrong, good and evil, eternal life and sin. As disciples of Jesus Christ we are called to choose actions that show our love for God, others, and ourselves. And the process by which we make these choices is called **moral decision-making**.

Faith Word
moral decision-making

God has given each of us the gift of conscience to help us to make decisions and our actions. Our conscience helps us to determine the morality of our actions—that is, whether our actions are right or wrong, good or sinful. Conscience is the inner voice that can guide us in making good moral decisions, choices that bring us closer to God and one another. "Conscience is the most secret core and sanctuary of a man. There he is alone with God, whose voice echoes in his depths." (*Pastoral Constitution on the Church in the Modern World*, 16)

As we make moral decisions, our conscience is at work:

- **before** we make decisions, helping us to know what is good and to consider the results of our possible choices
- **during** the decision-making process, bringing the feelings of peace or discomfort, depending on the choices we are making

- **after** we have made decisions, enabling us to judge as good or evil the decisions that we have made and to accept responsibility for our choices.

Thus, our conscience is our moral compass, directing us in our moral decision-making. And relying on our conscience is a powerful expression of our dignity as human beings made in the image and likeness of God. To deny the voice of our conscience is to lose our dignity and to forget who we really are. As the *Catechism* reminds us, "Living a moral life bears witness to the dignity of the person" (1706).

Activity One way that our conscience can help us during the decision-making process is by bringing a feeling of peace when we have chosen what is good, or a feeling of discomfort when we have made a sinful choice. Under the appropriate heading below, list other feelings associated with making choices.

Making a sinful choice

Choosing what is good

How can we tell if an act is morally good?

To determine the morality of an act, it is helpful to pray for the guidance of the Holy Spirit and ask what Jesus would call us to do. We can also consider three specific elements of the act, asking ourselves:

1. What is the "object" of the act? What is the very nature of the act itself? Is the act itself good or evil, in the very nature it is, or is it selfish or hurtful to others?

2. What is my "intention" of the act? What is the purpose of committing the act? Is the act meant to do good for others, or is it selfish or hurtful to others?

3. What are the "circumstances" of the act? Under what conditions or situations is the act taking place—where, when, and how?

Thus, even if our intentions are good, if the act itself is not by its very nature a good act, then it cannot be judged morally good. And some acts, by their very nature, are always wrong to choose—no matter what the intentions or circumstances.

Can you think of some examples?

For any act to be morally good, its object, intention, and circumstances must all be good.

We are responsible for forming our conscience.

Determining what is good and what is sinful may not always be easy. Because sin and its effects are very real in our world, there are many negative influences in life that can affect our conscience. Peer pressure or popular culture may try to convince us that certain things are good when they're not. And there may be other factors that can cause our conscience to have the wrong information. Acting on this information may cause us to make sinful choices. So, to be able to rely on our conscience for help, we need it to clearly tell us what is sinful and what is good. It must be a well-formed conscience, a conscience that is educated so that it is able to recognize what is good and then direct us to act on that good.

> "Living a moral life bears witness to the dignity of the person." (CCC, 1706)

A well-formed conscience helps us to follow the teachings of Christ, living as his disciples and growing closer to the Blessed Trinity and to one another. But a well-formed conscience does not come naturally. We continue to form it throughout life. And the Church teaches that we are obliged to do so. It is our responsibility to seek the guidance of God's word in Scripture, to listen to the teachings of the pope and bishops, to fill our minds and hearts with the love and wisdom of our Catholic faith, to look to the guidance of faithful Catholics among us, and to pray for the guidance of the Holy Spirit. These are all sources that help to form our conscience, bringing it reliable information that can be used in making right judgments.

Faith Word
well-formed conscience

Forming our conscience prepares us to make good moral decisions. Acting on those good moral decisions also strengthens and develops our conscience. If we fail to care for our conscience and continually act against it, we can weaken and even eventually destroy our conscience. In our lives we may have already seen or felt the effects of people who seem to have "no conscience."

Acting against our conscience is acting against ourselves, because our conscience represents our dignity, our character, and our honor and integrity as persons created by God. And though it may take courage to be the persons God created us to be, when we act in good conscience, we are never alone: God is always guiding us.

Activity The verses of the psalm below ask God for help and guidance. For each verse, write your own response. Then pray the verses together, saying responses chosen by your group from among those written.

Reader: "Your word is a lamp for my feet, a light for my path." (Psalm 119:105)

All: _____

Reader: "I have examined my ways and returned my steps to your decrees." (Psalm 119:59)

All: _____

Reader: "You are good and do what is good; teach me your laws." (Psalm 119:68)

All: _____

24

BELIEVING...

God gives us the gifts of forgiveness and grace.

What happens when we don't choose to do what is right?

In life there are many decisions that we need to make and many tough choices that we face. We can always talk to God about our fears and uncertainties. We can listen as the Holy Spirit guides us and strengthens us. We can also seek the guidance of those who show faithfulness in their discipleship to Christ and wisdom in their moral decision-making. Yet, sometimes, even with all this help, we can fail and give in to the temptation to sin. But God in his mercy sent Jesus Christ, his only Son, to save us from sin. And God continues to show his mercy, his love and forgiveness, through a special Sacrament of Healing that Jesus Christ gave to the Church, the Sacrament of Penance and Reconciliation.

To prepare for this sacrament, commonly called the Sacrament of Penance, we examine our conscience. This means that we think about whether our decisions were based on the actions and teachings of Jesus. We determine whether or not our choices have shown love for God, others, and ourselves. And we ask the Holy Spirit to help us to judge the goodness of our thoughts, words, and actions.

Through the Sacrament of Penance we can be reconciled with God and with the Church. We go before a priest who acts in Jesus' name, and we acknowledge our sins. These sins may be acts, wrongs that we have committed, or omissions, failures to do the good that we were called to do. We then express our sorrow for any wrongdoing or any lack of love for God and others. We show repentance by promising not to repeat our sins and by taking action to show that we are truly sorry for our sins.

In a special way, through the Sacrament of Penance, we receive not only the gift of God's forgiveness, but the gift of his grace. "Grace is first and foremost the gift of the Spirit who justifies and sanctifies us." (CCC, 2003) God's grace helps us to make good moral decisions, to lead good moral lives, and to resist the temptation to sin. Thus, our relationship with God and the Church is strengthened or restored. Through the grace that we receive in this and all the sacraments, we, all the members of the Church, are enabled to live as God calls us to live.

Activity Design a feature for your parish Web site inviting people to receive the Sacrament of Penance.

The effects of Penance

The Sacrament of Penance has these wonderful effects in our lives:

- restoring or strengthening our relationship with God
- reconciling us with the Church
- excusing us from eternal punishment for the mortal sins rejoined
- lessening the purification necessary for our sins after death
- granting us peace and serenity of conscience
- comforting us
- strengthening us to continue living a moral life.

Even if we have not committed mortal sin, we are encouraged to receive the Sacrament of Penance regularly. It helps us to grow in our ability to make good moral decisions.

CATHOLIC IDENTITY
Pray a prayer of thanks for the Sacrament of Penance.

Jesus calls the whole Church to follow his example.

Through the power of the Holy Spirit, our unity as the Church strengthens us as we follow Jesus' teachings together, receive the grace of the sacraments, and grow in holiness. Strengthened by the Eucharist, sustained by the word of God in the liturgy, and guided by the Holy Spirit and Church teachings, we continue our lives of discipleship. And as the community of Jesus' disciples, the Church, we are called to be aware of the effects of our sins on the human community.

Created in God's image, we all share the same human dignity. This makes us one human community. And we must realize that while choosing to disobey God and failing to love him may be a personal sin, over time these personal sins affect the entire human community. These sins can give rise to "structures of sin," to unjust situations and conditions that negatively impact society and its institutions. This is social sin. Prejudice, poverty, homelessness, crime, violence, and discrimination against people on the basis of their race or ethnicity are just a few of the unjust situations and conditions in society that sin has caused.

> "Grace is first and foremost the gift of the Spirit who justifies and sanctifies us." (CCC, 2003)

Faith Word
social sin

During his lifetime Jesus recognized the problems in society. And Jesus took action:

- Jesus stood up for those treated unjustly because they were ill or poor.
- Jesus protected people who could not protect themselves.
- Jesus offered the peace and freedom that come from God's love and forgiveness.

As Jesus' disciples, each of us is called to follow his example in word and deed. So, we must be aware

of all of our sins, asking God for mercy and opposing all social sin in the same way that we avoid personal sin. We are called, in whatever way possible for us, to work to change the things in society that allow unjust behaviors or conditions to exist. We don't have to say yes to sin, either personally or as a society. Jesus has liberated us from its power.

In the same way that Jesus worked among the people—teaching them about the love of God his Father and encouraging them to turn to God—the Church, the whole community of Jesus' disciples, is called to work among the people. And one of the ways that the Church does this is by speaking out against social sin and encouraging all people to turn to God and love and respect one another throughout their lives.

Activity Find out how programs in your parish or diocese are helping to address unjust situations in society. Brainstorm ways to support these programs.

26   27

An activity helps me to apply what I have learned to my own life and relationships.

Features give interesting details about an aspect of the chapter.

In the BELIEVING section, I learn more about the Catholic faith and ways to live out my discipleship as a member of the Church.

Great photos and beautiful artwork help me to understand the Catholic faith.

Specific aspects of the Catholic faith strengthen my identity as a Catholic.

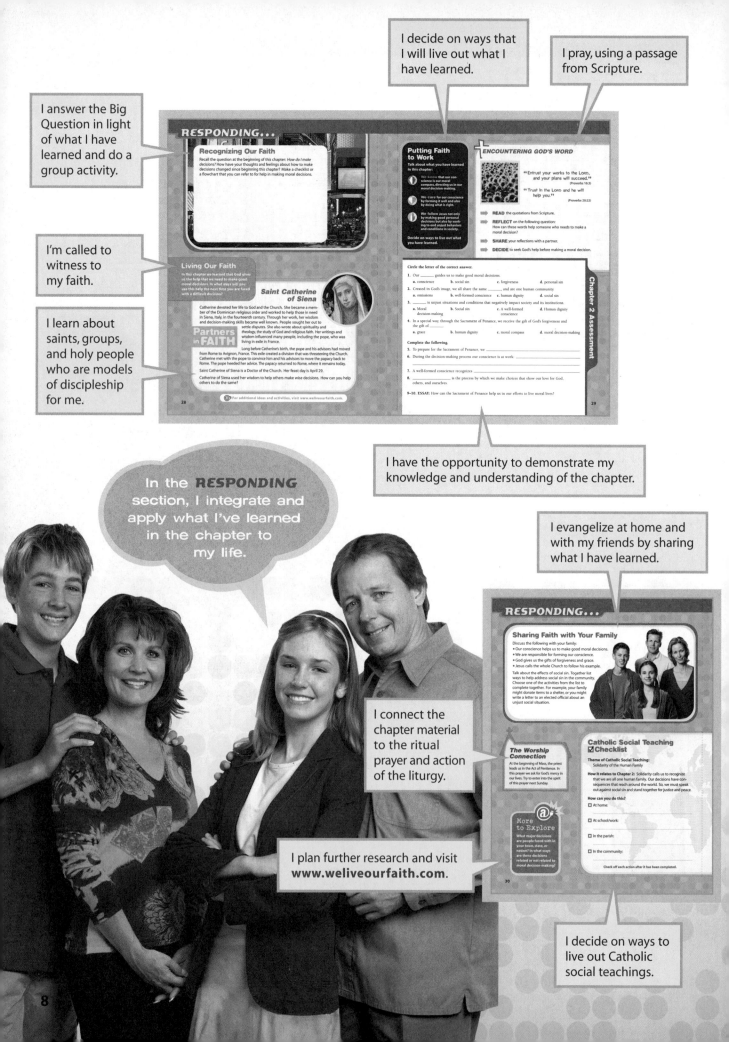

Throughout the year we will learn about many saints, holy people, and Catholic organizations, including:

Sister Thea Bowman

Saint Catherine of Siena

Saint Ignatius of Loyola

Blessed Pier Giorgio Frassati

The Sisters of Life

Thomas Merton

Women of the Early Church

Saint Ambrose

Saint Columba

Saints Francis and Dominic

Diane Bowers

Women of Renewal

"Father Farmer" Ferdinand Steinmeyer

Blessed Noel Pinot

Venerable John Henry Cardinal Newman

Blessed Pope John XXIII

Pope John Paul I

Dorothy Day

Saint María de Jesús Sacramentado

Danny Thomas

Saint Alberto Hurtado Cruchaga

Blessed Teresa of Calcutta

Saint Charles Lwanga

The Seven Martyrs of Thailand

We Live Our Faith has many great features that will help us to grow as Jesus' disciples and members of the Church.

We visit **www.weliveourfaith.com** to find:

surveys

quizzes

games

chapter resources

magazines

community outreach

. . . and much more!

We Live Our Faith is filled with great activities, including:

discussions and reflections

games

role-plays

timelines

quizzes

polls and surveys

puzzles

teamwork

outreach projects

artwork

creative writing

prayer services

We pray by using:

Scripture readings

meditations

prayers from the Mass and the sacraments

traditional Catholic prayers

prayers from many cultures

prayer in our own words

psalms

songs

We learn more by using these helpful resources:

Bible Basics

Prayers and Practices

Glossary

Index

Unit 1

How Do We Nourish God's Gift of Faith?

1

We Respond to God's Love

"Whoever is without love does not know God, for God is love."

(1 John 4:8)

✚ **Leader:** There is a very important truth in our lives that we may not always be aware of: *God loves us.* Let us take time now to remember and reflect on God's love.

Reader 1: "We have come to know and to believe in the love God has for us."
(1 John 4:16)
(silent reflection)

Reader 2: "For God so loved the world that he gave his only Son, so that everyone who believes in him might not perish but might have eternal life." (John 3:16)
(silent reflection)

Reader 3: No obstacle "will be able to separate us from the love of God in Christ Jesus our Lord" (Romans 8:39).
(silent reflection)

Leader: Thank you, God, for your great love for us. We pray that we may live our lives as a response to your love.

All: God,
I want to be present.
I want to be ready.
I want to share what I have—my life,
my laughter, my love, my joy.
I want to give to you as I receive
from you.
Amen.

(based on a prayer by Sister Thea Bowman)

@✸ **Visit www.weliveourfaith.com to find appropriate music and songs.**

The BiG QuEstion:

How can I be true to myself?

Discover some messages that may motivate you to be true to yourself. Decode each text message.

"There's nobdy lk U, + U cn mak a diff."

"Do somit gud 4 sum 1 U lk lEst 2day."

"D futR wl B diFrent f we mak D presnt diFrent."

Answers:

"There's nobody like you, and you can make a difference."
(The Christophers, a non-profit organization that communicates messages of hope and understanding to all people)
"Do something good for someone you like least today."
(quotation attributed to Saint Anthony of Padua)
"The future will be different if we make the present different."
(Peter Maurin, founder of the Catholic Worker Movement)

Now write a motivational text message of your own.

Share your text message with a partner. Decode and discuss the meaning of each other's messages.

In this chapter we learn that we are created to respond to the goodness and love of God—Father, Son, and Holy Spirit. We do this by truly being ourselves—human beings who reflect the image of God. Through this chapter, we hope

to understand that we have human dignity

to appreciate that a great sign of our dignity is our conscience, through which we can recognize God's law and respond to God's love

to respond to Jesus' call to holiness by imitating his example, accepting God's mercy, and proclaiming the good news.

Did you realize that right now, at this very moment, without having to do anything special, you are a worthy, valuable, and remarkable person? You simply need to *be*, to exist, for this to be true. No grand achievements are required. So, just sit there for a minute . . . and close your eyes . . . and without thinking about anything extraordinary—or doing anything special—just **be**.

Activity Have you ever considered how important your very existence is to the lives of those around you? Think of one friend or one family member whom you believe values you as a person. What qualities do you have that make you mean so much to this person?

> **"**To the world, you might be just one other person. But to one other person, you just might mean the world.**"**
> (Anonymous)

We reflect the goodness of God.

We've all heard the advice "Just be yourself." But at times we're so busy trying to fit in, or simply figuring out who we are, that we may not follow this advice. Yet "being ourselves" can have new meaning for us when we realize just how valuable and worthy we are as human beings. In Scripture we read, "God is love" (1 John 4:8). And because God created us in his image and likeness, we reflect his love and eternal goodness. The value and worth that we share because of this is our **human dignity**.

A great sign of our dignity is our ability to choose right over wrong. We have this ability because when God created us, he placed his law into our hearts. This law of God within us, known by human reason, is called the **natural law**. The natural law is understood through our *conscience*. Our **conscience** is our ability to know the difference between good and evil, right and wrong. It enables us to make right choices. And when we choose to follow God's law and do what is good, we are simply being ourselves, human beings who have dignity.

In fact, as human beings who have dignity, we are created to respond to God's goodness and love. It is natural for us to want to return God's love, to do what is pleasing to God, and to help one another. Through God's gift of **free will**, the freedom and ability to choose what to do, we can choose to love and praise God and also act kindly and lovingly toward one another. What a great sign of our dignity this is! We have the freedom and ability to *choose* to live in God's image.

Yet since we have the ability to *choose* to live in God's image, we can also choose not to. We can deny our human dignity by turning away from God. The first human beings used their free will and decided to turn from God. This turning from God was the first sin. And this first sin committed by the first human beings is called **original sin**. As their descendants we have been born with this original sin. But God the Father fulfilled his promise to send a savior.

Faith Words

human dignity
natural law
conscience
free will
original sin

God sent his only Son, Jesus Christ. Through his suffering, death, Resurrection, and Ascension, Christ offers us freedom from sin and the hope of eternal salvation. Through his example, Jesus Christ showed us that we can *truly* be ourselves: human beings who reflect the image of God. And God the Holy Spirit inspires us and enables us to truly reflect God.

An examination of conscience

An *examination of conscience* is the practice of thinking about our choices and determining whether we have followed God's law and the teachings and example of Jesus. Every night before sleeping, take a few moments to ask yourself: Did my choices today show love for God and others? Or did they contribute to the sinfulness and suffering in the world? Thank Jesus for your good choices. Ask Jesus to forgive you for any sinful choices. Plan to ask those you may have hurt for forgiveness, too.

Ask Jesus to help you to follow your conscience and his example each day.

Activity Write a slogan to encourage young people to turn to God and value their human dignity.

God forgives our sins.

Because of original sin, we are subject to ignorance, suffering, and death, and we have a tendency to use our free will to turn from God and from his laws. When we do this, we sin. *Sin* is any thought, word, deed, or omission against God's law. And just as original sin destroyed the harmony with God that the first humans had, so the sins that we commit, our personal sins, also weaken or destroy God's life in us. But in the Sacrament of Baptism God offers us the hope of **eternal life**, a life of happiness with him forever. God frees us from original sin, and our personal sins are forgiven. God also gives us his **grace**, a participation, or a sharing, in God's life and friendship. And as we read in the *Catechism of the Catholic Church*, God's grace "restores what sin had damaged in us" (1708). Yet we can still sometimes say no to God and to the goodness and life that he offers us.

Jesus Christ "saved us and called us to a holy life" (2 Timothy 1:9).

And sin, when very serious, may completely take away God's grace, his very life in us. This very serious sin that breaks our friendship with God is *mortal sin*. Since mortal sin separates us from God, we have no hope of eternal life with God until we turn back to him—until we repent and ask his forgiveness in the Sacrament of Penance. Sin is mortal only when these three conditions are present: (1) the sin is about a serious matter; (2) we commit the sin knowing that it is seriously wrong; and (3) we commit the sin completely of our own free will. A less serious sin that weakens our friendship with God is *venial sin*. But even though venial sins do not turn us completely away from God, they still hurt us and others. If we keep repeating venial sins, they can lead us further away from God and the **Church**, the community of people who believe in Jesus Christ, have been baptized in him, and follow his teachings. And over time, all sins, whether mortal or venial, have destructive effects in our lives if we do not make the effort to turn away from them and from the things that lead us to them.

But through his mercy, especially in the Sacrament of Penance, God forgives our sins if we are sorry and have a firm desire not to sin again. Through the Sacrament of Penance, the life of grace in us is strengthened when we are absolved of venial sins, or restored when we are absolved of mortal sins. We are reconciled with the Church and strengthened to live by the Ten Commandments and by Jesus' teaching to love one another as he loved us. And as we respond to the grace of the sacraments, we can come to realize that Jesus Christ "saved us and called us to a holy life" (2 Timothy 1:9).

Faith Words

eternal life
grace
Church

Activity Design a prayer card to remind you of God's forgiveness and love. You may want to use one of these Scripture quotations on your card:

"The LORD is gracious and merciful,
    slow to anger and abounding in love."
    (Psalm 145:8)

"Everyone who calls on the name of the Lord
    will be saved." (Romans 10:13)

"If we acknowledge our sins, he is faithful and
    just and will forgive our sins." (1 John 1:9)

Pray the words on your prayer card before or after receiving the Sacrament of Penance.

We live holy lives.

How can we be all that God calls us to be—reflections of his goodness and holiness?

Holiness is a participation in God's goodness and a response to God's love by the way that we live. God alone is holy, but through grace he calls us to share in his holiness. The grace that we receive, the sharing in God's life, unites us to the Blessed Trinity—one God in three Persons: God the Father, God the Son, and God the Holy Spirit. God the Son, Jesus Christ, gave us the perfect example of living in holiness, saying, "I have given you a model to follow, so that as I have

done for you, you should also do" (John 13:15). Through Jesus Christ, the second Person of the Blessed Trinity, God fully reveals who he is, shows us how he wants us to live, and offers us forgiveness and salvation. The coming of Jesus Christ is good news for all people and for all time. Jesus' life was lived in total love for God the Father and service to others.

Throughout Jesus' public ministry, his work among the people, he showed that he truly believed that all human life should be respected and treasured. He constantly reached out to those who were poor and in need and to those who were weak and defenseless. Truly, Jesus called people to live their lives more fully, relying on God's love and loving others. And Jesus promised eternal life to those who lived as he did and wanted to grow in holiness.

The Holy Spirit, the third Person of the Blessed Trinity, guides us to holiness. The Holy Spirit makes the truth clear to us, reminding us of Jesus' teachings, helping us to understand God's word, and helping us to do good and to avoid sin.

> **Faith Word**
>
> holiness

As we read in the *Catechism*, "All are called to holiness" (2013). As disciples of Jesus Christ, we work together to respond to this call. Supporting one another as the Church, with God's grace and the guidance of the Holy Spirit, we can live as Jesus lived.

The Blessed Trinity

The truth of the Blessed Trinity sheds light on all of our beliefs and guides us in all areas of our lives. The whole life of the Church revolves around our belief in the Blessed Trinity. The words *Father*, *Son*, and *Holy Spirit* express the relationship among the three Divine Persons of God and are central to our relationship with God. We are baptized "in the name of the Father, and of the Son, and of the Holy Spirit" (Rite of Baptism). And just as the Father, Son, and Holy Spirit are one, all who are baptized become one with God and one another. God continues to be with us and is active in our lives as Father, Son, and Holy Spirit, through the grace of all the sacraments that we receive. And in our prayer and liturgy—especially in the Mass—we become one with the Father, Son, and Holy Spirit, and our unity with one another is strengthened.

CATHOLIC IDENTITY

Listen for references to the Blessed Trinity at Mass this week.

Activity Jesus gave us the perfect example of living in holiness. On a separate sheet of paper, write a dialogue in which you interview Jesus about how he lives in holiness and how you can do the same. What does Jesus say to you?

We give witness to Jesus.

Jesus' first disciples gave witness to Jesus by showing that they believed in him. They went everywhere with him. They were his apprentices.

An *apprentice* is a pupil who learns a specific skill or trade under the guidance of a master teacher. Jesus was the master teacher who encouraged his disciples to develop their God-given gifts, learn his teachings, and continue his work of sharing God's love. Jesus invited them to trust in God his Father and to obey God's laws.

> Learning about and living out our Catholic faith is **"an initiation and apprenticeship"** (*General Directory for Catechesis*, 30).

Jesus showed his followers that through discipleship to him they would share love, freedom, justice, and peace in this life, and would also be choosing *eternal life* over sin and eternal death. In response, Jesus' disciples worked with him to share God's love and spread God's Kingdom. The **Kingdom of God** is the power of God's love active in our lives and in our world. We will share in the fullness of God's Kingdom in eternal life.

Having learned from Jesus, the disciples would go on to proclaim the good news of Jesus Christ to the whole world. We are Jesus' disciples. And as members of the Church today, God calls each of us to proclaim the good news of Christ by what we say and do. As disciples, we too give witness to Jesus and live our faith as apprentices. Learning about and living out our Catholic faith is "an initiation and apprenticeship" (*General Directory for Catechesis*, 30). Jesus is our master teacher, encouraging us to develop our God-given gifts, learn his teachings, and continue his mission—sharing the good news and spreading God's Kingdom.

Then we too will be "choosing life" here on earth and, in so doing, choosing eternal life with God forever.

Faith Word
Kingdom of God

Activity Write a "Help Wanted" ad for the position of a disciple of Jesus.

In what ways do you qualify for this position?

17

Recognizing Our Faith

Recall the question at the beginning of this chapter: *How can I be true to myself?* Write a fifty-word reflection on the way that living as Jesus' disciple helps you to be true to yourself.

Living Our Faith

In this chapter we learned that we are all called to holiness. Think of one thing you can do to respond to this call, and then carry it out.

Sister Thea Bowman

Born in 1937, Thea Bowman was the granddaughter of a slave. Raised by Methodist parents, she attended Catholic school to obtain a better education and then converted to Catholicism. As a teenager she became a member of the Franciscan Sisters of Perpetual Adoration.

Gifted with a beautiful voice, an energetic personality, and wit, Sister Thea shared the message of God's love through a teaching career. She not only had a doctorate in English, but also was the first African-American woman to receive an honorary doctoral degree in theology from Boston College. She began giving presentations combining songs, the Gospels, poetry, prayer, and storytelling. She encouraged people to communicate, to learn about and accept all cultures, and to live with hope, love, and justice.

In 1984 Sister Thea was diagnosed with bone cancer. Seated in a wheelchair, she continued to be true to herself, working against prejudice, suspicion, hatred, and things that drive people apart. She continued to give witness to Jesus until her death in 1990.

How does the life of Sister Thea Bowman motivate you to be true to yourself?

@ For additional ideas and activities, visit www.weliveourfaith.com.

Putting Faith to Work

Talk about what you have learned in this chapter:

 We understand that we have human dignity.

We appreciate that a great sign of our dignity is our conscience, through which we can recognize God's law and respond to God's love.

We respond to Jesus' call to holiness by imitating his example, accepting God's mercy, and proclaiming the good news.

Decide on ways to live out what you have learned.

✝ ENCOUNTERING GOD'S WORD

❝ As he who called you is holy, be holy yourselves in every aspect of your conduct. ❞
(1 Peter 1:15)

➡ **READ** the quotation from Scripture.

➡ **REFLECT** on these questions:
Does the call to be holy in every aspect of your conduct seem challenging? As Jesus' disciples, what help have we been given to meet this challenge?

➡ **SHARE** your reflections with a partner.

➡ **DECIDE** today on a way that your conduct can better reflect the holiness of Jesus.

Write the letter that best defines each term.

1. _____ holiness

2. _____ conscience

3. _____ human dignity

4. _____ Kingdom of God

a. the value and worth that we share because God created us in his image and likeness

b. the ability to know the difference between good and evil, right and wrong

c. a participation in God's goodness and a response to God's love by the way that we live

d. the law of God within us, which is known by human reason

e. the power of God's love active in our lives and in our world

Write *True* or *False* next to the following sentences. On a separate sheet of paper, change the false sentences to make them true.

5. _____ Venial sin is a very serious sin that completely breaks our friendship with God.

6. _____ The law of God within us, which is known by human reason, is called free will.

7. _____ The first sin committed by the first human beings is called mortal sin.

8. _____ The Church is the community of people who believe in Jesus Christ, have been baptized in him, and follow his teachings.

9–10. ESSAY: In what ways can you respond to God's love?

Chapter 1 Assessment

RESPONDING...

Sharing Faith with Your Family

Discuss the following with your family:
- We reflect the goodness of God.
- God forgives our sins.
- We live holy lives.
- We give witness to Jesus.

Each person in your family has dignity. As a family, do something simple this week to show that you respect each other's dignity. Offer to do a favor; leave a small, unexpected gift; write a kind note; pay a compliment; lend a listening ear, and so on.

The Worship Connection

The "Holy, Holy, Holy" is a hymn that we sing at Mass. It is a song of praise for Jesus that comes from Isaiah 6:3, Revelation 4:8, and Matthew 21:9. This hymn prepares us to receive Jesus Christ in Holy Communion.

More to Explore

Saints are disciples of Christ who lived lives of holiness on earth and now share in eternal life with God in heaven. What saint would you like to know more about? Research this person online.

Catholic Social Teaching ☑ Checklist

Theme of Catholic Social Teaching:
Life and Dignity of the Human Person

How it relates to Chapter 1: This chapter explored human dignity. As Catholics, we are called to respect one another's human dignity—seeking peace and justice for one another and helping one another.

How can you do this?

☐ At home:

_____

☐ At school/work:

_____

☐ In the parish:

_____

☐ In the community:

_____

Check off each action after it has been completed.

GATHERING...

"The aim . . . is love from a pure heart, a good conscience, and a sincere faith."

(1 Timothy 1:5)

✙ **Leader:** Lord, our lives are filled with important choices that we can make in response to your great love. We ask you to guide us through these many important decisions as we pray together.

All: I praise you as my constant helper and call on you as my loving protector.
Guide me by your wisdom, correct me with your justice, comfort me with your mercy, protect me with your power.

I want to do what you ask of me:
in the way you ask,
for as long as you ask,
because you ask it.

Lord, I believe in you: increase my faith.
I trust in you: strengthen my trust.
I love you: let me love you more
and more.
Amen.

(from the "Universal Prayer," attributed to Pope Clement XI)

Visit www.weliveourfaith.com to find appropriate music and songs.

21

The BiG Question:

How do I make decisions?

Discover how everyday decisions can be affected by fear. The list below names some fears that people may have of everyday situations and objects. These fears are called *phobias*. A *phobia* is a persistent, irrational fear of a specific object, activity, or situation. Identify the phobia by choosing a name from the box and writing it on the line.

acrophobia	pyrophobia
claustrophobia	phonophobia
felinophobia	aquaphobia
triskaidekaphobia	

1 fear of speaking aloud _____

2 fear of water _____

3 fear of the number 13 _____

4 fear of fire _____

5 fear of heights _____

6 fear of closed spaces _____

7 fear of cats _____

Answers:
1. phonophobia 2. aquaphobia 3. triskaidekaphobia 4. pyrophobia 5. acrophobia 6. claustrophobia 7. felinophobia

The fear of making a decision is called *decidophobia*. Making a decision can be difficult, overwhelming, and even downright scary at times. Think about some decisions that seem overwhelming to you.

In this chapter
we learn more about the process of moral decision-making that is essential to our lives as Jesus' disciples. Through this chapter, we hope

to know
that our conscience is our moral compass, directing us in our moral decision-making

to care
for our conscience by forming it well and also by doing what is right

to follow
Jesus not only by making good personal decisions but also by working to end unjust behaviors and conditions in society.

Arianna was really upset. Her so-called best friend Nicole was spreading rumors about her. Arianna could not figure out why Nicole would do something like that. She called Nicole to talk about it, but things only got worse. Soon Arianna was getting really hateful text messages from students she didn't even know! She didn't know what to do to make them stop.

Paula was also friendly with Arianna and Nicole. She heard the rumors about Arianna and knew that they were false, but Nicole was pressuring her to "join the fight against Arianna." Nicole even wanted her to post lies about Arianna on a Web site. Paula was afraid that if she didn't do what Nicole wanted, she would be Nicole's next target.

Paula had a decision to make.

Activity What decision does Paula have to make? What do you think she should do? Finish the story.

66We all must try to be the best person we can: by making the best choices, by making the most of the talents we've been given, by treating others as we would like to be treated,99 said Mary Lou Retton (1968–   ), Olympic gold medalist in gymnastics.

Our conscience helps us to make good moral decisions.

Throughout our lives we constantly face choices between right and wrong, good and evil, eternal life and sin. As disciples of Jesus Christ we are called to choose actions that show our love for God, others, and ourselves. And the process by which we make these choices is called **moral decision-making**.

> **Faith Word**
>
> **moral decision-making**

God has given each of us the gift of conscience to help us to make decisions and to judge our decisions and our actions. Our conscience helps us to determine the morality of our actions—that is, whether our actions are right or wrong, good or sinful. Conscience is the inner voice that can guide us in making good moral decisions, choices that bring us closer to God and one another. "Conscience is the most secret core and sanctuary of a man. There he is alone with God, whose voice echoes in his depths." (*Pastoral Constitution on the Church in the Modern World,* 16)

As we make moral decisions, our conscience is at work:

- *before* we make decisions, helping us to know what is good and to consider the results of our possible choices

- *during* the decision-making process, bringing the feelings of peace or discomfort, depending on the choices we are making

- *after* we have made decisions, enabling us to judge as good or evil the decisions that we have made and to accept responsibility for our choices.

Thus, our conscience is our moral compass, directing us in our moral decision-making. And relying on our conscience is a powerful expression of our dignity as human beings made in the image and likeness of God. To deny the voice of our conscience is to lose our dignity and to forget who we really are. As the *Catechism* reminds us, "Living a moral life bears witness to the dignity of the person" (1706).

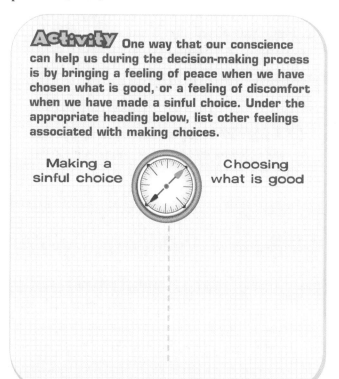

Activity One way that our conscience can help us during the decision-making process is by bringing a feeling of peace when we have chosen what is good, or a feeling of discomfort when we have made a sinful choice. Under the appropriate heading below, list other feelings associated with making choices.

Making a sinful choice

Choosing what is good

How can we tell if an act is morally good?

To determine the morality of an act, it is helpful to pray for the guidance of the Holy Spirit and ask what Jesus would call us to do. We can also consider three specific elements of the act, asking ourselves:

1 What is the "object" of the act? What is the *nature* of the act itself? Is the act itself good or is the act by its very nature wrong?

2 What is the "intention" of the act? What is the *purpose* of committing the act? Is the act meant to do good for others, or is it selfish or hurtful to others?

3 What are the "circumstances" of the act? What are the act's *consequences* or results—harm or good?

For any act to be morally good, its object, intention, and circumstances must all be good.

Thus, even if our intentions are good, if the act itself is not by its very nature a good act, then it cannot be judged morally good. And some acts, by their very nature, are *always* wrong to choose—no matter what the intentions or circumstances.

Can you think of some examples?

We are responsible for forming our conscience.

Determining what is good and what is sinful may not always be easy. Because sin and its effects are very real in our world, there are many negative influences in life that can affect our conscience. Peer pressure or popular culture may try to convince us that certain things are good when they're not. And there may be other factors that can cause our conscience to have the wrong information. Acting on this information may cause us to make sinful choices. So, to be able to rely on our conscience for help, we need it to clearly tell us what is sinful and what is good. It must be a **well-formed conscience**, a conscience that is educated so that it is able to recognize what is good and then direct us to act on that good.

> "Living a moral life bears witness to the dignity of the person."
> (CCC, 1706)

A well-formed conscience helps us to follow the teachings of Christ, living as his disciples and growing closer to the Blessed Trinity and to one another. But a well-formed conscience does not come naturally. We continue to form it throughout life. And the Church teaches that we are obliged to do so. It is our responsibility to seek the guidance of God's word in Scripture, to listen to the teachings of the pope and bishops, to fill our minds and hearts with the love and wisdom of our Catholic faith, to look to the guidance of faithful Catholics among us, and to pray for the guidance of the Holy Spirit. These are all sources that help to form our conscience, bringing it reliable information that can be used in making right judgments.

Faith Word

well-formed conscience

Forming our conscience prepares us to make good moral decisions. Acting on those good moral decisions also strengthens and develops our conscience. If we fail to care for our conscience and continually act against it, we can weaken and even eventually destroy our conscience. In our lives we may have already seen or felt the effects of people who seem to have "no conscience."

Acting against our conscience is acting against ourselves, because our conscience represents our dignity, our character, and our honor and integrity as persons created by God. And though it may take courage to be the persons God created us to be, when we act in good conscience, we are never alone: God is always guiding us.

Activity The verses of the psalm below ask God for help and guidance. For each verse, write your own response. Then pray the verses together, saying responses chosen by your group from among those written.

Reader: "Your word is a lamp for my feet, a light for my path." (Psalm 119:105)

All: _____

Reader: "I have examined my ways and turned my steps to your decrees." (Psalm 119:59)

All: _____

Reader: "You are good and do what is good; teach me your laws." (Psalm 119:68)

All: _____

The effects of Penance

The Sacrament of Penance has these wonderful effects in our lives:

- restoring or strengthening our relationship with God
- reconciling us with the Church
- excusing us from eternal punishment for the mortal sins repented
- lessening the purification necessary for our sins after death
- granting us peace and serenity of conscience
- comforting us
- strengthening us to continue living a moral life.

Even if we have not committed mortal sin, we are encouraged to receive the Sacrament of Penance regularly. It helps us to grow in our ability to make good moral decisions.

CATHOLIC IDENTITY

Pray a prayer of thanks for the Sacrament of Penance.

God gives us the gifts of forgiveness and grace.

What happens when we don't choose to do what is right?

In life there are many decisions that we need to make and many tough choices that we face. We can always talk to God about our fears and uncertainties. We can listen as the Holy Spirit guides us and strengthens us. We can also seek the guidance of those who show faithfulness in their discipleship to Christ and wisdom in their moral decision-making. Yet, sometimes, even with all this help, we can fail and give in to the temptation to sin. But God in his mercy sent Jesus Christ, his only Son, to save us from sin. And God continues to show his mercy, his love and forgiveness, through a special Sacrament of Healing that Jesus Christ gave to the Church, the Sacrament of Penance and Reconciliation.

To prepare for this sacrament, commonly called the Sacrament of Penance, we examine our conscience. This means that we think about whether our decisions were based on the actions and teachings of Jesus. We determine whether or not our choices have shown love for God, others, and ourselves. And we ask the Holy Spirit to help us to judge the goodness of our thoughts, words, and actions.

Through the Sacrament of Penance we can be reconciled with God and with the Church. We go before a priest who acts in Jesus' name, and we acknowledge our sins. These sins may be *acts*, wrongs that we have committed, or *omissions*, failures to do the good that we were called to do. We then express our sorrow for any wrongdoing or any lack of love for God and others. We show repentance by promising not to repeat our sins and by taking action to show that we are truly sorry for our sins.

In a special way, through the Sacrament of Penance, we receive not only the gift of God's forgiveness, but the gift of his grace. "Grace is first and foremost the gift of the Spirit who justifies and sanctifies us." (*CCC*, 2003) God's grace helps us to make good moral decisions, to lead good moral lives, and to resist the temptation to sin. Thus, our relationship with God and the Church is strengthened or restored. Through the grace that we receive in this and all the sacraments, we, all the members of the Church, are enabled to live as God calls us to live.

Activity Design a feature for your parish Web site inviting people to receive the Sacrament of Penance.

Jesus calls the whole Church to follow his example.

Through the power of the Holy Spirit, our unity as the Church strengthens us as we follow Jesus' teachings together, receive the grace of the sacraments, and grow in holiness. Strengthened by the Eucharist, sustained by the word of God in the liturgy, and guided by the Holy Spirit and Church teachings, we continue our lives of discipleship. And as the community of Jesus' disciples, the Church, we are called to be aware of the effects of our sins on the human community.

Created in God's image, we all share the same human dignity. This makes us one human community. And we must realize that while choosing to disobey God and failing to love him may be a personal sin, over time these personal sins affect the entire human community. These sins can give rise to "structures of sin," to unjust situations and conditions that negatively impact society and its institutions. This is **social sin**. Prejudice, poverty, homelessness, crime, violence, and discrimination against people on the basis of their race or ethnicity are just a few of the unjust situations and conditions in society that sin has caused.

> **"Grace is first and foremost the gift of the Spirit who justifies and sanctifies us."**
> (CCC, 2003)

Faith Word

social sin

During his lifetime Jesus recognized the problems in society. And Jesus took action:

- Jesus stood up for those treated unjustly because they were ill or poor.

- Jesus protected people who could not protect themselves.

- Jesus offered the peace and freedom that come from God's love and forgiveness.

As Jesus' disciples, each of us is called to follow his example in word and deed. So, we must be aware of all of our sins, asking God for mercy and opposing all social sin in the same way that we avoid personal sin. We are called, in whatever way possible for us, to work to change the things in society that allow unjust behaviors or conditions to exist. We don't have to say yes to sin, either personally or as a society; Jesus has liberated us from its power.

In the same way that Jesus worked among the people—teaching them about the love of God his Father and encouraging them to turn to God—the Church, the whole community of Jesus' disciples, is called to work among the people. And one of the ways that the Church does this is by speaking out against social sin and encouraging all people to turn to God and love and respect one another throughout their lives.

Activity Find out how programs in your parish or diocese are helping to address unjust situations in society. Brainstorm ways to support these programs.

27

Recognizing Our Faith

Recall the question at the beginning of this chapter: *How do I make decisions?* How have your thoughts and feelings about ways to make decisions changed since beginning this chapter? Make a checklist or a flowchart that you can refer to for help in making moral decisions.

Living Our Faith

In this chapter we learned that God gives us the help that we need to make good moral decisions. In what ways will you use this help the next time you are faced with a difficult decision?

Saint Catherine of Siena

Catherine devoted her life to God and the Church. She became a member of the Dominican religious order and worked to help those in need in Siena, Italy, in the fourteenth century. Through her work, her wisdom and decision-making skills became well known. People sought her out to settle disputes. She also wrote about spirituality and *theology*, the study of God and religious faith. Her writings and wisdom influenced many people, including the pope, who was living in exile in France.

Long before Catherine's birth, the pope and his advisors had moved from Rome to Avignon, France. This exile created a division that was threatening the Church. Catherine met with the pope to convince him and his advisors to move the papacy back to Rome. The pope heeded her advice. The papacy returned to Rome, where it remains today.

Saint Catherine of Siena is a Doctor of the Church. Her feast day is April 29.

Catherine of Siena used her wisdom to help others make wise decisions. How can you help others to do the same?

Putting Faith to Work

Talk about what you have learned in this chapter:

We know that our conscience is our moral compass, directing us in our moral decision-making.

We care for our conscience by forming it well and also by doing what is right.

We follow Jesus not only by making good personal decisions but also by working to end unjust behaviors and conditions in society.

Decide on ways to live out what you have learned.

✝ ENCOUNTERING GOD'S WORD

"Entrust your works to the LORD, and your plans will succeed."
(Proverbs 16:3)

"Trust in the LORD and he will help you."
(Proverbs 20:22)

➡ **READ** the quotations from Scripture.

➡ **REFLECT** on the following question:
How can these words help someone who needs to make a moral decision?

➡ **SHARE** your reflections with a partner.

➡ **DECIDE** to seek God's help before making a moral decision.

Circle the letter of the correct answer.

1. Our _____ guides us to make good moral decisions.

   a. conscience   **b.** social sin   **c.** forgiveness   **d.** personal sin

2. Created in God's image, we all share the same _____, and are one human community.

   a. omissions   **b.** well-formed conscience   **c.** human dignity   **d.** social sin

3. _____ is unjust situations and conditions that negatively impact society and its institutions.

   a. Moral decision-making   **b.** Social sin   **c.** A well-formed conscience   **d.** Human dignity

4. In a special way, through the Sacrament of Penance, we receive the gift of God's forgiveness and the gift of _____.

   a. grace   **b.** human dignity   **c.** moral compass   **d.** moral decision-making

Complete the following.

5. To prepare for the Sacrament of Penance, we _____.

6. During the decision-making process our conscience is at work: _____
   _____.

7. A well-formed conscience recognizes _____.

8. _____ is the process by which we make choices that show our love for God, others, and ourselves.

9–10. ESSAY: How can the Sacrament of Penance help us in our efforts to live moral lives?

RESPONDING...

Sharing Faith with Your Family

Discuss the following with your family:

- Our conscience helps us to make good moral decisions.
- We are responsible for forming our conscience.
- God gives us the gifts of forgiveness and grace.
- Jesus calls the whole Church to follow his example.

Talk about the effects of social sin. Together list ways to help address social sin in the community. Choose one of the activities from the list to complete together. For example, your family might donate items to a shelter, or you might write a letter to an elected official about an unjust social situation.

The Worship Connection

At the beginning of Mass, the priest leads us in the Act of Penitence. In this prayer we ask for God's mercy in our lives. Try to enter into the spirit of this prayer next Sunday.

More to Explore

What major decisions are people faced with in your town, state, or nation? In what ways are these decisions related or not related to moral decision-making?

Catholic Social Teaching ☑ Checklist

Theme of Catholic Social Teaching:
Solidarity of the Human Family

How it relates to Chapter 2: Solidarity calls us to recognize that we are all one human family. Our decisions have consequences that reach around the world. So, we must speak out against social sin and stand together for justice and peace.

How can you do this?

☐ At home:
_____

☐ At school/work:
_____

☐ In the parish:
_____

☐ In the community:
_____

Check off each action after it has been completed.

3

We Follow God's Law

"If you love me, you will keep my commandments."

(John 14:15)

✝ **Leader:** Let us pray some verses from Psalm 119.

Group 1: "Blessed are you, O LORD;
    teach me your laws.
    With all my heart I seek you;
    do not let me stray from
      your commands."

(Psalm 119:12, 10)

Group 2: "LORD, teach me the way of
    your laws;
    I shall observe them with care.
    Give me insight to observe
      your teaching,
    to keep it with all my heart."

(Psalm 119:33–34)

Group 1: "I keep my steps from every
      evil path,
    that I may obey your word.
    From your edicts I do not turn,
      for you have taught them
      to me."

(Psalm 119:101–102)

Group 2: "Your decrees are my heritage
      forever;
    they are the joy of my heart.
    My heart is set on fulfilling your
      laws;
    they are my reward forever."

(Psalm 119:111–112)

Leader: Thank you, Lord, for your laws.
    Guide us so that we may follow them
    with all our hearts.

All: Glory to the Father, and to the Son,
    and to the Holy Spirit:
    as it was in the beginning,
    is now, and will be for ever. Amen.

 Visit www.weliveourfaith.com to find appropriate music and songs.

GATHERING...

The BiG QuEstion:

Why do I need to follow laws?

Discover some unusual laws. Believe it or not, the following are actual laws that were made!

1 It is unlawful to lend your vacuum cleaner to your next-door neighbor in Denver, Colorado.

2 No one may catch fish with bare hands in the state of Kansas.

3 It is unlawful to walk backwards after sunset in Devon, Connecticut.

4 The state law of Pennsylvania prohibits singing in the bathtub.

Now write four city or state laws that seem more logical than these do.

1. _____

_____

2. _____

_____

3. _____

_____

4. _____

_____

Look back at the laws you wrote. Which one do you think would be the most important to follow? Why?

In this chapter
we learn that true happiness is found in turning to God and in following God's law. Through this chapter, we hope

 to know
that by following Jesus we can be faithful to God's law and find true happiness

 to accept
the commandments as the law of God's covenant

 to love
God, others, and ourselves by keeping the commandments and living as disciples of Jesus.

*N*o more laws! Michael thought. He was expecting a fun day ahead now that there were no more laws in his hometown in the county of Lawless. Just the night before, the town council had voted to do away with all the laws in town. Michael laughed to himself, thinking that he didn't even have to take the bus to school if he didn't feel like it. Maybe he would even skip school altogether and go break some laws—wait, there were no laws to break! Michael laughed again as he went to grab his bike . . .

But when he got to the bike rack, he found that his bike chain was cut and his bike had been stolen! That wasn't cool. *I guess I'll have to walk*, he thought. So, he put on his headphones to listen to music as he walked. But within minutes someone walked by, grabbed his music player, and took off with it. "Hey!" he shouted. "Get back here!" But it was no use. There were no laws to protect him anymore or to guide anyone else . . .

66 Where there is no law, there is no freedom, 99 wrote philosopher John Locke (1632–1704).

Following God's law leads to peace, love, and joy.

It might seem that life would be more fun without laws. But, in reality, each day many of the rules or laws that we encounter help to make things safer or better for us. And, ideally, all the laws and rules that we follow should help us to live up to our best potential as human beings. That's what God, above all, wants—what's best for us. God loves us and wants us to be able to live in his image, with peace, love, and joy in our lives.

As we can read in the Book of Exodus, when God gave his law to Moses on Mount Sinai, God made a *covenant*, or agreement, with Moses and the Israelites. God promised Moses that he would be their God, and they would be his people. He told Moses that to keep this covenant relationship the people had to live by the Ten Commandments. And, after Moses shared God's laws with the people, they agreed to follow these laws.

The Ten Commandments are the law of God's covenant. Even Jesus Christ, God's only Son, who became one of us, accepted this law as his guide. By the way he lived his earthly life Jesus showed his disciples how to live their covenant relationship with

The Ten Commandments	
I	I am the LORD your God: you shall not have strange gods before me.
II	You shall not take the name of the LORD your God in vain.
III	Remember to keep holy the LORD's Day.
IV	Honor your father and your mother.
V	You shall not kill.
VI	You shall not commit adultery.
VII	You shall not steal.
VIII	You shall not bear false witness against your neighbor.
IX	You shall not covet your neighbor's wife.
X	You shall not covet your neighbor's goods.

God, how to act justly, and how to love God, themselves, and others. And, when Jesus shared God's love, it was always within the context of living by God's law. Jesus told his followers, "Do not think that I have come to abolish the law or the prophets. I have come not to abolish but to fulfill" (Matthew 5:17).

The Ten Commandments explain the ways in which we can be faithful to the loving, covenant relationship into which God has called humankind throughout the ages. And as Jesus' disciples today we are called to follow the Ten Commandments, living out our covenant with God—Father, Son, and Holy Spirit.

The law within us

The natural law, the law of God within us, enables us to sense what is good and what is evil. The commandments express in words the natural law that God has already placed within us. And "the natural law is a participation in God's wisdom and goodness.... It expresses the dignity of the human person and forms the basis of his fundamental rights and duties" (*CCC*, 1978). Society is called to base its laws on the natural law, found in the commandments, for this law comes from God, helps us to know right from wrong, and expresses our dignity.

CATHOLIC IDENTITY

What is an example of how following God's law can help people to live up to their full potential as human beings?

Activity Imagine that a new community is being established. What would be your top five laws to help the people of this new community live in peace and happiness? How do your laws reflect the Ten Commandments?

Jesus calls us to conversion.

Many of us may think that happiness is just something that "happens" to us if and when we get the things that we want. Possessions, pleasure, luxury, power, or fame can bring us happiness, but is that the happiness that brings us lasting joy?

In one of his parables, Jesus told his disciples about a man who had two sons. In the story the younger son asked his father for his share of the family's fortune. Maybe this young man was looking for happiness. But certainly he wanted something more from life than what he had. And when his father gave him his inheritance he set off to live life on his own. Would it be a happy, carefree life? Maybe for a while, but after the young man spent all his money, he realized that the things that had brought him happiness were gone. He was hungry and alone. He wanted to go home, even if it was only to be treated as a hired worker.

The Return of the Prodigal Son, Lionella Spada (1576–1622)

So, the young man decided that he would journey back and tell his father, "Father, I have sinned against heaven and against you" (Luke 15:18). When the father saw his son coming, he ran to him and greeted him. The father was full of love and forgiveness. The son admitted that he had sinned against his father, but the father quickly embraced him. The father made a feast and invited all to celebrate the return of his son, saying, "This son of mine was dead, and has come to life again; he was lost, and has been found" (Luke 15:24).

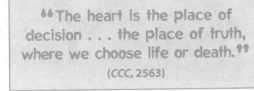

> **"The heart is the place of decision . . . the place of truth, where we choose life or death."**
> *(CCC, 2563)*

In this parable, the younger son's actions show his *conversion*. He turned back to his father. He was sorry and was forgiven. He again had the opportunity to share in his father's life and love. And, in this parable, the father's actions remind us of God's mercy. God waits for us to come back to him. God wants us to experience the lasting joy of his presence. And he rejoices when we decide to turn back to him and accept his love.

Jesus called his first disciples to **conversion**, turning back to God with all one's heart. And he calls us, his disciples today, to continual conversion, too. Jesus leads us to God our Father, inviting us to change our lives and turn to God completely. Our lifelong conversion involves a constant change of heart, since "the heart is the place of decision . . . the place of truth, where we choose life or death" (*CCC*, 2563). And through God the Holy Spirit we are given the desire to change and grow. We are given the grace to begin again. We can find a new life of happiness, sharing in God's life and love each day. We can look forward to the lasting joy of eternal salvation.

Faith Word

conversion

Activity Rewrite the parable about the younger son as if it were taking place in today's world. Take turns reading or performing your modern-day versions of the parable. Discuss the way conversion is shown in each parable.

Following Jesus' teachings leads to true happiness.

How does God's law lead us to happiness?

As Catholics, knowing the laws and teachings of our faith helps us to love the good things of the world properly. That is the whole point of our moral life as followers of Jesus Christ—learning to love all good things in all the right ways. For each of us, the greatest challenge of the moral life is in discovering how to do this, because by doing this we can find *true* happiness.

One day, while teaching on a mountainside, Jesus told us what true happiness is and what we must do to find it. He said:

"Blessed are the poor in spirit,
  for theirs is the kingdom of heaven.
Blessed are they who mourn,
  for they will be comforted.
Blessed are the meek,
  for they will inherit the land.
Blessed are they who hunger and thirst
    for righteousness,
  for they will be satisfied.
Blessed are the merciful,
  for they will be shown mercy.
Blessed are the clean of heart,
  for they will see God.
Blessed are the peacemakers,
  for they will be called children of God.
Blessed are they who are persecuted for
    the sake of righteousness,
  for theirs is the kingdom of heaven."
(Matthew 5:3–10)

Jesus taught about the blessings, the fulfillment of promises, that come to those who follow his example of living and trusting in God's care. Jesus' teaching is called the *Beatitudes*. In the Old Testament when people were faithful to God they were called *blessed*. Each of the Beatitudes expresses the message that we will be blessed, or happy, when we are faithful to God. And when we are patient, kind, respectful, and forgiving, when we recognize our dependence on God and live as he wants us to live, when we do not desire material possessions but fill our hearts with love for God and others, we are living out that faithfulness. We are following Jesus' example of living and trusting in God's care.

When we live out the message of the Beatitudes, we can find true happiness in God. This happiness is not just something for the future, for after we die, but something for today. By living as Jesus' disciples, we experience God's friendship and love each day, as we work to spread God's Kingdom here on earth and look forward to lasting joy—the happiness of the kingdom in heaven. As it is explained in the *Catechism*, happiness is found "in God alone, the source of every good and of all love" (1723).

Activity Discuss how Jesus' message is the same or different from media messages you hear about finding happiness in your daily life.

Jesus' Sermon on the Mount from the movie *King of Kings* (1961)

A perfect world?

Media and popular culture seem to be obsessed with the idea of a "perfect world." There are movies and books with plots about perfect worlds. There are even video games where entire realities and characters can be created according to one's idea of perfection. Can you name some? Why do you think so much time and effort are dedicated to creating these imaginary perfect worlds? How can following the Ten Commandments and the Beatitudes help you to make our world a more perfect place?

Following Jesus means loving as he did.

In Jesus Christ, the second Person of the Blessed Trinity, God fully revealed himself. Jesus treated all people equally and respected the dignity of each person. He cared about the human rights of all people. He protected people who could not protect themselves. He spoke out for the freedom of all people and especially for those who were treated unjustly. He listened to those who were lonely and went out of his way to help people in need. And through Jesus we learn of the great love God the Father has for all people. Jesus was a perfect example of God's unconditional love—offered even when people did not respond to it.

So, it is not surprising that on the night before he died, Jesus told his disciples, "I give you a new commandment: love one another. As I have loved you, so you also should love one another. This is how all will know that you are my disciples, if you have love for one another" (John 13:34–35). This command from Jesus to his disciples is known as the **New Commandment**. Jesus wanted his disciples to love as he loved and to act as they knew he would act so that everyone they met would know him through them. And, in living out this commandment, they would be recognizable as his disciples.

Through the New Commandment Jesus called his disciples to live by the Ten Commandments, not just out of obedience, but out of love. Thus, Jesus taught his disciples that God's love and the call to respond to God's love are the bases for truly being able to live out God's law. He taught that all the laws and teachings he had given were to be lived in love—the kind of love with which he had loved them. And this is a very challenging kind of love—one that respects the human rights of others and values everyone's human dignity unconditionally.

> **The entire Law of the Gospel is contained in the 'new commandment' of Jesus, to love one another as he has loved us.**
> (CCC, 1970)

Jesus calls each of us as his disciples today to live the New Commandment, loving as he loved us. For "the entire Law of the Gospel is contained in the 'new commandment' of Jesus, to love one another as he has loved us" (CCC, 1970). And it is through the example of Jesus' life that we find the way he wants us to love: praying and worshiping God, valuing each person's life, seeking peace and justice, living with honesty and integrity, appreciating God's creation, cherishing family and friends, caring about the good of the community, defending people's rights, and including everyone without exception. By the way we live, we too must be recognizable as Jesus' disciples.

Faith Word

New Commandment

Activity Discuss what the world would be like if everyone truly followed Jesus' New Commandment. What is one thing your group can do today to bring about this kind of world?

RESPONDING...

Recognizing Our Faith

Recall the question at the beginning of this chapter: *Why do I need to follow laws?* Design a screensaver that uses a catchy slogan to express the importance of following God's law.

Living Our Faith

What is one way you can show your love for God and others by following the commandments and the teachings of Jesus? Make a commitment to do so this week.

Partners in FAITH

Saint Ignatius of Loyola

Saint Ignatius of Loyola was born into a wealthy, noble Spanish family. He was not very religious. But his life changed when he received a severe leg injury as a soldier battling the French army in 1521. Unable to walk, he spent time reading while he recovered from his injury. One of the books that he read was about Christ and the saints. Ignatius began to reflect upon the role of Christ in his life. He decided to make some changes in his life, making an effort to follow God's law.

After recovering from his injury, Ignatius made a pilgrimage to Jerusalem where he spent time in a spiritual retreat. While on this pilgrimage he developed a method of prayer known as the Spiritual Exercises. He studied theology and was ordained a priest in 1537. In 1540 he founded the Society of Jesus, or Jesuits, men who live in service to God and God's greater glory.

The Church remembers Saint Ignatius of Loyola, the patron saint of spiritual retreats, on July 31.

What changes might you make in order to more fully follow God's law?

Putting Faith to Work

Talk about what you have learned in this chapter:

 We know that by following Jesus we can be faithful to God's law and find true happiness.

 We accept the commandments as the law of God's covenant.

We love God, others, and ourselves by keeping the commandments and living as disciples of Jesus.

Decide on ways to live out what you have learned.

✝ ENCOUNTERING GOD'S WORD

"If you keep my commandments, you will remain in my love."
(John 15:10)

➡ **READ** the quotation from Scripture.

➡ **REFLECT** on the following question:
How can keeping God's commandments bring about love in the world?

➡ **SHARE** your reflections with a partner.

➡ **DECIDE** on one way you can truly live out God's commandments this week.

Underline the correct answer.

1. Jesus called his first disciples to (**covenant/conversion/community**), which is turning back to God with all one's heart.

2. Each of the (**Beatitudes/Ten Commandments/parables**) expresses this message: We will be blessed, or happy, when we are faithful to God.

3. God made a (**covet/conversion/covenant**) with Moses and the Israelites.

4. The teaching "Love one another. As I have loved you, so you also should love one another" (John 13:34) is known as the (**Beatitudes/New Commandment/Ten Commandments**).

Short Answers

5. How can we live out the New Commandment? _____

6. Name the teaching of Jesus that tells us what true happiness is and what we must do to find it.

7. What do we call the law of God's covenant? _____

8. In Jesus' parable about the man with two sons, whose actions remind us of God's mercy?

9–10. ESSAY: Based upon what you have learned in this chapter, explain how true happiness is found.

RESPONDING...

Sharing Faith with Your Family

Discuss the following with your family:

- Following God's law leads to peace, love, and joy.
- Jesus calls us to conversion.
- Following Jesus' teachings leads to true happiness.
- Following Jesus means loving as he did.

What are some rules that your family follows? Why do they follow those laws? With your family, talk about your answers to these questions.

The Worship Connection

The Ten Commandments call us to keep holy the Lord's Day. On the Lord's Day, or Sunday, we join together to worship God and celebrate the Eucharist.

More to Explore

Find out about laws under consideration in the local, state, or federal government. How will these laws affect your life?

Catholic Social Teaching ☑ Checklist

Theme of Catholic Social Teaching:
Rights and Responsibilities of the Human Person

How it relates to Chapter 3: We have a responsibility to make sure that people's basic rights—food, shelter, clothing, religious freedom, and life itself—are upheld. Following the commandments is one way to fulfill this responsibility.

How can you do this?

☐ At home:

_____

☐ At school/work:

_____

☐ In the parish:

_____

☐ In the community:

_____

Check off each action after it has been completed.

4

We Love God and Others

> "Shout joyfully to God, all you on earth;
> sing of his glorious name;
> give him glorious praise."
>
> (Psalm 66:1–2)

Leader: Let us now praise God in the words of a Church hymn from the fourth century, a great song of praise and thanksgiving to God.

Group 1: You are God: we praise you;
You are the Lord: we acclaim you;
You are the eternal Father:
All creation worships you.

Group 2: To you all angels, all the powers of heaven,
Cherubim and Seraphim, sing in endless praise:
Holy, holy, holy Lord, God of power and might,
heaven and earth are full of your glory.

Group 1: The glorious company of apostles praise you.
The noble fellowship of prophets praise you.
The white-robed army of martyrs praise you.

Group 2: Throughout the world the holy Church acclaims you:
Father, of majesty unbounded,
your true and only Son, worthy of all worship,
and the Holy Spirit, advocate and guide.

Group 1: You, Christ, are the king of glory,
the eternal Son of the Father.

When you became man to set us free,
you did not spurn the Virgin's womb.

Group 2: You overcame the sting of death,
and opened the kingdom of heaven to all believers.

You are seated at God's right hand in glory.
We believe that you will come, and be our judge.

All: Come then, Lord, and help your people, bought with the price of your own blood, and bring us with your saints to glory everlasting. Amen.

(Te Deum)

Visit www.weliveourfaith.com to find appropriate music and songs.

41

The BiG Question:

How do I honor those I love?

iscover the story behind your name. Have you ever wondered why your parents selected your name? Perhaps you were named to honor a saint, a family member, or a friend. Or perhaps your parents selected your name just because it seemed right for you!

Take a survey of your group. How many members know the story behind their own names?

Most popular baby names in the United States in recent years

Girls	Boys
1. Emily	1. Jacob
2. Emma	2. Michael
3. Madison	3. Joshua
4. Olivia	4. Matthew
5. Hannah	5. Ethan
6. Abigail	6. Andrew
7. Isabella	7. Daniel
8. Ashley	8. William
9. Samantha	9. Joseph
10. Elizabeth	10. Christopher

If you had to choose your name today, what would it be? Why?

HELLO
my name is

In this chapter we learn about Jesus' Great Commandment and the first three commandments of the Ten Commandments. Through this chapter, we hope

to understand Jesus' Great Commandment and the first three of the Ten Commandments

to respect the obligations and challenges these commandments place on us

to respond to these commandments by following them in our everyday lives.

"This memorial is for those who have died, and for us to remember them." (Maya Lin, architect of the Vietnam Veterans Memorial)

In 1982 the Vietnam Veterans Memorial was dedicated in Washington, D.C., to honor veterans who served in the Vietnam War. The most famous part of this popular monument is "The Wall," which is inscribed with the names of more than 58,000 men and women who died or went missing during the Vietnam War.

Visitors to the monument commonly use paper to take rubbings of the names of their loved ones. They also leave offerings of cards, poems, pictures, medals, and other mementos. Currently there are more than 64,000 offerings stored at the Museum Resource Center. The leaving of keepsakes serves to honor and actively remember loved ones. And honoring their names helps us to remember their sacrifices and their lives.

Activity What other memorials do you know of? Whom do they honor?

The Wall, Vietnam Veterans Memorial, Washington, D.C.

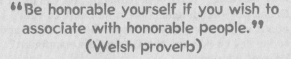

"Be honorable yourself if you wish to associate with honorable people." (Welsh proverb)

43

BELIEVING...

Jesus teaches us the Great Commandment.

As a young Jewish boy growing up in Nazareth, Jesus studied the teachings of the Old Testament. He studied about the covenant God made with his people and about the Ten Commandments. To celebrate religious holidays, he and his family sometimes went to the **Temple**, the holy place in Jerusalem where Jewish people gathered to worship God. There, as a young boy celebrating Passover with his family one year, Jesus listened to and questioned the teachers about the law and about Scripture. And "all who heard him were astounded at his understanding and his answers" (Luke 2:47). Later in his public life, while teaching in the synagogue, Jesus again astonished people with his teaching, "for he taught them as one having authority and not as the scribes" (Mark 1:22).

Yet throughout Jesus' public life there was growing hostility toward him from some religious leaders. The chief priests, the **scribes**, or scholars of the law, and the elders wanted to know who gave Jesus the authority to speak and act the way he did. And as Jesus carried out his ministry, his teachings continued to astonish and alarm some leaders, for he taught about the righteousness, or moral conduct in agreement with God's will, that "surpasses that of the scribes and Pharisees" (Matthew 5:20). Thus, people sometimes tried to entrap Jesus, hoping he would say something that they could use against him. This may have been the case one day in the Temple area, when one of the scribes posed this question to Jesus: "Teacher, which commandment in the law is the greatest?" (Matthew 22:36).

Jesus said, "You shall love the Lord, your God, with all your heart, with all your soul, and with all your mind. This is the greatest and the first commandment. The second is like it: You shall love your neighbor as yourself" (Matthew 22:37–39). Jesus' answer to the scribe is called the **Great Commandment**, and by his response Jesus demonstrated his deep knowledge of Scripture. For the Great Commandment combined the *Shema*, a prayer from the Book of Deuteronomy, and a teaching from the Book of Leviticus. The *Shema* reminded the Jewish people to love God with all their heart, soul, and strength. And the teaching from Leviticus, which had been used since the beginning of the people's covenant with God, instructed God's people about loving their neighbors as themselves. So, the Great Commandment encompasses all the demands of the Ten Commandments, the **Decalogue**. And the Decalogue, God's "ten words," "must be interpreted in light of this twofold yet single commandment of love, the fullness of the Law" (*CCC*, 2055).

This love, the fullness of the law, was evident in Jesus Christ. He lived the twofold message of the Great Commandment, loving God, and loving and serving others. And Jesus invites us to do the same.

Faith Words
Temple
scribes
Great Commandment
Shema
Decalogue

Activity Read and highlight the words of the Great Commandment. Take a moment to really think about what these words mean. Do you think people today try to live out the Great Commandment? Why or why not?

We live out the first commandment.

Whether they are stated as directives or as restrictions, the commandments make God's will known to us. The commandments bring into a single focus the religious and social dimensions of our lives—the first three instruct us in loving God and the other seven instruct us in loving others. Yet if we disregard any one of the commandments, it affects the way we live out all of them. For we cannot love one another without loving God, who created us, and we cannot love God without loving all of his creatures!

When God gave the Israelites the Ten Commandments, it was after freeing them from their slavery in Egypt. He brought them into the desert of Sinai and, calling Moses to the mountain, said, "I, the LORD, am your God, who brought you out of the land of Egypt, that place of slavery" (Exodus 20:2). After this reminder of his power, love, and gift of freedom, God stated the first commandment, "You shall not have other gods besides me" (Exodus 20:3). Through this commandment God reveals that he is the one and true God, who brought his people freedom so that he could be their God

Moses receives tablets (Germany, 11th century)

> **" God has loved us first. "**
> (CCC, 2083)

and they could be his people. Yet only a short time later, when Moses went back up Mount Sinai for more instruction from God, the people grew restless, melted down their gold, made an idol in the shape of a calf, and worshiped before it. In doing this they disobeyed the first commandment. They committed the sin of **idolatry**, giving worship to a creature or thing instead of God.

Faith Words
idolatry
atheism

In our lives, when we make anything more important than God, it becomes an idol. Today we may not worship images of a calf, but there might be other things that we worship. We might make things like popularity or money far too important, maybe even more important than God. Some people even reject or deny God's existence, which is the sin of **atheism**. To live out the first commandment we must believe in God and put him first in our lives. The very reason that we are here and have been created in God's own image is that "God has loved us first" (CCC, 2083). In living out the first commandment, we recall God's love for us and respond to God with love. We honor God by believing in him, praying to him, worshiping him, and loving others because they are made in his image. We put God first, acting in God's image and likeness and living out our love for God so that others can see that God is among us.

Activity Complete a day planner for tomorrow. Slot in events that show that God is important in your life.

Theological virtues

Faith, hope, and love are called *theological virtues*, or habits of doing good. In Greek, *theos* means "God." These virtues are gifts from God. They make it possible for us to have a relationship with God—the Father, the Son, and the Holy Spirit.

The first commandment calls us to put God first by believing in him, hoping in him, and loving him above everything. We express our connection to God through faith, hope, and charity, or love.

The first commandment calls us not to doubt but to nourish and protect our faith, not to despair but to hope in God's goodness and justice, and not to be indifferent or ungrateful but to love God who is the source of all things.

Pray the Acts of Faith, Hope, and Love. (See page 308.)

CATHOLIC IDENTITY

45

We live out the second commandment.

How do you feel when someone disrespects your name?

Showing a deep respect for God's holy name is an outcome of putting God at the center of our lives. So, the second commandment, "You shall not take the name of the LORD, your God, in vain" (Exodus 20:7), follows from the first. Through the second commandment God reveals that his name is **sacred**, or holy.

When God called Moses to lead the Israelites out of Egypt, Moses asked, "When I go to the Israelites and say to them, 'The God of your fathers has sent me to you,' if they ask me, 'What is his name?' what am I to tell them?' God replied, 'I am who am'" (Exodus 3:13–14). The Hebrew letters of God's response form the name *Yahweh*. The Israelites knew that God was holy and understood that his name was holy, too. So, out of respect for God's holiness they did not say the name Yahweh aloud. Instead they called upon God as *Lord* and used God's name only when absolutely necessary and with great **reverence**, or honor, love, and respect.

Yet, we hear of many abuses of God's name. There are many sins by which people disregard the second commandment. There is **blasphemy**, a thought, word, or act that makes fun of or shows contempt or hatred for God, the Church and the saints, or sacred objects. There is also **perjury**, or the act of making a false oath. In an oath, often in a courtroom, people swear, with God as their witness, that what they are about to say is true. But perjury calls on God to be a witness to a lie and thus violates the sacredness of God's name. **Cursing**, which means calling on God to do harm to someone, also violates the second commandment.

As people who believe in God, we are called to obey the second commandment. We are called to always show reverence for God's name, never using it in a disrespectful or unnecessary way, but always speaking it with a sense of awe that acknowledges

Faith Words

sacred
reverence
blasphemy
perjury
cursing

God's power and love for us. We are called to hold God's name in our minds and hearts in a silent, loving way and only speak it to bless, praise, or glorify God.

As Catholics, we are baptized in the name of the Father and of the Son and of the Holy Spirit—in the name of the Blessed Trinity. And as we live out the second commandment, we revere the many titles used to call upon God the Father, God the Son—Jesus Christ—and God the Holy Spirit. We respect the names of Mary and the saints. Each of our names is sacred, too, for we are called as God's children. Thus, as a sign of our human dignity, we use our names and the names of others with respect. As God himself has told us,

"I have called you by name: you are mine" (Isaiah 43:1).

Activity Think about your day. Did you use God's name? Was it with reverence?

We live out the third commandment.

In the story of creation, in six days God created the heavens, the earth, and all that is in them, and "God blessed the seventh day and made it holy, because on it he rested from all the work he had done in creation" (Genesis 2:3). Thus, the Israelites set apart the seventh day to rest and honor God. They kept this day as their **Sabbath**. And this day became a memorial of their freedom from slavery in Egypt and was set aside as a sign of the covenant they had made with God when they accepted the Ten Commandments. For in the third commandment God said to the people, "Remember to keep holy the sabbath day" (Exodus 20:8). God added, "Six days you may labor and do all your work, but the seventh day is the sabbath of the LORD, your God" (Exodus 20:9–10).

God revealed in the third commandment that we must keep a day holy for the Lord, a day of praising him, resting from our work, and doing good things for ourselves and others. As Catholics we celebrate this holy day of rest on Sunday, the first day of the week. For it was on this day that Jesus Christ rose from the dead. We call this day the Lord's Day. The Lord's Day is the first day of the new creation, begun by Christ's Resurrection, which brings us the hope of life forever with God in heaven.

In living out the third commandment, we, as members of the Church, must gather for Mass every Sunday—or the evening before—with our parish community. This celebration of the Eucharist is the very center of our life and worship as Catholics. It is the most important way to keep the Lord's Day holy. In this celebration, we give God thanks and praise, listen to God's word, and remember and celebrate Jesus' **Paschal Mystery**, his suffering, death, Resurrection, and Ascension. We celebrate Jesus' gift of himself in the Eucharist, receive Jesus in Holy Communion, and go out to share his love, serve others, and build a better community.

As Catholics we must also participate in Mass on the *holy days of obligation*. And on Sundays and these special holy days we must recognize and honor God through worship, remember that we depend on God for everything, take rest for our bodies and spirits, and renew our efforts to live as disciples of Jesus, refocusing on what matters most, the Lord our God!

> **"God replied, 'I am who am.'"**
> (Exodus 3:14)

Activity Use some form of the words *recognize*, *remember*, *rest*, *renew*, and *refocus* in a paragraph that describes ways to keep the third commandment.

Faith Words
Sabbath
Paschal Mystery

שבת Shabbat

The Jewish people celebrate the Sabbath, or *Shabbat* (meaning "to rest") in Hebrew, in specific ways. *Shabbat*:

- is celebrated from sundown on Fridays until sunset on Saturdays
- was a new concept. In ancient times days of rest were usually for the wealthy and the elite. The working class, which included the majority of people, worked every day.
- includes a brief religious service on Friday evenings, and a longer service on Saturdays
- frequently involves a precooked meal (since cooking for most Jews is prohibited during *Shabbat*)
- incorporates a prayer before the meal and grace after the meal
- officially ends at nightfall, when three stars are visible, approximately 40–60 minutes after sunset
- concludes with a blessing called *Havdalah* that symbolically marks the separation between the Sabbath and the rest of the week.

In what ways is *Shabbat* the same as or different from the Lord's Day for Christians?

RESPONDING...

Recognizing Our Faith

Recall the question at the beginning of this chapter: *How do I honor those I love?* Think of someone you love. Write an inscription on this plaque honoring that person.

Think of your love for God. How will you honor him this week?

Living Our Faith

Look back at the day planner you made on page 45. Did you take time for God? Explain your answer.

Blessed Pier Giorgio Frassati

Pier Giorgio Frassati was born April 6, 1901, in Turin, Italy. Known among his friends as a practical joker and a natural leader, Pier Giorgio lived an adventurous life while developing a deep spiritual life. As a student, he joined the Society of St. Vincent de Paul and other organizations, such as Catholic Action, dedicating much of his spare time to serving those in need.

At age twenty-four, Pier Giorgio became sick with polio, a disabling disease, which caused his death. When he died, more than 1,000 people honored Pier Giorgio's life and works by attending his funeral! He had helped many people and had given so much of his time and resources to help the poor families he met.

Pope John Paul II honored Pier Giorgio's life and works on May 20, 1990. Pier Giorgio was *beatified*, recognized by the Church for having lived an outstanding Christian life. Blessed Pier Giorgio Frassati may someday be *canonized*, or named a saint.

Pier Giorgio honored God and all the people in his life. How can you do the same?

Putting Faith to Work

Talk about what you have learned in this chapter:

 We understand Jesus' Great Commandment and the first three of the Ten Commandments.

 We respect the obligations and challenges these commandments place on us.

 We respond to these commandments by following them in our everyday lives.

Decide on ways to live out what you have learned.

✝ ENCOUNTERING GOD'S WORD

Jesus explained that honoring God meant keeping God's law in both great and small ways:

❝You . . . have neglected the weightier things of the law: judgment and mercy and fidelity. [But] these you should have done, without neglecting the others❞
(Matthew 23:23).

➡ **READ** the quotation from Scripture.

➡ **REFLECT** on the following:
Think of what we can do to honor God in our daily lives in both great and small ways.

➡ **SHARE** your reflections with a partner.

➡ **DECIDE** on two ways to honor God this week.

Write the letter that best defines each term.

1. _____ Temple

2. _____ sacred

3. _____ Sabbath

4. _____ reverence

a. honor, love, and respect

b. giving worship to a creature or thing instead of God

c. holy

d. a day set apart to rest and honor God

e. the holy place in Jerusalem where Jewish people gathered to worship God

Complete the following.

5. Through the first commandment, God reveals that _____.

6. Through the second commandment, God reveals that _____.

7. Through the third commandment, God reveals that _____.

8. The Paschal Mystery refers to Jesus' _____.

9–10. ESSAY: Explain the twofold message of Jesus' Great Commandment.

RESPONDING...

Sharing Faith with Your Family

Discuss the following with your family:

- Jesus teaches us the Great Commandment.
- We live out the first commandment: I AM THE LORD YOUR GOD: YOU SHALL NOT HAVE STRANGE GODS BEFORE ME.
- We live out the second commandment: YOU SHALL NOT TAKE THE NAME OF THE LORD YOUR GOD IN VAIN.
- We live out the third commandment: REMEMBER TO KEEP HOLY THE LORD'S DAY.

Design a family plaque. Include at least three ways your family honors God, one another, and other people.

THE WILSON FAMILY

The Wilson family honors God by believing in him.

The Worship Connection

Pay attention to the actions by which we show reverence at Mass: standing for the Gospel reading, bowing our heads, and kneeling. Honor God by prayerfully entering into these actions.

More to Explore

Use the Internet or library to find cities, towns, or communities that are named in honor of saints or holy people.

Catholic Social Teaching ☑ Checklist

Theme of Catholic Social Teaching:
Care for God's Creation

How it relates to Chapter 4: The first three commandments instruct us in ways to show our love for God. In following these commandments, we can show respect for God and all that he has created.

How can you do this?

☐ At home:

_____

☐ At school/work:

_____

☐ In the parish:

_____

☐ In the community:

_____

Check off each action after it has been completed.

"**Choose life, then, that you and your descendants may live.**"

(Deuteronomy 30:19)

Leader: We all depend on others to help us through life. And they depend on us. Let us pray to be open and respectful toward all the people in our lives.

Reader 1: "The LORD God formed man out of the clay of the ground and blew into his nostrils the breath of life, and so man became a living being." (Genesis 2:7)

Leader: Lord God, we honor you as our creator. Help us to respect the life that you gave to every one of us.

We ask this in the name of Jesus Christ.

All: Amen.

Reader 2: "Hear, my son, your father's instruction,
and reject not your mother's teaching." (Proverbs 1:8)

Leader: Lord God, you have given us parents and guardians to care for us and to teach us how to live as your children. Help us to listen to their teaching, appreciate all that they do for us, and bring them joy and honor.

We ask this in the name of Jesus Christ.

All: Amen.

Reader 3: "Each one of you should love his wife as himself, and the wife should respect her husband." (Ephesians 5:33)

Leader: Lord God, help all wives and husbands to love and respect each other. Help each of us to make our contribution to happy and loving relationships.

We ask this in the name of Jesus Christ.

All: Amen.

@ Visit www.weliveourfaith.com to find appropriate music and songs.

The BiG QuEstion:

Whom do I respect?

Discover some examples of respect. Using the letters of the word *respect* below, list some things you can do or say to show respect for yourself and others.

R _____

E _____

S _____

P _____

E _____

C _____

T _____

Look back at the examples of respect you have listed. Identify one way that you will be more respectful in your life this week.

In this chapter
we learn that the fourth, fifth, and sixth commandments require us to respect ourselves and others in specific ways. Through this chapter, we hope

 to understand that Jesus taught us to fulfill the commandments out of love for God, others, and ourselves

 to express this love in the specific ways taught by the fourth, fifth, and sixth commandments

 to choose life by obeying these commandments with love and respect for God, ourselves, and others.

Born in 1929, Anne Frank was thirteen when she, her family, and four others went into hiding in the attic above her father's office in the Netherlands during World War II. They were protecting themselves from the Nazi troops who were occupying their country and arresting and killing Jews. Though hidden away, Anne, her family, and those living with them listened to radio broadcasts and knew the horrors of the Holocaust taking place around them.

As many young people do, Anne recorded her feelings and experiences in a diary. Her words address and challenge discrimination, intolerance, and violence in a way that still touches our lives today. She wrote, "It's utterly impossible for me to build my life on a foundation of chaos, suffering and death. I see the world being slowly transformed into a wilderness, I hear the approaching thunder that, one day, will destroy us too, I feel the suffering of millions. And yet, when I look up at the sky, I somehow feel that everything will change for the better, that this cruelty too shall end, that peace and tranquility will return once more."

After two years, the Nazis raided the secret hideaway. Anne, her family, and the others were sent to concentration camps. At the age of fifteen, Anne died at a concentration camp. But her diary survived. So did her father, who, out of love and respect for his daughter, published excerpts from the diary that expressed so much love and respect for everyone and everything around her.

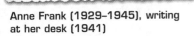

Anne Frank (1929–1945), writing at her desk (1941)

Room in the hideaway where Anne Frank stayed

"It's a wonder I haven't abandoned all my ideals, they seem so absurd and impractical. Yet I cling to them because I still believe, in spite of everything, that people are truly good at heart."

Those were the words that Anne Frank, a German-Jewish teenager forced into hiding during the Holocaust, wrote in her diary on July 15, 1944. The *Holocaust* is the name for the mass murder, during World War II, of Europe's Jews by the Nazis, led by German dictator Adolf Hitler. Since *The Diary of Anne Frank* was first published in 1947, its powerful message of respect for life, for other people, and for oneself has helped to make it one of the most popular books of our time. More than 31 million copies have sold worldwide, and it is available in more than sixty-seven languages.

Activity How can you show that you respect your own life? that you respect the lives of others?

"Respect starts with yourself."
(Anonymous)

We are called to choose life.

The Ten Commandments are the laws of God's covenant. In the Old Testament God reminds the Israelites: "If you obey the commandments of the LORD, your God, . . . loving him, and walking in his ways, . . . you will live . . . and the LORD, your God, will bless you. . . . I have set before you life and death, . . . Choose life" (Deuteronomy 30:16, 19). It is not surprising, then, that in the Gospels of Matthew, Mark, and Luke we find a rich young man asking Jesus what he would have to do to "gain eternal life" (Matthew 19:16).

Jesus told this young man, "If you wish to enter into life, keep the commandments" (Matthew 19:17). When the young man asked which commandments, Jesus replied, "'You shall not kill; you shall not commit adultery; you shall not steal; you shall not bear false witness; honor your father and your mother'; and 'you shall love your neighbor as yourself'" (Matthew 19:18–19). Then, when the young man explained that he had kept these commandments, Jesus said, "If you wish to be perfect, go, sell what you have and give to [the] poor, and you will have treasure in heaven. Then come, follow me" (Matthew 19:21). Jesus' words to this young man point out that the New Law, the Law of the Gospel, "'fulfills,' refines, surpasses, and leads the Old Law to its perfection" (*CCC*, 1967).

Jesus had already explained to his disciples that he had not come to do away with the laws that God had given to Moses, but to fulfill them. Jesus taught his disciples to live out the commandments as an expression of love for God, for themselves, and for their neighbors. He also taught them that love of neighbor extended even to their enemies and to those who persecuted them. Jesus called his disciples to "be perfect, just as your heavenly Father is perfect" (Matthew 5:48). In Luke 6:36, where this same teaching of Jesus is also given, the word *perfect* has been replaced by the word *merciful*. Thus, as Jesus called his disciples to be perfect, he also called them to imitate the example of God, his Father, who is all-merciful. Jesus called them to a life filled with mercy toward others—a life of caring for everyone; of giving to those who were poor; of being kind, generous, and compassionate toward all people; and of showing God's mercy, his love and forgiveness, to everyone.

Jesus calls us, too, to keep the commandments and to live as his disciples. He calls us to follow him and to be perfect—to be merciful in all of our dealings with others. He teaches us that we can live out our discipleship by loving and forgiving all people—even those who are hard to love and hard to forgive. Jesus teaches that God's love, and the call to respond to God's love, are at the center of the commandments. And Jesus shows us that in living out the commandments we are able to choose "life" by loving God and walking in his ways, as Jesus himself did.

Activity Compare and contrast Jesus' call to be "perfect" with our society's understanding of what it means to be "perfect." Complete the chart below.

Society's view of being perfect	Jesus' vision of being perfect

We live out the fourth commandment.

The commandments are part of God's Revelation. Yet they also express what is instinctively, or naturally, moral to each of us. Thus, as we look closely at the fourth through tenth commandments, we recognize the fundamental rights of all human beings and our obligation to respect those rights by loving each of our neighbors.

When God gave the fourth commandment, he said, "Honor your father and your mother, that you may have a long life in the land which the Lord, your God, is giving you" (Exodus 20:12). How fitting that God called people to first honor and respect those who are most closely connected to them: their parents, brothers, sisters, grandparents, aunts, uncles, cousins, other relatives, and friends. How fitting, too, that Jesus' own life showed us how to live out the fourth commandment. In his early life, within the Holy Family, we find that Jesus "went down with them and came to Nazareth, and was obedient to them" (Luke 2:51). The Gospels recount, too, that throughout his whole life Jesus lived in loving obedience to the will of God, his Father, and called all of his disciples to do the same.

> "Keep the commandments."
> (Matthew 19:17)

As Jesus' disciples we try to show our love by living out the commandments. We can live out the fourth commandment by:

- appreciating and obeying our parents, guardians, other family members, and all those who lead and serve us

- continually being grateful to our parents for all they have given us

- eventually supporting our families and helping to care for our parents in their old age

- respecting those who are our elders, appreciating their wisdom as valued members of our communities, and avoiding any form of discrimination that causes us to treat older people as less than equal to everyone else

- valuing and listening with respect to parents, guardians, family members, friends, teachers, pastors, bishops, the pope, those with whom we work, those who govern our lands, all those who help us to see God's will for us, and our neighbors everywhere.

We must always be aware, though, that God our Father never asks us to be obedient to those who direct us to do what is morally wrong.

Activity In groups brainstorm ways to better live out the fourth commandment at home, at school, and in your neighborhood.

Civil authority

The fourth commandment requires civil authorities to use their authority justly, fairly, and respectfully. They are to respect the rights of everyone. And they are never to command what is "contrary to the dignity of persons and the natural law" (CCC, 2235). They cannot dismiss anyone's rights as a citizen without a legitimate, justifiable reason.

As citizens, we, along with our civil authorities, are responsible for building up society in a spirit of truth, justice, solidarity, and freedom. Thus, we have a moral obligation to pay taxes, to exercise our right to vote, and to defend our country when necessary.

If you were the mayor of your town, how would you use your authority to respect the rights of everyone?

We live out the fifth commandment.

How can we show love for our neighbors?

Out of all of his creation, God has chosen to share his own life with humanity and has called us to the special responsibility of loving, caring for, and protecting his gift of life. This responsibility requires us to live out the fifth commandment, "You shall not kill" (Exodus 20:13). This commandment is based on the truth that all life is sacred, created by God.

Pro-life flyer, United States Conference of Catholic Bishops' Secretariat for Pro-Life Activities

And the fact that Jesus Christ, the Son of God, took on our human life is the greatest testimony we have to the dignity and sacredness of human life.

The right to life, from the moment of conception to the moment of natural death, is the most basic human right. Following the fifth commandment demands that we respect and protect human life in all that we say and do.

As Catholics we recognize that some forms of violence are always wrong:

abortion—The direct termination of the life of an unborn baby is always wrong. The Supreme Court of the United States has legalized abortion, but we must remember that what is legal is not always morally right. We should work to change laws in society that allow abortion.

euthanasia, or *mercy killing*—We can never deliberately kill someone, even in cases of great suffering. Our faith requires us to take ordinary measures to preserve life. A dying patient, however, may refuse "'over-zealous' treatment" (*CCC,* 2278).

murder—The deliberate taking of a life is not our right.

suicide—The taking of one's own life is an offense against God, who gave each of us the gift of life.

terrorism and related violence that intentionally targets innocent civilians—Misusing political views and personal beliefs to intimidate or attack others is wrong.

There are many other forms of violence. Catholic teaching should shape our decisions on these:

war—We should always try to use nonviolent means to resolve conflicts. War should be a last resort when other means fail to protect the innocent against fundamental injustice. Our American Catholic bishops have declared, "We do not perceive any situation in which the deliberate initiation of nuclear warfare . . . can be morally justified" (*The Challenge of Peace,* 1983, 150).

the death penalty—The *Catechism* states, "The cases in which the execution of the offender is an absolute necessity 'are very rare, if not practically non-existent'" (2267).

domestic violence—People are often violated in their own homes by their own families. Domestic violence is an assault against human dignity, and those who commit it should seek professional help.

environmental waste and pollution—This is the destruction of those things in creation that God gave us to support life. To pollute the environment is to poison ourselves and to take away the possibilities of life for the generations that will come after us.

scandal—This is "an attitude or behavior which leads another to do evil" (*CCC,* 2284). It is wrong when individuals or groups use their power and influence to tempt others to disrespect life in any way.

God's mercy is greater than the actions of any person. Through God's grace each of us can find the power to heal, to build up, and to choose life.

Activity Make a timeline of the various stages of the average person's life. Note ways to show respect for people at each stage of their lives.

Dealing with anger

Jesus' words to his disciples in his Sermon on the Mount give us a deeper understanding of the ways we are to follow the fifth commandment. Jesus said, "You have heard that it was said to your ancestors, 'You shall not kill; and whoever kills will be liable to judgment.' But I say to you, whoever is angry with his brother will be liable to judgment" (Matthew 5:21–22). Anger can lead us to act in violent ways—to destroy things and to harm or injure others. And violence against others can lead us to a complete disregard for human life.

Brainstorm some positive ways of dealing with anger.

CATHOLIC IDENTITY

We live out the sixth commandment.

God created humanity in his image, giving us the human dignity that makes us all equal. And he created us with **human sexuality**, the gift of being able to feel, think, choose, love, and act as the male or female person God created us to be. Our human sexuality makes us female or male, and our sexuality is an important part of everything about us. Our human sexuality is a good and beautiful gift from God that gives us the capacity to form bonds of unity, love, and communion with others.

> ❝Through God's grace each of us can find the power to heal, to build up, and to choose life.❞

The sixth commandment is "You shall not commit adultery" (Exodus 20:14). **Adultery** is infidelity in marriage, unfaithfulness to one's husband or wife. Married couples promise, or vow, to commit their whole lives to each other while showing their love for each other in a beautiful, physical way. This full expression of sexual intimacy is reserved for marriage, and married couples vow to share this love only with each other. The sexual union of husband and wife bonds them into a covenant of life and love that is open to the responsibility of procreation—bringing God's gift of new life into the world.

Married couples are obliged to love and protect each other and their relationship. Divorce is the breaking of the marriage contract between a man and woman. The sixth commandment obliges married couples to be faithful to each other until death, both physically and emotionally. They must be open to the children with whom God may bless them, never artificially preventing the conception of a child. The sixth

commandment also obliges each of us to honor the love a husband and wife have for each other and to honor their promise to be faithful. The sixth commandment obliges us to grow in loving ourselves, in respecting our bodies, in loving our family and friends, and in properly showing our feelings of love.

As we live out the sixth commandment, we refrain from these and all offenses against the dignity of marriage and the commitment of relationships:

polygamy—the practice of having two or more spouses at the same time

incest—sexual relations with family members

free union—living together and having sexual relations without the commitment of marriage

fornication—sexual relations outside of marriage, including premarital sex

lust—an excessive or uncontrollable desire for inappropriate sexual enjoyment or pleasure

masturbation—deliberately stimulating one's sexual organs by oneself

pornography—the degrading portrayal of human sexuality in words, movies, or pictures

promiscuity—a casual approach to sexual love with no regard to faithful commitment

prostitution—the buying and selling of sex

rape—the violent act of forcing someone into sexual intimacy

homosexual acts—sexual relations between persons of the same sex.

The sixth commandment also reminds us of our vocation to love as God calls us to love, remaining faithful to our baptismal promises. It reminds us to practice the virtue, or good habit, of chastity. **Chastity** is the use of our human sexuality in a responsible and faithful way, a way in which we integrate our sexuality and our spirituality in a unity of body and spirit. Whether we are single, married, ordained priests, or religious sisters and brothers leading consecrated lives, Christ is the model of chastity for all of us.

Faith Words
human sexuality
adultery
chastity

Activity What could you say to someone your own age to emphasize the positive nature of chastity?

RESPONDING...

Recognizing Our Faith

Recall the question at the beginning of this chapter: *Whom do I respect?* Whom did you list as you began the chapter? Would you add others to your list after working on this chapter? If so, whom does the list include now?

Living Our Faith

Discuss ways to honor life and creation. Choose one way and make it part of your life today.

The Sisters of Life

Partners in FAITH

The Sisters of Life are a community of religious women who devote their lives to promoting respect for every human life. In addition to taking the three traditional religious vows of poverty, chastity, and obedience, the Sisters of Life take a special, fourth vow to protect and enhance the sacredness of every human life.

This religious order was founded in 1991 by a New York archbishop, John Cardinal O'Connor. In the archdiocesan newspaper, he had published a special request: "Help Wanted: Sisters of Life." Many women responded to this call, and on June 1, 1991, eight women entered this new religious order. Within a few years the Sisters of Life had established several convents in the New York area and were actively helping pregnant women, offering retreats, and assisting families in need. In 2002 New York Archbishop Edward Cardinal Egan appointed these sisters to run the Family Life/Respect Life Office of the Archdiocese of New York.

In what ways can you devote some time to promoting respect for every human life?

For additional ideas and activities, visit www.weliveourfaith.com.

Putting Faith to Work

Talk about what you have learned in this chapter:

 We understand that Jesus taught us to fulfill the commandments out of love for God, others, and ourselves.

 We express this love in the specific ways taught by the fourth, fifth, and sixth commandments.

 We choose life by obeying these commandments with love and respect for God, ourselves, and others.

Decide on ways to live out what you have learned.

ENCOUNTERING GOD'S WORD

Jesus said:

"I have told you this so that my joy might be in you and your joy might be complete. This is my commandment: love one another as I love you"

(John 15:11–12).

➡ **READ** the quotation from Scripture.

➡ **REFLECT** on the following:
Jesus wants us to love as he loved. How did Jesus show his love? How can we show love and respect for one another, no matter what our age or role in life?

➡ **SHARE** your reflections with a partner.

➡ **DECIDE** to show love and respect to others in the ways that Jesus taught us.

Write the letter of the answer that best defines each term.

1. _____ chastity

2. _____ right to life

3. _____ human sexuality

4. _____ adultery

a. the gift of being able to feel, think, choose, love, and act as the male or female person God created us to be

b. discrimination that causes us to treat older people as less than equal to everyone else

c. infidelity in marriage, unfaithfulness to one's husband or wife

d. the most basic human right

e. the virtue by which we use our human sexuality in a responsible and faithful way

Write True or False next to the following sentences. On a separate sheet of paper, change the false sentences to make them true.

5. _____ Jesus came to do away with the laws God had given to Moses.

6. _____ The fourth commandment requires that we obey all those who lead and serve us, except when they direct us to do something that is morally wrong.

7. _____ The fifth commandment demands that we respect and protect human life.

8. _____ The sixth commandment and its requirement of chastity apply only to those who are married.

9–10. ESSAY: What are three ways to show that we are living out the fourth commandment?

RESPONDING...

Sharing Faith with Your Family

Discuss the following with your family:

- We are called to choose life.
- We live out the fourth commandment: HONOR YOUR FATHER AND YOUR MOTHER.
- We live out the fifth commandment: YOU SHALL NOT KILL.
- We live out the sixth commandment: YOU SHALL NOT COMMIT ADULTERY.

Together think of a mission statement for your family, summarizing the way you can live out the fourth, fifth, and sixth commandments.

The Worship Connection

In the offertory at Mass, we give thanks to God for giving us the gifts of the earth and the dignity of our human lives. Be attentive to this prayer of thanks at Mass.

More to Explore

In books, movies, or TV shows, try to find role models for living out the fourth, fifth, and sixth commandments. Share your findings with your group.

Catholic Social Teaching ☑ Checklist

Theme of Catholic Social Teaching:
Call to Family, Community, and Participation

How it relates to Chapter 5: As we learned in this chapter, we, as citizens, are responsible for building up society in a spirit of truth, justice, solidarity, and freedom. We are to participate in public life, working for the good of all people in society.

How can you do this?

☐ At home:

_____

☐ At school/work:

_____

☐ In the parish:

_____

☐ In the community:

_____

Check off each action after it has been completed.

6

We Respect All People

"**Therefore, putting away falsehood, speak the truth, each one to his neighbor, for we are members one of another.**"

(Ephesians 4:25)

Reader: "Owe nothing to anyone, except to love one another; for the one who loves another has fulfilled the law. The commandments, 'You shall not commit adultery; you shall not kill; you shall not steal; you shall not covet,' and whatever other commandment there may be, are summed up in this saying, [namely] 'You shall love your neighbor as yourself.' Love does no evil to the neighbor; hence, love is the fulfillment of the law." (Romans 13:8–10)

Leader: Help us, Lord Jesus, to love as you did, for in so doing we will keep the commandments.

All: May we owe nothing to anyone, except love.

Leader: Help us, Lord Jesus, to fulfill your law and to do no evil to our neighbors.

All: May we show that love is the fulfillment of the law.

Leader: Help us, Lord Jesus, to love our neighbors as we love ourselves.

All: May we respect all people and love them as our neighbors.

Leader: We ask these things in your name, Lord Jesus, you who live and reign with the Father and the Holy Spirit.

All: Amen.

@ Visit www.weliveourfaith.com to find appropriate music and songs.

The BiG QuEStion:

Who is my neighbor?

 iscover which of the following quotations about one's neighbor are from the Bible. Turn this page upside down and learn the source of each quote.

1 "Good fences make good neighbors."

2 "Love your neighbor as yourself."

3 "Let each of us please our neighbor for the good, for building up."

4 "I want you to be concerned about your next-door neighbor. Do you know your next-door neighbor?"

5 "Love thy neighbor—and if he happens to be tall, debonair and devastating, it will be that much easier."

6 "As man draws nearer to the stars, why should he not also draw nearer to his neighbor?"

7 "Virtue is not solitary; it is bound to have neighbors."

Answers:
1. American poet Robert Frost (1874-1963), from the poem "Mending Wall" 2. The Bible (Leviticus 19:18, Matthew 22:39, and Mark 12:31) 3. The Bible (Romans 15:2) 4. Blessed Mother Teresa of Calcutta (1910-1997) 5. Actress Mae West (1893-1980) 6. Lyndon B. Johnson (1908-1973), thirty-sixth president of the United States 7. Chinese philosopher Confucius (551-479 b.c.)

Write your own quotation. Share it with your group.

In this chapter
we learn about our obligations to our neighbor as commanded by the seventh, eighth, ninth, and tenth commandments. Through this chapter, we hope

 to consider seriously the obligations of the seventh through tenth commandments and to apply them to our own lives

to focus our hearts on God as we learn to love our neighbors as ourselves

to share our love and our gifts with others generously.

Hurricane Katrina devastated vast regions of the Gulf Coast in the United States in 2005. Thousands of neighborhoods were destroyed, and people were suddenly without homes, food, and the basic necessities of life. Many hurricane victims set off to other parts of the country in search of help and resources. Several hundred made a 1,600-mile journey to settle on a military base in Middletown, Rhode Island, which was offering shelter to people affected by the hurricane.

Like people in so many other communities, these Rhode Island residents came together to welcome the people affected by the hurricane and provide resources for them. They donated food, toys, and clothing. They volunteered their time to watch the children of those applying for jobs in their new community. The people who had fled the hurricane, in turn, came together to help one another. They volunteered their time to sort and oversee the food pantry at the shelter. If they had cars, they loaned them to their new neighbors to transport needed items.

Despite desperate circumstances, a new community of neighbors was forged and strengthened by the efforts of many.

Aerial view of neighborhoods in New Orleans, Louisiana flooded by Hurricane Katrina

Activity Complete the following.

The Rhode Island residents and the Gulf Coast residents were "neighbors" because they:

I have been a neighbor to others by:

66 One needs a neighbor on whom to practice compassion, 99 wrote Phyllis McGinley (1905–1978), American Catholic poet and author.

We live out the seventh commandment.

Stealing is any action that unjustly takes away the property or rights of others. What does it mean to steal from someone? Our answer to this question can enlighten us about how well we are living out the seventh commandment. The seventh commandment is "You shall not steal" (Exodus 20:15). It is based on **justice**—respecting the rights of others and giving them what is rightfully theirs.

Living according to the seventh commandment means giving people the things that are rightfully theirs by:

- being God's stewards of creation—caring for the world that God has given us, protecting our environment, using the gifts of creation in a responsible way, and remembering that the world's resources are not only God's gift to us but also to the generations of people to come
- caring for the things that belong to us and respecting what belongs to others
- not taking things that are not ours, even things such as the answers to a test, someone else's homework, or the ideas of others
- treating all people as valuable and important, no matter who they are
- appreciating human work as a participation in the work of creation
- showing respect for the goods and property of others and not damaging the property of others on purpose
- working to help all people, especially those who are poor and powerless, to share in the gifts of the earth and sharing our own goods, as necessary, with others who are in need
- giving alms as a work of justice
- making reparation, or amends, for injustices.

Faith Words

stealing
justice

Jesus lived his life exemplifying the way to live justly and fairly. And he asks us to do the same. Striving to live the moral life that God has called us to live and working for justice are not simply choices for disciples of Jesus and members of the Church; they are requirements.

Activity Take a few moments to think about ways you have followed the seventh commandment. How have you:

- cared for the gifts of creation?
- taken care of your belongings?
- respected the property of others?
- been honest in taking tests and playing games?
- shared what you have with those who are in need?
- worked with your family, parish, or school to care for those who are poor and make their lives better?
- performed acts of kindness and service for others?

Justice for all

The seventh commandment not only commands us not to steal. It requires respect for human beings, their goods and possessions, and the created world. The good things of the world are gifts from God that belong to everyone. Individuals can own things as private property, but what we own, we own as *stewards,* or caregivers. The idea that the goods of creation are meant for the benefit of all people is called the "universal destination of created goods." True justice in society means making sure that all people have the goods they need to live, whether they have money or not. We must take care that the economy, or society's rules and structures for buying and selling, is organized and run in a way that ensures that human needs are met.

The seventh commandment also requires that contracts and promises be kept if they are morally just. It also requires that stolen goods, or their equivalent in money or goods, be returned. The seventh commandment also forbids the enslavement of human beings. It is against human dignity to buy and sell human beings like merchandise. Other offenses against the seventh commandment are: deliberately keeping what is loaned to you, fraud in business, paying unjust wages, and "price gouging" (charging high prices to take advantage of another's ignorance or in times of hardship).

Gambling or games of chance, though not immoral in themselves, are against the seventh commandment if they deprive someone of the means to provide for his or her needs or the needs of others.

Make a list of the requirements of, and sins against, the seventh commandment that you learned about and that you did not know before. Think of a current example for each one.

We live out the eighth commandment.

The Old Testament is full of accounts showing that God was faithful and true, keeping all of his promises to his people. And when God brought the Israelites to Mount Sinai, they, in turn, promised to be his people—to live out the commandments and to give witness to the truth of God's great love for them.

To give witness means to have personal knowledge of a person or event and to tell others the truth about it. The eighth commandment states, "You shall not bear false witness against your neighbor" (Exodus 20:16). Giving false witness can harm others; often, it can harm the whole community. When false witness is given under oath it even threatens fair legal decisions. So, the eighth commandment teaches us about the need for the truth. Truth is the foundation of all positive human relationships. The eighth commandment obliges us:

- to witness to the truth of Jesus by the things we say and do

- to tell the truth

- to respect the privacy of others

- to honor the good names of others and avoid anything that would harm their reputations.

The eighth commandment forbids us to **lie**—to speak or act falsely with the intention of deceiving others. Some lies that hurt the good names of others are *rash judgment*, or assuming that something about another person is true while not having sufficient information to judge; *detraction*, or telling, without reason, someone's faults and failings to those who do not know them; *calumny*, or lying about someone, thus hurting that person's reputation and causing others to judge him or her falsely. *Boasting,*

or bragging, is also an offense against truth, as is *sarcasm* when it is used to make fun of people.

No matter what the reason, lying makes situations worse. Lying damages our own name, makes us lose respect for ourselves, and hurts other people. When we lie, we need to admit it, tell the truth, and try to make up for any harm our lie has caused. We also must make reparation for any words and actions against the dignity of another person.

The eighth commandment also teaches us about keeping promises. If we promise to keep a secret by giving our word to another person, that person trusts us. It is wrong to break that person's trust. There might be times, however, when we are asked to keep a secret about something that is harmful or dangerous to someone. In these cases we must tell people we trust and get help for the person in danger. Doing this is courageous and is also an act of friendship. And though we must always tell the truth, we cannot set out to hurt someone's good name. Thus, we should avoid *gossip* and *rumors*—information that we hear but do not know to be true. And at certain times we should just keep the truth to ourselves, if sharing it would only hurt people's feelings and make them sad, or even sick, for no reason.

Once, when Jesus was teaching about the eighth commandment, he explained it very simply. He said, "Let your 'Yes' mean 'Yes,' and your 'No' mean 'No'" (Matthew 5:37). Jesus expects us, as his disciples, to follow his advice and keep our words and actions true.

> **"Let your 'Yes' mean 'Yes,' and your 'No' mean 'No.'"**
> (Matthew 5:37)

Faith Word
lie

Activity Debate this popular saying: "Sticks and stones may break my bones, but names will never hurt me." How does the eighth commandment enter into your debate?

BELIEVING...

We live out the ninth commandment.

Do you respect others and their relationships?

Throughout our lives we grow to understand how our human emotions, or feelings, affect the habits we form. The ways we express our feelings should guide us to act in loving and respectful ways, not ways that lead us to sin. With the help of the Holy Spirit, we can overcome **temptation**, the attraction to choose sin. With God's grace, we can form virtues, or good habits rather than vices, or bad habits that cloud our judgment of what is good and what is evil.

The ninth commandment is "You shall not covet your neighbor's wife" (Exodus 20:17). To **covet** is to wrongly desire someone or something. When we desire, or want, something unreasonably, our thoughts and feelings can lead us to do things we should not do. The ninth commandment obliges us to become more aware of the gift of human sexuality that God has given us and of the emotions,

feelings, desires, and even temptations that may go with it. This gift of human sexuality enables us to love others and to show them our affection. The sixth commandment teaches us the proper ways to show love and affection, calling us to respect and be in control of our bodies. The ninth commandment calls us to protect even our desires—our feelings and intentions. So, we must:

- keep our instincts and desires within the limits of what is good and honorable
- respect and protect the fidelity of the marriage commitment
- practice the cardinal virtue of **temperance**, which moderates the attraction of pleasures and helps us to bring our desires into balance
- trust in God's ways and value our human sexuality
- practice the virtue of chastity and the virtue of **modesty**, which means thinking, speaking, acting, and dressing in ways that show respect for ourselves and others
- try to know and follow God's will
- avoid thoughts and feelings that lead us away from following God's commandments
- pray, receive the sacraments, and keep our hearts focused on God.

In all these ways we are **pure of heart**—living in the love of God, our Father, just as his Son, Jesus Christ, calls us to do, and allowing the Holy Spirit to fill us with goodness and love.

Abstinence programs

As Catholics, we are all called to chastity. The Church teaches us that chastity "is a moral virtue. It is also a gift from God, a *grace*, a fruit of spiritual effort" (CCC, 2345). Our relationship with God can give us the strength to make the right choices regarding ourselves and our bodies.

Statistics on teen pregnancies and sexually transmitted diseases can be alarming. Abstinence programs are one way that we can learn about the importance of living a chaste life. One Christian program, the Silver Ring Thing (SRT), features an abstinence program designed for Catholic schools and parish youth groups. SRT uses humor and technology to communicate the message of practicing abstinence. Being a part of SRT involves making a pledge to live a chaste life and wearing a silver ring as a sign of this pledge.

CATHOLIC IDENTITY

Discover ways SRT and other abstinence programs might help you live out the virtue of chastity.

> ### Faith Words
> temptation
> covet
> temperance
> modesty
> pure of heart

Activity With your group, plan a 30-second television ad promoting the ninth commandment.

66

We live out the tenth commandment.

The tenth commandment, like the ninth commandment, teaches us to look into our hearts and to examine our thoughts and feelings, especially our feelings toward the possessions, qualities, and abilities of others. The tenth commandment also relates to the seventh commandment because it too deals with the property of others. In the tenth commandment—"You shall not covet your neighbor's house. . . . nor anything else that belongs to him" (Exodus 20:17)—we are reminded that we are obliged not to desire wrongly, or covet, the things that do not belong to us.

The tenth commandment obliges us to thank God for what we have, to work for what we need, and to help others to have what they need. We all need certain things to have a happy and healthy life, and God wants us to have those things. But we must not get caught up in wanting things unnecessarily. **Greed** is an excessive desire to have or own things. When people are greedy, they want more and more of something—money or clothing, for example. People can want things so much that they forget what is important in life. Jesus told us, "Take care to guard against all greed, for though one may be rich, one's life does not consist of possessions" (Luke 12:15).

> "The ways we express our feelings should guide us to act in loving and respectful ways."

In living out the tenth commandment, we trust in God, knowing that his love is more important than money or success. We work to live the way that Jesus taught us to live, knowing that true happiness comes from loving God, ourselves, and others. We restrain ourselves from being envious of others. **Envy** is a feeling of sadness when someone else has the things we want for ourselves. Envy can lead us to take what belongs to someone else. It makes us think mostly about ourselves and makes us unhappy about the success of others. When we are envious, we have a hard time seeing what we already have and being grateful for it.

When we rely on God and are grateful for the many gifts he has given us, we are able to think of others in a loving and giving way. Relying on God enables us to develop a generous heart.

The tenth commandment reminds us to become **poor in spirit**, depending on God and making God more important than anyone or anything else in our life. We remember the things that are important: God and his love, people and their needs, the Church community in which we worship and grow in faith, and God's gifts of creation that we share with all people. These are the things that should fill our hearts.

Faith Words

greed
envy
poor in spirit

Activity How can you tell that someone is "poor in spirit"? How can you be "poor in spirit"?

Recognizing Our Faith

Recall the question at the beginning of this chapter: *Who is my neighbor?* What have you learned in this chapter that can help you to be more loving to your neighbor?

Living Our Faith

Think of a neighbor whom you will help today. Make a plan for helping him or her.

Thomas Merton

Although he was not raised Catholic, Thomas Merton had a conversion experience as a young adult and became a member of the Catholic Church. He received bachelor's and master's degrees from Columbia University in New York and eventually taught at the university level, but he desired to live a more spiritual life. He became a member of the Abbey of Gethsemani, a monastic community in Trappist, Kentucky. He lived as a monk in this community and often focused on the phrase inscribed on the monastery gate: *GOD ALONE*. Yet while living in the community, he wrote about a variety of subjects, including God's presence, prayer, social problems, Christian responsibilities, nuclear war, violence, and race relations. His writings expressed concern for his neighbors around the world.

Thomas Merton was a man who put his trust in God, as we can read in his autobiography, *The Seven Storey Mountain*. He died on December 10, 1968, while attending a meeting of religious leaders in Thailand.

How can you, too, focus on God alone yet show love for your neighbors?

For additional ideas and activities, visit www.weliveourfaith.com.

Putting Faith to Work

Talk about what you have learned in this chapter:

We consider seriously the obligations of the seventh through tenth commandments and to apply them to our own lives.

We focus our hearts on God as we learn to love our neighbors as ourselves.

We share our love and our gifts with others generously.

Decide on ways to live out what you have learned.

✝ ENCOUNTERING GOD'S WORD

" Finally, brothers, whatever is true, whatever is honorable, whatever is just, whatever is pure, whatever is lovely, whatever is gracious, if there is any excellence and if there is anything worthy of praise, think about these things. . . . Then the God of peace will be with you. "

(Philippians 4:8–9)

➡ **READ** the quotation from Scripture.

➡ **REFLECT** on these questions:
How might this advice help you to keep your heart pure and at peace? How can you remind yourself to turn your thoughts toward true, just, lovely, gracious, or excellent things?

➡ **SHARE** your reflections with a partner.

➡ **DECIDE** to turn your thoughts today toward truth and peace, and toward love of God and neighbor.

Complete the following.

1. A feeling of sadness when someone else has the things we want for ourselves is called _____.

2. Being pure of heart is living in the love of _____.

3. Respecting the rights of others and giving them what is rightfully theirs is _____.

4. The virtue that moderates the attraction of pleasures and helps us to bring our desires into balance is called _____.

Define.

5. poor in spirit _____

6. temptation _____

7. covet _____

8. greed _____

9–10. ESSAY: Name at least four ways to live out the seventh commandment.

RESPONDING...

Sharing Faith with Your Family

Discuss the following with your family:
- We live out the seventh commandment: YOU SHALL NOT STEAL.
- We live out the eighth commandment: YOU SHALL NOT BEAR FALSE WITNESS AGAINST YOUR NEIGHBOR.
- We live out the ninth commandment: YOU SHALL NOT COVET YOUR NEIGHBOR'S WIFE.
- We live out the tenth commandment: YOU SHALL NOT COVET YOUR NEIGHBOR'S GOODS.

The seventh through tenth commandments call us to respect the rights of our neighbors. They remind us to put God first in our lives and to be grateful for what God has given us. The next time you are gathered with your family, spend time counting your blessings as a family.

The Worship Connection

At Mass, at the end of the Liturgy of the Word, we pray the prayer of the faithful: for our pope and bishops, our country, city, town, and parish, and all of our neighbors in need. Be sure to join in this prayer.

More to Explore

Explore the Internet for Catholic service organizations. Find out ways that our neighbors around the world are helped. How can you help, too?

Catholic Social Teaching Checklist

Theme of Catholic Social Teaching: Option for the Poor and Vulnerable

How it relates to Chapter 6: As Catholics we are called to have special care and concern for those among us who are the least fortunate and the most in need. We must join together to serve these neighbors who need our help and support.

How can you do this?

☐ At home:

_____

☐ At school/work:

_____

☐ In the parish:

_____

☐ In the community:

_____

Check off each action after it has been completed.

70

Complete each sentence with a term from the box. Capitalize terms as needed.

free will	Beatitudes	sin	chastity
conscience	New Commandment	idolatry	social sin

1. In the _____, Jesus tells us what true happiness is and what we must do to find it.

2. _____ is any thought, word, deed, or omission against God's law.

3. Giving worship to a creature or thing instead of God is known as the sin of _____.

4. God gave us the gift of _____, the freedom and ability to choose what to do.

5. _____ is the virtue by which we use our human sexuality in a responsible and faithful way.

6. _____ is unjust situations and conditions that negatively impact society and its institutions.

Write *True* or *False* next to the following sentences. Then, on the lines provided, change the false sentences to make them true.

7. _____ The sixth commandment is based on justice—respecting the rights of others and giving them what is rightfully theirs.

_____

_____

8. _____ In living out the third commandment, we must gather for Mass every Sunday—or the evening before—with our parish community.

_____

_____

9. _____ In living out the eighth commandment, we trust in God, knowing that his love is more important than money or success.

_____

_____

10. _____ The fourth commandment demands that we respect and protect human life.

_____

_____

11. _____ The tenth commandment forbids us to lie.

_____

_____

12. _____ Through the second commandment God reveals that his name is sacred, or holy.

_____

_____

Define the following.

13. conversion _____

_____

14. reverence _____

_____

15. Decalogue _____

_____

16. natural law _____

_____

17. temptation _____

_____

18. moral decision-making _____

_____

Respond to the following.

19. Choose one of the "Big Questions" from this unit (_How can I be true to myself?_, _How do I make decisions?_, _Why do I need to follow laws?_, _How do I honor those I love?_, _Whom do I respect?_, or _Who is my neighbor?_) and answer it in an essay. Use at least three Faith Words from the unit in your essay.

_____

_____

_____

_____

20. Using what you have learned in this unit, describe ways you will live your faith each day.

_____

_____

_____

_____

ALTERNATIVE ASSESSMENT

Based upon what you have learned in Unit 1, build a flow chart that represents the moral decision-making process. Apply the teachings from Unit 1, for example the Great Commandment, the New Commandment, the Ten Commandments, examination of conscience, and sin, to your flow chart.

Use your flow chart the next time you have a decision to make.

Unit 2

Who Are Our Ancestors in Faith?

GATHERING...

The Early Church
(A.D. 30–313)

"The community of believers was of one heart and mind."

(Acts of the Apostles 4:32)

Leader: How did the first Christians pray?

Reader: Those who came to Christianity as Jews prayed by marking the Jewish times of prayer. They did this by gathering together and singing psalms. As we read in the Acts of the Apostles, "Peter and John were going up to the temple area for the three o'clock hour of prayer" (Acts of the Apostles 3:1). These hours of prayer were the foundation for the Christian practice of prayer that we call the *Liturgy of the Hours.*

Leader: Let us pray together in this ancient tradition now.

Group 1: Our soul waits for the LORD, who is our help and shield.

Group 2: For in God our hearts rejoice; in your holy name we trust.

Group 1: May your kindness, LORD, be upon us; we have put our hope in you.

(Psalm 33:20–22)

Group 2: Glory to the Father and to the Son, and to the Holy Spirit:

Group 1: As it was in the beginning, is now, and will be for ever. Amen.

Leader: Let us now pray as Jesus taught us:
(All pray the Lord's Prayer.)

Lord, be our help always. May our hearts rejoice in you. May we, the people whom you have gathered into your Church, trust in your holy name and hope always in your kindness. We ask this in your name, Lord Jesus.

All: Amen.

Visit www.weliveourfaith.com to find appropriate music and songs.

GATHERING...

The BiG QuEStion:
What connects me to a community?

Discover how much you know about the first Christian community. Answer these questions about the disciples of Jesus Christ. (You might want to use your Bible.)

1 Who were they?

_____

_____

2 Where did they come from?

_____

_____

3 Why did they come together?

_____

_____

4 What happened to them after Jesus died? after he rose from the dead? after he ascended to his Father?

_____

_____

_____

How are you connected to Jesus' first disciples? How is your life similar to theirs? different from theirs?

In this chapter we will explore the origins of the Church and her expansion into the world. Through this chapter, we hope

 to understand the history behind the spread of the early Church

 to appreciate the faith and courage of the early Christian believers

to resolve to follow Jesus as they did, in sincerity of heart.

Labor Day in Bungalowville by Charles Wysocki (1929–2002)

hink about all of the different types of communities, small and large, that exist in the world. Communities can consist of people linked together by many different things. A community may be made up of people with common interests or hobbies. Or a community may simply be a group of people that live in the same area. A group of people who actively cooperate with one another is also considered a community. A group of people who share the same religious beliefs is a community, too. Though their members may be scattered throughout the world, they are united by their beliefs. The word *community* can also be used to describe a group of people who share similar economic or political backgrounds. People with a common profession also can form a community; for example, doctors make up the medical community.

> **"**There are no strangers in this world, only friends we haven't met yet.**"**
> (Anonymous)

Activity Right now you belong to several communities. Below, list the communities that you are a part of—those of which you are a member by choice and those to which you belong by circumstance. Then, consider why each of these communities is important to you. How does each community influence your life, and how do you affect each community?

BELIEVING...

The Church begins and grows.

Imagine that you were living in Jerusalem around the year 30—the year of Jesus' death. From a political point of view you were living in the Roman Empire, a vast grouping of territories controlled and governed by Roman rule. And ultimately the Roman emperor had the highest authority. But you were also part of the first Christian community. What might you have experienced at that time? Perhaps you saw and heard Jesus teach. Perhaps you witnessed the horrors of his suffering and death and then rejoiced at the news of his Resurrection from the dead and Ascension into heaven. Perhaps, too, you were present on the morning of Pentecost when the Holy Spirit descended on the community of Jesus' disciples.

On that morning, Peter and the other disciples were gathered together in a house in Jerusalem. Suddenly, "there came from the sky a noise like a strong driving wind, and it filled the entire house in which they were. Then there appeared to them tongues as of fire, which parted and came to rest on

each one of them" (Acts of the Apostles 2:2–3). At that moment the disciples were filled with the Holy Spirit. They were strengthened to proclaim the good news of Jesus Christ to the world. It was then that "the Church was openly displayed to the crowds and the spread of the Gospel among the nations, through preaching, was begun" (*CCC*, 767).

Peter told the people of Jerusalem, "Let the whole house of Israel know for certain that God has made him both Lord and Messiah, this Jesus whom you crucified" (Acts of the Apostles 2:36). When people in the crowd asked, "What are we to do?" Peter answered, "Repent and be baptized, every one of you, in the name of Jesus Christ for the forgiveness of your sins; and you will receive the gift of the holy Spirit" (Acts of the Apostles 2:37, 38). Amazingly, as we can read in the Acts of the Apostles, about three thousand people were baptized that very day. All those who were baptized received the Holy Spirit.

The Holy Spirit was with the members of the first Christian community, guiding them to believe in Jesus and helping them to remember and live out Jesus' teachings. And the members of this first Christian community, the early Church, "devoted themselves to the teaching of the apostles and to the communal life, to the breaking of the bread and to the prayers. . . . All who believed were together and had all things in common; they would sell their property and possessions and divide them among all according to each one's need. Every day they devoted themselves to meeting together in the temple area and to breaking bread in their homes" (Acts of the Apostles 2:42, 44–46).

With the help and guidance of the Holy Spirit, the community of Jesus' disciples had become something that we can recognize today, over two thousand years later: the Catholic Church growing and working as a community to share the good news of Jesus Christ.

> **Activity** What are some ways that, with the help of the Holy Spirit, you proclaim the good news of Jesus Christ in the communities to which you belong?

Early Christians are martyred for their faith.

The world in which Christianity began offered some advantages to those who wanted to spread the Gospel. The Roman Empire was at peace, with networks of good roads and safe harbors. Romans spoke Latin but also favored the widely spoken Greek language. Thus, Christian missionaries who spoke Greek could preach far and wide and be understood by many. The most famous of these Christian missionaries was Paul. After a conversion to belief in Jesus Christ, Paul spread the Gospel throughout the Roman Empire. The Lord said of Paul, "This man is a chosen instrument of mine to carry my name before Gentiles, kings, and Israelites" (Acts of the Apostles 9:15).

> **"You will receive the gift of the holy Spirit."**
> (Acts of the Apostles 2:38)

But Paul and the other early Christian missionaries faced many challenges. One was the tension that emerged with the Christians' Jewish neighbors. This tension was evidenced when the disciple Stephen was put to death in Jerusalem, falsely accused of "speaking blasphemous words against Moses and God" (Acts of the Apostles 6:11). Stephen became a martyr by witnessing to the faith and dying rather than denying his belief in Christ.

There was also tension with the Roman authorities. They did not require Jews within the empire to worship the Roman gods. So, at first they also ignored the early Christians who seemed to be a group within Judaism. But the Romans soon became suspicious of the Christians. And, in time, the authorities began to fear that Christianity, with its emphasis on the dignity and equality of all people in God's eyes, might also be a revolutionary political movement.

When the Christians refused to worship the Roman gods and denied that the Roman emperor was himself a god, the Romans started to persecute the Christians. The first recorded persecution of Christians began in Rome around A.D. 64, under the Emperor Nero. Other persecutions followed, and thousands of Christians accepted death rather than deny their faith. But the more the Romans persecuted the Christians, the more the number of converts to Christianity grew.

Activity Name some ways that people today are persecuted. How can our communities work together against these kinds of persecutions?

Saints Peter and Paul

Every year on June 29, the Church celebrates the feast day of Saints Peter and Paul. This feast day is noted on even the oldest existing Roman calendar, which dates back to A.D. 354.

Peter was entrusted by Jesus to lead the Apostles and to guide the growing Church. In the Acts of the Apostles we find that, when any major decisions were to be made, it was Peter to whom the other Apostles and leaders of the early Church turned. And Paul constantly journeyed to bring the good news of salvation to the world:

• On Paul's first journey he traveled to the island of Cyprus in the eastern Mediterranean, to the city of Antioch in Asia Minor (modern-day Turkey), and to other cities in what are now Turkey and Syria.

• On his second and longest journey, he traveled to Greece, where he established a center of Christian faith in the city of Corinth.

• On his third journey he returned to Asia Minor, where he helped set up other Christian communities, including one in the city of Ephesus.

Nothing could stop Paul from preaching the Gospel. When he couldn't travel to a community to share the Christian faith, he would write a letter.

Both Peter and Paul died in Rome as martyrs. Their courage and witness are important for Catholics everywhere to honor and celebrate. Pray a prayer of thanksgiving for them.

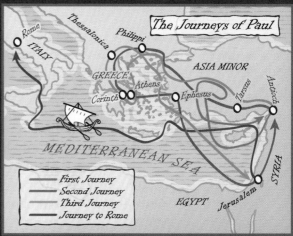

The Journeys of Paul

First Journey
Second Journey
Third Journey
Journey to Rome

BELIEVING...

The Church meets at the Council of Jerusalem.

When have you had to stand up for your faith?

The young Christian community, the early Church, not only faced external problems, but also faced many issues and questions from within. It was toward the end of his first missionary journey that Paul and a disciple named Barnabas visited the Christian community at

Model of ancient Jerusalem at the time of Herod the Great (first century B.C.)

Antioch. And in Antioch, in about the year 40, the word *Christian* was first used to refer to the followers of Jesus Christ. But many of these Christians were **Gentiles**, or people who, like the Romans and the Greeks, were not Jews. So, at Antioch, a controversy arose. People were asking whether Gentiles first needed to become Jews before becoming Christians. So, "it was decided that Paul, Barnabas, and some of the others should go up to Jerusalem" to ask the leaders of the Church about this question (Acts of the Apostles 15:2). In Jerusalem the Christians of Antioch were to present their dispute to the Apostles and to a new generation of leaders called *presbyters*—men whom Catholics today would call priests. When they reached Jerusalem, however, Paul and Barnabas discovered that the Church leaders there were struggling with the same question.

As good Jews, the earliest Christians had always respected and obeyed the **Torah**, the sacred law of faith given by God to Moses. Now people were asking whether men and women who had not been born Jews could be excused from some of the requirements of Jewish law. So, "the apostles and the presbyters met together to see about this matter" (Acts of the Apostles 15:6). They were confident that, with the guidance of the Holy Spirit, they could make the right decision. This meeting became known as the Council of Jerusalem, the first great council of the Catholic Church. It took place in Jerusalem in about the year 49. As the arguments

Faith Words
Gentiles
Torah

went back and forth, the Apostle Peter told the council that "God, who knows the heart," granted Gentiles "the holy Spirit just as he did us" (Acts of Apostles 15:8). Peter also reminded the council that "we are saved through the grace of the Lord Jesus, in the same way as they" (Acts of the Apostles 15:11).

Then the Apostle James spoke up to present the position that the council accepted. This position has been the law of the Church ever since. Many aspects of the law of Moses—the Ten Commandments and certain marriage laws, for example—would still be the law for all Christians. But some Torah requirements—for instance, circumcision for men— would be done away with for Gentile converts, those who did not come to Christianity through Judaism. The council leaders sent Paul, Barnabas, and two other delegates back to Antioch with a letter describing the council's decision. When the delegates arrived in Antioch, "they called the assembly together and delivered the letter. When the people read it, they were delighted" (Acts of the Apostles 15:30–31).

At the Council of Jerusalem, the Holy Spirit worked through the community of the Church, helping the leaders to decide on important matters about which Jesus had left no specific instruction. And with the Holy Spirit's guidance, the Christian faith was now on its way to becoming a faith for the whole world.

Activity Pray together a prayer to the Holy Spirit to guide the Church today in all of her decisions.

The Church is inspired by the Holy Spirit.

The good news of Jesus was conveyed by word of mouth from the first believers to those who followed. But as the first eyewitness Christians began to die, the Christian community became aware that future generations would need something more than this existing oral tradition. So, the early Christians began to write things down. Many scholars agree on the following timeline.

The Gospel of Mark was the first account of Jesus' life and teachings to be written down, sometime around the year 70. The Gospels of Matthew and Luke were written down next, between A.D. 80 and 90. Matthew and Luke based their accounts on that of Mark as well as on other early Christian sources. These three Gospels are closely related, with many similarities. The fourth Gospel, the Gospel of John, was written later, probably around A.D. 100. This Gospel describes words and deeds of Jesus that are similar to those recorded by the other three Gospel writers, but it also addresses incidents and issues that are not included in the other three Gospels.

> **"We are saved through the grace of the Lord Jesus."**
> (Acts of the Apostles 15:11)

Other books of the New Testament were also written at this time. Fourteen of these, said to be the oldest books in the New Testament, are *epistles*, or letters, to the early Christian communities that were written by, or at least attributed to, Saint Paul. Seven are letters that were written by other leaders of the early Church. There is also an account of the very earliest days of the Church—the Acts of the Apostles—and a book called the Book of Revelation, which is the last book of the Bible and calls believers in Christ to look forward with hope to eternal glory. The human authors of these sacred texts, just as the authors of existing Scripture, were inspired by God the Holy Spirit to write what would faithfully present God's saving truth. And as the early Christians lived their faith, facing issues that were unknown to earlier generations, the Holy Spirit was also working in the Church, guiding the

development of Tradition. Tradition refers to the written and spoken beliefs and practices that have been passed down to us from the time of Christ and the Apostles. Together, Tradition and Scripture make up "a single sacred deposit of the Word of God" (*CCC*, 97). As the Church relies on the Bible as a book of faith, the Church looks to Tradition as a living witness of faith.

For more information on Scripture, see "Bible Basics" on pages 310–311.

Activity Reread this page to find out how many books there are in the New Testament. Share with a partner a New Testament passage that has particular meaning for you.

The Magisterium

The pope today can trace his authority directly back to Saint Peter, and our bishops can trace their authority directly back to the first Apostles. This is what we mean when we speak of "apostolic succession." Under the guidance of the Holy Spirit, the pope and the bishops lead the Church to be faithful to God's original Revelation in Jesus and to the developments in Tradition that have taken place over the long history of the Church.

We call the teaching authority of the pope and the bishops the *Magisterium*, the living teaching office of the Church. The Magisterium's presence in the Church guarantees the continuing guidance of the Holy Spirit through apostolic succession.

Through letters, statements, and documents for the whole Church, the Magisterium continually teaches us about the truth. And when the Church encounters new circumstances, questions, and issues of importance to our faith, the Holy Spirit guides the Magisterium and the whole Church to develop its understanding of Divine Revelation in Scripture and Tradition.

In what ways do the pope and bishops guide the Church today?

CATHOLIC IDENTITY

RESPONDING...

Recognizing Our Faith

Recall the question at the beginning of this chapter: *What connects me to a community?* What connects you to your family? your neighbors? your parish? the world?

Living Our Faith

How will you share the good news of Jesus Christ with others?

Partners in FAITH

Women of the Early Church

The lives of Lydia, Prisca, and Perpetua give us some of the greatest examples of the role of women in the early Church. Lydia was baptized by Saint Paul. Her conversion to Christianity was very important because she was one of the first prominent Gentiles to accept Christian belief.

Prisca, also called Priscilla, was a Gentile married to Aquila, a Jew. They became Christians at a time when Christianity was not accepted by the Romans. Forced to leave Rome, the couple relocated to Corinth, in Greece, and became involved in Saint Paul's mission to share the good news of Jesus Christ. In his letter to the Romans, Paul called this couple "my co-workers in Christ Jesus" (Romans 16:3).

Perpetua, an early Christian living in North Africa, and her servant Felicity were arrested and imprisoned for practicing their Christianity. Perpetua's wealthy father visited her and begged her to give up the faith. Yet she refused. Eventually, the Roman emperor ordered the deaths of Perpetua and Felicity. They became martyrs of the early Church.

Who are some women who share the good news of Jesus Christ today?

For additional ideas and activities, visit www.weliveourfaith.com.

Putting Faith to Work

Talk about what you have learned in this chapter:

 We understand the history behind the spread of the early Church.

 We appreciate the faith and courage of the early Christian believers.

We resolve to follow Jesus as they did, in sincerity of heart.

Decide on ways to live out what you have learned.

✝ ENCOUNTERING GOD'S WORD

Life in the early Christian community is described in the Acts of the Apostles:

❝ **The community of believers was of one heart and mind, and . . . had everything in common** ❞
(Acts of the Apostles 4:32).

➡ **READ** the quotation from Scripture.

➡ **REFLECT** on the following question:
What are some ways your parish fulfills this Scripture passage?

➡ **SHARE** your reflections with a partner.

➡ **DECIDE** on ways to help other young people in your parish become part of a "community of believers."

Choose four events discussed in this chapter and explain their significance to the Church then and now.

1. _____
   _____

2. _____
   _____

3. _____
   _____

4. _____
   _____

Write *True* or *False* next to the following sentences. On a separate sheet of paper, change the false sentences to make them true.

5. _____ Scripture is the only means by which God's Revelation comes to us.

6. _____ At the Council of Jerusalem, the Apostles made a decision that is no longer the law of the Church today.

7. _____ The fourteen letters, or epistles, that are attributed to Paul are said to be the oldest books of the New Testament.

8. _____ As the Church relies on the Bible as a book of faith, the Church looks to Tradition as a living witness of faith.

9–10. ESSAY: Explain the importance of the coming of the Holy Spirit upon the community of Jesus' disciples.

Chapter 7 Assessment

Sharing Faith with Your Family

Discuss the following with your family:

- The Church begins and grows.
- Early Christians are martyred for their faith.
- The Church meets at the Council of Jerusalem.
- The Church is inspired by the Holy Spirit.

Spend a week with Saint Paul. Each day this week, look up one of the Scripture passages referenced here. Each is from one of Saint Paul's letters. Copy each reference on a separate index card and display the card as you read and discuss the Scripture passage together.

1 Corinthians 13:13	Ephesians 4:32	1 Thessalonians 5:18
Romans 8:31	2 Corinthians 5:7	Philippians 4:4
	Galatians 2:20	

The Worship Connection

Many of our Catholic liturgical practices have their origin in Jewish worship. The reciting and singing of the psalms is one such practice. During Mass pay special attention to the *responsorial psalm* that follows the first reading.

More to Explore

Research Catholic people and organizations who are helping to fight persecution throughout the world.

Catholic Social Teaching ☑ Checklist

Theme of Catholic Social Teaching:
Solidarity of the Human Family

How it relates to Chapter 7: As Catholics we respect and care for all human beings as one human community, one human family—no matter where they live.

How can you do this?

☐ At home:

_____

☐ At school/work:

_____

☐ In the parish:

_____

☐ In the community:

_____

Check off each action after it has been completed.

8
Christians of the Roman Empire
(A.D. 313–476)

"Guide me in your truth and teach me, for you are God my savior."

(Psalm 25:5)

✝ **Leader:** Saint Helena was the mother of Emperor Constantine. She is remembered for helping to found churches and serving poor people. According to legend, she visited Palestine in the year A.D. 326 and found the true cross of Christ. In the reign of her son, the cross of Christ became a sign of victory for all Christians. Let us pray with Saint Helena:

Reader 1: That the Church may always glory in the cross of our Lord Jesus Christ, who is our life and Resurrection, let us pray:

Reader 2: We adore you, O Christ, and we bless you,

All: Because by your holy cross, you have redeemed the world.

Reader 1: That all those who suffer may find courage in the cross of Christ and hope in the love of God that it symbolizes, let us pray:

Reader 2: We adore you, O Christ, and we bless you,

All: Because by your holy cross, you have redeemed the world.

Reader 1: That we may show respect for the cross of Christ, in our homes, in our churches, and as we bless ourselves with the sign of the cross, let us pray:

Reader 2: We adore you, O Christ, and we bless you,

All: Because by your holy cross, you have redeemed the world.

Leader: Let us conclude our prayer by blessing ourselves with the sign of the cross—in the name of the Father, and of the Son, and of the Holy Spirit.

(All make the sign of the cross.)

All: Amen.

@ Visit www.weliveourfaith.com to find appropriate music and songs.

The BiG QuEStion:
Who or what leads me to the truth?

iscover how astounding the truth can be! Which of the following do you think are true?

1 The elephant is the only land-based mammal that cannot jump.

2 There is an underwater hotel off the coast of Florida that guests must enter by diving.

3 Geckos can see through their eyelids.

4 More bats are found in the tropics than any other mammal.

5 An average of eighteen major earthquakes occur each year in the world.

6 Twenty-five percent of the bones in your body are in your feet.

Answers:
It's hard to believe, but all are true.

In this chapter we will learn how the Church sought to define and proclaim the truths of our faith. Through this chapter, we hope

 to consider the people and events through which the Holy Spirit worked to define the faith of the Church

to understand the various ways in which the truths of our faith have been handed down to us

to proclaim —especially by our actions— the truths of faith we hold as Christians.

Do you know the truth about deoxyribonucleic acid (DNA)? It is a nucleic acid that contains the genetic instructions specifying the biological development of all cellular forms of life. It is responsible for the genetic formation of most inherited traits. And it has been around forever!

Yet finding out the truth about DNA took centuries of thinking, questioning, and researching and depended upon many earlier discoveries. In fact, the existence of DNA was not even discovered until the mid-nineteenth century. And it was only in the twentieth century that researchers began suggesting that DNA might store genetic information. Here are some of the discoveries that led to our present understanding of DNA:

• In 1665 a scientist named Robert Hooke made an observation that eventually led to the establishment of the cell theory, which states that all organisms are composed of similar units.

• In the 1830s Robert Brown observed a small and dark-staining sphere inside plant cells and called this structure a nucleus. This was a key step in the development of the basic cell theory.

• Around 1865 Gregor Mendel, who was a monk, did an experiment that explained the patterns of inheritance. He is considered to be "the father of genetics" because, without his information about inheritance, the idea of heredity would never have developed, and, without the idea of heredity, nobody would know about DNA.

• In 1928 an Army medical officer named Frederick Griffith, trying to find a vaccine, made a breakthrough in the world of heredity. And his experiment taught us about hereditary transformation.

• Oswald Avery and his colleagues expanded the investigation that Griffith started. And, in 1944, they reported that DNA, not protein, was the hereditary substance.

• Erwin Chargaff, a biochemist, first figured out the equation for the different bases in DNA.

• In 1951 James Watson and Francis Crick began to examine DNA's structure. In 1953, using X-ray photos of DNA fibers taken by Maurice Wilkins and Rosalind Franklin, Watson and Crick discovered that DNA has an X shape and came up with the "double helix" structure that is associated with DNA. They produced the first three-dimensional model of the structure of DNA that is still in use today.

Activity Think about all the steps that led to what we know about DNA today. Do you think we'll learn more in the future? Why?

"The right to search for the truth implies also a duty; one must not conceal any part of what one has recognized to be the truth," said physicist Albert Einstein (1879–1955).

Computer artwork of the double helix of DNA viewed from the inside

BELIEVING...

An empire turns to Christ.

Jesus had commissioned the first disciples to "go, therefore, and make disciples of all nations" (Matthew 28:19). But in following Jesus' call, the earliest Christians endured many persecutions. Two of the worst persecutions occurred under the Roman emperors Decius, who ruled from 249 to 251, and Diocletian, who ruled from 284 to 305. Decius tried to consolidate his power by having the people worship him as a god. But the Christians of the empire refused, and their persecution soon followed. The Emperor Diocletian also wanted to be worshiped as a god. In the year 303 he issued edicts, or orders, that led to what we now call the "Great Persecution"

Emperor Constantine (306–337)

which continued until 311 under Diocletian's successor Galerius.

During this persecution thousands of Christians were martyred for their faith. Church property was confiscated, and Christian books were burned. Yet, in spite of the persecutions, the Christian faith continued to spread to every corner of the empire and beyond.

Then, from 312 to 337, the Emperor Constantine ruled the Roman Empire. He became emperor after winning a great battle, the battle of the Milvian Bridge. Fortunately for Christians, Constantine attributed this victory to his soldiers' display of the cross on their shields and banners. Thus, though he did not officially become a Christian until the end of his life, the Emperor Constantine favored Christianity from early in his reign. In 313 he issued the Edict of Milan, granting religious tolerance throughout the Roman Empire and giving Christians the freedom to worship openly. He also returned much of the Church property that had been seized during the Great Persecution.

Encouraged by his Christian mother, Helena, Constantine made Rome a Christian city. He built a great basilica over the tomb of Saint Peter and gave many government buildings to the Christians to be used as places of worship. He declared every Sunday a government holiday and made official holidays of both Easter and Christmas. He also worked to restore the holy places in Jerusalem and banned many forms of pagan worship, or the worship of false gods.

Eventually, one of Constantine's successors, the Emperor Theodosius I (379–395), made Christianity the official religion of the Roman Empire. Amazingly, Christianity was no longer a suspect and persecuted faith. And the early Christians experienced again that the Holy Spirit is at work in the world.

Activity Highlight or underline the contributions that Constantine made to Christianity.

Saint Augustine

Saint Augustine was among the great teachers of the early Church whom we now honor with the title "Church Fathers." Born in A.D. 354, he was a skilled writer and preacher who went on to become the bishop of Hippo, a city in North Africa. His father was a pagan, or one who worshiped false gods. Yet his mother, celebrated today as Saint Monica, was a devout Christian who never stopped praying for Augustine's conversion to Christianity. And her prayers were answered; Augustine became a faithful Christian. But not only that, he became a great Christian scholar, a theologian. In his spiritual autobiography, *The Confessions,* he gives us the account of his own conversion, or turning to Jesus Christ with all his heart, mind, soul, and body.

Augustine's writings express a deep faith and love of Jesus Christ combined with a talent for logical thinking. Exploring the mystery of God, he wrote, "If you understood him, it would not be God"—and many other powerful words that continue to build up the faith of the Church today. Research to discover some of these powerful words of Saint Augustine.

The Church relies on the word of God.

One of the tasks facing the early Church was to decide which sacred writings should be considered part of the Christian Bible. In the second century a scholar named Marcion tried to convince the Church to exclude the Old Testament. The Church condemned Marcion's ideas and accepted the Old Testament as part of the Christian Bible. And because the early Christians used the Greek translation of the Hebrew Bible, they accepted the forty-six Old Testament books that are still part of our Catholic Bibles today. These books recall God's relationship with the people of Israel, from creation through the formation of the covenant, to the laws and beliefs of the Israelites, to the history of Israel and God's role in everyday life, to the writings of the prophets who spoke God's word to his people.

The entire Bible is a collection of books concerned with God's covenant: the agreement that God made with the people of Israel (the old covenant) and the agreement brought to fulfillment in Jesus (the new covenant). *Testament* is another word for "covenant." As part of their work, the early Christians had to determine which writings should be included in the New Testament, the part of the Bible that recalls the story of Jesus, his mission, his first followers, and the beginnings of the Church. The work was slow and complex. But gradually, under the guidance of the Holy Spirit, the Church developed its New Testament of twenty-seven books. And, in approximately 367, in a letter written by Saint Athanasius (about 296–373), the Bishop of Alexandria, Egypt, we find what seems to be the first written list of New Testament books. Thus, these early Christians compiled for the Church the official list, or *canon*, of Sacred Scripture. And even today our Catholic Bible consists of those seventy-three books, divided into two parts called testaments.

> **"The early Christians experienced . . . that the Holy Spirit is at work in the world."**

Activity The names of thirty books of the Bible are hidden in the text below. Work with a partner to find them. (For a list of the books of the Bible, see page 310.)

This is a most remarkable puzzle. It was found by a gentleman in an airplane seat pocket, on a flight from Los Angeles to Honolulu, keeping him occupied for hours. He enjoyed it so much, he passed it on to some friends. One friend from Illinois worked on this while fishing from his john boat. Another friend studied it while playing his banjo. Elaine Taylor, a columnist friend, was so intrigued by it she mentioned it in her weekly newspaper column. Another friend judges the job of solving this puzzle so involving, she brews a cup of tea to help her nerves. There will be some names that are really easy to spot. That's a fact. Some people, however, will soon find themselves in a jam, especially since the book names are not necessarily capitalized. Truthfully, from answers we get, we are forced to admit it usually takes a minister or a scholar to see some of them at the worst. Research has shown that something in our genes is responsible for the difficulty we have in seeing the books in this paragraph. During a recent fundraising event, which featured this puzzle, the Alpha Delta Phi lemonade booth set a new record. The local paper, the *Chronicle*, surveyed more than two hundred patrons who reported that this puzzle was one of the most difficult they had ever seen. As Daniel Humana humbly puts it, "The books are all right here in plain view hidden from sight." Those able to find all of them will hear great lamentations from those who have to be shown. One revelation that may help is that books like Timothy and Samuel may occur without their numbers. Also, keep in mind that punctuation and spaces in the middle are normal. A chipper attitude will help you compete really well against those who claim to know the answers. Remember, there is no need for a mad exodus; there really are thirty books of the Bible lurking somewhere in this paragraph waiting to be found.

The Church defends the truth.

What contributes to your understanding of your faith?

It was also during these first centuries of Christianity that many notable scholars and writers contributed to the understanding of the Christian faith. Because of the importance of their work to the life and growth of the Church, we honor these men today as the Fathers of the Church. Among these men were:

- Origen (about 185–254), who studied and explained Scripture

- Tertullian (about 155–222), who developed a vocabulary of terms with which to describe the faith

- Saint John Chrysostom (about 347–407), a great preacher whose name, *Chrysostom*, means "golden-mouthed"

- Saint Jerome (about 347–420), who translated the Bible into Latin from Hebrew and Greek.

In the early centuries of the Church, many heresies emerged to challenge the Christian faith. A *heresy* is a belief or collection of beliefs that rejects one or more of the revealed truths of the faith. But the Church's long struggle against these false beliefs also played a positive role in the development of the faith. Some of the most important works of the Fathers of the Church were written to defend the truths of the faith against heretics.

The following are some of the groups whose beliefs were heretical.

Gnostics—They claimed that God's real revelation was available only as secret knowledge to a select few. The Church knew, however, that Jesus welcomed everyone, telling his disciples to bring his Gospel to all nations.

Docetists—They claimed that Jesus only pretended to be human and so didn't really suffer on the cross. The Church teaches, however, that Jesus was fully human and fully divine. His sufferings were real.

Manichees—They claimed that the material world is evil and that it was created by an evil spirit. The Church knew and taught that all of creation is good because it was made by God, who is all-good.

Marcionites—They were the followers of Marcion, who rejected the Old Testament. The Church, however, recognized that the Old Testament is truly the revealed word of God.

Donatists—They claimed that only "saints" can belong to the Church. But the Church knew that her mission was to welcome both saints and sinners—everyday people, such as ourselves, who strive for holiness of life.

Arians—They claimed that Jesus was less than divine.

Monophysites—They claimed that Jesus was only divine and thus not fully human.

To combat these last two heresies, the Church knew that it had to make clear to the faithful that Jesus was both fully human and fully divine.

The Church's need to combat heresy also gave rise to the first ecumenical councils. The word *ecumenical* comes from the Greek and means "of the whole world." These councils of the Church, both ancient and modern, stand out as expressions of the guidance of the Holy Spirit. An ecumenical council brings together the bishops of the whole world with the bishop of Rome, the pope—the successor of Peter—to guide the Church in matters of faith and life in Jesus Christ. Thus, ecumenical councils are examples of the teaching power that the Apostles possessed and passed on to their successors throughout the ages. Because of this, the teachings of these councils are reliable guides to authentic Catholic faith.

Activity Choose one of the heretical groups discussed on this page, and prepare and present a message defending the truth against this group's heresy.

The Church is strengthened by her councils.

At the beginning of the fourth century, a priest from Alexandria named Arius was preaching that Jesus was a little more than human but not fully divine. Arius's teachings soon became popular throughout the Roman Empire, and his followers became known as Arians. The argument over Jesus' divinity and humanity became so intense that it began to threaten the peace of the empire. In 325, to settle the dispute caused by this Arian heresy, the Emperor Constantine summoned all the bishops of the Church to a council in the city of Nicaea, in modern-day Turkey. More than two hundred bishops were present at this council, which was the first ecumenical council. The argument against the Arian heresy was put forward by a young deacon named Athanasius. He explained that Jesus had to be fully human to represent humanity before God and also had to be fully God to have the power to save us. This argument was accepted by the assembled bishops. The Arian heresy was condemned. The council then set down a creed—a statement of Christian belief—to express clearly the full divinity and full humanity of Jesus.

> ❝The Church . . . perpetuates and hands on to all generations all that she herself is, all that she believes.❞
> (*Dogmatic Constitution on Divine Revelation*, 8)

But the controversy continued. In 381 this prompted the Emperor Theodosius I to call a council at Constantinople—modern-day Istanbul. There the bishops repeated the teaching of Nicaea and reiterated the truth that the Holy Spirit, like Jesus, is also fully divine. Our salvation is the work of one God, but that God exists in three divine Persons—the Father, the Son, and the Holy Spirit. This truth of the Blessed Trinity is "the central mystery of Christian faith and life" (*CCC*, 234). Thus, the creed that was written at Nicaea was added to at Constantinople. It is the same Nicene Creed that we proclaim today at Mass. In this creed we proclaim our faith, first in God the Father, then in God the Son, and then in God the Holy Spirit. Yet all that we proclaim flows from this creed's first line, "We believe in one God."

As the years went on, new controversies arose and new councils were called to deal with them. Nestorius, a bishop of Constantinople, claimed that Jesus was really two different persons, one human and one divine, and that people should not speak of Mary as the Mother of God, but only as the mother of the human Jesus. The Council at Ephesus, in modern Turkey, was called in 431 to deal with this heresy. The council condemned Nestorius, affirmed that Mary gave birth to Jesus Christ, the Son of God, and declared that Mary truly can be called "Mother of God." The council at Chalcedon in 451 is considered the greatest of the first four ecumenical councils. There the bishops affirmed the teaching of Pope Leo the Great that Jesus was one person with two natures—divine and human—and that the two natures did not interfere with or compromise each other.

Through the ecumenical councils the life of the Church continued in truth, for "the Church, in her teaching, life, and worship, perpetuates and hands on to all generations all that she herself is, all that she believes" (*Dogmatic Constitution on Divine Revelation*, 8).

Ecumenical councils

Twenty-one ecumenical councils have been held in the history of the Church. They call together the pope and bishops of the whole world. At the first ecumenical council, the Council of Nicaea, more than two hundred bishops were present. If an ecumenical council were held today, there would be more than 4,500 bishops gathered! At each council they live out their role as teachers, guiding the faithful of the Church and helping to express and clarify the Church's doctrines and faith in every age.

Research the last ecumenical council.

CATHOLIC IDENTITY

Activity What are some ways that the Church today communicates the truth to your generation?

Recognizing Our Faith

Recall the question at the beginning of this chapter: *Who or what leads me to the truth?* What surprised you the most in learning about the early Christians' constant striving for the truth? How has their example enriched your answer to this question? enriched your faith?

Living Our Faith

Decide on ways to live and share the truths of your faith this week.

Saint Ambrose

Ambrose was a lawyer and also the governor of a Roman province that included the city of Milan. When the bishop of Milan died in 374, a group of heretics who did not believe in the divinity of Christ wanted a new bishop who shared their beliefs. When representatives of the true Church and the heretics met in the basilica of Milan to elect a new bishop, the election soon threatened to become a riot. As governor, Ambrose went to the basilica to try to restore order. His faith, wisdom, and courage impressed many people. He was elected as the new bishop. Ambrose was stunned and at first protested that he was not a priest; in fact, he was not even baptized! But he was urged to accept the election. Ambrose agreed, was baptized, and was later ordained a priest and eventually a bishop.

As bishop of Milan, Ambrose defended the truth of Christ's divinity against the Arian heresy. His homilies were eloquent and persuasive. Among the people he converted and baptized was Saint Augustine of Hippo, who went on to become a great saint. Ambrose died in 397. The Church has named him a saint and celebrates his feast day on December 7.

Who are the teachers of truths of the faith in your life?

@ For additional ideas and activities, visit www.weliveourfaith.com.

Putting Faith to Work

Talk about what you have learned in this chapter:

 We consider the people and events through which the Holy Spirit worked to define the faith of the Church.

 We understand the various ways in which the truths of our faith have been handed down to us.

We proclaim—especially by our actions—the truths of faith we hold as Christians.

Decide on ways to live out what you have learned.

✝ ENCOUNTERING GOD'S WORD

Jesus said:

"**I am the way and the truth and the life**"

(John 14:6).

➡ **READ** the quotation from Scripture.

➡ **REFLECT** on these questions:
How does following Jesus lead you to truth? How does following Jesus lead you to a fuller life?

➡ **SHARE** your reflections with a partner.

➡ **DECIDE** to do something each day to witness to Jesus—the way, the truth, and the life for you.

Choose four people discussed in this chapter and write brief descriptions to explain their contributions to the Church.

1. _____

2. _____

3. _____

4. _____

Short Answers.

5. What is a heresy? _____

6. What is a creed? _____

7. Which ecumenical council had the task of writing a creed to express the full divinity and full humanity of Jesus? _____

8. The Fathers of the Church were great scholars and writers who contributed to the understanding of the Christian faith. Name two Church Fathers and what they contributed to the Catholic faith.

_____

_____

9–10. ESSAY: Use what you learned in this chapter to explain this statement: *The early Christians experienced the Holy Spirit at work in the world.*

Sharing Faith with Your Family

Discuss the following with your family:
- An empire turns to Christ.
- The Church relies on the word of God.
- The Church defends the truth.
- The Church is strengthened by her councils.

With your family, pray that the Church will always stay true to Christ's teachings and continue to express the truth.

The Worship Connection

At the Sunday Eucharist, we proclaim our faith in the words of the Nicene Creed. This week listen and think about each truth of faith as the assembly proclaims this creed together.

More to Explore

Learn more about the councils mentioned in this chapter by researching them on the Internet or in your library.

Catholic Social Teaching
☑ Checklist

Theme of Catholic Social Teaching:
The Dignity of Work and the Rights of Workers

How it relates to Chapter 8: Our work is a sign of participation in God's work. So, no matter what work people do, they and their work should be respected.

How can you do this?

☐ At home:

_____

☐ At school/work:

_____

☐ In the parish:

_____

☐ In the community:

_____

Check off each action after it has been completed.

9

Christians of the Early Middle Ages

(A.D. 476–1054)

"The Lord is my life's refuge."
(Psalm 27:1)

Leader: Monks, nuns, and many other holy men and women of the Church have made God the focus of their lives. They have shared all they have, claiming nothing as their own.

That we will be generous in sharing what we have with others in our everyday lives, let us pray,

All: All you holy men and women, pray for us.

That we and our families will respond generously to parish efforts in sharing food, clothing, and other necessities with those in need, let us pray:

All: (repeat response)

Leader: That the people of the world, not as owners but as caretakers, will learn to share natural resources and manufactured goods with others who need them, let us pray:

All: (repeat response)

Leader: That we will learn to distinguish between our wants and our true needs, let us pray:

All: (repeat response)

Leader: Lord, may we make you the focus of our lives, and "turn away from evil and do good; seek after peace and pursue it" (prologue to the Rule of Saint Benedict).

We ask this in your name, Lord Jesus.

All: Amen.

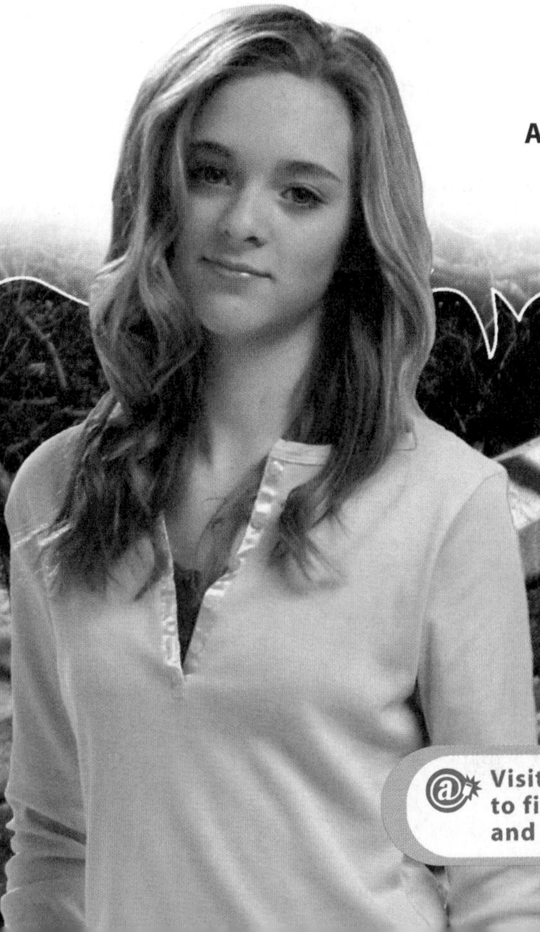

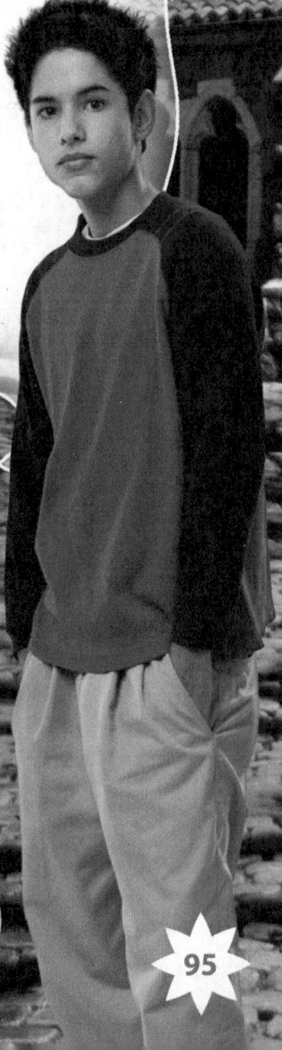

Visit www.weliveourfaith.com to find appropriate music and songs.

The BiG Question:

What helps me to focus on what's important?

iscover a list of some things that will not help you to focus on what's important! Read the list below.

How to Be Perfectly Miserable

1. Always think about yourself.

2. Always talk about yourself.

3. Use the personal pronoun *I* as often as possible in your conversations.

4. Continually base your perceptions on the opinions of others.

5. Focus on what people say about you.

6. Sulk if people are not grateful to you for what you've done for them.

7. Never forget the things you've done for others.

8. Expect to be appreciated.

9. Be suspicious.

10. Be sensitive to slights.

11. Be jealous and envious.

12. Insist that people agree with your views on everything.

13. Never forget a criticism.

14. Trust nobody but yourself.

Now write your own "how-to" list, describing ways to be happy.

In this chapter we learn that, despite difficulties and upheaval, the Church grew and expanded. Through this chapter, we hope

to understand the religious and political forces at work in the world in A.D. 476–1054

to treasure and focus on the enduring values lived by the faithful people of the early Middle Ages

to reach out to all in service and love, focusing on what's really important in this life.

In Florence, Italy, in the fall of 1966, the weather had been wet for weeks. Rain fell constantly, and the Arno River ran high and fast beneath the bridges of the ancient city. Then, in early November, a new storm drenched the hills above Florence. More than a foot and a half of rain fell in less than forty-eight hours, and the river could no longer contain the flood. The Arno burst its banks, and a wall of muddy water roared down from the hills to submerge the city.

The following day, the world awoke to the news that one of Europe's most historic cities lay under seven to twenty feet of mud and filthy water. Mercifully, and thanks to countless acts of selfless heroism, the death toll in the city was small; but thousands of Florentine families were now homeless. And throughout the city, in historic churches, museums, and libraries, hundreds of works of art and millions of rare manuscripts and books lay buried in water and mud.

City authorities worked quickly to aid those whose homes and businesses had been lost, to restore basic services, and to prevent the spread of disease. Then, with the waters receding and the population safe, an international effort to rescue and restore the city's damaged artwork and books began. Soon, in response to the city's urgent request, thousands of art experts, students, and concerned young people from around the world gathered in Florence and went to work. Thanks to the selfless efforts of these "mud angels," as the Florentines called them, many of the city's irreplaceable treasures were saved.

On the thirtieth anniversary of the flood, the mayor of Florence remembered the international effort to preserve Florence's artwork and books. He praised the work of the "mud angels" and noted that "this became clearer every day, that we were not working for ourselves but for . . . our grandchildren. . . . What we were doing was dictated by the desire to give back the traces of . . . the past to future generations."

Activity List some things that individuals or organizations are doing today around the world to preserve what is important and to be considerate of future generations.

"Everyone needs reminders that the fact of their being on this earth is important and that each life changes everything," wrote Marge Kennedy (1950–), U.S. author.

Monasteries are established throughout the Christian world.

After Christianity became the official religion of the Roman Empire, some people began to view Baptism as a way to gain social status and advantages within the empire. Others, however, resisted this trend, knowing that in Baptism they received grace and began a new life in Christ. Some even began to set themselves apart from society in order to live their lives of faith more fully.

At first these people lived alone as hermits, often in desert regions. Then, in about the year 300, Anthony of Egypt (251–356) brought together a group of these solitary hermits to live in community, supporting each other in leading holy lives. Thus, *monasticism* began. **Monastic life** is a life dedicated to prayer, work, study, and the needs of society.

Eventually, systems of "rules" began to govern each **monastery**, or place where monks or nuns live, to guide the lives of those in the monastic life.

Monastic life

Many men and women continue to live the monastic life, following a "rule of life" within a community of monks or nuns. They are very important to the Church, offering their lives, prayer, and work to God for all of us.

Monks and nuns may be contemplative, meaning that they remain within their monasteries, dedicated to prayer, work, and study. They often support themselves by their own labor, which may include farmwork or manufacturing goods such as candy, cake, wine, and bread.

Some monks and nuns support their communities through sculpture, religious paintings, and icons. Some may also teach in schools and colleges or may work in nursing, social work, and parish ministry.

Find out more about specific monastic communities and the way they follow the rules of their founders.

Basil the Great (329–379), who lived in the eastern part of the Roman Empire, was a great theologian whose writings helped to defeat the Arians at the Council of Constantinople in 381. Basil was also a holy monk who developed a great "rule of life" for monks, calling them to a life dedicated to serving God in other people, especially those who were poor. Under Basil's rule the monks vowed, or promised, to practice poverty, chastity, and obedience, which are called the **evangelical counsels**. The monks also followed a daily routine of community prayer, manual labor, contemplation, and service to those in need.

Faith Words

monastic life
monastery
evangelical counsels

Benedict of Nursia (480–550) lived in the western part of the Roman Empire. He founded a monastery at Monte Cassino, Italy, around 529. His sister, Scholastica (480–543), founded a nearby monastery for nuns. Building on the work of Basil, Benedict wrote a rule for his monks and for Scholastica's nuns. Benedict lived by the motto *Ora et labora,* or "Pray and work," and his "rule" named seven specific times each day for community prayer.

In the Benedictine system each monastery was independent, with monks following the rules of their abbot, and nuns of their abbess. Under good and saintly leaders this worked very well, but this was not always the case. Thus, in the tenth century a movement to reorganize, or reform, monastic life began at the French monastery of Cluny. The abbot here directed his monks to a life of prayer centered on Benedict's original rule. Other monasteries soon decided to do the same. Later an even more demanding reform was led by Bernard of Clairvaux (1090–1153), who founded the Cistercian order. His monks followed an extremely strict rule of prayer, manual labor, and simple living. Soon thousands of monasteries became centers of prayer and service to others. The holy lives of the monks and nuns inspired many positive changes in both the Church and the world.

Activity With your group brainstorm some "rules of life" that would help you to serve God and others.

The Church brings the good news to pagan tribes.

Though monasteries were growing and flourishing, the Roman Empire was showing signs of weakening, even signs of beginning to collapse. The empire did not have the strength of leadership that it once had, and there was widespread corruption. Much of this came from the immoral ways in which leaders were behaving.

From the fifth century onward, tribes from outside the empire began to invade Roman territories. The Romans called these invaders "barbarians" because of their lack of education and culture. Fierce Germanic tribes—Goths, Visigoths, Vandals, and Huns—came across the Danube and the Rhine rivers, which marked the borders of the empire. Armies of Franks and Vikings also came to plunder and conquer what had been Roman provinces. The western part of the empire collapsed and the eastern part of the empire barely survived.

With these invasions came much uncertainty. Standards of housing, security, and healthcare declined, and food was often scarce. Death was never far away. Many schools and centers of learning across the Roman world were destroyed or abandoned. For a while it looked as if civilization itself might be wiped out. The invading tribes also brought with them the practice of paganism. And because the Church and the empire had long been so closely linked, the invasions threatened the Christian faith. Thus, Christian leaders like Pope Gregory the Great reached out to the pagan tribes and began the work of their conversion. Gregory made treaties with their leaders and sent Christian missionaries to their homelands.

Gregory also helped to reform the Church. He contributed to canon law, a grouping of laws that would be used to govern the Church and would provide for

Sixth century Gospel manuscript sent by Pope Gregory the Great to spread the good news

> **"Pray and work."**
> motto of the Order of Saint Benedict

good order in **ecclesial**, or Church, governance. Gregory was involved in the development of the *Gregorian Sacramentary*, a book that would guide the celebration of Mass and the other sacraments for many centuries to come. And his name is associated with the beginnings of Church music. Throughout the ages, the beautiful music that has been chanted at the Liturgy of the Hours and other liturgical and traditional celebrations is called, in Gregory's honor, Gregorian chant.

Throughout the years of the barbarian invasions, there were monasteries scattered across the occupied countryside. The pagan invaders were impressed by the kindness and virtue of the monks and nuns. Soon the invaders and their leaders wanted to know more about the faith that inspired these holy men and women. One of these leaders was Clovis, King of the Franks (466–511). The Franks lived in a Roman province called Gaul, known today as France. Clovis converted to Christianity and laid the foundation for a new Christian empire in what was the western part of the known world. Later, in the ninth century, two Greek brothers, Cyril (827–869) and Methodius (825–884), brought the good news of Jesus Christ to the territory from which many of the invading tribes had come. Thus, by the year 1000, most of what had been "barbarian" Europe was Christian.

> **Faith Word**
> ecclesial

Activity Role-play the parts of a Christian missionary and an invader as the missionary tries to convert the invader to Christianity.

Charlemagne strengthens the Church.

How does the Church strengthen the world today?

Like Constantine some five hundred years earlier, the Emperor Charlemagne became a major figure in the history of the Church. Over several centuries the Franks had gradually conquered all of what had been the western part of the Roman Empire. In Rome, on Christmas Day, 800, Pope Leo III crowned Charlemagne, the leader of the Franks, as Holy Roman

Portrait bust of Charlemagne

Emperor. Charlemagne immediately began a reform of both the Church and the state. In fact, he did not distinguish between the two but saw politics and religion as the two halves that formed his Holy Roman Empire.

Historians suspect that Charlemagne realized that Christianity could bind his empire together. Working through combined Church and civil courts, Charlemagne launched a program of reform that included the defense of Christian doctrine, a reorganization of the Church's *hierarchy*, or governing body, and the strict observance of all of the Church's rules and practices.

Charlemagne's most lasting contribution was to education. He decreed that all monasteries should open schools to everyone, not just to those studying to become monks and nuns. He also encouraged monastic libraries to preserve and copy ancient manuscripts. And he appointed a monk named Alcuin from England to set up a school of religious studies at his palace at Aachen, in modern-day Germany—reestablishing the importance of Christian scholarship.

The "'family of God' is gradually formed and takes shape during the stages of human history, in keeping with the Father's plan" (*CCC*, 759). And by the end of the first thousand years, or *millennium,* many monasteries and cathedral schools provided education and preserved ancient culture. Charlemagne had reformed and strengthened the position of the Church's bishops and had enabled the pope to have greater power and status. In fact, it was commonly assumed that the pope, who crowned the emperor, was the true ruler of the Roman Empire—having power over both spiritual and worldly affairs. This close partnership between Church and state affected all parts of life and faith.

Activity Imagine that you are trying to strengthen the Church and the role of faith in society. Name some of the things that you would do.

Forms of prayer

The spirituality of our ancestors in faith can help us to realize that our whole lives can be offered as prayer. But we still need to set aside specific times for prayer. These times include gathering with our parish community to celebrate the Eucharist and the other sacraments, as well as time for personal prayer.

With the guidance of the Holy Spirit, each of us can offer God our prayer. In our prayers of *blessing* we dedicate someone or something to God or ask that something be made holy in God's name. Because God has blessed us, we can ask God to bless other people and things. In prayers of *petition* we ask something of God, usually for ourselves. Often these are prayers in which we ask God for forgiveness. Prayers of *intercession* are also types of prayers of petition. In prayers of intercession we ask God for something on behalf of another person, group of people, or the world. In prayers of *thanksgiving* we show God our gratitude for all he has given us. We show our gratitude for the life, death, Resurrection, and Ascension of Jesus Christ. We do this most especially every time we join in the greatest prayer of the Church, the Eucharist. In prayers of *praise* we give glory to God simply for being God.

CATHOLIC IDENTITY

Using one of the forms of prayer described, pray to God for the Church.

The Church encounters division.

Throughout the seventh and eighth centuries, great armies of Muslims, followers of the prophet Muhammad (570–632), arose in Arabia. These armies conquered much of the Middle East, including the holy sites in Jerusalem. These Muslim invaders began to be seen as a serious threat to Christianity. They conquered the Christian areas of Northern Africa and, by the end of the eighth century, conquered Spain, which had also been a Christian land. Spain then remained under Muslim rule for almost another eight hundred years.

> The "'family of God' is gradually formed and takes shape during the stages of human history, in keeping with the Father's plan"
> (CCC, 759).

At the same time, there was a deepening division in the Church in the eastern and western parts of the Roman Empire. Up until this time, all those who had followed Christ in the Church shared the same creed, the same canon of Scripture, the same respect for the teachings of the Church councils, the same sacraments, and the same moral code and were united under the same pope. But the growing cultural and political differences between the eastern and western parts of the Roman Empire clouded this unity in faith. And in 1054 a division, or *schism*, took place in Catholicism, separating the Church in the eastern and western parts of the Roman Empire. In the earliest days of the Church, there had been no official "Eastern" or "Western" (Roman) Church. But due to this schism, the Church in the western part of the empire would grow into what we know today as the Roman Catholic Church, remaining under the leadership of the pope, or the Roman pontiff.

The Eastern Churches that chose to remain in union with or were later reunited with the Roman Catholic pope and bishops would be called the Eastern Catholic Churches. They are *Churches* because each Church follows its own ancient tradition, retaining its own bishops, language, and liturgical customs. So, the Catholic Church today consists of twenty-two Churches: the Roman Catholic Church and twenty-one Eastern Catholic Churches.

The Church in the eastern part of the empire, choosing not to accept the pope's leadership, would grow into what we know today as the Eastern Orthodox Church. Due to the differences that created tensions between the Churches of the East and the Church in Rome, the schism has lasted to this day. Yet one of the greatest hopes of the pope and the whole Church today is unity with the Eastern Orthodox Church.

Activity Write a prayer for the unity of the Catholic Church.

Hagia Sofia (The Church of the Holy Wisdom), Istanbul, Turkey

Recognizing Our Faith

Recall the question at the beginning of this chapter: *What helps me to focus on what's important?* Reflect on what your answer to this question was at the beginning of this chapter and what your answer is now. In what ways do these answers differ? What might your answer be ten years from now, and what might be important to you then? List your ideas here.

Living Our Faith

When during this coming week will you make time to focus on the important things in life?

Saint Columba

Saint Columba (A.D. 521–597) was an Irish monk, abbot, and missionary. After founding monasteries in Ireland, in the counties of Derry, Durrow, and Kells, he and twelve companions sailed to the island of Iona, off the coast of Scotland, in order to spread the Gospel. There they founded an influential center of monastic life. Saint Columba was also a poet and a scribe. Copying manuscripts was important work for monks, as it preserved the libraries of the ancient world that otherwise might have been destroyed or lost. It is said that Columba was always praying, reading, or copying manuscripts and was personally responsible for copying more than three hundred books. Three of his poems (written in Latin) survive. His feast day is June 9.

Today, there is still a monastic community living on the island of Iona—an ecumenical community of laypeople. The community strives to seek new ways of living the Gospel of Jesus in today's world, while drawing on the heritage of Saint Columba and Irish monastic life.

A prayer that Columba wrote asks God to grant us a love that may never die. In what ways can you focus on the importance of love in your own life?

@* For additional ideas and activities, visit www.weliveourfaith.com.

Putting Faith to Work

Talk about what you have learned in this chapter:

We understand the religious and political forces at work in the world in A.D. 476–1054.

We treasure and focus on the enduring values lived by the faithful people of the early Middle Ages.

We reach out to all in service and love, focusing on what's really important in this life.

Decide on ways to live out what you have learned.

ENCOUNTERING GOD'S WORD

In the prologue to his rule, Saint Benedict quotes these words of Jesus:

" Everyone who listens to these words of mine and acts on them will be like a wise man who built his house on rock. The rain fell, the floods came, and the winds blew and buffeted the house. But it did not collapse; it had been set solidly on rock **"**

(Matthew 7:24–25).

➡ **READ** the quotation from Scripture.

➡ **REFLECT** on the following question: How can Jesus' words help us in our daily lives?

➡ **SHARE** your reflections with a partner.

➡ **DECIDE** to pray, before every reading of the Gospel, "Lord, what do you want me to hear?" This can help you to focus on what's important.

Circle the letter of the correct answer.

1. _____ wrote a rule for monks and lived by the motto *Ora et labora* ("Pray and work").

   a. Basil the Great   **b.** Benedict of Nursia   **c.** Charlemagne   **d.** Bernard of Clairvaux

2. _____ is associated with the beginnings of Church music.

   a. Pope Gregory the Great   **b.** Scholastica   **c.** Anthony of Egypt   **d.** Clovis

3. _____ brought together a group of solitary hermits, thus beginning monastic life.

   a. Basil the Great   **b.** Benedict of Nursia   **c.** Anthony of Egypt   **d.** Scholastica

4. In 1054 a division, or schism, took place in Catholicism, separating the Church in the _____ parts of the Roman Empire.

   a. northern and southern   **b.** eastern and western   **c.** southern and western   **d.** northern and eastern

Write the letter of the answer that best defines each term.

5. _____ monastic life

6. _____ evangelical counsels

7. _____ ecclesial

8. _____ monastery

   a. of or relating to the Church

   b. a life dedicated to prayer, work, study, and the needs of society

   c. a place where monks or nuns live

   d. poverty, chastity, and obedience

   e. a division

9–10. ESSAY: What was Charlemagne's most lasting contribution to the Church?

RESPONDING...

Sharing Faith with Your Family

Discuss the following with your family:

- Monasteries are established throughout the Christian world.
- The Church brings the good news to pagan tribes.
- Charlemagne strengthens the Church.
- The Church encounters division.

What are the cultural or ethnic customs and traditions that are important to the faith of your family? Why are they important to your family? Make a family plan to help preserve these customs and traditions and share them with others.

The Worship Connection

Saint Benedict's rule said, "Let us take part in the psalmody [the singing and praying of the psalms] in such a way that our mind may be in harmony with our voice." Be attentive and responsive to how the responsorial psalm and the songs at Mass contribute to the richness and meaning of the liturgy.

More to Explore

Explore the Internet for the Web sites of Catholic monasteries and learn about the history and mission of each one.

Catholic Social Teaching ☑ Checklist

Theme of Catholic Social Teaching:
Option for the Poor and Vulnerable

How it relates to Chapter 9: As we learned in this chapter, monasteries focused on what was important and served those who were poor. As Catholics we are called to have special care and concern for the poorest among us and to help them.

How can you do this?

☐ At home:

_____

☐ At school/work:

_____

☐ In the parish:

_____

☐ In the community:

_____

Check off each action after it has been completed.

❝Your light must shine before others, that they may see your good deeds and glorify your heavenly Father.❞

(Matthew 5:16)

✝ **Leader:** Saint Francis of Assisi lived in A.D. 1181–1226. As a young man from a wealthy family, he became a soldier and fought for his town in Italy, but later he chose a life of poverty and prayer. Let us pray this well-known prayer for peace that is attributed to him.

All: Lord, make me an instrument of your peace:
where there is hatred, let me sow love;

Group 1: where there is injury, pardon;
where there is doubt, faith;

Group 2: where there is despair, hope;
where there is darkness, light;
where there is sadness, joy.

All: O divine Master, grant that I may not so much seek
to be consoled as to console,

Group 1: to be understood as to understand,
to be loved as to love.

Group 2: For it is in giving that we receive,
it is in pardoning that we are pardoned,

All: it is in dying that we are born to eternal life. Amen.

(Saint Francis of Assisi)

@✷ Visit www.weliveourfaith.com to find appropriate music and songs.

The BiG Question:

Do I welcome change, or do I fear it?

D iscover some inventions that changed the way people lived in the Middle Ages.

In 1268, the first spectacles, made of thick convex lenses, were developed in Italy. These spectacles, or eyeglasses, only helped people who were farsighted.

The first use of a glass mirror was recorded around the year 1180.

Buttons were invented in 1200. They were first used as decorations for clothing.

The first mechanical clock was invented in 1280.

What are some recent inventions that have changed the way we live?

In this chapter we learn that during the period of the High Middle Ages, the Church flourished in Europe as the Catholic faith came to influence every aspect of people's lives. Through this chapter, we hope

 to recognize the ways that Christians in the High Middle Ages sought to live and spread the Gospel message

to appreciate the great contributions that Christians of the High Middle Ages made to the life of the Church

 to live Christ's message of peace as we work to share his Gospel.

s a church building different from other kinds of buildings? Can a church's design express faith and beliefs? Can its architecture reflect changing times within the history of the Catholic Church?

If you were to ask someone living in the Middle Ages these questions, they would probably respond with an enthusiastic *yes.* In Europe during the Middle Ages, the period covering approximately the fifth to the fifteenth centuries and also called the *medieval* period, Gothic cathedrals may have been the grandest expression of faith shown through art. Designed to express the glory and power of God, they featured architectural innovations such as tall, thin walls with large windows that were held in place by structures called flying buttresses. They also had beautiful stained glass and *cruciform,* or cross-shaped, floor plans. Many of these features were developed in the Middle Ages to add deeper religious meaning and greater physical beauty to the existing style of churches.

Nearly every feature of a medieval cathedral was built for a sacred purpose. Magnificent stained glass served not only to allow more light into the building but also to illustrate stories from the Bible and the lives of saints. This was especially important because many Christians at the time could not read. Now they were able to "read" stories of the lives of Jesus, Mary, and the saints in the windows of these great churches.

The cruciform design of a cathedral emphasized its role as a "house of God." To form the shape of the cross, the *nave,* a long central section where the public gathers for Mass, intersected with the *transept,* an aisle that runs across the interior. Thus, a cross shape

Illustration of Notre Dame Cathedral in Paris, France

is seen in aerial views of medieval cathedrals, many of which still stand today—a stunning reminder of the medieval Church's collective mind and heart raised toward God.

In what ways have church buildings changed since this period? How are they still the same?

Activity Think of the unique features of your own church. Draw some of them here. What sacred purpose do these features seem to have?

"Art must show the world as changeable. And help to change it," said Ernst Fischer (1899–1972), an Austrian editor, poet, and art critic.

107

BELIEVING...

The Church fights to recover the Holy Land.

From the earliest days of the Church, many Christians followed the spiritual practice of going on a **pilgrimage**, a journey to a shrine or other holy place for spiritual and devotional reasons. But, during A.D. 1000–1200 the Holy Land—the land where Jesus Christ had lived, died, and risen from the dead, including the holy city of Jerusalem—fell into the hands of Muslim conquerors. This caused great anxiety throughout the Christian world. Many feared that, if these conquerors were not stopped, the Muslim armies might sweep into the heart of Europe.

The Battle of Jaffa, a battle won by the crusaders in 1102, by Henri Auguste Calixte César Serrur (1794–1865)

In 1095 Pope Urban II called on all Christian rulers to organize a crusade. *Crusade* is from the Latin word *crux,* or "cross," and, on their crusade, Christians were to "take back the cross," freeing the Holy Land and its sacred sites. Soldiers, nobles, and *knights,* professional military men of high rank, volunteered to fight in the battles known as the *Crusades*. They acted out of faith, hoping to save Christianity. There were four major crusades between 1097 and 1204. The First Crusade was the most successful, with the Christian armies taking control of Jerusalem and the surrounding lands in 1099. But by 1187 Jerusalem had fallen again, this time to a great Muslim general named Saladin. Other crusades followed, but Jerusalem remained under Muslim control until 1917, when it was captured by the British during the First World War.

> **Faith Word**
>
> pilgrimage

It is often thought that the Crusades reflected a misguided faith. Many crusaders used their religious commitment as an excuse to kill Muslims, Jews, or others not considered followers of Christianity. Over time, many of those who supported or fought the Crusades somehow forgot that using force to spread the Gospel is contrary to everything for which Christianity stands. They forgot God's commandment to protect human life—not take it!

The excesses of the Crusades hurt non-Christians and Christians alike. In 1204 the armies of the Fourth Crusade attacked and looted Constantinople, a city in the eastern part of the Christian world. There was no reason for this terrible act of violence, and, thus, the ill-will between Christians of the east and west only grew deeper.

Activity Discuss: If you were to make a pilgrimage to a holy place or shrine, where would you go? Why?

A changing society

Life in medieval Europe was ruled by *feudalism,* a system that organized society strictly by social class and land ownership. In feudalism, *serfs* were peasants who had the lowest positions in society. They farmed land and were bound to it, but they did not own it. *Vassals,* who had a higher position in society than serfs, held the land, but in exchange for the land they had to give military or other services to *overlords*—the actual landowners and the most powerful class in society.

Most people did not question feudalism, believing that this was the way God meant things to be. The Crusades, however, brought about change. Though destructive to human dignity in many ways, the Crusades helped to promote cultural, economic, and technological growth throughout Europe. Crusaders brought back new ideas, inventions, and renewed appreciation for ancient learning. Soon, manufacturing and other nonagricultural businesses in the towns expanded.

Peasants began moving to the towns, hoping to find freedom from the drudgery of farmwork. And as the towns expanded, great universities were founded. These centers of learning became places for great advances in human knowledge.

Compare and contrast life in feudal society with life in modern society.

The Church struggles with corruption.

During the Middle Ages the Church's power had increased, and most of the world looked to the leader of the Church, the pope, for moral and spiritual leadership. The pope was recognized as Europe's supreme ruler, ruling on all matters—both worldly, or secular, and spiritual. And it was even commonly accepted that the pope had authority from God to give power to kings, princes, and other civil rulers.

Yet at this time in the Church there was much corruption. Some bishops and abbots were living like princes, concerned only about money and power. And the actual kings and princes were insisting on appointing the bishops and abbots within their kingdoms. This illicit practice by secular leaders—laypeople, not ordained bishops—to invest, or empower, a Church leader with authority was known as **lay investiture**. This practice opposed Church teaching, since bishops are successors of the Apostles. As explained in the *Catechism*, "The risen Christ, by giving the Holy Spirit to the apostles, entrusted to them his power of sanctifying: they became sacramental signs of Christ. By the power of the same Holy Spirit they entrusted this power to their successors. This 'apostolic succession' structures the whole liturgical life of the Church and is itself sacramental, handed on by the sacrament of Holy Orders" (1087).

At this time the papacy, too, seemed to become the possession of a few noble Roman families. These powerful families quarreled among themselves over who would hold the power of the papal throne. Finally, however, a great and saintly pope, Pope Gregory VII, was elected. He guided the Church from 1073 to 1085 and started what we now call "the Gregorian reforms." Gregory forbade lay investiture. He also insisted on celibacy for priests in the Roman Catholic Church. He banned all forms of **simony**, the buying and selling of spiritual things, spiritual services, or Church offices. In some cases, under the practice of simony, even entire dioceses and abbeys had been sold to the highest bidder. Gregory's reforms were supported by thousands of reform-minded clergy, and by the laity all over Europe.

Pope Gregory VII, engraving, 1754

> **"'Apostolic succession' structures the whole liturgical life of the Church and is itself sacramental, handed on by the sacrament of Holy Orders."**
> (CCC, 1087)

But reform was a difficult task, and Gregory found that demanding that the emperor, Henry IV, submit to his reforms was indeed difficult. Henry would not obey. Gregory sentenced him to **excommunication**, a severe penalty imposed by the Church for serious sins against the Catholic religion. Thus, Henry was excluded from participation in the sacramental life of the Church. Later, when Henry pretended to be sorry, Gregory lifted the penalty of excommunication. But the Holy Roman Emperor Henry IV returned to Germany and, putting together an army, drove Gregory from Rome. Gregory eventually died in exile, but the Gregorian reforms survived and are still in place in the Church today.

Faith Words

simony
excommunication
lay investiture

Activity Imagine that you are a member of the reform-minded clergy or laity. On a separate sheet of paper, write a letter of support to Pope Gregory VII for his reforms.

BELIEVING...

Fearing heresy, the Church launches the Inquisition.

How does being Catholic influence your daily life?

Many people refer to this time in history as the High Middle Ages. If one word could categorize this period, it would probably be *Christendom*. *Christendom* is not the same as *Christianity*, the religion of the followers of Jesus Christ. **Christendom** refers to a cultural and political atmosphere that came into existence during this period in Europe when nearly everyone was Catholic and Catholicism influenced every aspect of people's lives.

The reign, or rule, of Pope Innocent III (1198–1216) marked the high point of papal power. In the year 1215 Pope Innocent III gathered about 1,200 bishops, abbots, and other Church leaders for a great ecumenical council, the Fourth Lateran Council. At this council, which met in Rome, every aspect of Catholic life was discussed and regulated by decree. Among the decisions of the council were the rulings that:

- Catholics must receive Holy Communion at least once a year

- **transubstantiation** would be the term used to describe the changing of the bread and wine into the Body and Blood of Christ that takes place at Mass during the consecration, by the power of the Holy Spirit and through the words and actions of the priest.

As the Church moved into the later Middle Ages, the world was a place of strict order and conformity. But because civil law and Church law were so closely related, secular and spiritual leaders alike began to fear that any threat to the faith was a threat to all of society. Thus, the leaders of the Church began to defend the faith against heresy. Those who taught false doctrines, and sometimes even those who criticized the Church in a positive and faithful way, were identified as heretics.

In order to investigate suspected heretics, in 1231 Pope Gregory IX set up an official court called the *Inquisition*. This court investigated people who were accused of heresy. It had the authority to impose fines, imprison people, and even condemn unrepentant heretics to death. In 1252, during the pontificate of Pope Innocent IV, suspected heretics were even tortured to make them confess their beliefs against Church teaching. And, in Spain, the Spanish Inquisition, launched by King Ferdinand and Queen Isabella in 1497, was particularly vicious. Going beyond simply finding and punishing people who were suspected of heresy, the Spanish authorities also targeted Jewish and Muslim converts to Christianity, accusing them of secretly practicing their former religions.

It is not easy for us to understand how, in the name of the Gospel, people could be so cruelly punished. Yet we know that fear can cloud a good conscience and alter good judgment. And the leaders of the Inquisition acted out of fear as well as faith. Fear and other vices, both personal and communal, steered those in power to give in to unjust and even inhuman practices that were common in that period of history. All of this gave rise to unjust situations and conditions that had a negative impact on society and its institutions, including the Church. The excesses of the Inquisition mark a sad episode in history. Again, as in the Crusades, some people forgot that Jesus' message is one of love for all people, not violence.

Activity Design a screensaver or logo that shares Jesus' message of love for all people. How can you live out this message?

Friars witness to Christ.

When peasants began to relocate from farms to towns during the High Middle Ages, a huge increase in the number of poor people in the cities resulted. There were no social structures in place to care for them. This shift in population also led to an increase in the types of social problems that accompany urban poverty. Many of those who left farms and villages to go to towns also began to fall away from their faith. To make things worse, many priests were poorly trained and could not explain or defend the truths of the faith. Some of these priests even led noticeably unholy lives. It was clear that the Church was in need of reform.

As has been the case throughout history, God saw the Church's need. With the guidance of the Holy Spirit there arose those who found a new way to help Christians to live the Gospel—a new form of religious life. The men who came together to live this new religious life called themselves friars. The word *friar* comes from the Latin word *frater*, meaning "brother." Unlike the monks of the monasteries, who owned property and lived a life apart from the world, the friars were *mendicant*, a word taken from *mendicus*, the Latin word for "beggar." They would do their work out in the world, and they would depend entirely on the generosity of other people for their daily needs. They would work directly with and among the poor and would travel from town to town, preaching the Gospel.

The friars dedicated themselves to following Jesus' invitation to "sell all that you have and distribute it to the poor" (Luke 18:22). They saw the social responsibilities of the Christian faith as an essential part of humanity's partnership with God. But in addition to living as witnesses to Christ in the world, the friars also committed themselves to being well educated in their faith. They understood, explained,

> **"Sell all that you have and distribute it to the poor."**
>
> (Luke 18:22)

and defended the faith to all who would hear. Two great orders of friars that began at this time were the Franciscans and the Dominicans.

Activity Reflect on Jesus' invitation to "sell all that you have and distribute it to the poor" (Luke 18:22). How would accepting this invitation change your life?

Saint Thomas Aquinas

Theology

The word *theology* comes from *theos*, the Greek word for "god." It literally means "the study of God." Theology is a way of using our human reason to reflect on the mystery of God and understand the teachings of our faith. This helps us to live our faith. In the later Middle Ages, theology became an important area of study. The greatest *theologian*, or scholar studying theology, at this time was Saint Thomas Aquinas (1225–1274).

As a young boy in Italy, Thomas earned the nickname "the dumb ox" because he was large for his age and quiet as well. But after becoming a Dominican friar, he went on to become a great scholar and a professor at the University of Paris. Thomas, convinced that all truth was based in God, was not afraid to study the works of the ancient Greek philosopher Aristotle and other pagan authors. Using these writers' ancient logical arguments and his own powerful gift of reason, he defended the Christian faith and helped people to gain a better understanding of it. His best-known work is called, in Latin, *Summa Theologica*—the most important points of theology.

Today, the Congregation for the Doctrine of the Faith examines the teachings of Catholic theologians, encouraging faithfulness to the Tradition of the Church, which includes the teachings of Saint Thomas Aquinas. Find out about this congregation's recent work for the Church.

CATHOLIC IDENTITY

RESPONDING...

Recognizing Our Faith

Recall the question at the beginning of this chapter: *Do I welcome change, or do I fear it?* Make a list of notable changes in your life or in the world around you during the past year. How did you feel about each of these changes? How did God help you through each one?

Living Our Faith

Make a decision to rely on your relationship with God through all the changes you encounter in life.

Partners in FAITH

Saints Francis and Dominic

Saint Francis of Assisi (1181–1226) and Saint Dominic de Guzman (1170–1221) are saints whose lives as mendicant friars in the Middle Ages continue to have a powerful influence on the Church today. Francis, the son of a wealthy merchant in Assisi, Italy, chose to live a holy life in absolute poverty as a mendicant friar. He never intended to found a religious order, but he soon realized that many people wanted to follow him and share his way of life. He gradually developed a rule to guide his followers in living simple, holy lives. He called his followers the Order of Friars Minor, better known as the Franciscans.

Dominic was born in Spain. As a priest he worked hard to combat a spreading heresy that claimed that the material world and the human body were, by nature, evil. To discourage this heresy, he established an order of nuns, and then an order of mendicant friars to travel far and wide to preach the Gospel. He called his community the Order of Preachers, better known as the Dominicans. They became famous for teaching the Christian faith. Saint Dominic is also believed to have contributed to the development of the rosary.

What can you learn from Saints Francis and Dominic about being unafraid of change?

@ For additional ideas and activities, visit www.weliveourfaith.com.

Putting Faith to Work

Talk about what you have learned in this chapter:

 We recognize the ways that Christians in the High Middle Ages sought to live and spread the Gospel message.

 We appreciate the great contributions that Christians of the High Middle Ages made to the life of the Church.

 We live Christ's message of peace as we work to share his Gospel.

Decide on ways to live out what you have learned.

✝ ENCOUNTERING GOD'S WORD

In his Sermon on the Mount, Jesus taught:

❝ **Blessed are the peacemakers, for they will be called children of God** ❞

(Matthew 5:9).

 READ the quotation from Scripture.

REFLECT on the following:
By sharing the peace that comes from loving God, our Father, and trusting in his will, we can change the world. As peacemakers, we can bring joy where there is sorrow, pardon where there is injury, and love where there is hatred.

SHARE your reflections with a partner.

DECIDE on one way you will try, in the coming week, to change the world by living as an instrument of God's peace.

Write *True* or *False* next to the following sentences. On a separate sheet of paper, change the false sentences to make them true.

1. _____ Pope Gregory VII encouraged simony—the buying and selling of spiritual things, spiritual services, or Church offices.

2. _____ The word *excommunication* refers to a severe penalty imposed by the Church for serious sins against the Catholic religion; it brings exclusion from participation in the sacramental life of the Church.

3. _____ During the High Middle Ages, many peasants relocated from farms to towns, which resulted in an increase in the number of poor people in the cities.

4. _____ In 1231 Pope Gregory IX set up an official court called the Inquisition to "take back the cross" and free the Holy Land and its sacred sites.

Short Answers

5. Name two reforms that were made by Pope Gregory VII. _____

   _____

6. Write a brief description of a friar. _____

7. What does the term *Christendom* refer to? _____

8. Name a Church ruling that was made in 1215 by the Fourth Lateran Council. _____

   _____

9–10. ESSAY: Use what you have learned in this chapter to explain this statement: *People forgot that Jesus' message is one of love for all people, not violence.*

RESPONDING...

Sharing Faith with Your Family

Discuss the following with your family:

- The Church fights to recover the Holy Land.
- The Church struggles with corruption.
- Fearing heresy, the Church launches the Inquisition.
- Friars witness to Christ.

Have a family discussion about changes or reforms that took place at this time in the Church. Then, discuss some reforms or changes that can improve the relationships in your family and in the life and faith you share together.

The Worship Connection

Through the power of the Holy Spirit and the words and actions of the priest, the bread and wine become the Body and Blood of Christ. Be prayerfully attentive to the words of consecration prayed by the priest at Mass.

More to Explore

Use the Internet to research pilgrimages to holy places and shrines around the world.

Catholic Social Teaching ☑ Checklist

Theme of Catholic Social Teaching:
Life and Dignity of the Human Person

How it relates to Chapter 10: This period in Church history reminds us that we need to be faithful to Jesus' teaching to respect the life and dignity of all human beings. We must treat human life as sacred because it is a gift from God.

How can you do this?

☐ At home:

_____

☐ At school/work:

_____

☐ In the parish:

_____

☐ In the community:

_____

Check off each action after it has been completed.

GATHERING...

"**The LORD is my light and my salvation; whom do I fear?**"
(Psalm 27:1)

✚ **Leader:** Let us reflect on one of the mysteries of the rosary, praying that Christ will shine his light on the Church in all times, through all changes.

The fifth mystery of light: the Institution of the Eucharist

Reader: A reading from the holy Gospel according to Luke

"Then he [Jesus] took the bread, said the blessing, broke it, and gave it to them, saying, 'This is my body, which will be given for you; do this in memory of me.' And likewise the cup after they had eaten, saying, 'This cup is the new covenant in my blood, which will be shed for you.'"
(Luke 22:19–20)

The Gospel of the Lord.

All: Praise to you, Lord Jesus Christ.

Leader: Our Father,

All: who art in heaven . . . .
(finish praying the Lord's Prayer). Amen.

Leader: Hail Mary, full of grace,

All: the Lord is with you. Blessed are you . . . .
(finish praying the Hail Mary). Amen.

Leader: Glory to the Father, and to the Son, and to the Holy Spirit:

All: As it was in the beginning, is now, and will be for ever. Amen.

@ Visit www.weliveourfaith.com to find appropriate music and songs.

115

The BiG QuEStion:

How do I respond in times of crisis?

Discover some tactics for responding to a problem. Read the paragraph below. Then devise a plan to help the farmer solve his problem.

A farmer has to transport a fox, a goose, and a sack of grain from his farm to a place across the river. But his boat is so small that he can only cross the river with one item at a time. This is a problem because, if he leaves the fox and goose together, the fox will kill the goose, and if he leaves the goose and the sack of grain together, the goose will eat the grain. How can the farmer get the fox, the goose, and the sack of grain all to the other side of the river?

Answer:

The farmer must take four trips to get the fox, the goose, and the sack of grain to the other side of the river. First trip: Leaving behind the fox and the grain, the farmer takes only the goose to the other side of the river. He then returns to his farm. Second trip: The farmer takes the fox to the other side of the river. But he brings the goose back to the farm. Third trip: Leaving the goose behind, the farmer takes the grain to the other side of the river. He returns to the farm. Fourth and final trip: The farmer takes the goose from the farm to the other side of the river. Mission accomplished!

What problem-solving suggestions might you have for people who are trying to respond to difficult situations in life?

In this chapter
we learn that the Church endured the crisis of the Black Plague, divisions caused by the election of antipopes, and setbacks in the understanding of the Catholic faith. Through this chapter, we hope

 to recognize that the decisions of human beings affect society

to appreciate that the Church endures because it was founded on Christ

to continue the work of Christ as members of the Church—which, even with human problems and flaws, is sustained by grace.

In the days after terrorists attacked the United States on September 11, 2001, New Yorkers remarked at how amazing it was that an old church directly across from the World Trade Center had survived the attacks on the Trade Center's twin towers. When the towers collapsed, sending debris all around the area, St. Paul's Chapel—an Episcopal church built more than two hundred years ago and New York City's oldest public building still in active use—remained relatively unharmed. What helped the church to withstand such a crisis?

A seventy-year-old sycamore tree, it turned out, had shielded the church from the falling debris. This deeply rooted tree took the brunt of the damage from the towers' collapse. As a result, the church remained intact . . . and became the site of an extraordinary volunteer relief effort to help people hurt by the attacks.

Activity List some things that can help to keep you "rooted in faith" when a crisis arises. Share your thoughts with your group.

Sculpture of *Trinity Root*, a sculpture of the tree that saved St. Paul's Chapel, by Steve Tobin (1957–   )

A cloud of dust, debris, and smoke overwhelms St. Paul's Chapel after the terrorist attacks on September 11, 2001.

"Faithless is he that says farewell when the road darkens," wrote British novelist and scholar J.R.R. Tolkien (1892–1973) in *The Lord of the Rings.*

117

The faith of the Church is shaken by the Black Death.

The years 1300–1500 A.D. are often called the late Middle Ages. Unlike the glorious age of faith before, this was a time of disease, disorder, and great change for the Church and the world. A deadly disease was spreading from south to north and from east to west—throughout all of Europe and beyond. This highly contagious disease, or *plague*, was known as the *Black Death*; its victims became extremely ill and sometimes even looked bruised, or "black-and-blue." Those who contracted the plague died a painful death, and doctors were powerless against the disease. Scientists today believe that most of those who died from the Black Death had contracted a form of what we now call the *bubonic plague*. At the time, there was no vaccination to prevent the Black Death and no known cure for the disease.

Medieval book cover depicting the Black Death, 1437

Historians believe that the plague started in Asia and was spread by traders and armies, transmitted by the fleas and rats that were on their ships or in their caravans. Eventually the plague overran Europe, and within years there were so many deaths that it would take about four hundred years to restore the world's population to what it was before the plague began. The economy was hard hit because so many working-class people died. Existing social structures—including feudalism—broke down completely. Poor laborers began to demand higher wages. Crops and animals were neglected, and some people did not even want to care for their own children, fearing they might catch the plague from them.

In fact, people who were well were constantly worried, knowing that this illness could strike them at any time. As a result, people's views on life and faith totally changed. They had seen so much death and wanted to enjoy what was left of life. Often, people even roamed the land, taking what they wanted and acting unjustly toward those who were poor, sick, or disabled. Even faithful people despaired, taking out their anger on God and blaming him for all that was happening. As Catholics, we know that "faith gives us the certainty that God would not permit an evil if he did not cause a good to come from that very evil, by ways that we shall fully know only in eternal life" (*CCC*, 324). But this concept was difficult for people to understand or accept because of the devastation that was all around them. It would take time for people to see God's plan and to reaffirm their faith.

Europe was in a time of crisis—the plague was raging, England and France were at war with each other, Germany was suffering under weak and ineffective rulers, and Muslim armies were advancing on Europe. By 1453 the Muslim Turks had taken over the great Christian capital of Constantinople, and by 1529 Muslim armies had conquered all of southeastern Europe—even attacking the Austrian city of Vienna, deep inside Europe, and raising fears that western Europe would be next.

Activity Identify ways that illnesses and hardships affect people's faith today. How does the Church support people during these times?

The Church faces setbacks in the understanding of the Catholic faith.

During the spread of the Black Death, priests visited and administered the sacraments to those dying of this horrible disease. Many of these priests also contracted the plague and died. Since so many people were dying, priests were constantly busy devoting their time to private Masses for the dead. Some priests grew rich by collecting fees for these Masses.

The devotion to the Christian faith that had grown during the Gregorian reform movement was falling away. The study of theology in the universities was disappearing. A major problem in the Church was that there was a lack of understanding of the real meaning of the Eucharist, which should be the center of every Christian's spiritual life. The Mass became an unclear and distant rite even to those who attended it faithfully. Moreover, the Mass was still in Latin, but, by this time, few laypeople spoke Latin. Only those who were highly educated could even understand it. Most Europeans spoke early versions of French, German, English, or other local languages. So, everyone except the very educated sat through Mass in silence. And it became common practice for even the most religious Christians to receive Holy Communion only a few times a year.

Many priests were poorly educated in the faith and thus could not teach the faith to others. Fewer and fewer priests preached on a regular basis or were able to provide religious instruction for all their parish members. As a result, when Catholics so desperately needed their faith, more and more of them did not even know the basics of Catholicism. And before long, many Catholics did not know the meaning of the Creed or the Ten Commandments and could not even pray the most common prayers, such as the Lord's Prayer and the Hail Mary.

During this era, the choices that were made and the events that took place caused Europe to lose the valued ideals of Christendom. And as Christendom began to weaken, the once powerful papacy began to decline. Catholics should have been able to look to the pope and bishops for strength and guidance in these times of crises and change. But during the late Middle Ages, the Church's leadership, even the papacy itself, became one of the Church's many problems—proving that in every age, the choices that individuals make, and that groups or institutions make, affect society as a whole.

> "God would not permit an evil if he did not cause a good to come from that very evil."
>
> (CCC, 324)

Activity In groups list ways that your parish helps people to understand the Catholic faith. Add to the list as you find new examples.

Women of the Church

During this troubled era the work of two women provided hope: Saint Catherine of Siena (1347–1380) and Blessed Julian of Norwich (1342–approximately 1420).

Catherine was known for her holiness and also for her wisdom. She called for Church reform and for more faithful practice of the sacraments. Princes and bishops sought her advice, and she helped to negotiate peace in wartime. She is also credited with convincing Pope Gregory XI to return the papacy to Rome. Catherine was named a saint in 1461. And in 1970, Pope Paul VI declared her a Doctor of the Church, a special honor given to saints whose writings help us to grow in our understanding of the Catholic faith.

Julian of Norwich was a holy woman who became seriously ill in 1373. As she recovered, she began to have visions. She meditated on them and collected them in a book. This great work, *Revelations of Divine Love*, was the first book written in English by a woman. In it Julian speaks of God's unconditional love for all people.

Pray that you too may be a sign of hope to others.

CATHOLIC IDENTITY

The Church's leadership suffers as a result of the Great Schism of the West.

Where do you go for strength and guidance in times of crisis?

The *Catechism* states, "The *Pope*, Bishop of Rome and Peter's successor, 'is the perpetual and visible source and foundation of the unity both of the bishops and of the whole company of the faithful'" (882). And, as the Bishop of Rome, the pope had always lived in Rome. But in 1305 a French cardinal was elected pope and became Pope Clement V. Rather than moving to Rome, Clement V lived in Avignon, a small city in southeastern France. During his papacy (1305–1314) he appointed mostly French cardinals, who, in turn, continued to elect French popes. All of these popes continued to reside in Avignon, and, though they were not bad or immoral men, they harmed the Church by appearing to place the papacy under the control of the French king, a civil ruler.

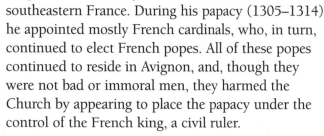
Great Schism of the West (1378–1417)

Pope Gregory XI finally moved the papacy back to Rome in 1377. Later that year, after Pope Gregory's death, the cardinals elected an Italian pope who took the name Urban VI. When Pope Urban VI proposed reforms that the cardinals disliked, they claimed that they had been forced by the Roman mob to vote for the Italian pope and that Urban VI, therefore, was not the true pope. These cardinals then held another election for a pope, selecting the nephew of the French king. This man, who took the name Clement VII, was an **antipope**—not the true pope. Clement VII, unable to seize Rome but recognized as pope by the king of France, returned to Avignon and established his own papal court. But Pope Urban VI, still in Rome, would not step down.

The cardinals had caused a schism in the Church: Two men were claiming to be pope. Across Europe, everyone took sides—with both the pope and the antipope appointing bishops and abbots to various dioceses and monasteries. When Urban VI and Clement VII died, competing groups of cardinals elected two new popes, each one claiming to be the real pope. This situation within the Church was known as the **Great Schism of the West**. Finally, in 1409, the cardinals from both sides met at a council in Pisa, Italy. They dethroned both popes and elected another, who took the name Alexander V. But the two deposed popes refused to step aside. Now there were three rival popes, with Alexander V setting up his papacy in Pisa, Italy.

Eventually, under the influence of the Holy Roman Emperor Sigismund, a general council of the Church met from 1414 to 1418 in the city of Constance, Switzerland. This council decided to set aside all three rival popes. In 1417 a new pope was elected, Pope Martin V, who was accepted by the Western Church.

Thus, after almost forty years, the Great Schism of the West was over. The true lineage of the papacy was restored. But the power of the papacy had been weakened, and the advice and intervention of the popes would no longer be important to many civil leaders. Succeeding popes, only beginning to understand that civil governments were separate from Church governance, would have a difficult time carrying out much-needed reforms in the Church.

Faith Words

antipope
Great Schism of the West

Activity Plan a prayer service to ask for God's blessing upon the Church and her leaders. Write your notes and ideas here.

The Renaissance and humanism influence the life of the Church.

The transitional period between the end of the Middle Ages and the start of the Modern Age is known as the **Renaissance**. The French word *renaissance* means "rebirth." This was a time of rediscovery of ancient Greek and Roman cultures and revival of European culture.

During the Renaissance, the Church became a great patron of the arts—commissioning works of Christian art and architecture. Christian scholars again became interested in the culture of the ancient Christian world, reading Scripture in its original Hebrew and Greek forms and searching monastic libraries for the manuscripts of the Fathers of the Church. And many aspects of Renaissance philosophy were compatible with Christian faith.

One philosophy was called **humanism**. It placed an increased emphasis on the importance of the person. Many great Christian scholars began to devise a "Christian humanism," which helped the Church to rediscover the humanism that lies at the heart of the Gospel message. The Christian humanists emphasized again that everyone is made in God's own image and likeness. Christian humanism has become a lasting legacy. As noted in one of the documents of the Second Vatican Council (1962–1965), we are "witnesses of the birth of a new humanism" and have a duty to "build a better world based upon truth and justice" (*Pastoral Constitution on the Church in the Modern World*, 55).

> We have a duty to **"build a better world based upon truth and justice"**
> (*Pastoral Constitution on the Church in the Modern World*, 55).

Christian humanists of the Renaissance period were concerned about the ignorance and corruption that they saw around them. Many of the Renaissance popes seemed more interested in being patrons of the arts and living lives of luxury than in serving God and his people. And the secular spirit of the Renaissance promoted individual choices and desires more than Christian morality. Christian humanists hoped that a renewed clergy would improve the spirituality and the faith of the whole Church.

Yet, the thriving life of the Church during this era reminds us that even in the worst of times and with poor leadership, the Church survives. The Church, instituted by Christ, guided by the Spirit, and sustained by God's grace, always remains.

Faith Words

Renaissance
humanism

Activity Imagine what the world would be like if people took Christian humanism more seriously. On a separate sheet of paper, express your ideas in a poem.

Renaissance art

The interior of the Sistine Chapel in Rome gives an extraordinary example of Renaissance art. Two of its paintings show the Arch of Constantine, an arch built in the year 315 to commemorate the Emperor Constantine's triumph at the battle of the Milvian Bridge. The Renaissance artists and their papal patron wanted everyone who visited the Sistine Chapel to remember Constantine, the Roman emperor who gave Christians the right to worship openly and who made Rome a Christian city. They also wanted to emphasize the continuity of papal authority over the centuries.

Such works of art clearly show that the Renaissance commemorated our ancestors in faith and celebrated the important role played by the Church in preserving some of the finest aspects of ancient art and culture.

What role does art play in our faith today?

Recognizing Our Faith

Recall the question at the beginning of this chapter: *How do I respond in times of crisis?* How did the Church respond to crises in the late Middle Ages? How does the Church respond to crises today? Display your findings on a poster.

Living Our Faith

Find out how your parish or diocese helps people in times of crisis. What can you do to participate in these efforts?

Diane Bowers

Partners in FAITH

Managing a restaurant was Diane Bowers's dream career, and, at thirty-four, she was finally living it. But then she was diagnosed with fatal brain cancer, with only about five years to live. Anyone would find this diagnosis to be a major crisis—but for Bowers it was the beginning of a spiritual journey.

Bowers didn't always profess a specific faith. But restaurant customers regularly witnessed her kindness and hospitality. One of them invited her to Sunday Mass, and Bowers was so moved by the worship experience that she decided to become Catholic. She then became an active parishioner. While still being treated for cancer, she also took on the roles of catechist and pastoral council member.

When Bowers's mother became ill with cancer, she cared for her mother until her death. And when her own cancer spread and left her paralyzed on one side, Bowers shared her kindness with other patients at the care center where she spent her final months. Even after her death, Bowers's strength, courage, and faith in God lived on for all whose lives she touched.

Think about someone coping with a crisis. How can you help them?

For additional ideas and activities, visit www.weliveourfaith.com.

Putting Faith to Work

Talk about what you have learned in this chapter:

 We recognize that the decisions of human beings affect society.

 We appreciate that the Church endures because it was founded on Christ.

We continue the work of Christ as members of the Church—which, even with human problems and flaws, is sustained by grace.

Decide on ways to live out what you have learned.

✝ ENCOUNTERING GOD'S WORD

❝ Behold, God's dwelling is with the human race. He will dwell with them. . . . He will wipe every tear from their eyes. ❞

(Revelation 21:3–4)

➡ **READ** the quotation from Scripture.

➡ **REFLECT** on these questions:
How did God dwell with his people during the sufferings of the Black Death? during the confusing elections of the antipopes? How is God with you in times of crisis and confusion?

➡ **SHARE** your reflections with a partner.

➡ **DECIDE** to pray for God's grace the next time you experience crisis or confusion in your life.

Define the following.

1. humanism _____

2. Great Schism of the West _____

3. antipope _____

4. Black Death _____

Circle the letter of the correct answer.

5. The French word _____ means "rebirth."

   a. *humanism*   b. *renaissance*   c. *plague*   d. *feudalism*

6. As the bishop of Rome, the pope had always lived in Rome. However, from 1305 to 1377 the pope lived in _____.

   a. Constantinople   b. Florence   c. Avignon   d. Pisa

7. The _____ of the Renaissance emphasized that everyone is made in God's own image and likeness.

   a. antipopes   b. Christian humanists   c. civil leaders   d. civil governments

8. In the late Middle Ages it became common practice for even the most religious Christians to receive Holy Communion _____.

   a. daily   b. weekly   c. monthly   d. a few times a year

9–10. ESSAY: How did the Black Death affect the faith of Catholics of that time?

Sharing Faith with Your Family

Discuss the following with your family:

- The faith of the Church is shaken by the Black Death.
- The Church faces setbacks in the understanding of the Catholic faith.
- The Church's leadership suffers as a result of the Great Schism of the West.
- The Renaissance and humanism influence the life of the Church.

Talk with your family about ways to cope with problems that the Church is facing today. Discuss ways your family can continue to support the Church by living out your faith.

The Worship Connection

The practice of raising the Host after the consecration so that all could see it began during this period in Church history. At Communion, thank Jesus for your opportunity to not only see and believe, but also to receive the Body and Blood of Jesus Christ.

More to Explore

Use the Internet to research the papal election process.

Catholic Social Teaching ☑ Checklist

Theme of Catholic Social Teaching:
Rights and Responsibilities of the Human Person

How it relates to Chapter 11: This chapter revealed some ways that choices can affect society as a whole. We must work to ensure that people's human rights are upheld, especially in times of crisis when people are most vulnerable.

How can you do this?

☐ At home:

_____

☐ At school/work:

_____

☐ In the parish:

_____

☐ In the community:

_____

Check off each action after it has been completed.

"A clean heart create for me, God; renew in me a steadfast spirit."
(Psalm 51:12)

✚ **Leader:** Let us pray in the words of Saint Thomas More, a courageous person of faith during this period of Church history. As lord chancellor of England, Thomas was martyred by the king of England in 1535 because he challenged the king's rejections of the Catholic Church.

All: O Lord,
give us a mind
that is humble, quiet, peaceable,
patient and charitable,
and a taste of your Holy Spirit
in all our thoughts, words, and deeds.
O Lord,
give us a lively faith, a firm hope,
a fervent charity, a love of you. . . .

Give us fervor and delight in thinking
of you,
your grace, and your tender
compassion toward us.
Give us,
good Lord,
the grace to work for
the things we pray for.
Amen.

("Prayer for Fervor in Thinking of God" by Saint Thomas More [1478–1535])

⊕✹ **Visit www.weliveourfaith.com to find appropriate music and songs.**

GATHERING...

The BiG QuEStion:
How can a challenge be an opportunity?

Discover whether you can find opportunities in the challenges you face.

1 **You receive a failing grade on your math test. You**
  (a) start thinking of ways to warn your parents about the inevitable bad report card.
  (b) pledge to study harder next time.
  (c) talk to your teacher about extra-credit possibilities.

2 **You lost the race for class president, so you**
  (a) do nothing; you lost.
  (b) congratulate the winner.
  (c) join a committee; even if you aren't president, you can still be involved.

3 **You break your leg during soccer season. You**
  (a) quit the team.
  (b) suit up and sit on the bench; even if you can't play, you can cheer.
  (c) volunteer to keep score and help out during practices and games.

4 **After your big move to a new town, your afterschool routine includes**
  (a) going straight home since you don't have any friends to hang out with.
  (b) observing classmates in hopes of finding someone to befriend you.
  (c) joining a club to meet new people and make new friends.

Scoring:

If your answers were mostly:	you find challenges to be:
a's	really tough to handle. Try to look at them in an optimistic way and think about the possibilities that they may hold!
b's	manageable, but only when necessary. Perhaps you can listen for opportunity knocking the next time you face a challenge.
c's	opportunities for growth. Keep up your great outlook!

What strengths do you have that you can draw on to face challenges?

In this chapter
we learn that the Church was renewed and strengthened as she answered the challenge of the Protestant Reformation. Through this chapter, we hope

 to understand what the Protestant reformers were seeking and what the Church did in response

to appreciate the teachings of the Council of Trent, which reaffirmed the importance of both Scripture and Tradition

to respond to the challenges of today's world with strength and courage.

From the time Poland was formed in the middle of the tenth century, it encountered almost constant invasions and claims to its territory. Sandwiched between Germany and Russia, Poland achieved only a short-lived independence after World War I. Then Germany invaded it in September 1939, launching World War II. After this war, Poland fell behind the "Iron Curtain"—the powerful communist regime governing the Soviet Union.

TIME
DECEMBER 29, 1980
Shaking Up Communism
OUTLOOK '81
More Recession Ahead
Poland's Lech Walesa

detainment by the government for his activism, Walesa was able to lead the National Committee of Solidarity, an independent trade union that stood up for the freedoms and rights of the people. Walesa, a devout Roman Catholic, was supported by Pope John Paul II and the Catholic Church in his efforts.

For helping to lead the Polish people out of communism, Walesa was named *TIME Magazine's* 1981 "Man of the Year" and awarded the Nobel Peace Prize in 1983. He also became Poland's first popularly elected president in 1990. His contribution to the end of communism in Europe stands as a testament to his ability to turn a challenge into an opportunity.

Polish citizens struggled under the pro-Soviet communist government. The economy was failing. The people were oppressed. Their communist government did not allow free speech or religious freedom. It also regulated the price of food, strictly controlled employment and wages, took political prisoners, and limited citizens' rights. By the mid-1970s Poland's economy was in a terrible decline. It was in this unsettled environment that Lech Walesa lived and grew.

Born in 1943 into a working class family, Walesa received a primary education and training as an electrician. He began working as an electrician for a shipyard in Gdansk, Poland, in 1967. By this time, Polish workers were beginning to protest the poor living conditions in Poland. Strikes and protests in Gdansk eventually led to Walesa's organization of a noncommunist trade union for the workers. In time, despite the challenges of job loss and

Activity Think of someone you know who was able to turn a challenge into an opportunity. List some questions that you could ask this person about his or her ability to meet a challenge this way. Then set aside some time to interview this person.

"We can choose to turn a crisis into an opportunity or into a negative experience," wrote Virginia Satir (1916–1988), U.S. family therapist and author.

BELIEVING...

Abuses and scandals weaken the Church.

In the late Middle Ages the Church faced great challenges. General councils were called to deal with many crises, including the Great Schism of the West. At the Council of Constance the claim was actually made that such councils should have supreme authority in the Church, superior even to that of the pope. Pope Martin V refused to accept this claim, and the Church later officially condemned this idea, which is called *conciliarism*.

In addition to these internal questions, the Church also had to face questions from outside—questions that were brought on by the Renaissance. In universities across Europe, debates were occurring about the nature of the Church. There was widespread discussion about the origin and extent of the authority of the pope, the councils, and Europe's many princes. The papacy was still weak as a result of the Great Schism of the West. Often bishops lived in luxury, away from their dioceses. Some local priests did not lead holy lives and were poorly educated in the faith. Because of this, most ordinary Catholics

Village fair in Schelle by Jan the Elder Brueghel (1568–1625)

were not taught the truths of the faith. Yet people were hungry for a more personal relationship with God—one that was free from the control of what they saw as a corrupt Church. As the *Catechism* explains, the "mystery of the faith . . . requires that the faithful believe in it, that they celebrate it, and that they live from it in a vital and personal relationship with the living and true God" (2558).

At this time people began to think about their own individual rights. They began to feel angry about having to submit to traditional authority. Even Europe's princes started to resent the taxes they had to pay to the Church and to the Holy Roman Empire. Many local rulers began to envy the wealth of the Church and began to covet her land and buildings. At all levels of society, people began to call for change, or reform. And much of the talk of reform centered on corruption and scandal in the Church.

In Germany an Augustinian priest named Martin Luther (1483–1546) was angered by the many abuses and scandals that he saw in the Church. Luther worried about his salvation and found it hard to believe that a corrupt Church could be much help in saving souls. With Christian Europe longing for change, the beliefs of Martin Luther would prove to be the "kindling wood" that would be just enough to start the fire of a religious revolution. Few suspected that events were coming that would lead so many away from the Church.

Faith and good works

The Catholic Church has always taught that our good works on earth do matter. God's grace, working through us, enables us to cooperate in Jesus' work of salvation. Through Baptism we are saved by our faith in God and in his Son, Jesus Christ, our Savior; but we also must express our faith through good works. In fact, the Church teaches that God's gift of grace gives us a *responsibility* to do good works on earth—a *responsibility* to live our earthly lives as Jesus lived his.

"The charity of Christ is the source in us of all our merits before God. Grace, by uniting us to Christ in active love, ensures the supernatural quality of our acts and . . . their merit before God and before men." (CCC, 2011)

CATHOLIC IDENTITY

How have you lived by both faith and good works in your own life?

Activity What challenges did the Church face during this period? Underline or highlight them on this page.

The Church faces the Protestant Reformation.

In the Catholic Church *indulgences* are "closely linked to the effects of the sacrament of Penance" (*CCC*, 1471). An **indulgence** is the remission of the temporal punishment due to sins already forgiven by God. Through certain good works or prayers, Catholics obtain indulgences from the Church for themselves or for the souls in purgatory. But, unfortunately, during the late Middle Ages, the granting of indulgences also became a way for some to raise money for various purposes within the Church. And that practice led to abuses.

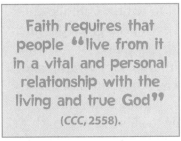

Faith requires that people "live from it in a vital and personal relationship with the living and true God"
(*CCC*, 2558).

Pope Leo X approved an indulgence for anyone who made a contribution of money for the building of Saint Peter's Basilica in Rome. Martin Luther, meanwhile, believed that salvation was purely a gift from God and that it was not possible for a person to earn salvation. Thus, when preachers told the German people that they could automatically free their deceased relatives from purgatory by obtaining this particular indulgence for them, Luther was infuriated. He saw this as the sale of indulgences. Luther made a list describing this and other Church-related issues that he felt were in need of reform. On October 31, 1517, Luther nailed his list, called his Ninety-five Theses, to the door of the church in the German city of Wittenberg.

Luther's Ninety-five Theses were meant to be an appeal to the local bishop to correct certain abuses. But when the bishop did not respond to him, Luther appealed

Martin Luther's 95 Theses by Ferdinand Pauwels (1830–1904)

to the pope. The pope sent a cardinal to meet with Luther. That meeting broke up in anger, turning points of disagreement into a standoff. Now there was little possibility of Luther and the Church finding any common ground. Thus, the chain of events that followed the posting of Luther's Ninety-five Theses started the great *protest* against the Church. This protest would spread through Western Europe and would become the *Protestant Reformation*—a great revolt against the Catholic Church.

Over the years Luther's calls for reform grew more extreme. Emphasizing the importance of Scripture and even translating it into German, he dismissed the authority of Tradition in Christian life. He rejected the Latin Mass and wrote his own communion service in German. He rejected the ordained priesthood, the monastic life, most of the sacraments, and the authority of the pope. He encouraged civil rulers to set up their own national churches. He also wrote many stirring hymns whose lyrics proclaimed his new doctrines. In 1520 Pope Leo X excommunicated Luther from the Church. And in the city of Worms, in Germany, Emperor Charles V had the governing body of the Holy Roman Empire, called the *Diet*, declare Luther an outlaw. But Martin Luther continued to write and to promote his reforms. Many people left the Catholic Church, followed Luther's teachings, and formed a new Christian community, called *Lutherans*.

Emperor Charles V wanted to wipe out the beliefs of Luther and bring Germany back to the Catholic Church. But constant wars with the French and invasions by the Muslim Turks made this an impossible task. It was not until 1547 that Charles could bring his army to Germany to do battle with the Lutheran princes. By that time millions of Germans had already become Lutherans, as did these princes. And though Luther himself had died the year before, the Protestant Reformation continued to grow.

Faith Word
indulgence

Activity Imagine that you are a journalist in Wittenberg during this period. Report on the events taking place.

BELIEVING...

A spirit of reform sweeps Europe.

What in society needs reform?

The invention of the printing press around the year 1450 allowed ideas to be quickly documented and shared. Thus, the spirit of the Protestant Reformation traveled far and fast. As it spread across Europe, it took on different forms.

In Switzerland a reformer named Huldrych Zwingli (1484–1531) rejected the Real Presence of Christ in the Eucharist, a truth that Luther had defended. Zwingli replaced the Mass with a memorial service commemorating the Last Supper. He also declared that the Bible was the only source of faith and encouraged ordinary people to interpret Scripture for themselves.

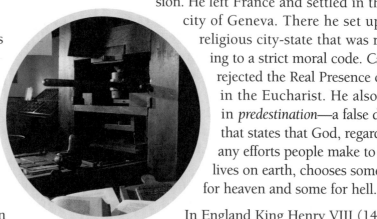

Printing press, circa 1450

Luther thought that Zwingli was too radical. Yet other Protestant reformers were even more radical. Some of these were known as Anabaptists, or "rebaptizers." Since they rejected the validity of infant Baptism they baptized adults again. The Anabaptists complained that Zwingli did things not specifically approved in the Bible, such as baptizing infants and collecting church taxes, or tithes. The Anabaptists also rejected both the authority of the Church and civil government. They wanted to live their lives in their own isolated communities. Some Anabaptists, such as the Amish and the Mennonites, eventually came to America in search of religious freedom.

Defending the faith

Pope Paul III approved a new society in 1540. The Society of Jesus—also known as the Jesuits—soon became famous for their scholarship in defense of the faith and for their missionary zeal. Ignatius of Loyola (1491–1556), Francis Xavier (1506–1552), Peter Canisius (1521–1597), Robert Bellarmine (1542–1621), Edmund Campion (1540–1581) are among the many famous Jesuits. Research how these men and other Jesuits have contributed to the growth of the Church.

Another reformer was a Frenchman, John Calvin (1509–1564). In 1533 Calvin experienced a conversion. He left France and settled in the Swiss city of Geneva. There he set up a kind of religious city-state that was run according to a strict moral code. Calvin rejected the Real Presence of Christ in the Eucharist. He also believed in *predestination*—a false doctrine that states that God, regardless of any efforts people make to live good lives on earth, chooses some people for heaven and some for hell.

In England King Henry VIII (1491–1547) did not set out to reform Catholic doctrine. He had even been given the title "Defender of the Faith" by the pope for speaking out against Luther's claim that only Baptism and Eucharist were valid sacraments. But when Henry's marriage did not produce a son, he became angry with the pope for refusing to allow his marriage to be annulled, or dissolved, so that he could marry again. Henry, taking matters into his own hands, persuaded Thomas Cranmer, the Archbishop of Canterbury, to declare the royal marriage invalid. The pope excommunicated Henry, but the king responded by having the English parliament name him supreme head of the Church in England. The king's actions did not sit well with his lord chancellor, Sir Thomas More (1478–1535), a devout Catholic. More refused to attend the coronation of Henry's new wife and to recognize Henry as the supreme head of the Church in England. More paid a high price for his courage: being executed by the king. Sir Thomas More was named a saint in 1886.

From 1547 to 1553 events that would truly change the Church in England took place. Under Henry's son, the child-king Edward VI, Archbishop Cranmer and other reformers would refashion the English Church into something distinctly not Catholic. The rejections of the Catholic Church during this period were setbacks to the unity of Christian faith once shared throughout Europe.

Activity What would you do to live up to the title "Defender of the Faith"?

The Church responds with the Counter-Reformation.

The Protestant revolt shocked the Catholic Church. At first the Church's internal crises kept it from responding effectively. Under Pope Paul III, the Church answered the reformers' challenge by calling a general council in Trent, Italy. The Council of Trent met from 1545 to 1563, in three sessions under the leadership of three popes—Paul III, Julius III, and Pius IV. It proved to be an important general council.

The Council of Trent focused on confronting the need for reform within the Church and disproving Protestant beliefs. In answer to John Calvin's belief, the Council of Trent affirmed that, though human beings are capable of terrible sin, humanity is not essentially evil—God's grace works through each person, enabling that person's cooperation in the work of salvation. The Council of Trent also affirmed that there are seven sacraments and upheld the truth of the Real Presence of Christ in the Eucharist. Another belief reaffirmed at Trent was that people need the Church to guide them in their efforts to live a Christian life. Thus, people must interpret Scripture only within the faith community; they need the guidance of Tradition as well as Scripture to truly understand and live out their faith.

The Council of Trent by Nicolo Dorigati (1692–1748)

> **"God's grace works through each person."**

The council made clear that we are, as the reformers emphasized, saved by our faith in God and in Jesus Christ, his only Son. But the council also stated that faith must be expressed in good works. Although we depend entirely on God's grace, that grace gives us a responsibility to follow Jesus. The Council of Trent also upheld the practice of praying to the saints and for souls in purgatory, thus reiterating that the bond of Baptism joins all the members of the Church—those who are living and those who are dead.

The Council of Trent required all bishops to work to reform the Church. The council asked them to do this by living within their dioceses, caring for the spiritual welfare of their people, preaching regularly, visiting every parish at least once a year, watching over monasteries and convents, supervising hospitals and charitable institutions, and setting an example of good Christian conduct. The council also put in place a system for selecting bishops, free from the interference of local princes. It also ordered that seminaries be established to give future priests a good education and a strong spiritual formation.

Significantly, the council also called for the publication of a universal catechism, a summary of Catholic faith to guide the whole Church. A papal commission headed by Saint Charles Borromeo completed this task, and the *Roman Catechism* was issued by Pope Pius V in 1566. Thus, the Council of Trent set forth the official teaching of the Church on all important matters, signaling the beginning of a substantial program of reform within the Church itself. This enabled the Church to answer, or counter, the crisis begun by the Protestant Reformation. Because of this, this period in history is known as the **Counter-Reformation**.

> **Faith Word**
> **Counter-Reformation**

Activity On a separate sheet of paper make a two-column chart that lists Protestant reformers and their ideas, and the ways the Church responded to these ideas at the Council of Trent.

RESPONDING...

Recognizing Our Faith

Recall the question at the beginning of this chapter: *How can a challenge be an opportunity?* In light of this chapter, list some challenges that can present new opportunities for you to grow in and strengthen your faith.

Living Our Faith

Find a community situation that is a challenge. Work with your parish members to turn it into an opportunity.

Women of Renewal

Partners in FAITH

One source of renewal for the Catholic Church during the fifteenth and sixteenth centuries was the formation of women's religious orders. From these came notable women leaders in the Church who were strong and educated in their faith. They dedicated their lives to defending and spreading the Catholic faith in Europe and around the world. Here are just a few of them:

Saint Angela de Merici (1474–1540) was born in Italy. In 1531 she started the Order of Saint Ursula—the Ursulines—dedicated specifically to the teaching of girls. Saint Teresa of Ávila (1515–1582) was from a noble Spanish family. A brilliant spiritual writer, she helped to reform her religious order, the Carmelites. In 1970 Pope Paul VI declared her a Doctor of the Church. Saint Jane Frances de Chantal (1572–1641) was from a noble French family. In 1610 she founded the Order of the Visitation of Our Lady, who today still live lives of prayer and service around the world. These women helped to lead the Church through reform and renewal.

What women today are examples of service to the Church?

@* For additional ideas and activities, visit www.weliveourfaith.com.

Putting Faith to Work

Talk about what you have learned in this chapter:

 We understand what the Protestant reformers were seeking and what the Church did in response.

We appreciate the teachings of the Council of Trent, which reaffirmed the importance of both Scripture and Tradition.

 We respond to the challenges of today's world with strength and courage.

Decide on ways to live out what you have learned.

ENCOUNTERING GOD'S WORD

Speaking of Jesus, Saint Paul wrote:

❝ **For he is our peace, he who made both one and broke down the dividing wall of enmity** ❞
(Ephesians 2:14).

➡ **READ** the quotation from Scripture.

➡ **REFLECT** on the following:
By the word *both*, Saint Paul means "both the Jews and the Gentiles who had become one through belief in Jesus." What are some divisions among believers today? What are some ways their faith in Jesus Christ can unite them?

➡ **SHARE** your reflections with a partner.

➡ **DECIDE** to follow Jesus Christ by bringing his peace and unity into your everyday life.

Write *True* or *False* next to the following sentences. On a separate sheet of paper, change the false sentences to make them true.

1. _____ An indulgence is the remission of the temporal punishment due to sins already forgiven by God.

2. _____ The great protest against the Church in the sixteenth century was known as the Counter-Reformation.

3. _____ Reformation is a false doctrine that states that God, regardless of any efforts people make to live good lives on earth, chooses some people for heaven and some for hell.

4. _____ The invention of the printing press had a negative impact on the Protestant Reformation.

Complete each statement with the name of a person discussed in this chapter.

5. _____ wrote a list of Church-related issues in need of reform known as the Ninety-five Theses and believed that salvation was purely a gift from God, not possible to earn.

6. _____ approved an indulgence for anyone who made a contribution of money for the building of Saint Peter's Basilica in Rome.

7. _____ rejected the Real Presence of Christ in the Eucharist, believed in predestination, and in Geneva set up a kind of religious city-state that was run according to a strict moral code.

8. _____ headed the papal commission to complete the publication of a universal catechism, a summary of Catholic faith to guide the whole Church.

9–10. **ESSAY:** The Council of Trent (1545–1563) proved to be an important general council. What were some things that the Council of Trent focused on?

RESPONDING...

Sharing Faith with Your Family

Discuss the following with your family:

- Abuses and scandals weaken the Church.
- The Church faces the Protestant Reformation.
- A spirit of reform sweeps Europe.
- The Church responds with the Counter-Reformation.

Suggest that your family set a date for a special dinner together. This dinner could be at home or a local restaurant. During your time together, invite family members to discuss the challenges that they are facing as followers of Jesus Christ. Talk about ways to work together to help change these challenges into opportunities.

The Worship Connection

From January 18 to January 25 each year, Catholic parishes join with other Christian communities to pray for Christian unity. In light of the history of divisions, we are all called to pray and work for Christian unity.

More to Explore

Use the Internet or encyclopedias to research one of the councils mentioned in this chapter. Share your findings with your family or group.

Catholic Social Teaching ☑ Checklist

Theme of Catholic Social Teaching:
Care of God's Creation

How it relates to Chapter 12: The world around us is in a state of constant reform and renewal. We are challenged to care for and respect the environment, protecting it for future generations.

How can you do this?

☐ At home:

_____

☐ At school/work:

_____

☐ In the parish:

_____

☐ In the community:

_____

Check off each action after it has been completed.

Write the letter of the answer that best defines each term.

1. _____ pilgrimage

2. _____ antipope

3. _____ monastic life

4. _____ ecclesial

5. _____ evangelical counsels

6. _____ simony

a. of or relating to the Church

b. a life dedicated to prayer, work, study, and the needs of society

c. a journey to a shrine or other holy place for spiritual and devotional reasons

d. the buying and selling of spiritual things, spiritual services, or Church offices

e. the sacred law of faith given by God to Moses

f. not the true pope

g. a place where monks or nuns live

h. poverty, chastity, and obedience

Complete the following.

7. Saint Basil the Great developed a _____ for monks, calling them to a life dedicated to serving God in other people, especially those who were poor.

8. The term _____ refers to a cultural and political atmosphere that came into existence during the High Middle Ages in Europe when nearly everyone was Catholic and Catholicism influenced every aspect of people's lives.

9. _____ wrote a list of Church-related issues that he felt were in need of reform, called the Ninety-five Theses.

10. _____ translated the Bible into Latin from Hebrew and Greek.

11. Fourteen books of the New Testament are epistles, or letters, which were written by, or at least attributed to _____, one of the most famous early Christian missionaries.

12. _____, the sister of Saint Benedict of Nursia, founded a monastery for nuns.

Use numbers to order the following events discussed in Unit 2.

13. _____ The Great Schism of the West developed in the late 1300s when competing cardinals elected two new popes, each one claiming to be the real pope.

14. _____ Pope Innocent III gathered about 1,200 bishops, abbots, and other Church leaders for a great ecumenical council, the Fourth Lateran Council.

15. _____ Peter and the other disciples were filled with the Holy Spirit and strengthened to proclaim the good news of Jesus Christ to the world.

16. _____ Constantine made Rome a Christian city.

17. _____ In 1054 a schism separated the Church in the eastern and western parts of the Roman Empire.

18. _____ The Council of Trent called for the publication of a universal catechism, a summary of Catholic faith to guide the Church.

Respond to the following.

19. Choose two women of the Church discussed in Unit 2, and describe the impact of their work.

_____

_____

_____

_____

20. Summarize the outcomes of one of the Church councils discussed in this unit.

_____

_____

_____

_____

Design a visual timeline depicting the major events that took place in Unit 2. You may wish to illustrate using drawing, collage, PowerPoint, or digital imagery. Use captions to describe the important people and events you choose to include. List the people, events, and visuals that you plan to use in the space below.

Choose six Faith Words from the box and write the definition for each.

natural law	temptation	eternal life	reverence	Decalogue
pure of heart	original sin	Counter-Reformation	monastery	pilgrimage

1. _____

_____

2. _____

_____

3. _____

_____

4. _____

_____

5. _____

_____

6. _____

_____

Fill in the circle beside the correct answer.

7. The Emperor _____ made Christianity the official religion of the Roman Empire.

   ○ Nero   ○ Constantine   ○ Charlemagne   ○ Theodosius I

8. _____, an emperor of the Holy Roman Empire, decreed that all monasteries should open schools to everyone and encouraged monastic libraries to preserve and copy ancient manuscripts.

   ○ Nero   ○ Constantine   ○ Charlemagne   ○ Theodosius I

9. The _____ reaffirmed the teaching of Pope Leo the Great that Jesus was one person with two natures—divine and human—and that the two natures did not interfere with or compromise each other.

   ○ Council of   ○ Council of   ○ Council at   ○ Fourth Lateran
   Jerusalem   Trent   Chalcedon   Council

10. The _____ brought reform after the Protestant Reformation.

   ○ Council of   ○ Council of   ○ Council at   ○ Fourth Lateran
   Jerusalem   Trent   Chalcedon   Council

11. The _____ ruled that Catholics must receive Holy Communion at least once a year.

   ○ Council of   ○ Council of   ○ Council at   ○ Fourth Lateran
   Jerusalem   Trent   Chalcedon   Council

12. The _____ was the first great council of the Catholic Church.

  ○ Council of   ○ Council of   ○ Council at   ○ Fourth Lateran
     Jerusalem   Trent   Chalcedon   Council

Choose six people discussed in Units 1 and 2 and briefly describe their impact on the Church.

13. _____

_____

14. _____

_____

15. _____

_____

16. _____

_____

17. _____

_____

18. _____

_____

Respond to the following.

19. What is the message of the Great Commandment? How do the Ten Commandments relate to this message? Use one commandment from the first through third commandments and one commandment from the fourth through tenth commandments to explain your answer to the second question.

_____

_____

_____

_____

20. Choose one of the following topics discussed in Unit 2: *heresies, the Great Schism of the West, the Black Death, the Protestant Reformation.* Explain its impact on the Church.

_____

_____

_____

_____

Unit 3

How Can the Church's Heritage Give Us Hope?

13
Keeping Faith in a Changing World
(A.D. 1648–1789)

"**Working night and day . . . we proclaimed to you the gospel of God.**"

(1 Thessalonians 2:9)

✚ **Leader:** Let us listen to some words of Saint Paul about the need to evangelize people who have not heard the Gospel.

Reader: A reading from the Letter of Saint Paul to the Romans

"For 'everyone who calls on the name of the Lord will be saved.'

"But how can they call on him in whom they have not believed? And how can they believe in him of whom they have not heard? And how can they hear without someone to preach? And how can people preach unless they are sent? . . . Thus faith comes from what is heard, and what is heard comes through the word of Christ."

(Romans 10:13–15, 17)

The word of the Lord.

All: Thanks be to God.

Leader: Let us pray.

All: God our Father,
you will all men to be saved
and come to the knowledge of your
    truth.
Send workers into your great harvest
that the gospel may be preached to
    every creature
and your people, gathered together
    by the word of life
and strengthened by the power of
    the sacraments,
may advance in the way of salvation
    and love.

We ask this through our Lord Jesus
    Christ, your Son,
who lives and reigns with you and
    the Holy Spirit,
one God, for ever and ever.

Amen.

(collect, Mass for the Spread of the Gospel)

@ **Visit www.weliveourfaith.com to find appropriate music and songs.**

The BiG QuEStion:

How do I keep my faith in a world full of changes?

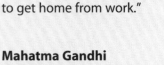iscover people who lived during times of great change and played an influential role in history. Match the person and his or her quote to the historical change to which he or she contributed.

1 **Rosa Parks (1913–2005)**
"All I was doing was trying to get home from work."

2  **Mahatma Gandhi (1869–1948)**
"Nonviolence is the first article of my faith. It is also the last article of my creed."

3 **Alice Paul (1885–1977)**
"If the women of the world had not been excluded from world affairs, things today might have been different."

4  **César Chávez (1927–1993)**
"The fight is never about grapes or lettuce. It is always about people."

____ **a.** the U.S. women's rights movement

____ **b.** India's movement to break free from British control

____ **c.** the movement to uphold the rights of migrant Mexican farmworkers

____ **d.** the U.S. civil rights movement

Answers:

1.d 2.b 3.a 4.c

How do I respond to times of great change?

In this chapter
we learn about difficult changes that the Church faced in evangelization, politics, and scientific thought. Through this chapter, we hope

 to examine the challenges to faith that the Church faced in 1648–1789

to appreciate the faithful response that was demanded of the Church at this time

 to respond in faith and love to the challenges we face today.

Le Gourmet (The Greedy Child), 1901

Pablo Picasso (1881–1973)

THE ROSE PERIOD

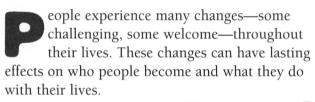

Jeune Ecuyere (Young Horseback Rider), 1905

People experience many changes—some challenging, some welcome—throughout their lives. These changes can have lasting effects on who people become and what they do with their lives.

In many ways, the paintings of artist Pablo Picasso reflect the changes in his life. Pablo Picasso was born Pablo Ruiz Blasco in Spain in 1881. He created his first oil painting at the age of eight. He began studying art in 1892, and his early works show his developing skill and talent.

In his late teens Picasso moved from his home in Barcelona, Spain, to Paris, France. Living conditions were very poor in Picasso's new neighborhood. And, around this time, a close friend of his died. The paintings that he created during this period reflect the great impact of these changes on his emotions. This period of time is called Picasso's "blue" period, not only because of the blue paint he used liberally in his paintings from this period, but also because of his paintings' somber tone. He painted sad, desolate subjects in lonely, depressing, and abandoned

> "Time does not change us. It just unfolds us," said Max Frisch (1911–1991), Swiss author and critic.

situations. It was during this time that he began signing his art with his mother's name, Picasso.

Around 1905 Picasso began painting in pink, or rose. For this reason the period beginning in 1905 is known as his "rose" period. The subjects of his paintings at this time were less depressing and more lighthearted, depicting subjects such as harlequins or clowns.

In 1906 Picasso began painting in a truly innovative style in which strong geometric shapes were used to express space. These works marked the beginning of his "cubist" period.

World War I also brought change to Picasso's style of painting, which started to reflect his disillusionment with war. In the late 1930s, Picasso, then the world's most famous artist, used his art to depict the brutality of the Spanish civil war. He also painted the important people in his life during this time, continuing to develop his cubist style. Picasso remained an active painter until his death in 1973.

Activity Use art to express your emotions or thoughts about current events or world situations that are now unfolding.

BELIEVING...

The Church evangelizes the world.

Peter and the other Apostles and all of Jesus' disciples spread the good news of Christ throughout the known world, which at that time included Europe, Asia, and North Africa. The Church had truly become *catholic*, or universal, because she included people of all races, languages, and nationalities. Saint Ignatius of Antioch, around the year 110, even referred to the Church as the Catholic Church. But the rise of Islam in the seventh century changed the boundaries of Christianity. And by the time of the Protestant Reformation, it seemed as if Catholicism existed almost exclusively on the continent of Europe.

When explorers began to voyage to faraway lands, Pope Alexander VI, whose pontificate was from 1492 to 1503, asked these explorers to **evangelize**, or proclaim the good news of Christ to people everywhere. Thus, the mission of the Church to spread the good news of Jesus Christ to the world was renewed. And missionaries, those officially sent by the Church, brought the Gospel of Christ to all nations.

Starting in 1492 with the first voyage of Christopher Columbus, Spain and Portugal launched explorations that led into the Caribbean and the Americas. Missionary priests traveled with the explorers and preached to the native peoples. The Church saw her mission expanding with each voyage; the call now was to bring the Gospel of Jesus Christ to the "New World." By 1600 there were millions of Christians throughout this region.

Yet some of the explorers forgot that we, "redeemed by the sacrifice of Christ, all . . . enjoy an equal dignity" (*CCC*, 1934). Some committed violent acts against the native populations and even enslaved them. The Spanish government and the pope himself wanted the natives of the newly discovered countries protected. But laws meant to protect the people were hard to enforce from so far away. However, great Christian missionaries, such as the Spanish Dominicans Antonio Montesino (1468–1530) and Bartolomé de las Casas (1474–1566), boldly defended the human rights of America's native peoples.

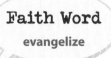

Faith Word

evangelize

Even under the protection of these missionaries, many native peoples still suffered. Without immunity to the diseases brought by European settlers and explorers, millions of them died. It was then that some Spanish and Portuguese settlers began to bring in slaves from Africa to replace the native workers in the mines and on the plantations. The slaves were reduced "by violence to their productive value or to a source of profit" (*CCC*, 2414). And this enslavement was completely against Christianity—against Jesus' command to "love one another" (John 15:17).

Yet other faithful followers brought the good news of Jesus Christ into many other parts of the world. Spanish missionaries brought the faith to the Philippines, which today is the only predominantly Catholic country in Asia. The Jesuit missionary Francis Xavier, arriving in India in 1542, baptized many people in Goa. Francis also traveled to Japan and taught and baptized many people there. Japanese Catholics brought the faith to Vietnam and other parts of Southeast Asia, where French and Portuguese missionaries assisted them. Lay missionaries brought the Christian faith to Korea. And Portuguese and French missionaries were active in Africa, even though the slave trade and the continued advance of Islam slowed their efforts.

Activity In groups, discuss: Where in the world is evangelization most needed? How can you do your part?

Christianity in Africa

The Christian faith originally spread to Africa during the first century. In fact, North Africa gave the Church some of her greatest scholars. One of them was Saint Augustine of Hippo (354–430). Yet it was not until around 1800 that the Church launched new efforts to evangelize Africa. Many missionary orders were founded to aid in this mission. Today there are almost 400 million Christians in Africa. Find out how many of these Christians are Catholic.

Catholics and Protestants yearn for religious freedom.

In Europe the Protestant Reformation led to deep religious differences between Protestants and Catholics. These differences were the basis of conflicts all across Europe between Protestant and Catholic armies, with each group fighting to defend its beliefs. These conflicts are known as the Thirty Years' War. They lasted from 1618 to 1648 and finally ended with the Peace of Westphalia. This series of treaties declared that the religion of the ruler of each area would also become the religion of the people of that area. Europe's kings and queens, or **absolute monarchs**, gained complete, or absolute, power over all aspects of the lives of their people, even deciding which religion they were to practice. Thus, the age of the absolute monarchs began.

In many Catholic countries the monarchs granted favors to the Church, such as control over schools and hospitals, release from the usual taxes, and permission to collect taxes from people for the Church. But, in granting these favors, the monarchs gained more control of the Church. Under the absolute monarchs, the Catholic Church lost her freedom of governance. So, while Catholicism was virtually wiped out in some Protestant countries, it also paid a heavy price in those countries where it was already well established.

King Louis XIV was an example of a Catholic absolute monarch. He ruled France, then the leading Catholic country in the world. In 1682 Louis XIV had the French bishops sign a document called the Gallican Articles, which enabled him to rule the Church in France as if he were more powerful than the pope. Later Emperor Joseph II, another Catholic monarch who ruled Austria, the second most important Catholic country of the time, interfered in Church matters even more than Louis XIV.

King Joseph II (1780–1790)

Faith Word
absolute monarchs

Joseph II actually abolished monasteries and put the state in charge of the seminaries. When Pope Pius VI traveled to Vienna to ask Joseph II to stop interfering in the governance of the Church, he paid no attention to the pope's pleas.

King Louis XIV (1643–1715)

> We, "redeemed by the sacrifice of Christ, all . . . enjoy an equal dignity" (*CCC*, 1934).

In many other Catholic countries, monarchs exercised unnecessary control over the Church. The Church longed to live as Jesus Christ had founded her—strengthened by the Holy Spirit and "governed by the successor of Peter and by the bishops in union with that successor" (*Dogmatic Constitution on the Church*, 8). Yet the age of absolute monarchs continued for one hundred and fifty years. Throughout this time, both Catholics and Protestants alike yearned for their religious freedom.

Activity Discuss: What reaction would you have if a ruler commanded you to change your religion? What would you say? What would you do?

BELIEVING...

Religious freedom advances.

Is religious freedom in danger today?

In the Americas, exploration led to new communities called settlements and colonies. In 1565 Spaniards founded the first Catholic settlement in North America in Saint Augustine, Florida. Spanish Franciscans continued to set up mission settlements, naming each after a saint. The path of these settlements can be traced on a map of America's West and Southwest. French Catholic missionaries also came to the New World in the 1600s. The land where they worked was called "New France," and it stretched from Quebec, in present-day Canada, through the American Midwest and down to New Orleans, Louisiana.

The English also came to settle in the New World. They came to Virginia in 1609. Then, in 1620, the Pilgrims, who came from England seeking religious freedom, settled in Massachusetts. But coming from a Protestant country that was extremely unfriendly toward Catholics, the English brought their dislike of Catholics to the New World.

An English nobleman named George Calvert, the first Lord Baltimore (1579–1632), was a convert to the Catholic faith. He saw how badly Catholics were being treated, both at home and in the colonies in America. So, he asked England's King Charles I for permission to establish a colony where English

Catholics could worship freely. The king granted permission, and in 1634 a group of settlers, both Catholic and Protestant, set sail across the Atlantic Ocean in two ships, the *Ark* and the *Dove*. Their new settlement was named Mary's Land in honor of the king's wife, Queen Henrietta Maria. Mary's Land, now called Maryland, promised freedom of worship to both Catholics and Protestants. But by the mid 1640s Protestants had gained power in the colony. And by 1654 Catholics in Maryland were being persecuted and sometimes even killed because of their faith. Catholics in most colonies were also denied the right to vote.

When the *Declaration of Independence* was signed, in 1776, the United States of America was the home of very few Catholics. Most of them still lived in Maryland, but many also lived in Pennsylvania, a colony founded in 1681 by William Penn. Pennsylvania had become a place of religious refuge, not only for Penn and his fellow Quakers, but also for the Amish and Mennonites, who were Anabaptists, and for Catholics. While the total number of Catholics in America was little more than 25,000 at that time—compared to more than 60 million today—more Catholics lived in Philadelphia, Pennsylvania, than any other city in America.

To coordinate the missionary work of the Church, in 1622 Pope Gregory XV founded the Congregation for the Propagation of the Faith. In 1784 Pope Pius VI began to organize the Church in America and chose Father John Carroll of Maryland (1735–1815) to be "Superior of the Mission" in the United States. In 1790 John Carroll was ordained the first bishop of Baltimore, Maryland—the first diocese of the Catholic Church in the United States. It included all thirteen states that were part of the United States at that time. Bishop John Carroll also founded the first Catholic college in the United States, known today as Georgetown University.

Missionary work

Today the Congregation for the Propagation of the Faith is called the Congregation for the Evangelization of Peoples. It promotes worldwide evangelization by fostering missionary vocations, advancing the education of catechists and clergy, and supervising the establishment of new churches. It sponsors three pontifical aid societies to raise funds for people and parishes in mission areas: the Society of St. Peter the Apostle, the Society for the Propagation of the Faith, and the Holy Childhood Association. What can you do to fulfill your role in the Church's mission of evangelization?

CATHOLIC IDENTITY

Activity List the religious freedoms that you would not have had in the seventeenth century.

Scientific instruments of Galileo Galilei (1564–1642)

The Enlightenment presents new challenges to Christian faith.

While European explorers were discovering civilizations and lands they never knew existed, scientists all across Europe were making discoveries about the natural world around them. New tools and instruments such as the telescope and microscope made it possible for people to look at the world in a new way. They began to seek a scientific understanding of the workings of the natural world. A *scientific revolution* had begun. But it caused many problems for Christians.

The problems began to arise when Italian scientist Galileo Galilei (1564–1642) proved the theory that the earth revolves around the sun. The Church at this time accepted the accounts of creation in the Book of Genesis as literally true. Galileo's discovery contradicted these accounts of creation. Thus, the Church condemned Galileo and asked him to sign a statement discrediting his discovery.

Also problematic for the Church at this time was the discovery of geological evidence that the earth could not have been created in six days, as the Book of Genesis states. Geologists had found that

the earth's rocks were millions of years old. Disagreements between scientists and theologians grew because the distinction between scientific truth and religious truth was not clear. Soon philosophers too began to question the literal truth of Genesis and even some of the basic beliefs of the Christian faith. Christians believe that human reason is God's gift, to be used to the fullest, but philosophers began to idolize reasoning itself. Their belief in the absolute authority of *critical reason*—a belief that by reason alone humans can know all truths, determine all rules, and solve all problems—became a real threat to the Christian faith.

By the eighteenth century people were calling this new age of science and reason "the Enlightenment," from the word *enlighten*, meaning "to give light or knowledge." The Enlightenment affected all of Europe and America, but its center was France. Leading thinkers of the Enlightenment began to portray faith as a kind of weakness, a refusal to think for oneself, or even something childish or immature. Enlightenment philosophers believed in *secularization*, the idea that religious faith had no place in society, science, or government. They saw religion and the truths of the Christian faith as enemies of human progress.

> **"Faith is always the foundation of people's lives, regardless of human progress."**

Yet, guided as always by the Holy Spirit, the Church continued to teach the truths of faith. The Church fought against secularization, continuing to affirm that faith is always the foundation of people's lives, regardless of human progress. The Church disagreed with the idea that critical reason alone was "enlightenment" and encouraged her own scholars to bring reason to the study of Scripture and Tradition. And eventually the Church made it clear that the Bible is not a book of science, but a book of faith that teaches great spiritual truths, among which is the truth that God is the loving creator of all things.

Activity Highlight or underline on this page the controversies that threatened people's faith. How did the Church respond to these controversies?

RESPONDING...

Recognizing Our Faith

Recall the question at the beginning of this chapter: *How do I keep my faith in a world full of changes?* With your group, think of different situations in the world today that can challenge your faith. Then role-play these scenarios, presenting different ways to respond to each situation as a person of faith.

Living Our Faith

This week, try to do something to encourage and build up the faith of a person or group who is facing challenges.

Partners in FAITH

"Father Farmer" Ferdinand Steinmeyer

Catholics living in the North American colonies before the American Revolution were often persecuted for practicing their faith. Father Ferdinand Steinmeyer, a German-born Jesuit, began working in 1752 as a missionary in Pennsylvania. There he ministered to Catholics in Philadelphia, but he also made many secret journeys into the colonies of New Jersey and New York, risking death for entering the British-ruled colonies. During twenty-eight years of ministry he faced great danger as he lived out his vocation. He used a false name to protect his identity: "Father Farmer." Father Farmer established the first Catholic congregation in New York City. He died in Philadelphia in 1786 and has been called "the Father of the Church in New York and New Jersey."

Father Farmer overcame the challenge of practicing his vocation in an environment which was not at all friendly to Catholics. What kinds of challenges must you overcome this week as you live out your faith?

@ For additional ideas and activities, visit www.weliveourfaith.com.

148

Putting Faith to Work

Talk about what you have learned in this chapter:

We examine the challenges to faith that the Church faced in 1648–1789.

We appreciate the faithful response that was demanded of the Church at this time.

We respond in faith and love to the challenges we face today.

Decide on ways to live out what you have learned.

✝ ENCOUNTERING GOD'S WORD

In the Old Testament the prophet Isaiah recounted his call to spread God's word, saying:

" **Then I heard the voice of the Lord saying, 'Whom shall I send? Who will go for us?' 'Here I am;' I said; 'send me!'** "

(Isaiah 6:8).

 READ the quotation from Scripture.

➡ **REFLECT** on the following:
Isaiah responded eagerly to God's call to spread his word. Where does God "send" you to spread his word? How are you responding to this call?

➡ **SHARE** your reflections with a partner.

➡ **DECIDE** on one way to spread God's word today.

Circle the correct answer.

1. To _____ means to proclaim the good news of Christ to people everywhere.

   a. *enlighten*   **b.** *reason*   **c.** *evangelize*   **d.** *secularize*

2. In 1790 John Carroll was ordained the first bishop of _____.

   a. Philadelphia, Pennsylvania   **b.** Baltimore, Maryland   **c.** Saint Augustine, Florida   **d.** New Orleans, Louisiana

3. The Jesuit missionary _____ brought the Catholic faith to India and Japan.

   a. Francis Xavier   **b.** Bartolomé de las Casas   **c.** Nicolaus Copernicus   **d.** Antonio Montesino

Short Answers

4. Where was the first Catholic settlement in North America? _____

5. What is an absolute monarch? _____

6. What is secularization? _____

7. Name two Catholic monarchs who interfered in Church matters in their countries.

   _____

8. How did George Calvert, Lord Baltimore, advance religious freedom in the New World?

   _____

9–10. ESSAY: How did the Church respond to the challenges of the scientific revolution and the Enlightenment?

RESPONDING...

Sharing Faith with Your Family

Discuss the following with your family:

- The Church evangelizes the world.
- Catholics and Protestants yearn for religious freedom.
- Religious freedom advances.
- The Enlightenment presents new challenges to Christian faith.

As a family, choose a favorite television show or movie that shows characters facing challenges to their faith. Afterward, discuss the show or movie. Encourage each family member to suggest advice that he or she would give to the characters.

The Worship Connection

At every Mass we pray for the Church everywhere. Listen for this or a similar prayer: "Lord, . . . grant [the Church] peace and unity throughout the world" (Eucharistic Prayer I).

More to Explore

Use the Internet to research ways the Church is evangelizing today.

Catholic Social Teaching ☑ Checklist

Theme of Catholic Social Teaching:
Solidarity of the Human Family

How it relates to Chapter 13: In this chapter we learned about the catholic, or universal, nature of the Church. As Catholics we respect and care for all human beings—no matter where they live—as one human community, one human family.

How can you do this?

☐ At home:

_____

☐ At school/work:

_____

☐ In the parish:

_____

☐ In the community:

_____

Check off each action after it has been completed.

14
Depending on God in Times of Fear
(A.D. 1789–1814)

> **"Neither death, nor life . . . will be able to separate us from the love of God in Christ Jesus our Lord."**
> (Romans 8:38–39)

✛ **Leader:** Reflect on some area of concern in the world, the Church, our nation, or your own life. Pray together with this concern in mind.

Leader: Lord, be merciful.

All: Lord, save your people.

Leader: From all evil,

All: Lord, save your people.

Leader: From every sin,

All: Lord, save your people.

Leader: From everlasting death,

All: Lord, save your people.

Leader: By your coming as man,

All: Lord, save your people.

Leader: By your death and rising to new life,

All: Lord, save your people.

Leader: By your gift of the Holy Spirit,

All: Lord, save your people.

Leader: Be merciful to us sinners.

All: Lord, hear our prayer.

Leader: Guide and protect your holy Church.

All: Lord, hear our prayer.

Leader: Keep the pope and all the clergy in faithful service to your Church.

All: Lord, hear our prayer.

Leader: Bring all peoples together in trust and peace.

All: Lord, hear our prayer.

Leader: Strengthen us in your service.

All: Lord, hear our prayer.

Leader: Jesus, Son of the living God,

All: Lord, hear our prayer.

Leader: Christ, hear us.

All: Christ, hear us.

Leader: Lord Jesus, hear our prayer.

All: Lord Jesus, hear our prayer.

(based on the Litany of the Saints)

Visit www.weliveourfaith.com to find appropriate music and songs.

The BiG Question:
What do I do to take charge of my life?

Discover what taking charge of life might mean to you. Imagine yourself in each of the following scenarios. Name two actions you would take, and one that you would not take, in each situation.

1 Tryouts for the soccer team will be very competitive because so many students are looking to make the team this season.

To ensure a spot on the team, I would _____ or _____, but I would *not* _____.

2 There is a style of jeans that everyone is wearing this year. You don't have the money to buy the jeans, but you really want them.

To have those jeans, I would _____ or _____, but I would *not* _____.

3 The grade for your science class will make or break your report card this quarter.

To get a passing grade in this class, I would _____ or _____, but I would *not* _____.

4 Your friends will all be going to a party that your parents say you cannot attend.

In handling this situation, I would _____ or _____, but I would *not* _____.

5 A new student at school asks you what you're doing after school. You've already made plans with friends.

To handle this situation, I would _____ or _____, but I would *not* _____.

Think about your responses. How does the way that you take charge of your life affect others?

In this chapter
we examine the causes and consequences of the French Revolution and the effects it had on society and on the Church. Through this chapter, we hope

 to understand the reasons for revolutionary turmoil, especially in France

to appreciate the courage of the Church in facing the turmoil and persecutions of this time

to choose to live as good Catholics and good citizens in the world today.

The word *revolution* comes from the Latin word *revolvere*, which means "to roll back" or "to turn around." All of the uses of this word suggest change or movement—for example, the *revolution* of the planets, or a *revolutionary* idea. The first time *revolution* was used in a political way was in seventeenth-century England, when it was used to describe the return or restoration of a former situation. It was not until the eighteenth century that in some countries *revolution* took on the meaning of overthrowing a government and replacing it with a new one.

Activity Make a list of revolutions that brought about new beginnings and revolutionaries who took charge and brought about improvements.

Washington Crossing the Delaware
(based on Emmanuel Leutze's painting)
by Eastman Johnson (1824–1906)

"Everyone thinks of changing the world, but no one thinks of changing himself," wrote Leo Tolstoy (1828–1910), one of Russia's greatest authors.

A Catholic revolutionary

Charles Carroll

It may be surprising to learn that Catholic ideals had significance in the American Revolution and other revolutionary events throughout the world. This is due, in part, to Charles Carroll (1737–1832), the only Catholic who signed the *Declaration of Independence*.

• A native of Maryland, he was educated by the Jesuits in France because anti-Catholic laws in the American colonies made Catholic education illegal.

• In France, he studied the writings of Catholic philosophers such as Saint Thomas Aquinas. These famous thinkers taught that natural law is God's law within us, a law greater than any human laws.

• His cousin was John Carroll, the first American archbishop.

• As a Maryland landowner, he requested that the English repeal laws that doubly taxed Catholics. When this was refused, he was convinced that the American colonies must become self-governing.

• He wrote a "Declaration of the Delegates of Maryland" in which he urged independence and argued for the right to life, liberty, and property.

• Some historians believe that Carroll contributed Catholic convictions about the natural law to the principles expressed in the *Declaration of Independence*, which states that the "Laws of Nature and of Nature's God" demand independence. Such ideals would, in turn, influence the French Revolution and the hopes of people for their own self-government for generations to come.

Who are some Catholics today who work to improve the world for generations to come?

CATHOLIC IDENTITY

BELIEVING...

The Church lacks defenses against the Enlightenment.

At the beginning of the eighteenth century, the two leading royal families of Catholic Europe were the Hapsburgs, who ruled in Austria, and the Bourbons, who ruled in France. These families, though closely related through marriage, were political rivals. But both families worked to influence the outcomes of papal elections, plotting each time for a weak pope who would not try to take away their power over the Church and her leaders. And they succeeded, since the elected popes at this time failed to stand up to these powerful Hapsburg and Bourbon rulers.

By the middle of the eighteenth century, some of Europe's powerful Catholic monarchs had begun to surround themselves with advisors and officials who were followers of the Enlightenment. So, they were persuaded that enlightened monarchs needed to keep the Church in a subordinate position. To complicate matters, many of Europe's bishops were willing to submit to the monarchs' power and were content to see the papacy decline into weakness.

But the Jesuits defended the papacy against these absolute monarchs and supported the doctrines of the Church against the antireligious teachings of the Enlightenment. All across Europe, in hundreds of schools, Jesuits were educating young men to live out their faith and to defend it. At the same time, in the Spanish and Portuguese colonies of the New World, Jesuits were working to protect the native peoples against slave traders and dishonorable colonial landowners. Thus, the "enlightened" Catholic monarchs of Europe began to see the Jesuits as a threat to both their power and their prosperity.

By the middle of the eighteenth century, Catholic monarchs were expelling Jesuits from their territories in both Europe and the Americas. The king of Portugal was the first to act, in 1759. The kings of France and Spain and the rulers of much of Italy soon followed. In 1773, in the face of conflicting reports and under pressure from secular rulers, Pope Clement XIV issued a decree suppressing the Jesuits in every Catholic country in the world. The Jesuits' schools, churches, and missions were all seized, and the priests of the order were banished. At a time when the Church might have benefited from the Jesuits' talents in combating the most dangerous outgrowths of the Enlightenment they were removed from the scene.

Activity Imagine that you were one of these people: a Jesuit, a native of the "New World", an absolute monarch, the pope, or a student in a Jesuit school. Give a short speech about what was happening to you at this time in history.

Revolution brings about division within the Church in France.

In France in May 1789 King Louis XVI called together the Estates-General, the governing body in France, to deal with his need to raise taxes. The Estates-General was made up of deputies of each of the three "estates" of the French population: the clergy; the nobles, or leaders; and the common citizens. While the king and his ministers wanted the Estates-General to get right down to the discussion of taxes, the deputies of the Third Estate, the common citizens, wanted to change the voting rules. Since these citizens made up 98 percent of France's population, they wanted the votes counted individually, with each deputy's vote holding equal weight rather than each estate's vote counting equally. They also wanted all three estates to meet and vote together rather than separately.

19th century French coin showing the revolutionary motto

> **The Catholic Church faced a terror not known since the persecutions of the early Christians.**

When the king took no action, the deputies of the Third Estate took matters into their own hands. On June 17, 1789, they renamed themselves the National Assembly—a unified assembly representing all the people of France—and invited the deputies of the other two estates to join them, calling for liberty, equality, and fraternity. Many of the clergy and a few of the nobles joined them, and the king reluctantly legalized the new assembly. The *French Revolution* had begun. The new National Assembly wanted France to adopt a constitutional monarchy, like that of England, with an elected parliament limiting the power of the monarch. And since the Church was so closely associated with the monarchy, the National Assembly also wanted to limit the Church's power.

The National Assembly quickly abolished taxes collected by the Church, took control of Church property, and dissolved all monastic orders. And in 1790 the National Assembly passed a law called the Civil Constitution of the Clergy. By this decree the boundaries of all dioceses were rearranged to match civil boundaries, bishops were appointed by the civil assemblies, and parish priests were even elected by civil assemblies. The pope had no say in any of these matters. And the king, while not wanting to sign this law, felt that he had to in order to protect his life and his family.

In November 1790 the National Assembly demanded that all clergy take an oath upholding the new Civil Constitution of the Clergy. Those who refused would lose their positions and, if they continued living as priests, would be prosecuted. The clergy waited for guidance from Pope Pius VI, but he was silent. Some bishops took the oath, and about half of France's priests agreed to the terms of the new law, thus forming a new constitutional Church. The bishops and priests who would not become a part of it were driven from their posts. Now the Catholic Church in France was divided, with two Churches—one the puppet of the revolutionary government, and the other, now illegal but still loyal to the pope.

Finally, in the spring of 1791, Pope Pius VI spoke out, condemning the Civil Constitution of the Clergy and denouncing the National Assembly for all that had happened from the onset of the revolution. The National Assembly quickly retaliated, taking over papal territories and cutting off relations with the Church in Rome. Now an enemy of the Revolution, the Catholic Church faced a terror not known since the persecutions of the early Christians.

Activity Discuss the way that people used their power during this time in history. Create some newspaper headlines that reflect ways people today use their power. How are they the same? different?

Pope Pius VI (1717–1799)

155

Turmoil in the French Church unleashes the Reign of Terror.

Why does the world need a strong Church?

By the spring of 1791 the French National Assembly had almost completed its draft of a new constitution. King Louis XVI did not like the direction the revolution was taking. He addressed the National Assembly and protested the Civil Constitution of the Clergy that was forced on him against his will. He did not want to have to sign a new constitution under similar conditions. So, like many members of the French nobility, he fled the country with his family. He hoped to rally support from the queen's Hapsburg relatives and from other sympathetic rulers and to regain his power. But, even though he was disguised, he was recognized and forced to return to Paris with his family. In September the king reluctantly agreed to the constitution.

But within eleven months the new constitution was overthrown. Violence increased. Thousands of people suspected of being sympathetic to the king were arrested. Mobs stormed the prisons and massacred the prisoners. In September 1792 a French Republic was declared. The government was now under the control of a National Convention. King Louis XVI was overthrown and found guilty of treason. In January 1793 he was executed by beheading, as was his wife, Queen Marie Antoinette.

The French Revolution now entered a period known as the *Reign of Terror*. At this point France was being run by Convention-appointed committees with tyrannical powers, including a powerful group called the Committee of Public Safety. During 1793 and 1794 tens of thousands of French citizens were killed. Nobles and anyone sympathetic to the king were killed. Those in charge were even fanatical enough to kill anyone whose allegiance to the French Republic could be questioned. Thousands of priests, brothers, and nuns were among the victims in a country now determined to erase Christianity as thoroughly as it had erased its monarchy. And by 1794, even those who had organized this Reign of Terror feared for their lives. Thus, they took steps to end this terrible bloodshed.

Eventually the National Convention that had ruled throughout the Terror was disbanded, and by October 1795 France had a new government called the Directory. The Directory ruled France from 1795 until 1799. By mid-1795 a series of decrees had restored freedom of worship, authorized the separation of Church and state, and allowed Catholics to worship in some church buildings that were still owned by the state. However, permission, payment, and loyalty oaths were required to hold religious services. And government security agents attended many Masses, ready to arrest anyone who might say something critical of the government. In addition, the French Church still needed to work out the divisions caused by the earlier Constitution of the Clergy.

Activity Role-play the situation of being accused of practicing Catholicism during the Reign of Terror. What evidence against you would your accusers find?

The Carmelite martyrs of Compiègne

During the Reign of Terror, religious communities were declared illegal because they did not pay taxes to the government. Many religious were executed when their attempts to continue their religious life in secret were discovered. Among these groups were the Carmelite sisters of Compiègne, France. Sixteen members of this community were executed by beheading in Paris on July 17, 1794. While they awaited their deaths, they renewed their baptismal promises and religious vows together and sang songs of praise. Their courageous witness has been remembered in Gertrud von le Fort's novel *Song of the Scaffold* and in François Poulenc's opera *Dialogues of the Carmelites*. The Church has also beatified these Carmelite martyrs. Their feast day is July 17.

Remember in prayer the Carmelite martyrs and all Catholics who have suffered for their faith.

Government unrest disrupts the Church.

From 1792 onward, while terror ruled at home, French armies conquered Belgium, the Netherlands, Switzerland, and much of Italy. The rulers in these countries were replaced with revolutionary governments. Some were more hostile to the Catholic Church than others, depending on the attitude of the French general in charge.

In 1798 the French army occupied Rome, capital of the **Papal States**, a section of central Italy that was governed by the pope. Pope Pius VI was taken prisoner and later forced to relocate to Tuscany. In 1799 the aged and ailing pope was deported to the French city of Valence, where on August 29, 1799, he died. The Church was without a pope for seven months. Many cardinals fled Rome, and the Church was in great disorder. Many people even feared for the survival of the Church. Then, finally, on March 14, 1800, in a conclave held in Venice, the cardinals elected a former monk who would become one of the greatest of all modern popes—Pope Pius VII. This new pope returned to Rome on July 3, 1800, and took up his duties.

The government of France had also undergone many changes. The Directory was gone and an ambitious young general named Napoleon Bonaparte was in power. He wanted the support of the French Catholics and hoped to find favor by showing respect for the pope. Napoleon, wanting to resolve the complicated problems of the divided French Church, entered into diplomatic negotiations with Pope Pius VII. The result, after many months of discussion, was a treaty called the Concordat of 1801. Through this treaty, the pope recognized the Republic as the legitimate government of France, and Napoleon recognized the pope as head of the French Church. Freedom of worship was again guaranteed to Catholics throughout France. The pope began to approve new French bishops after the voluntary resignation of the old ones and churches reopened throughout France and its territories. Seminaries, schools, hospitals, and charitable

> It was a time to **"revive and rebuild the Church in a changed world."**

Faith Word

Papal States

Le Sacre de Napoleon (The Coronation of Napoleon) by Jacques-Louis David (1748–1825)

institutions were opened. And many religious communities were begun or reestablished.

In May 1804 Napoleon declared himself emperor of France. He asked Pope Pius VII to crown him in the restored Cathedral of Notre Dame in Paris. But during the coronation ceremony, on December 2, 1804, Napoleon took the crown from the hands of the pope and placed it on his own head. And as the years went on, relations between the emperor and the pope grew more and more unsettled.

By 1806, as Napoleon's armies occupied most of Europe, he dreamed of also conquering Great Britain—demanding that Pius VII ally with him in this war. When the pope rejected this demand Napoleon ordered the occupation of Rome, also taking hold of the Papal States in 1809. Napoleon arrested Pius VII, first sending him to northern Italy and then bringing him to France, where the pope remained a prisoner until Napoleon's defeat in 1814.

On May 24, 1814, Pope Pius VII again returned to Rome amidst great rejoicing. One of his first acts upon returning to the Vatican was to restore the Society of Jesus, or the Jesuits, who had been suppressed by Pope Clement XIV in 1773. Now, in a Europe that Clement XIV would scarcely recognize, Pope Pius VII wanted the Jesuits back, to help him revive and rebuild the Church in a changed world.

Activity In groups, brainstorm a list of ways the Church can stay strong—and even positively influence the world—during times of political unrest.

RESPONDING...

Recognizing Our Faith

Recall the question at the beginning of this chapter: *What do I do to take charge of my life?* Share your answers as a group. Together do a skit to dramatize some of your responses. In the space below, write a script with dialogue and direction for the characters in your skit. Then perform it with your group.

Living Our Faith

What does your parish or diocese do to support people who are being oppressed? Find out and make a pledge to get involved.

Blessed Noel Pinot

Partners in FAITH

Father Noel Pinot was among a group of priests who refused to take the oath upholding the Civil Constitution of the Clergy in 1790. French government officials removed him from his parish and drove him from the town. But for the next two years, even while in hiding, Father Pinot continued to serve God.

Time after time, he returned to his parish, sometimes in disguise, to celebrate Mass and minister to his parishioners. He also convinced priests who had taken the oath to renounce their false vows. Sadly, in 1793 Father Pinot was betrayed. A man he had once helped told the French authorities that Father Pinot would be celebrating Mass at a particular place and time. That day, as Father Pinot put on his vestments for Mass, the police closed in. He was dragged off to prison, still wearing his vestments. After again refusing to take the oath, he was sentenced to death. On February 21, 1794, as he went to his death, he proclaimed, "*Introibo ad altare Dei,*" a Latin prayer from the Mass meaning "I will go in to the altar of God."

What qualities do you see in Blessed Noel Pinot that might help you to take charge of a difficult situation?

@ **For additional ideas and activities, visit www.weliveourfaith.com.**

158

Putting Faith to Work

Talk about what you have learned in this chapter:

 We understand the reasons for revolutionary turmoil, especially in France.

We appreciate the courage of the Church in facing the turmoil and persecutions of this time.

We choose to live as good Catholics and good citizens in the world today.

Decide on ways to live out what you have learned.

✝ ENCOUNTERING GOD'S WORD

Jesus said,

" Do not be afraid; just have faith "
(Mark 5:36).

➡ **READ** the quotation from Scripture.

➡ **REFLECT** on these questions:
In what ways does living our faith require us to overcome fears and have courage? How does faith help us to be good citizens of the world?

➡ **SHARE** your reflections with a partner.

➡ **DECIDE** to take charge of your fears and have faith in Jesus.

Write *True* or *False* next to the following sentences. On a separate sheet of paper, change the false sentences to make them true.

1. _____ In 1801 the Emperor Napoleon and Pope Pius VII signed a treaty known as the Civil Constitution of the Clergy.

2. _____ In 1773 Pope Clement XIV issued a decree suppressing the Jesuits in every Catholic country in the world.

3. _____ In 1790 the Civil Constitution of the Clergy required that bishops in France be appointed by the pope.

4. _____ In 1814 Pope Pius VII restored the Society of Jesus to help him revive and rebuild the Church.

Short Answers

5. In the eighteenth century, how did the royal families of Catholic Europe try to influence the Church?

_____

6. Name two actions the French National Assembly took to limit the power of the Church.

_____

7. What did the decrees passed in France by mid-1795 restore for Catholics?

_____

8. Briefly describe the events leading to the election of Pope Pius VII.

_____

9–10. ESSAY: Describe some of the changes brought about by the Concordat of 1801.

RESPONDING...

Sharing Faith with Your Family

Discuss the following with your family:

- The Church lacks defenses against the Enlightenment.
- Revolution brings about division within the Church in France.
- Turmoil in the French Church unleashes the Reign of Terror.
- Government unrest disrupts the Church.

Each of us is called to take charge of, or take responsibility for, the way we live our faith. What does your family do to take responsibility for the family's faith life? Hold a family council to examine this issue.

The Worship Connection

The next time you visit your parish church or participate in the Mass, say a special prayer of thanks for the freedom to practice your faith and to celebrate the sacraments.

More to Explore

Use the Internet or newspapers to find examples of people who stand up for a cause in a non-violent way.

Catholic Social Teaching ☑ Checklist

Theme of Catholic Social Teaching:
Rights and Responsibilities of the Human Person

How it relates to Chapter 14: As Catholics we have the responsibility to help one another, our families, and society and to protect the rights of all human beings. We are called to rise above fear and take charge of this responsibility.

How can you do this?

☐ At home:

_____

☐ At school/work:

_____

☐ In the parish:

_____

☐ In the community:

_____

Check off each action after it has been completed.

GATHERING...

"We, though many, are one body in Christ."
(Romans 12:5)

✝ **Leader:** Let us listen to the words of Venerable John Henry Cardinal Newman.

Reader 1: "God has created me to do him some definite service. He has committed some work to me which he has not committed to another. I have my mission."

Reader 2: "I am a link in a chain, a bond of connection between persons. He has not created me for naught. I shall do good, I shall do his work. I shall be an angel of peace, a preacher of truth in my own place, while not intending it, if I do but keep his commandments and serve him in my calling."

Reader 3: "Therefore I will trust him. Whatever, wherever I am, I can never be thrown away. If I am in sickness, my sickness may serve him; in perplexity, my perplexity may serve him; if I am in sorrow, my sorrow may serve him."
(The Newman Reader)

Leader: Meditate on these words of John Henry Cardinal Newman by silently answering the following questions:

Do you believe that God created you for a special mission?
Do you think of yourself as "a link in a chain, a bond of connection between persons"?
What are some ways that the problems of life—sickness, perplexity, sorrow—can become means of serving God?
What are some ways you can be a "preacher of truth in your own place" and teach others about Christ?

Now let us pray together:

All: "Therefore I will trust him." Amen.

@ Visit www.weliveourfaith.com to find appropriate music and songs.

161

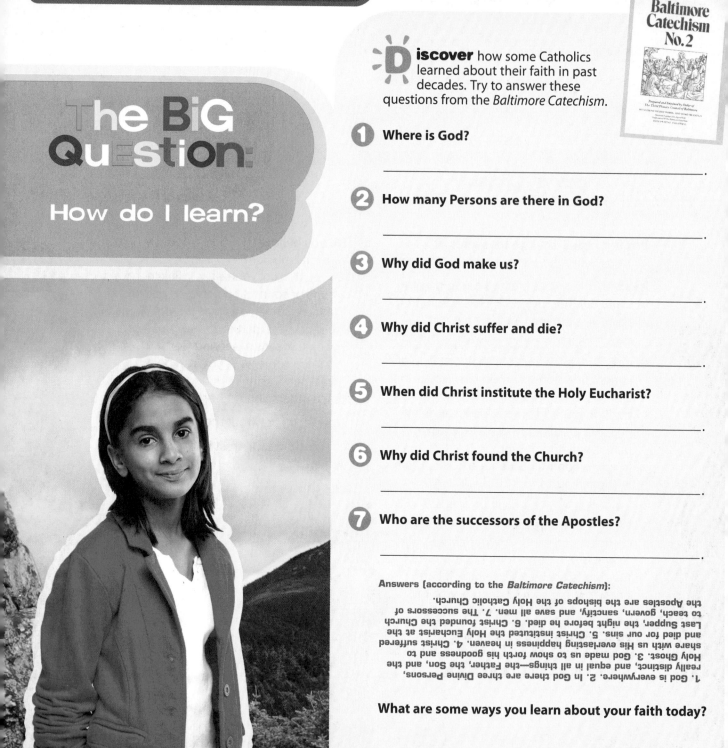

GATHERING...

The BiG Question:

How do I learn?

Discover how some Catholics learned about their faith in past decades. Try to answer these questions from the *Baltimore Catechism*.

1 **Where is God?**

_____

2 **How many Persons are there in God?**

_____

3 **Why did God make us?**

_____

4 **Why did Christ suffer and die?**

_____

5 **When did Christ institute the Holy Eucharist?**

_____

6 **Why did Christ found the Church?**

_____

7 **Who are the successors of the Apostles?**

_____

Answers (according to the *Baltimore Catechism*):

1. God is everywhere. 2. In God there are three Divine Persons, really distinct, and equal in all things—the Father, the Son, and the Holy Ghost. 3. God made us to show forth his goodness and to share with us His everlasting happiness in heaven. 4. Christ suffered and died for our sins. 5. Christ instituted the Holy Eucharist at the Last Supper, the night before he died. 6. Christ founded the Church to teach, govern, sanctify, and save all men. 7. The successors of the Apostles are the bishops of the Holy Catholic Church.

What are some ways you learn about your faith today?

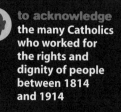

In this chapter
we learn that in a new, industrial age, the Church continued to bring the Gospel to all people. Through this chapter, we hope

to acknowledge
the many Catholics who worked for the rights and dignity of people between 1814 and 1914

to cherish
the selfless spirit of those who dedicated themselves to sharing the Gospel of Christ

to help
the Church to reach out to the poor and oppressed in today's world.

Have you ever experienced difficulty with a math problem that your friend easily understood? Or did you master a dance step while others needed more practice? Do creative, artistic ideas come easily to you, or would you rather be playing a sport than painting a picture? Not every person learns in the same way. Identifying where your skills lie may be the key to determining the way you learn.

Howard Gardner is an educational psychologist who has studied the ways in which people learn. Gardner suggests that there is not just one general intelligence, but at least eight different intelligences! These intelligences, Gardner said, work together to create an individual's unique combination of intelligence and learning style. His multiple intelligence theory includes the intelligences shown in the chart at right.

People with different intelligences learn in different ways. An interpersonal learner might prefer group work, while an intrapersonal learner might prefer to work independently. A musical learner might like to listen to the symphonies of an era in history, while a verbal/linguistic learner would rather read about that era in a history book. A visual/spatial learner, on the other hand, might prefer to create a timeline of historical events. And a bodily/kinesthetic learner might prefer to dramatize a historical event.

Activity Which of the intelligences below seem to be part of your unique combination of intelligences?

INTELLIGENCE	ABILITIES
Verbal/linguistic	Learns languages, writing, reading, and speaking
Logical/mathematical	Solves problems logically, scientifically, and mathematically
Musical	Creates, appreciates, and performs music, recognizing rhythm, tone, and pitch
Bodily/kinesthetic	Coordinates body movement and learns best by doing
Visual/spatial	Recognizes patterns and appreciates images, colors, and shapes
Naturalist	Recognizes and appreciates objects and events in the natural world
Interpersonal	Understands and communicates effectively with others
Intrapersonal	Understands one's own feelings and motivations

"Learn young, learn fair; learn old, learn more."
(Scottish proverb)

Catholic education

By the 1880s there were public schools in almost every city and town in the United States, but the values and beliefs taught in these schools were distinctly Protestant. Catholic parents worried that a public-school education might endanger the faith of their children. So, encouraged by the bishops, the Catholic Church in the United States set out to build what would become the largest independent school system in the world. By 1900 there were around 3,500 parish schools in the United States and about 100 Catholic high schools. By 1920 there were more than 8,000 Catholic elementary and high schools in the United States, and Catholic parishes were thriving. Many parishes in big cities were "national parishes" that served particular ethnic groups. In these parishes homilies were preached in the immigrants' home languages, and the special traditions and feast days of the "old countries" were honored and celebrated. By the 1960s there were 4.5 million students in America's Catholic elementary schools and a million more in Catholic high schools.

Talk to parents, grandparents, and older friends or relatives to find out about teaching and learning in their day.

Etching of the First Vatican Council (1869–1870), St. Peter's, Rome

New revolutions affect the Church.

After the defeat of Napoleon, the borders of European countries needed to be redrawn and order needed to be restored. Diplomats from all over Europe met in the city of Vienna, Austria, in October 1814 to take on these tasks. But, in March 1815, Napoleon returned to Paris with reinforced troops, hoping to regain his empire. In June 1815 he was finally defeated by the allied powers of Europe at Waterloo, Belgium. And by the end of 1815 Napoleon was exiled to the South Atlantic island of St. Helena.

A new era had begun. The world would never be the same as it had been before the French Revolution. Enlightenment ideas had taken root, and Europeans, newly freed from Napoleon's rule, grew more and more determined to govern their own lands. They wanted freedom from the restrictions placed on them by a distant emperor, by a congress of diplomats, and even by the Church.

In Italy, the Congress of Vienna reestablished the Church's rule over the Papal States and gave an assortment of Hapsburg, Bourbon, and other rulers reign over the rest of Italy. This did not please the Italian patriots who were hoping to build a new, united Italy. So, it was not surprising that, by the 1840s, revolutionary movements were breaking out all across Italy. By 1860 revolutionaries occupied all of the papal territories except the city of Rome and its immediate surroundings. The reigning pope, Pius IX (1846–1878), refused to recognize the authority of the new Italian government in Italy. But in 1861, a United Kingdom of Italy was proclaimed, with its rulers dreaming of making Rome their capital.

From December 1869 to October 1870 Pope Pius IX convened the First Vatican Council in Rome. This ecumenical council, the first since the Council of Trent, would unfortunately be interrupted by those banding together to unify Italy. In the summer of 1870, as bishops from around the world met at the Vatican, the remains of the Papal States and the city of Rome itself were taken over by Italian troops. Pope Pius IX had now lost the last of his worldly power. He dismissed the council fathers and retreated—shutting himself within the walls of the Vatican. For the rest of his long reign he would call himself the "prisoner of the Vatican."

Many European countries were also experiencing radical changes. After the Congress of Vienna the area now known as Germany became a confederation of small states under the rule of the emperor of Austria. But in 1871 Otto von Bismarck (1815–1898), a German statesman, succeeded in throwing off Austrian rule and uniting many of these states in a new German Empire. And as the empire's chancellor, Bismarck began a program of persecution against Catholics—known as the *Kulturkampf*, a German word meaning a "conflict of cultures." Bismarck claimed that the recent proclamation of the Vatican Council on **papal infallibility**, the divine guarantee that the pope's official statements of doctrine regarding faith and morals are free from error, would cause Catholics to disregard the German government. To further control the power of the Church in Germany, Bismarck initiated laws that severely restricted most Church ministries and required that the Jesuits leave the country.

Faith Word

papal infallibility

Activity Draw a political cartoon in support of the Church during this time.

The Church promotes justice in the modern world.

At this time factories were springing up all across Europe and America. Thousands of men, women, and children were leaving farms and villages to work in them, and in mines and mills. But this industrialization brought with it many social problems. Business owners often took advantage of their workers, making them work long hours for low wages. Living and working conditions were often dismal and dangerous.

Since factory owners had political influence, most civil governments did not protect the rights of the workers. Many angry workers looked to socialist and communist labor organizations for help. These groups promised workers justice, promoting a classless society and equal distribution of economic goods. But many of the communist organizers followed German philosopher Karl Marx (1818–1883), who taught that religion gave people an illusion of an unreal world, dulling their awareness of injustice. Thus, many workers gave up their religion as part of their fight for justice.

It was during this time that a new pope, Pope Leo XIII (1878–1903), was elected. Pope Leo XIII knew that the Church needed to proclaim her social teachings, or teachings about justice in society, and increase her efforts to bring about justice in the industrial age. He wrote eighty-five encyclicals. One of these, *Rerum Novarum*, issued in 1891, was the first great Catholic social justice encyclical. *Rerum Novarum* means "Of New Things," and in it Pope Leo XIII applied the Church's traditional doctrines to the conditions of the modern world. The "new things" that concerned the pope were the rights of workers in a new age of industrialization. The pope spoke forcefully about the dignity of work. He championed workers' right to a just wage and their right to form trade unions. And he called on governments to enact laws to protect workers' rights.

Pope Leo XIII (1810–1903)

> The Church worked to "increase her efforts to bring about justice in the industrial age."

When Leo XIII died, the next pope, Pius X (1903–1914), made important contributions to other aspects of Church teachings. Two of his very important contributions were in regard to the Eucharist. At this time in the Church, most Catholics would receive Holy Communion only a few times a year and children did not receive Holy Communion at all. But Pope Pius X declared that children should receive their First Holy Communion as soon as they were old enough to understand that Christ was truly present in the Eucharist. He encouraged Catholics to receive Holy Communion frequently, even daily.

Pope Pius X also called for reforms in the Church's liturgy, encouraging the revival of the Gregorian chant of the Middle Ages and welcoming the writing of appropriate new music. He encouraged bishops to make sure that priests received the best possible instruction, and he urged priests to preach clear and simple homilies. He also stated that parishioners should be able to participate actively at Mass, and he promoted reform and renewal of religious instruction for adult laypeople as well as children.

Pope Pius X (1835–1914)

Pope Pius X sowed the seeds for changes that would eventually take root in the Church. And in 1954 he was named a saint—the first canonized pope since Saint Pius V in 1712.

Activity Underline or highlight the reforms Pope Pius X made during his pontificate. How have these reforms affected your life?

165

BELIEVING...

Efforts to spread the Gospel grow.

What can I do to bring the Gospel to others?

Despite persecutions and political upheavals, the nineteenth century was a time of spiritual revival for the Church. Catholic schools and colleges were being founded. The Franciscans, Dominicans, Benedictines, and Jesuits had recovered from the horrors of the French Revolution. And many men and women of faith were now working for social justice in the modern age.

Among those spreading the good news of Jesus Christ were organizations of lay Catholic men and women, such as:

- the Center Party, organized by lay Catholics in Germany in the 1870s, to counter political oppression
- the Catholic Association, an organization begun in Ireland by Daniel O'Connell (1775–1847), a Catholic lawyer, to work for the civil rights of Catholics in Ireland and England
- the Society of St. Vincent de Paul, organized in France in 1833 by a university student named Antoine-Frédéric Ozanam (1813–1853) and his advisor, Sister Rosalie Rendu (1786–1856), to enable laypeople to serve the poor.

Setting out to spread the Gospel and work for social justice were missionaries such as:

- the Society of the African Missions, founded in France in 1856
- the St. Joseph's Society for Foreign Missions, or Mill Hill Missionaries, founded in England in 1866
- the Catholic Foreign Mission Society of America, or Maryknoll, founded in the United States in 1911
- the Missionary Society of St. Paul the Apostle, or the Paulists, founded in Rome and New York in 1858 by Father Isaac Thomas Hecker (1819–1888). One of the Paulists' first projects was to set up a publishing house to produce magazines and books about the Catholic faith for both adults and children.

New religious orders were also being established to meet the needs of the rapidly changing world. One was the Society of St. Francis de Sales, also known as the Salesians. It was started in Italy in 1859 by John Bosco (1815–1888). A few years later, with the help of Mary Mazzarello (1837–1881), John Bosco also founded an order of Salesian sisters,

Venerable Catherine McAuley   Venerable Cornelia Connelly   Saint Frances Xavier Cabrini   Saint Katharine Drexel

the Daughters of Mary, Help of Christians. The Salesians dedicated their lives to working with youth, especially the young men and women of industrial Europe's working classes. Both of their founders have since been named saints.

Other new orders of religious women included: the Sisters of Mercy, founded in Ireland in 1831 by Catherine McAuley (1778–1841); the Sisters of the Holy Child Jesus, founded in England in 1846 by an American, Cornelia Connelly (1809–1879); the Missionaries of the Sacred Heart of Jesus, founded in Italy in 1880 by Frances Xavier Cabrini (1850–1917); the Sisters of the Blessed Sacrament, founded in the United States in 1891 by Katharine Drexel (1858–1955).

Many women also joined existing religious communities such as the Ursulines, Sisters of Saint Joseph, and Sisters of Charity. All of these brave and holy women were striving, in the words of Cornelia Connelly, "to meet the wants of the age." In everything they did, in the schools, hospitals, and missions that they founded, these women promoted the Gospel of Christ.

Activity Imagine you were asked to found a new Catholic lay organization to spread the good news of Jesus Christ. What would your mission be? What needs would your organization address? How would you encourage others to join you in your efforts?

Catholicism grows with the United States.

In the early years of the nineteenth century, the United States was growing, both in population and in area. In 1803 Napoleon sold the Louisiana Territory—a tract of land that stretched from the Mississippi River to the Rocky Mountains—to the new nation for a total of $15 million. The United States was now twice as big as it had been at its founding.

In 1808 Pope Pius VII carved out four more dioceses from the original Baltimore diocese and named four new bishops to lead them. One of these was the bishop of Bardstown, Kentucky, Benedict Joseph Flaget (1763–1850). He did missionary work among the native peoples in his diocese and established colleges, convents, and other religious institutions.

> "The nineteenth century was a time of spiritual revival for the Church."

In 1811, even while being held captive by Napoleon, Pope Pius VII elevated John Carroll from bishop to archbishop of Baltimore. By the time of Archbishop Carroll's death, in 1815, the Catholic population of the United States had grown to between 100,000 and 150,000 people. Now, with the end of the Napoleonic wars, traveling between the old world and the new was again safe. All over Europe, war-weary people were looking to the United States as a land of hope and opportunity. Many Catholics in England, Ireland, and Germany were also looking to the United States as a haven from anti-Catholic prejudice and persecution. Thus, a great wave of immigrants, many of them Catholic, set out to reach America's shores.

In 1820 the pope established another new diocese, that of Charleston, South Carolina. Many of the Catholics in this diocese were poor Irish immigrants, and the first bishop was also an Irishman, John England (1786–1842). He started the first Catholic newspaper in the United States. He also opened a school for free African-American children and arranged for the religious instruction of slaves.

In the 1830s and 1840s the United States continued to add territory. In 1836 the independent Republic of Texas asked to join the United States; the final annexation took place in 1844. In 1846 Great Britain gave the United States full jurisdiction over the Oregon territories. In 1848, after a war with Mexico, the United States acquired the rest of Texas along with Colorado, Arizona, New Mexico, Wyoming, Nevada, Utah, and California. The diocese of Santa Fe, New Mexico, was formed in 1853. Its first bishop was a Frenchman named Jean Baptiste Lamy (1814–1888).

By 1850 there were 2 million Catholics in the United States, and Catholics had become the largest single religious group in the country. Among their strongest defenders was the new, Irish-born archbishop of New York, John Hughes (1797–1864), who worked tirelessly for social justice and civil rights for his largely poor, largely Irish flock.

Activity Discuss ways that your parish can welcome Catholics from other countries to your faith community.

Anti-Catholicism

Some Americans thought that immigrant Catholics arriving in the United States at this time would pledge their allegiance to the pope rather than to the United States. Anti-Catholic books and newspapers began to be published. Some Protestant clergy preached sermons denouncing the Catholic Church as un-American. With anti-Catholic prejudice on the rise, it was not surprising that violence soon followed.

In 1834 a mob looted and burned a convent in Massachusetts. In 1844 a series of riots by members of an anti-Catholic group rampaged through Philadelphia and nearby towns. The group set fire to homes of Irish Catholic immigrants, a seminary, and several Catholic churches. Some Irish Catholics were shot while trying to defend their homes and churches.

By 1852 many of the nation's anti-Catholic groups had banded together to form a secretive, nationwide political party. Its members came to be called "Know-Nothings" because they replied to outsiders' questions about their organization with the answer "I don't know." All across the United States Know-Nothing mobs burned Catholic churches while Know-Nothing candidates ran for election in the hope of passing anti-Catholic laws.

What can we do to discourage discrimination on the basis of race and religious beliefs today?

RESPONDING...

Recognizing Our Faith

Recall the question at the beginning of this chapter: *How do I learn?* In the space below, create a short lesson to teach a group of third graders about one aspect of the Catholic faith. Consider incorporating multiple intelligence methods on page 163 as you design your lesson.

Aspect of the Catholic faith you will teach about:

Lesson idea:

Living Our Faith

Find one new way that you can learn more about the Catholic faith.

Partners in FAITH

Venerable John Henry Cardinal Newman

One of the most influential Catholics of the nineteenth century was an Englishman of deep faith and great learning who began his career not as a Catholic, but as a priest of the Church of England—John Henry Newman (1801–1890). As a young Anglican priest Newman became one of the leaders of the Oxford Movement, a group of scholars and clergy who sought to renew the Church of England. Through his work in this movement, Newman became convinced that the Catholic Church was the true Church of Jesus Christ. Newman became a Catholic in 1845 and a Catholic priest the following year.

Over the next forty-five years John Henry Newman's many books, essays, homilies, and letters would influence both Catholics and non-Catholics in countries around the world. In 1879 Pope Leo XIII named John Henry Newman a cardinal. In 1991 Pope John Paul II declared him venerable, the first step toward sainthood.

Who are some other people who converted to Catholicism and now join in the Church's efforts to proclaim the Gospel?

For additional ideas and activities, visit www.weliveourfaith.com.

Putting Faith to Work

Talk about what you have learned in this chapter:

 We acknowledge the many Catholics who worked for the rights and dignity of people between 1814 and 1914.

 We cherish the selfless spirit of those who dedicated themselves to sharing the Gospel of Christ.

 We help the Church to reach out to the poor and oppressed in today's world.

Decide on ways to live out what you have learned.

✝ ENCOUNTERING GOD'S WORD

Just before his death, Jesus said to his disciples:

> **"In the world you will have trouble, but take courage, I have conquered the world"**
>
> (John 16:33).

➡ **READ** the quotation from Scripture.

➡ **REFLECT** on these questions:
What "trouble" do you see or face in the world today? How can you conquer such difficulties with Jesus' help?

➡ **SHARE** your reflections with a partner.

➡ **DECIDE** to have courage and know that Jesus is with you, helping you to share the Gospel message.

Complete each statement with a name.

1. In 1833 Antoine-Frédéric Ozanam and his advisor, _____, organized the Society of St. Vincent de Paul.

2. John Bosco, the founder of the Salesians, with the help of _____, founded an order of Salesian sisters known as the Daughters of Mary, Help of Christians.

3. From December 1869 to October 1870, _____ convened the First Vatican Council in Rome.

4. *Rerum Novarum,* the first great Catholic social justice encyclical, was written by _____.

Circle the letter of the correct answer.

5. The divine guarantee that the pope's official statements of doctrine regarding faith and morals are free from error is called _____.

   a. an encyclical   **b.** papal infallibility   **c.** *Kulturkampf*   **d.** "Of New Things"

6. _____ declared that children could receive their First Holy Communion as soon as they were old enough to understand that Christ was truly present in the Eucharist.

   a. Pope Leo XIII   **b.** Pope Pius IX   **c.** Pope Pius VII   **d.** Pope Pius X

7. The first bishop of Charleston, South Carolina, _____, started the first U.S. Catholic newspaper.

   a. John England   **b.** John Hughes   **c.** Joseph Flaget   **d.** John Bosco

8. By 1850 there were _____ Catholics in the United States.

   a. 100,000   **b.** 200,000   **c.** 1,000,000   **d.** 2,000,000

9–10. ESSAY: Describe a nineteenth-century religious order's or lay organization's efforts to proclaim the Gospel.

Sharing Faith with Your Family

Discuss the following with your family:

- New revolutions affect the Church.
- The Church promotes justice in the modern world.
- Efforts to spread the Gospel grow.
- Catholicism grows with the United States.

Check your parish bulletin to see what groups such as the Society of St. Vincent de Paul are doing in your diocese. Find ways your family can contribute to their work.

The Worship Connection

This Sunday pay close attention to the Gospel and reflect on the ways you may share its message with others throughout the week.

More to Explore

Use the Internet to find out more about Catholic religious orders that were founded during 1814–1914.

Catholic Social Teaching ☑ Checklist

Theme of Catholic Social Teaching:
Dignity of Work and the Rights of Workers

How it relates to Chapter 15: In this chapter we learned that Pope Leo XIII championed the rights of workers. All Catholics have the responsibility to uphold people's right to decent work, safe working conditions, and participation in decisions about their work.

How can you do this?

☐ At home:

_____

☐ At school/work:

_____

☐ In the parish:

_____

☐ In the community:

_____

Check off each action after it has been completed.

16

Renewing Our Relationship with Christ
(A.D. 1861–present)

"I am the way and the truth and the life."

(John 14:6)

✝ **Leader:** Let us pray now for help in understanding the challenges that face us in our lives, in our Church, in our country, and in our world.

Group 1: For all those in government, who have the responsibility to protect all our citizens—including those not yet born, those who are disabled, those who are poor, hungry, or homeless, and the elderly or very young, we pray to you, Lord Jesus:

All: Jesus, you are the way.

Group 2: For the leaders of our Church, our Holy Father and our bishops, that they may continue to guide us along right paths in the name of the Lord, we pray to you, Lord Jesus:

All: Jesus, you are the truth.

Group 3: For all those who work for peace and justice, that we may join them in their work in our everyday lives—through our prayers for the world and through our compassion for others, we pray to you, Lord Jesus:

All: Jesus, you are the life. We pray all of this in your name. Amen.

@ **Visit www.weliveourfaith.com to find appropriate music and songs.**

The BiG QuEStion:

Does my voice count?

Discover how challenging it can be to express yourself clearly. Tongue twisters are designed to be very difficult to say and repeat. Try to say the following tongue twisters to a partner!

1 One was a racehorse. Two was one, too. One won a race. Two won one, too.

2 She sells seashells by the seashore.

3 Pour a proper cup of coffee from a copper coffeepot.

4 How much wood would a woodchuck chuck if a woodchuck could chuck wood?

Were the tongue twisters easy to say, or was it a challenge to get the message across clearly? Think of a time when it was a challenge for you to voice a message. What would have helped you to get your message across?

In this chapter we learn about the growth of the U.S. Catholic Church and the work of the Second Vatican Council. Through this chapter, we hope

to understand some of the circumstances that influenced the growth of the Church in the United States from 1861 to the present

to appreciate the work of the Church in continuing to voice messages of justice, peace, and equality during times of political and social change

to share our faith with others as we meet the challenges of the present and the future.

hink for a moment about your voice. Your voice is the sound that is made by the vibration of your vocal cords. These vocal cords are part of your larynx, a muscular organ that forms an air passage to your lungs. Air passing out through the larynx brings the vocal cords closer together, creating sounds. These sounds together create words and language.

You probably use your voice for many things—for talking, for singing, for laughing, for screaming, and for crying. Your voice is not only your tool to convey information but also to express a vast array of emotions. Your voice can question, exclaim, state, and proclaim. It can show happiness, anger, surprise, and sadness. Your voice is an important tool to share your feelings and your emotions with the world. Yet messages can be voiced in many nonverbal ways, too. Sometimes people's actions can speak louder than words.

Activity Role-play some different ways people can voice their messages.

"The human voice. . . . is indeed the organ of the soul," wrote Henry Wadsworth Longfellow (1819–1892), an American poet.

Vatican Radio

In 1931 the Vatican began its own radio station. Vatican Radio became the voice of the Vatican and provided a central source from which to broadcast news coverage of Vatican events. The pope at that time, Pope Pius XI, viewed radio as a form of media through which to evangelize the modern world. He called on a renowned scientist, Guglielmo Marconi, to help him set up a Vatican radio station to spread the good news of Jesus Christ to all nations. Today Vatican Radio offers newscasts, live broadcasts of papal events, and other programming in forty different languages to listeners in Europe, Asia, Africa, North and South America, and the countries of the South Pacific. The Mass and other liturgical celebrations are also broadcast monthly in Italian, English, Russian, and Chinese, and in the various languages of the Eastern Catholic Churches. The Mass is also broadcast every morning in Latin, the official language of the Church. Now, in the twenty-first century, Vatican Radio's programming is sent out not only as radio broadcasts, but also via satellite and over the Internet. Today anyone, anywhere in the world, at any time of the day or night, can visit the Vatican Radio Web site to listen to past broadcasts of events such as the announcement of the election of Pope Benedict XVI and to download podcasts.

Tune in to Vatican Radio and find out what is being broadcast. Go to www.vatican.va for information.

CATHOLIC IDENTITY

The Catholic Church grows in a diverse nation.

At the time of the American Revolution, when neither the British nor the patriots were friendly toward Catholicism, American Catholics had a difficult choice to make. Most sided with the patriot cause and supported the Revolution. And when independence from England was won in 1783, Catholics shared the full religious freedom that was granted to everyone in America.

The entire country rose from the revolution as the "United States." But in the mid-nineteenth century all Americans were faced with a decision that would divide the country—whether or not to support human slavery. Somehow, even some Catholics, disregarding people's God-given dignity, supported slavery as a means to their own personal profit. So, when the Civil War broke out in 1861, Catholics, just as other Americans, were divided in their loyalties. Most Southern Catholics backed and fought with the Confederacy, and most Northern Catholics, the Union. Catholic priests served bravely in both armies as chaplains. More than 600,000 people were killed, and a million-plus more were wounded. But in 1865 as the Civil War ended, freedom for people of all races and creeds was proclaimed.

The U.S. bishops realized the need to call a meeting—a **plenary council**, a council to be attended by all the country's bishops—to address the needs of the Church in the newly reunited United States. So, in 1866, the bishops met in Baltimore at the Second Plenary Council. At the First Plenary Council, held in Baltimore in 1852, the bishops had issued recommendations that pastors teach Christian doctrine to the young people in their parishes and that every parish establish a Catholic school. Now, with the Catholic population of the United States reaching 4 million, the bishops reiterated this recommendation. By 1884, when the bishops gathered at Baltimore for the Third Plenary Council, they voted to establish a nationwide Catholic school system with the goal of having every Catholic child in the United States enrolled in a Catholic school. They also

> **Faith Word**
>
> plenary council

Third Plenary Council, Baltimore, Maryland (1884)

gave American Catholics the *Baltimore Catechism*. From its first publication in 1885 until the late 1960s, most young American Catholics learned their faith from this straightforward, question-and-answer text.

During these years of the late nineteenth and early twentieth centuries, bishops and other Catholics reached out to the 4 million slaves that had been freed in the United States, inviting them to become Catholics. Others concentrated on the multitudes of Catholics streaming into the United States from European countries such as Germany, Italy, Hungary, Lithuania, Poland, Croatia, Czechoslovakia, the Ukraine, and from the bordering countries of Mexico and Canada. Others ministered to those whose ancestors had arrived long before everyone else—the Native Americans. And many Catholic missionaries opened churches and schools for these native peoples who had shamefully been driven from their ancestral land and herded onto reservations.

By 1900 there were 12 million Catholics in the United States. And in 1908 the Vatican declared that the United States was no longer a mission country. It had, in a sense, finally "grown up."

Activity What is your cultural heritage? How has your faith enriched your heritage? How has your heritage enriched your faith?

Old St. Ferdinand Shrine, Florissant, Missouri

The world feels the effects of World War I and the Depression.

In 1914, as World War I engulfed Europe, newly elected Pope Benedict XV pleaded for peace and continued to do so throughout the war. But the leaders on both sides refused to listen. In 1917 the United States joined the war. Once again, brave Catholic chaplains served with the American troops, this time on battlefields far from home. By the time this war ended in 1918, more than 9 million soldiers had died and millions more had been wounded. Millions of civilians had also been killed.

In October 1929 another terrible event took place—the crash of the American stock market. As stock prices fell, people who owned stocks saw their life savings disappear. Businesses failed. Thousands of people lost their jobs. Prices plunged. Farmers couldn't sell their crops and lost their farms. People lost their homes when they could not pay the mortgage. Banks all across America began to fail. People who thought their savings were safe woke up to find their banks closed and their money gone. America had entered the period that we now know as the *Great Depression*.

> Pope Pius XI "restated the need to work for a just society."

Pope Pius XI

In 1922 the Church elected a new pope. He took the name Pius XI. Pope Pius XI (1922–1939), in response to the Great Depression, issued an encyclical in 1931 that was a direct reference to Pope Leo XIII's great social justice encyclical *Rerum Novarum*. In his encyclical titled *Quadragesimo Anno*, meaning "After Forty Years," Pope Pius XI summarized the positive impact of *Rerum Novarum* and restated the need to work for a just society.

At this time, European economies were also collapsing, and daily life was growing more uncertain. Europeans were looking for leaders who could restore their confidence and national pride. By 1933 Adolf Hitler (1889–1945) and his National Socialist Party—the Nazis—had gained control in Germany. Hitler modeled some of his political and economic policies on those of another dictator, Benito Mussolini (1883–1945), who had taken control of the Italian government in 1922.

In an attempt to secure rights for the Church, Pope Pius XI negotiated treaties with both Mussolini and Hitler. In the Lateran Treaty of 1929 the Italian government recognized Vatican City as an independent, sovereign state for the first time since 1870. And in a 1933 concordat between the Vatican and Hitler's Third Reich, Hitler agreed to respect the rights of the Church in Germany. But Hitler soon broke his promises. And as he stepped up his vicious persecution of Germany's Jews, Hitler also silenced and arrested Catholic priests and others who dared to speak out against his actions. In 1937 Pope Pius XI issued an encyclical condemning the Nazis' racist ideology.

Postwar prejudice

AL SMITH · A WINNER FOR YOU

After World War I there was a reaction against America's involvement in world affairs and a suspicion of foreigners in America. Laws were passed that limited immigration from southern and eastern Europe. Many Americans thought that these laws were meant to keep out Catholics and Jews. In the 1920s a secret society called the Ku Klux Klan began to attract hundreds of members all across America—but especially in the South. The Ku Klux Klan was anti-black, anti-Jewish, and anti-Catholic.

Despite this postwar rise of anti-Catholic and anti-immigrant sentiment, in 1928 the Democratic Party nominated a Catholic as its candidate for president of the United States: New York Governor Alfred E. Smith (1873–1944). It was the first time that a Catholic had gained the presidential nomination of one of the major parties. Smith lost the election, and most political writers agreed that anti-Catholic bias played a role in his defeat. Nevertheless, many Catholics saw the Smith candidacy as a sign of hope. Do you know of any Catholic men and women who help to lead our country today?

Activity With your group list ways to use your voices to convey a message of justice and peace to the world today. Implement one option from your list.

After World War II, the Iron Curtain falls across Europe.

In what ways can faith provide courage?

From 1939 to 1945 World War II ravaged the world. Hitler's forces overran much of Europe, and both German and Italian armies invaded parts of Africa. The army and navy of Japan were on the move into China and Southeast Asia and across the Pacific. At first the United States managed to stay out of the conflict. But on December 7, 1941, in a surprise attack, a Japanese air strike destroyed the United States battleship fleet at Pearl Harbor, Hawaii. More than 2,300 Americans died. The very next day, the United States declared war on Japan. On December 11, Germany and Italy declared war on the United States. Once again, Catholic chaplains accompanied American troops into battle.

A newly elected pope, Pius XII (1939–1958), led the Church through the horrors of World War II, which took some 40 million lives. Pius XII appointed an archbishop for the military services of the United States. His choice was Archbishop of New York Francis Cardinal Spellman (1889–1967), who during the war visited American servicemen and women in war zones around the world. And while Pius XII has often been criticized for not being stronger in his denunciations of Nazi war crimes, he strongly criticized the Nazis in his 1942 Christmas radio broadcast. Pope Pius XII also spoke out against communism in the postwar years.

In the years after World War II much of Europe lay in ruins. To make matters worse, a new barrier, referred to as the "Iron Curtain," divided the continent. In Western Europe, in countries liberated by British and American troops, people were free to rebuild their shattered lives. But in Eastern Europe, in countries such as Poland, Hungary, Yugoslavia, and Czechoslovakia, liberated by the advancing armies of the Soviet Union, people were now at the mercy of Soviet-controlled communist rulers and were not free. A new dividing line ran right through the heart of Germany. Where once there had been a single nation now there were two: one to the west, and one to the east that faced forty years of communist oppression.

Francis Cardinal Spellman gives Holy Communion to American troops in Italy. (1944)

Catholics in postwar Western Europe began to play a part in politics, hoping to bring the messages of *Rerum Novarum* and *Quadragesimo Anno* to their nations' civil governments. All across Western Europe laws were passed to improve the rights of workers and give people access to better housing and health care. But all over communist Eastern Europe, Catholics found themselves subject to persecution. Churches and schools were closed. Priests, bishops, and cardinals were convicted of treason against the state and sent to prison. Ordinary people who proclaimed their Catholic faith were barred from public life, good jobs, and good schools. And by 1949 Catholics were also under siege in China where communists had seized control, banished foreign missionaries, and begun to persecute Chinese Catholics.

Yet in postwar America, Catholics began to rise to leadership positions in law and medicine, in business, in politics, and in every area of American public life. An especially powerful symbol of Catholics' coming of age and being accepted in American society came in November of 1960 when John F. Kennedy (1917–1963) was elected as the first Catholic president of the United States.

Activity Give a presentation from the perspective of someone living in a country where Catholics are persecuted. Describe some things that you would do to sustain your faith.

The Second Vatican Council renews the life of the Church.

When Pius XII died, the cardinals of the Church gathered in Rome to elect a new pope. After four days of voting, they announced, "*Habemus papam*"— meaning "We have a pope!" The newly elected pope took the name John XXIII. As pope he convened the twenty-first ecumenical council in the history of the Church—the first ecumenical council since the Vatican Council of 1870. Pope John XXIII (1958–1963) used the Italian word *aggiornamento*— "bringing up to date"—to describe his intention for the council. This updating would be based in what some theologians call *ressourcement*—a French word meaning "returning to the sources." Pope John XXIII wanted the bishops who would gather in this council to study the unchanging truths of the Christian faith—the Scripture and the teachings of the early Fathers of the Church—and then communicate those truths in ways understandable to people in the modern world.

On October 11, 1962, at the opening session of the Second Vatican Council in Rome, 2,500 bishops from all over the world gathered together in St. Peter's Basilica. It was the largest gathering at any council in Church history and was the first truly worldwide council of the Church—including bishops from every inhabited continent on earth. The council fathers met in four general sessions between 1962 and 1965.

After planning the council and presiding over its first session, Pope John XXIII died, on June 3, 1963. But on June 21, 1963, the newly elected Pope Paul VI announced that he would continue the work that John XXIII had begun—the council would go on. And by the time the council ended on December 8, 1965, the bishops had issued sixteen documents about different aspects of the life of the Church.

Some of the Church's documents arising out of Vatican II are called *constitutions* because they concern the essential nature, or constitution, of the Church. Council documents that deal with other matters are called *decrees* or *declarations*. Some of the documents of the Second Vatican Council are: the *Dogmatic Constitution on the Church*, the *Dogmatic Constitution on Divine Revelation*, the *Constitution on the Sacred Liturgy*, the *Pastoral Constitution on the Church in the Modern World*, the *Declaration on the Relation of the Church to Non-Christian Religions*, the *Declaration on Religious Freedom*, the *Decree on Ecumenism*, and the *Decree on the Apostolate of the Laity*.

Find out more about these documents at www.vatican.va.

In addition to calling the Second Vatican Council, or Vatican II, Pope John XXIII wrote a number of encyclicals. Among these were two of the greatest social justice encyclicals in the history of the Church. The first was titled *Mater et Magistra*—Latin for "Mother and Teacher." It was issued in 1961. In it the pope discussed the teachings of Pope Leo XIII's encyclical *Rerum Novarum* in the context of the modern world. The second social justice encyclical was issued in 1963 and titled *Pacem in Terris*, or "Peace on Earth." In it Pope John XXIII spoke of "establishing universal peace in truth, justice, charity, and liberty." In these two important and influential encyclicals, the Church expanded her message of social justice. What was once a call for the rights of workers in an industrial society, as in *Rerum Novarum* and *Quadragesimo Anno,* had now become a call to wealthy societies to aid developing ones and a call for peace among nations in an age of weapons of mass destruction.

> The Church is called to work toward "establishing universal peace in truth, justice, charity, and liberty"
> (*Pacem in Terris*).

Activity In the spirit of Pope John XXIII, design a poster that celebrates the Church as "Mother and Teacher." Let your work be your voice!

RESPONDING...

Recognizing Our Faith

Recall the question at the beginning of this chapter: *Does my voice count?* Why is the voice of the Church important in the world today? How can you help the Church to proclaim the good news? Plan a 30-second commercial that urges people to listen to the voice of the Church. Storyboard your commercial here.

Living Our Faith

How can you add your voice to the proclamations of Vatican II in regard to the dignity of the human person?

Blessed Pope John XXIII

Partners in FAITH

Angelo Guiseppe Roncalli was born into a family of Italian peasant farmers in 1881. He was ordained a priest at the age of twenty-three. When he was elected pope, he took the name John XXIII. "Renewing Our Relationship with Christ" could have been a slogan for his papacy. He was elected pope in 1958, just before his seventy-seventh birthday. Because of his age, many people were taken by surprise when he called the Second Vatican Council. This meeting brought about many changes within the Church. Under the guidance and leadership of Pope John XXIII, the Church addressed, in light of modern times, issues of social justice, unity, world peace, and human rights. After the council many changes were implemented. Mass could now be celebrated in the local languages of Catholics around the world, though the official language of the Church was Latin.

Pope John XXIII died in 1963 at the age of eighty-three. He was beatified on September 3, 2000, by Pope John Paul II. Blessed Pope John XXIII's feast day is June 3. We remember his vision and optimism for the renewal of his beloved Church.

What are some ways to renew your relationship with Christ and the Church?

ⓐ For additional ideas and activities, visit www.weliveourfaith.com.

Putting Faith to Work

Talk about what you have learned in this chapter:

 We understand some of the circumstances that influenced the growth of the Church in the United States from 1861 to the present.

 We appreciate the work of the Church in continuing to voice messages of justice, peace, and equality during times of political and social change.

 We share our faith with others as we meet the challenges of the present and the future.

Decide on ways to live out what you have learned.

ENCOUNTERING GOD'S WORD

" The trumpeters and singers were heard as a single voice praising and giving thanks to the LORD, and . . . they raised the sound of the trumpets, cymbals and other musical instruments to 'give thanks to the LORD.' "

(2 Chronicles 5:13–14)

➡ **READ** the quotation from Scripture.

➡ **REFLECT** on the following question:
How do you use your voice to give thanks and praise to God?

➡ **SHARE** your reflections with a partner.

➡ **DECIDE** to use your voice this week to give thanks and praise to God.

Write *True or False* next to the following sentences. On a separate sheet of paper, change the false statements to make them true.

1. _____ In 1931, in response to the Great Depression, Pope Pius XI issued a social justice encyclical named *Rerum Novarum*, or "After Forty Years."

2. _____ One outcome of the Third Plenary Council was the publication of the *Baltimore Catechism* for American Catholics.

3. _____ A plenary council is a council to be attended by only some of the bishops of a specific country or region.

4. _____ In 1908 the Vatican declared that the United States was no longer a mission country.

Complete the following.

5. In 1960 _____ became the first Catholic president of the United States.

6. Pope _____ led the Catholic Church through the horrors of World War II.

7. Pope John XXIII wrote two great social justice encyclicals, *Mater et Magistra* and

_____.

8. After the death of Pope John XXIII, the work of the Second Vatican Council was carried on by

_____.

9–10. ESSAY: Two of the words used to describe the work of the Second Vatican Council are *aggiornamento* and *ressourcement*. What do these words mean, and why are they important?

RESPONDING...

Sharing Faith with Your Family

Discuss the following with your family:

- The Catholic Church grows in a diverse nation.
- The world feels the effects of World War I and the Depression.
- After World War II, the Iron Curtain falls across Europe.
- The Second Vatican Council renews the life of the Church.

Have a family discussion to find out if and how the events outlined in this chapter affected your family and your family's growth in faith.

The Worship Connection

At every Sunday Eucharist, in the prayer of the faithful, we voice our prayers for the needs of the world. We pray for our pope and bishops, our government, our parish community, and our own concerns. We also pray for those who are suffering, and for justice and peace in the world.

More to Explore

Use the Internet to find out more about the documents of the Second Vatican Council.

Catholic Social Teaching ☑ Checklist

Theme of Catholic Social Teaching:
Option for the Poor and Vulnerable

How it relates to Chapter 16: As the Church made clear during this period of history, Catholics are called to give special attention to those whose needs are greatest—poor, weakened, and oppressed people around the world.

How can you do this?

☐ At home:

_____

☐ At school/work:

_____

☐ In the parish:

_____

☐ In the community:

_____

Check off each action after it has been completed.

GATHERING...

"**Jesus said, 'Let the children come to me . . . for the kingdom of heaven belongs to such as these.'**"
(Matthew 19:14)

✛ **Leader:** Lord Jesus Christ, Savior of the world, you promised to remain with your Church until the end of time. Then your Kingdom will come: a new heaven and earth full of love, justice, and peace. This is our hope, our foundation.

All: Thanks be to you.

Reader 1: Lord, we pray: Bless the young people around the world. Make them architects of a new civilization of love and witnesses of hope for the whole world.

All: Thanks be to you.

Reader 2: Through them may you be with those who suffer from hunger, war, and violence. May they serve your Kingdom with the power of their faith and their love, and may they welcome their brothers and sisters from all over the world with open hearts.

All: Thanks be to you.

Reader 1: Bless your Church with new strength in these days, so that she can become a credible witness for you. We ask this through our Lord and God, living in unity with the Father and the Holy Spirit, reigning forever and ever.

All: Amen.

(excerpted from the Prayer in Preparation for World Youth Day 2005)

@ Visit www.weliveourfaith.com to find appropriate music and songs.

181

GATHERING...

The BiG QuEstion:
What can I do today to make a better tomorrow?

Discover the words of some people who helped to make a better tomorrow. Can you match the person to his or her words? Check your answers below.

Christa McAuliffe

Saint Francis of Assisi

Abraham Lincoln

Harriet Tubman

1 "Every great dream begins with a dreamer. Always remember, you have within you the strength, the patience, and the passion to reach for the stars to change the world."

2 "The best thing about the future is that it comes only one day at a time."

3 "Start by doing what's necessary; then do what's possible; and suddenly you are doing the impossible."

4 "I touch the future. I teach."

Answers:
1. Harriet Tubman (1820–1913), abolitionist
2. Abraham Lincoln (1809–1865), sixteenth U.S. president, who brought about the emancipation of slaves
3. Saint Francis of Assisi (1181–1226), founder of the Franciscans
4. Christa McAuliffe (1948–1986), American schoolteacher and astronaut

Who are some people today who are helping to make a better tomorrow?

In this chapter we learn that the Church and its leaders have encouraged peace, truth, and justice among peoples and nations. Through this chapter, we hope

 to recognize that, as members of the Church, we are called to practice peace, truth, and justice

 to desire peace, truth, and justice in our own lives and in the lives of all people

to become peaceful, truthful, and just so that we can help to change the world.

182

To learn about ancient times and civilizations, archeologists and historians spend lifetimes unearthing and studying artifacts, such as stone tools, pottery, jewelry, and clothing, left behind by ancient peoples. Piece by piece, artifacts give great insight into what life was like hundreds or even thousands of years ago.

Most ancient artifacts were left behind unintentionally. But some collections of objects were sealed away and hidden to be rediscovered later. We might consider these collections of artifacts to be "time capsules" because they preserve a period of time for us to study. For example, vaults of artifacts recovered in ancient Mesopotamian cities could be considered time capsules, though the term *time capsule* is modern.

In 1940 at Oglethorpe University, a huge time capsule, spanning an underground vault 20 feet long by 10 feet wide, was sealed. It contained objects ranging from two hundred books of fiction to Lincoln Logs™ to microfilm of texts on just about every subject known to humankind at the time. It even contained a Donald Duck toy and a tool to teach English to those who unseal the vault when it is supposed to be opened in the year 8113. Since then, many other time capsules have been created. Many individuals create time capsules with objects from their time and culture and also personal items such as photographs and letters or journal entries. Now time capsules can be registered with the International Time Capsule Society, which was created in 1990 to study and keep records of time capsules throughout the world.

Today, e-mail time capsules are the newest way to send information into the future. Web sites allow visitors to create an e-mail that will be delivered back to them in a year, five years, or even twenty years!

If you created a time capsule, what would you put inside to remind yourself, or to tell others, about yourself and the time in which you live?

> **"I look to the future because that's where I'm going to spend the rest of my life,"** wrote George Burns (1896–1996), an American comedian.

Activity What would you say to yourself in an e-mail time capsule to be delivered to you in the future? In this e-mail time capsule, list your goals for the future. What do you hope to achieve or do?

Dr. Thornwell Jacobs holds items to be placed into the time capsule at Oglethorpe University, including records and books. The time capsule is known as the "Crypt of Civilization."

183

Church leaders continue to call for justice and peace.

During the 1960s and 1970s, Pope Paul VI worked to show the Church's concern for international justice and world peace. In 1967 he issued an encyclical called *Populorum Progressio*, or "On the Development of Peoples." And a few years later, in 1971, he issued an apostolic letter called *Octogesima Adveniens*, or "Eightieth Anniversary." In this letter he honored the anniversary of Pope Leo XIII's great social justice encyclical *Rerum Novarum*, and he extended its teachings.

Pope Paul VI

Pope Paul VI died in 1978, a year that would come to be known as "the year of three popes." In August the cardinals came together in a **conclave**, the secret meeting in which they elect a pope. After two days of voting they chose a new pope. This pope took the name John Paul I in honor of John XXIII and Paul VI, the two popes who had preceded him. Sadly, the reign of Pope John Paul I was one of the shortest in Church history; he died after only thirty-three days as pope. So, the cardinals gathered in a conclave again in October 1978. After three days they announced that the new pope was Karol Wojtyla, the Archbishop of Krakow, Poland. At this, a gasp went up from the crowd waiting for the announcement

Faith Word

conclave

in Saint Peter's Square because this was the first non-Italian pope since the sixteenth century and also the youngest since Pope Pius IX in 1846.

The new pope took the name Pope John Paul II, and the call for social justice continued as the central theme of the pontificate. Among his many encyclicals were *Laborem Exercens*, or "Through Work," which he issued in 1981 to commemorate the ninetieth anniversary of *Rerum Novarum*. Another encyclical, *Sollicitudo Rei Socialis*, or "On Social Concern," was issued in 1987 to celebrate the twentieth anniversary of Pope Paul VI's *Populorum Progressio*. In 1991, on the one-hundredth anniversary of *Rerum Novarum*, Pope John Paul II issued the encyclical *Centesimus Annus*, or "Hundredth Year."

Throughout his reign of more than twenty-six years, Pope John Paul II placed new emphasis on human rights and religious freedom. Many people around the world give him credit for helping to bring an end to the long and brutal rule of Soviet communism in Russia and much of Eastern Europe. He called for solidarity among all peoples, including those in his own homeland, Poland.

Activity Work together in small groups to prepare a 30-second public service announcement based on these words of Pope John Paul II: "true development must be based on the love of God and neighbor, and must help to promote the relationships between individuals and society" (*Sollicitudo Rei Socialis*, 33).

Pope John Paul II appears for the first time on the balcony of St. Peter's Basilica (1978).

The pope calls the Church to worldwide fellowship and reconciliation.

Pope John Paul II especially reached out to members of the Jewish faith, whom he spoke of as "our *elder brothers in the faith*" (*Crossing the Threshold of Hope*, 99). In the year 2000, a "Jubilee Year" of the Church—marking the passage of 1,000 years since the last Jubilee Year—Pope John Paul II declared March 12, which was the First Sunday of Lent that year, a day of pardon. He asked forgiveness for the sins, past and present, of the "sons and daughters" of the Church.

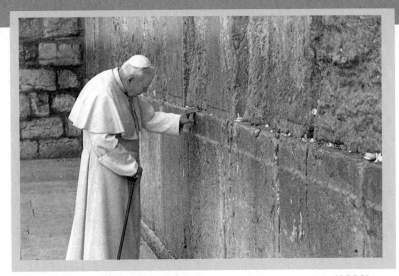

Pope John Paul II's pilgrimage to the Western Wall in Jerusalem (2000)

That same month Pope John Paul II made an historic visit to the Holy Land. There he made a pilgrimage to the Western Wall, considered to be a remnant of the Temple of Jerusalem and one of the holiest places on earth for people of the Jewish faith. During that trip, he also visited Damascus, Jordan, and the West Bank to reach out to all of the people of the area and to initiate dialogue with Muslims.

> **"He called them to live the Church's mission of reconciliation."**

Pope John Paul II's visit to the Holy Land was one of many historic trips that he made to offer fellowship to people around the world. John Paul II was, in fact, the most widely traveled pope in the history of the Church. Everywhere he went he proclaimed the mission of reconciliation.

Among his many memorable international visits were those he made to cities hosting World Youth Day celebrations. He established these celebrations to strengthen young people's faith. And he called them to live the Church's mission of reconciliation.

Activity Where do you think the current pope should travel? And what do you think his message should be?

Jewish-Christian relations today

On October 28, 1965, Pope Paul VI issued one of the most important documents of the Second Vatican Council, *Nostra Aetate* ("In Our Time"), which is also known as the *Declaration on the Relation of the Church to Non-Christian Religions*. In that document the council fathers said that "the Church . . . cannot forget that she received the revelation of the Old Testament through the people with whom God . . . concluded the Ancient Covenant" and that the Church "decries hatred, persecutions, displays of anti–Semitism, directed against Jews at any time and by anyone" (*Nostra Aetate*, 4).

In October 2005, on the fortieth anniversary of *Nostra Aetate*, Pope Benedict XVI issued a letter in which he expressed the need to continue to improve Jewish-Christian relations and stated his own determination to walk in the footsteps of Pope John Paul II. In August 2005 Pope Benedict XVI visited a Jewish synagogue in Cologne, Germany, as part of his celebration of World Youth Day. At the synagogue the pope paid tribute to the Jews who were killed during the Holocaust—the mass murder, during World War II, of Europe's Jews by the Nazis, led by German dictator Adolf Hitler. The pope spoke of the need to build a more just and peaceful world.

Where do you see the need for justice and peace today?

Catholics are called to defend life and faith.

How do I reach out to others?

Throughout his twenty-six years as pope, John Paul II repeatedly called Catholics to stand up for what he termed the "culture of life" in the face of the modern world's pervasive "culture of death." In his 1995 encyclical *Evangelium Vitae,* or "The Gospel of Life," he wrote powerfully and movingly about the

Pope John Paul II greets Cardinal Joseph Ratzinger (1995).

sacredness of all human life from conception to natural death. In his 1993 encyclical *Veritatis Splendor,* or "The Splendor of Truth," he described humanity's dependence on God and divine law while explaining that real freedom depends on the truth. Pope John Paul II called all Catholics to stand up for truth in the face of moral relativism. **Relativism** is the viewpoint that concepts such as right and wrong, good and evil, or truth and falsehood are not absolute but change from culture to culture and situation to situation.

In 1986 Pope John Paul II appointed a commission of twelve cardinals and bishops to preside over the writing of the new *Catechism of the Catholic Church,* a clear presentation of the truths of the faith. He chose the German theologian, Joseph Cardinal Ratzinger, to serve as chairman of that important commission. And the publication, in 1992, of the *Catechism of the Catholic Church* was one of Pope John Paul II's greatest accomplishments. In *Fidei Depositum,* or "Guarding the Deposit of Faith," a document he wrote that year to accompany the publication of the *Catechism,* Pope John Paul II called the new catechism "a sure norm for teaching the faith." He then prayed, "May it serve the renewal to which the Holy Spirit ceaselessly calls the Church."

Faith Word

relativism

In a 1998 encyclical called *Fides et Ratio,* or "Faith and Reason," Pope John Paul II dealt with a topic that has concerned philosophers since the Enlightenment: the relationship between faith and reason. In a 2003 encyclical called *Ecclesia De Eucharistia,* or "On the Eucharist in its Relationship to the Church," he wrote about the central place of the Eucharist in the life of the Church. The following year John Paul II declared a special "Year of the Eucharist" to run from October 2004 until October 2005.

Activity Work with a partner to design a slideshow of words, images, and sounds that bring to mind the many accomplishments of Pope John Paul II.

Canon Law

The Code of Canon Law is the body of laws that govern the Church. Another milestone during the papacy of John Paul II was the publication, in 1983, of a revised Code of Canon Law for the Roman Catholic Church. A separate code for Eastern Catholics was published in 1990. From the Middle Ages onward, people all across Europe turned to the Church and to Church law for judgments on spiritual and moral matters. In the sixteenth century the Council of Trent called for the writing of a comprehensive code of Church law, but this immense task was not undertaken until the early twentieth century, at the request of Pope Saint Pius X. That first Code of Canon Law was finally published in 1917 by Pope Benedict XV. Today the revised 1983 code, which contains 1,752 canons, or laws, is the official body of laws of the Catholic Church.

Think of some Church decisions that have been made that might be contained within the Code of Canon Law. Check the Vatican Web site at www.vatican.va for some ideas of what the code contains.

CATHOLIC IDENTITY

Catholics are called to witness to the truth and to change the world.

During the Second Vatican Council (1962–1965), Father Joseph Ratzinger had served as theological consultant to a German cardinal. After the council he taught theology at a series of German universities and soon gained an international reputation as a gifted theologian. In 1977 Pope Paul VI appointed Joseph Ratzinger Archbishop of Munich, Germany, and elevated him to the college of cardinals. Then in 1981 Pope John Paul II named Cardinal Ratzinger head of the Congregation for the Doctrine of the Faith, the Vatican department charged with upholding and safeguarding the doctrine of the Church. Cardinal Ratzinger served the Church in that position for twenty-four years.

> "True revolution consists in simply turning to God."
>
> (Pope Benedict XVI, World Youth Day speech, August 20, 2005)

When Pope John Paul II died, in April 2005, cardinals from around the world gathered in Rome to elect his successor. As dean of the college of cardinals, Joseph Ratzinger presided over the cardinals preparation for the conclave. On the second day, after four secret ballots, the cardinals elected Joseph Ratzinger as pope. He took as his name Benedict XVI, in honor of Pope Benedict XV (1854–1922), the pope who pleaded for peace at the time of the First World War, and Saint Benedict of Nursia (480–547), the great founder of monasticism in the Western Church. Shortly after becoming pope, Benedict XVI spoke of the authority—and responsibility—of his new role:

"The Pope is not an absolute monarch whose thoughts and desires are law. On the contrary: the Pope's ministry is a guarantee of obedience to Christ and to his Word. He must not proclaim his own ideas, but rather constantly bind himself and the Church to obedience to God's Word, in the face of every attempt to adapt it or water it down" (Pope Benedict XVI's homily, Mass of Possession of the Chair of the Bishop of Rome, May 7, 2005).

Like John Paul II before him, Pope Benedict XVI continues to urge Catholics to stand up for the truth in the face of today's "culture of relativism." To the young people gathered at Cologne, Germany, for World Youth Day 2005, Benedict XVI said, "Only from God does true revolution come, the definitive way to change the world. . . . True revolution consists in simply turning to God who is the measure of what is right and who at the same time is everlasting love" (Pope Benedict XVI's World Youth Day speech, August 20, 2005).

Several days later, as he stood at the Cologne airport before flying back to Rome, the pope praised the young people he had encountered at World Youth Day—young men and women who, in his words, "have shown us a young Church, one that seeks with imagination and courage to shape the face of a more just and generous humanity" (Pope Benedict XVI's address at Cologne Airport, August 21, 2005).

Activity In small groups, discuss ways that young Catholics in your area can help to change the world. Make a plan to put one thing you have discussed into action.

Pope Benedict XVI waves from a balcony of St. Peter's Basilica after being elected pope (2005).

RESPONDING...

Recognizing Our Faith

Recall the question at the beginning of this chapter: *What can I do today to make a better tomorrow?* Look back at the e-mail you wrote to yourself on page 183. Look at your goals for the future. List ways you can accomplish these goals.

Living Our Faith

Be conscious of the decisions you make today. Consider how these decisions will affect tomorrow. How does your faith affect your decisions?

Pope John Paul I

Albino Luciani was born in 1912. He was ordained a priest in 1935. After three decades of service he became patriarch of Venice in 1969 and then was made cardinal in 1973. On August 26, 1978, he was elected pope, head of the worldwide Catholic Church. He combined the names of his two immediate predecessors, Pope Paul VI and Pope John XXIII, to become Pope John Paul I. His time as leader of the Catholic Church was short. On September 28, 1978, Pope John Paul I died of a heart attack, only thirty-three days after his election.

When the beatification process opened for Pope John Paul I in 2003, Pope Benedict XVI, who was a cardinal at the time, said of Pope John Paul I, "I am totally convinced he was a saint because of his great goodness, simplicity, humanity, and great courage."

Say a prayer for our Church leaders of yesterday and today.

Partners in FAITH

Putting Faith to Work

Talk about what you have learned in this chapter:

 We recognize that, as members of the Church, we are called to practice peace, truth, and justice.

 We desire peace, truth, and justice in our own lives and in the lives of all people.

 We become peaceful, truthful, and just so that we can help to change the world.

Decide on ways to live out what you have learned.

✝ ENCOUNTERING GOD'S WORD

The prophet Micah reminded the people of what God required:

❝ **Only to do the right and to love goodness, and to walk humbly with your God** ❞

(Micah 6:8).

➡ **READ** the quotation from Scripture.

➡ **REFLECT** on these questions:
How have the popes of recent decades been prophets for us? What good and right things have they asked of us and the people of the world? How can we walk with God in our own times?

➡ **SHARE** your reflections with a partner.

➡ **DECIDE** on one way to "do the right" in your own life today.

Complete each statement with the name of the pope to whom it refers.

1. In March 2000, _____ made an historic visit to the Holy Land.

2. In 1967 _____ issued a social justice encyclical called *Populorum Progressio*, or "On the Development of Peoples."

3. When Cardinal Joseph Ratzinger was elected pope in 2005, he took as his name

   _____.

4. The reign of _____ was one of the shortest in Church history—only thirty-three days.

Write *True* or *False* next to the following sentences. On a separate sheet of paper, change the false sentences to make them true.

5. _____ In his 1995 encyclical *Evangelium Vitae*, or "The Gospel of Life," Pope John Paul II wrote about the sacredness of all human life from conception to natural death.

6. _____ The new *Catechism of the Catholic Church*, published in 1992, was one of Pope Paul VI's greatest accomplishments.

7. _____ At World Youth Day 2005 in Cologne, Germany, Pope John Paul II told the young people gathered there that "true revolution consists in simply turning to God."

8. _____ In 2000, during the Church's Jubilee Year, Pope Benedict XVI visited Israel.

9–10. ESSAY: Define *relativism* and describe what both Pope John Paul II and Pope Benedict XVI called on Catholics to do regarding it.

Chapter 17 Assessment

RESPONDING...

Sharing Faith with Your Family

Discuss the following with your family:

- Church leaders continue to call for justice and peace.
- The pope calls the Church to worldwide fellowship and reconciliation.
- Catholics are called to defend life and faith.
- Catholics are called to witness to the truth and to change the world.

Gather family members for a discussion. Invite everyone to share his or her memories of Pope John XXIII, Paul VI, John Paul I, John Paul II, or Benedict XVI. Lead the discussion by asking what these popes and their messages mean to each family member. How has the work of these popes affected our families and our world?

The Worship Connection

At every Mass, we hear the word of God in Scripture. Listen carefully and consider how the word of God calls you to peace, justice, and truth in your life.

More to Explore

Read more about the encyclicals of Pope John Paul II, which are found on the Vatican Web site: www.vatican.va.

Catholic Social Teaching
☑ Checklist

Theme of Catholic Social Teaching:
Life and Dignity of the Human Person

How it relates to Chapter 17: We are all God's children and we share the same human dignity, which comes from being made in the image and likeness of God. As Christians we respect all people and defend human life from conception to natural death.

How can you do this?

☐ At home:

_____

☐ At school/work:

_____

☐ In the parish:

_____

☐ In the community:

_____

Check off each action after it has been completed.

18 Transforming the World Through Faith

"**What good is it, my brothers, if someone says he has faith but does not have works?**"

(James 2:14)

Leader: Jesus said that putting our faith into action was like building a home on a strong foundation.

Reader: A reading from the holy Gospel according to Luke

"I will show you what someone is like who comes to me, listens to my words, and acts on them. That one is like a person building a house, who dug deeply and laid the foundation on rock; when the flood came, the river burst against that house but could not shake it because it had been well built. But the one who listens and does not act is like a person who built a house on the ground without a foundation. When the river burst against it, it collapsed at once and was completely destroyed." (Luke 6:47–49)

The Gospel of the Lord.

All: Praise to you, Lord Jesus Christ.

Leader: Lord Jesus, you want your disciples not only to listen to your teachings, but to live them out. You want us to share our faith with the world through our actions.

All: When we look at the world
we see so much need, suffering,
despair—even hate.
May our lives be built on the strong
foundation of your teachings
so that our actions may transform
this world
with your justice, comfort, peace, joy,
and love.

Amen.

@ Visit www.weliveourfaith.com to find appropriate music and songs.

191

The BiG QuEstion:

What are the most important things in my life?

Discover your real priorities in life. Complete the following statements.

Three ways I spend my time are:

1. _____
2. _____
3. _____.

Three ways I spend my money are:

1. _____
2. _____
3. _____.

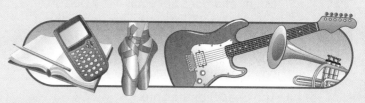

Three ways I use my talents and abilities are:

1. _____
2. _____
3. _____.

Survey members of your group and compare your responses. What are the most common responses? What do they tell you about what your group considers important?

In this chapter we learn that the Church supports us and encourages us as we live and share our faith in the modern world. Through this chapter, we hope

 to recognize the importance of our full participation in the liturgy

to respect the sacredness of all human life and the dignity of the human person

to build upon the efforts of the Church in transforming the world through faith.

Vincent Capodanno was born in Staten Island, New York on February 13, 1929. At the age of 28 he was ordained a priest. He served the first eight years of his priesthood as a missionary in Taiwan and Hong Kong. After being commissioned as a lieutenant in the United States Navy, he asked to serve as battalion chaplain to the Marines in Vietnam. He was known as the "Grunt Padre." The word *grunt* is slang for a member of the Marine infantry. Father Vincent's original tour of duty was only supposed to last twelve months but he asked to stay another six to continue serving the Marines by hearing confessions, celebrating the Mass, and anointing the sick.

> "Most of the important things in the world have been accomplished by people who have kept on trying when there seemed no hope at all," wrote Dale Carnegie (1888–1955), American lecturer and author.

A medal, known as a Purple Heart, is given to a soldier wounded or killed while serving in the U.S. Military. The day Father Vincent died he became eligible for three Purple Hearts. First, he was shot in the hand and then, after refusing to leave his battalion, he was shot in the arm. Still unwilling to leave his men, he made his rounds to hear wounded soldier's confessions. Since his right hand was so badly hurt, he had to use his left hand to support his right to give absolution. Then as a soldier was knocked down by a burst from a machine gun, Father Vincent ran over and stood between the soldier and the enemy troops. When the enemy troops fired again, Father Vincent was fatally wounded. After his death, Father Vincent was awarded the Medal of Honor, the highest military honor in the United States.

Father Vincent is a powerful example of a model of faith who lived out his vocation as a priest and a soldier. He cared for the spiritual needs and wounds of the Marines he served. He inspires us to live more deeply our own vocation with continued courage.

The Marines' motto is *"Semper Fidelis,"* which is Latin for *"Always Faithful."* Father Vincent was truly always faithful, ultimately giving up his life to help his fellow man.

Activity Among the important things in Father Vincent's life were his faith in God, his vocation, and a commitment to serving others. How do these priorities compare with your own?

Father Vincent leading field prayer for Marines of 1st Batallion, 7th Marines (1/7) in the Muo Douc Area, Vietnam (1966)

We are nourished by participation in the liturgy.

In the years following the close of the Second Vatican Council, the Catholic Church in the United States faced many challenges. The bishops who had taken part in the council returned home from Rome knowing that they had much to do. They began to bring the *aggiornamento* and *ressourcement* of the council to their dioceses.

In 1964 American Catholics began to celebrate the Eucharist in a new way. For centuries, priests had celebrated Mass with their backs to the assembly. Now, they stood facing the people. And something else had begun to change, too. Everywhere in the world, wherever Mass was celebrated, it had always been celebrated in Latin, the Church's universal, official language. But now, some of the prayers of the Mass were being prayed for the first time in the language of the people.

In 1970 the Church published—for the entire world—a new, revised Roman Missal, which sets out the Order of the Mass. With this 1970 publication the bishops in every country were directed to produce authorized translations of the Mass into local languages. National conferences of bishops undertook this job, and soon Catholics everywhere were celebrating Mass in their own languages. The Church also published a book called the *General Instruction of the Roman Missal* to teach bishops, priests, and others the proper way to celebrate the revised liturgy.

Much more active participation in the Mass by the assembly was called for. Laypeople could now serve as lectors, reading God's word at Mass, and as extraordinary ministers of Holy Communion, distributing Holy Communion at Mass. Previously, these roles were reserved for members of the clergy and candidates for the priesthood. Additionally, with Mass now being celebrated in the languages of the people, new liturgical music was needed. Talented composers began to write new musical settings for the prayers of the Mass and new songs of worship with which to praise God.

These changes were being made in response to the Second Vatican Council's *Constitution on the Sacred Liturgy*. In that document the bishops of the council had stated that the Church "desires that all the faithful be led to that full, conscious, and active participation in liturgical celebrations, which is demanded by the very nature of the liturgy. Such participation . . . is their right and duty by reason of their baptism. . . . this full and active participation by all the people . . . is the primary and indispensable source from which the faithful are to derive the true Christian spirit" (*Constitution on the Sacred Liturgy*, 14).

Activity Reflect on the actions, prayers, and rituals that are part of the Mass. How do you fully and actively participate in the liturgy? Make a list of some ways here.

We are a community committed to justice.

In the years since the Second Vatican Council, the U.S. Catholic bishops—encouraged by the social justice teachings of papal encyclicals and other council documents—have become a bold voice in our culture, speaking out for world peace and social justice for all people. In 1983, when the possibility of a nuclear war between the United States and the Soviet Union seemed to be a very real threat, the American bishops issued a pastoral letter called *The Challenge of Peace*. In that letter the bishops stated, "We are called to be a Church at the service of peace" (*The Challenge of Peace*, 23). They also described the conditions necessary for a war to be just, set forth principles on the use of nuclear weapons, and pointed out that true peace calls for reverence for life: "No society can live in peace with itself, or with the world, without a full awareness of the worth and dignity of every human person, and of the sacredness of all human life" (*The Challenge of Peace*, 285).

In 1986 the bishops issued *Economic Justice for All*, a pastoral letter about Catholic social teaching and

> **"Followers of Christ must avoid a tragic separation between faith and everyday life."**
> (*Economic Justice for All, 5*)

the American economy. In this important letter the bishops reminded Catholics that "followers of Christ must avoid a tragic separation between faith and everyday life" (*Economic Justice for All*, 5) and that "the obligation to 'love our neighbor' has an individual dimension, but it also requires a broader social commitment to the common good" (*Economic Justice for All*, 14).

Speaking of the basic moral principles that should guide a just and loving society, the bishops noted that "every economic decision and institution must be judged in light of whether it protects or undermines the dignity of the human person. . . . How we organize our society . . . directly affects human dignity and the capacity of individuals to grow in community" (*Economic Justice for All*, 13, 14). And in this letter the bishops called Catholics to say no to negative trends in our culture that conflict with faith, love, and justice.

Activity The bishops have told us that how we organize society directly affects our human dignity. What organizations in our culture promote human dignity? How can you as a young person help to aid and strengthen these organizations? Make a plan to help.

We respect and defend the sacredness of all human life.

How do your values affect the way you live?

A central principal of the natural law and a basic teaching of the Catholic Church is that every human life is sacred from the moment of conception to the moment of natural death. "God alone is the Lord of life from its beginning until its end: no one can, in any circumstance, claim for himself the right to destroy directly an innocent human being." (*Instruction on Respect for Human Life in Its Origin, Congregation for the Doctrine of the Faith*, 5). In March 1995 Pope John Paul II, in *Evangelium Vitae* ("The Gospel of Life"), reiterated the Church's teachings on the sacredness of human life.

The bishops of the United States have spoken out repeatedly in defense of the right to life—the most basic of all human rights. In 1972 they even established the first Sunday of October as Respect Life Sunday. Every year on that Sunday parishes across the country focus on such life issues as abortion, the rights of the elderly and persons with disabilities, and the death penalty. In November 1998, they issued *Living the Gospel of Life*, which urged American Catholics to accept the responsibilities to which *Evangelium Vitae* called them. The bishops encouraged Catholics to defend human life and protect human dignity in all of the roles they play in both their private and public lives. They explained that "the basic principle is simple: *We must begin with a commitment never to intentionally kill, or collude in*

the killing, of any innocent human life, no matter how broken, unformed, disabled or desperate that life may seem. . . . Direct abortion is *never* a morally tolerable option. It is *always* a grave act of violence against a woman and her unborn child" (*Living the Gospel of Life*, 21). They added, "Similarly, euthanasia and assisted suicide are *never* acceptable acts of mercy. They *always* gravely exploit the suffering and desperate, extinguishing life in the name of the 'quality of life' itself. This same teaching against direct killing of the innocent condemns all direct attacks on innocent civilians in time of war" (*Living the Gospel of Life*, 21).

These calls to defend human life and dignity and to work for greater justice and peace continue to be major concerns for the bishops of the United States—and for all Catholics everywhere.

Activity In groups, choose one of the following issues: abortion, rights of the elderly, rights of the disabled, or the death penalty. Use art, music, or drama to communicate ways to uphold the sacredness of life concerning this issue.

Protecting life

Life

CATHOLIC IDENTITY

On January 22, 1973, the Supreme Court of the United States ruled that abortion—the direct termination of the life of an unborn baby—was legal throughout the United States. By this ruling the court declared that an act contrary to God's law was, in fact, protected by civil law. In the years since the court's ruling, the U.S. Catholic bishops have been in the forefront in the fight for the right to life of every unborn child.

A comprehensive program in support and defense of human life—called the *Pastoral Plan for Pro-Life Activities*—was issued by the bishops in 1975 and revised and updated in 1985 and 2001. It states, "Only with prayer . . . will the culture of death that surrounds us today be replaced with a culture of life."

In November 2002, as the thirtieth anniversary of the Supreme Court's abortion decision approached, the U.S. Catholic bishops issued a pro-life statement called *A Matter of the Heart*. In it

they expressed hope for the future: "The pro-life movement is brimming with the vibrancy of youth. . . . Young people know that the future is in their hands, and their hearts yearn to bring a message of hope and healing to a culture in great need of hearing it."

Every January, on the anniversary of the Supreme Court's abortion ruling, the National Prayer Vigil for Life is held in Washington, D.C., at the National Shrine of the Immaculate Conception.

What specific things are being done in your parish and diocese to ensure that all life is protected?

We treasure and proclaim the rich legacy of faith.

The Church, guided by the Holy Spirit in every age, continues to proclaim the good news of Jesus Christ and to invite all people into a deeper relationship with the Blessed Trinity. Through her liturgy, her teaching, her life in community, and through service and social justice, the Church proclaims the risen Christ each day. As we participate in this rich legacy of faith, we are strengthened for the mission of evangelization.

The Church's document, *On Evangelization in the Modern World*, names five specific qualities that we need to develop to be effective in proclaiming the good news of Jesus Christ. We must:

- witness to Jesus Christ by the way we live
- be united as Catholics and as Christians by working to heal our divisions
- embrace the truth by studying, praying, and seeking the wisdom of people of faith
- have a deep love for those we evangelize, which is shown through respect for their culture and their life situations
- share enthusiastically the joy and hope that we find in Jesus, as evangelizers have done throughout the Church's history. (*On Evangelization in the Modern World*, 76–80)

These qualities prepare us to take on the mission entrusted to the Church by Jesus Christ—to make disciples of all nations. Our responsibility today as disciples of Christ and members of the Catholic Church is to invite others to learn about Jesus Christ and what it means to follow him.

> **"God alone is the Lord of life."**
> (*Instruction on Respect for Human Life in Its Origin*, 5)

Activity With your group, choose one of the qualities of an effective evangelizer. Prepare a skit to demonstrate ways that living out this quality might affect others.

Sending a message

To help them in the mission of evangelization and to share the rich legacy of the Catholic faith with the world, the U.S. Catholic bishops established a department of communication. The department is organized into four divisions, each with its own special mission.

- The *Catholic Communication Campaign* develops radio and television programs and other resources that promote Gospel values.
- The *Catholic News Service* provides news articles, photographs, and other features to Catholic newspapers and magazines across the country.
- The *Office of Media Relations* prepares and distributes the bishops' statements and other documents to the media, arranges for interviews with bishops, organizes press conferences, and responds to questions from the media.
- The *Office for Film and Broadcasting* distributes reviews of new movies and television programs, which are written from a Catholic viewpoint.

What issue do you hope this department will address?

Recognizing Our Faith

Recall the question at the beginning of this chapter: *What are the most important things in my life?* Write a slogan for young people throughout the world, encouraging them to use their time, money, and talents and abilities in putting their faith to work.

Living Our Faith

What ways of transforming the world through faith have you discovered in this chapter? Choose one and live it out this week.

Dorothy Day

Dorothy Day (1897–1980) was a journalist and writer who converted to Catholicism in 1927. With Peter Maurin, she founded a newspaper called *The Catholic Worker*. This newspaper began to print articles on Catholic social teaching, especially peace, justice for workers, and concern for the poor. Gradually, a lay community, called the Catholic Worker movement, developed. The community put faith into action by opening soup kitchens and "houses of hospitality" for those in need all across the United States. The soup kitchens and houses of the Catholic Worker movement were especially needed during the Great Depression, and many still exist today.

Partners in FAITH

The Catholic Worker movement has been committed to peace and social justice since the time of its founding. *The Catholic Worker* is still printed today and is sold for the same price: one cent per copy!

Why is it important for you, too, to find ways to commit yourself to working for peace and social justice?

@ **For additional ideas and activities, visit www.weliveourfaith.com.**

Putting Faith to Work

Talk about what you have learned in this chapter:

 We recognize the importance of our full participation in the liturgy.

 We respect the sacredness of all human life and the dignity of the human person.

 We build upon the efforts of the Church in transforming the world through faith.

Decide on ways to live out what you have learned.

✝ ENCOUNTERING GOD'S WORD

"Faith of itself, if it does not have works, is dead."

(James 2:17)

➡ **READ** the quotation from Scripture.

➡ **REFLECT** on the following:
Perhaps you have heard the saying "You can't just talk the talk; you have to walk the walk." How does that compare to this Scripture quotation? Can you think of other sayings that are similar?

➡ **SHARE** your reflections with a partner.

➡ **DECIDE** on one way to "walk the walk" in your own life today.

Complete the following.

1. In *Economic Justice for All*, the U.S. bishops called Catholics to avoid negative trends that conflict with

   _____, _____, and justice.

2. In 1970 the Church published—for the entire world—a new, revised _____ which sets out the Order of the Mass.

3. Every human life is sacred from _____ to _____.

4. Through her liturgy, her teaching, her life in community, and through service and social justice, the Church

   proclaims the _____ each day.

Short Answers

5. What is Respect Life Sunday? _____

6. Name one change that resulted from the Second Vatican Council. _____

   _____

7. Who is entitled to the right to life? _____

8. Describe one thing the American bishops talked about in their letter *The Challenge of Peace*. _____

   _____

9–10. **ESSAY:** What are the five specific qualities that we need to develop to be effective in proclaiming the good news of Jesus Christ?

RESPONDING...

Sharing Faith with Your Family

Discuss the following with your family:

- We are nourished by participation in the liturgy.
- We are a community committed to justice.
- We respect and defend the sacredness of all human life.
- We treasure and proclaim the rich legacy of faith.

Think of these two questions: "What's in it for me?" and "How can I help?" How would your family life change if everyone in your family asked the second question more often than the first? Make a decision as a family to do so this week.

The Worship Connection

At Mass we often pray with the priest as he speaks to God our Father: "All life, all holiness comes from you" (Eucharistic Prayer II). Reflect on these words and pray that all life will be respected and protected.

More to Explore

Learn more about the United States Conference of Catholic Bishops (USCCB) at www.usccb.org.

Catholic Social Teaching ☑ Checklist

Theme of Catholic Social Teaching:
   Call to Family, Community, and Participation

How it relates to Chapter 18: As this chapter reminds us, Catholics have an obligation to participate in public life, bringing their faith to the world.

How can you do this?

☐ At home:

_____

☐ At school/work:

_____

☐ In the parish:

_____

☐ In the community:

_____

Check off each action after it has been completed.

Write the letter that best defines each term.

1. _____ evangelize

2. _____ conclave

3. _____ Papal States

4. _____ plenary council

5. _____ relativism

6. _____ papal infallibility

a. is the viewpoint that concepts such as right and wrong, good and evil, or truth and falsehood are not absolute but change from culture to culture and situation to situation

b. a council to be attended by all the bishops of a specific country or region

c. to proclaim the good news of Christ to people everywhere

d. the secret meeting in which the cardinals elect a pope

e. a section of central Italy governed by the pope

f. the divine guarantee that the pope's official statements of doctrine regarding faith and morals are free from error

g. a Renaissance philosophy that placed an increased emphasis on the importance of the person

Use the names in the box to complete the sentences.

John Paul I	John XXIII	Pius X	Leo XIII
Benedict XVI	Pius IX	Paul VI	John Paul II

7. Pope _____ convened the Second Vatican Council.

8. Pope _____ wrote the first great Catholic social justice encyclical.

9. Pope _____ died after only thirty-three days as pope, making his pontificate one of the shortest in Church history.

10. Pope _____ was the most widely traveled pope in the history of the Church, and one who placed new emphasis on human rights and religious freedom.

11. Pope _____ declared that children should receive their First Holy Communion as soon as they were old enough to understand that Christ was truly present in the Eucharist, and also encouraged Catholics to receive Holy Communion frequently.

12. Pope _____ served as head of the Congregation for the Doctrine of the Faith before being elected pope.

Write *True* or *False* next to the following sentences. Then, on the lines provided, change the false sentences to make them true.

13. _____ Human life is sacred from the moment of conception to the moment of natural death.

_____

_____

14. _____ In France, the Jesuits abolished taxes collected by the Church, took control of Church property, and dissolved all monastic orders.

_____

_____

15. _____ Enlightenment philosophers believed in *secularization*, the idea that critical reason had no place in society, science, or government.

_____

_____

16. _____ Absolute monarchs gained complete control over all aspects of the lives of their people.

_____

_____

17. _____ *Evangelium Vitae* is an encyclical about the worker and the dignity of work.

_____

_____

18. _____ Baltimore, Maryland was the first diocese of the Catholic Church in the United States.

_____

_____

Respond to the following.

19. Choose one encyclical discussed in this unit and describe its message.

_____

_____

_____

20. Explain the role that either (1) evangelization or (2) Catholic social teaching played in the period of Church history discussed in this unit.

_____

_____

_____

_____

ALTERNATIVE ASSESSMENT

Design a "Guess Who" game in which you write a series of clues to reveal the identities of four key people in Unit 3. Write your clues on the cards below.

GUESS WHO?

1. _____
_____
2. _____
_____
3. _____
4. _____
5. _____

Name of person: _____

GUESS WHO?

1. _____
_____
2. _____
_____
3. _____
4. _____
5. _____

Name of person: _____

GUESS WHO?

1. _____
_____
2. _____
3. _____
4. _____
5. _____

Name of person: _____

GUESS WHO?

1. _____
_____
2. _____
3. _____
4. _____
5. _____

Name of person: _____

Play your game with a partner or with your group.

Unit 4

What Does It Mean to Be Catholic?

Chapter 19
Caring for the Whole Human Family
The Big Question:
What does it mean to be human?

Chapter 20
Seeking God's Life and Love As a Church
The Big Question:
What helps me to achieve my goals?

Chapter 21
Living As the Body of Christ
The Big Question:
What are my roles in life?

Chapter 22
Witnessing to Our Relationship with Christ
The Big Question:
How do I nurture my relationships?

Chapter 23
Growing in Faith Together
The Big Question:
Where am I going in life?

Chapter 24
Belonging to the Communion of Saints
The Big Question:
In what ways do I live my Catholic faith?

GATHERING...

19
Caring for the Whole Human Family

"If possible, on your part, live at peace with all. . . . Do not be conquered by evil but conquer evil with good."

(Romans 12:18, 21)

✛ **Leader:** Jesus taught us that all people are our brothers and sisters. We are one human family. Let us pray for the grace to live the way that Jesus did—with love, concern, and respect for the dignity of all human beings.

All: Almighty and eternal God,
may your grace enkindle in all of us
a love for the many unfortunate people
whom poverty and misery
reduce to a condition of life
unworthy of human beings.

Arouse in the hearts of those who call you Father
a hunger and thirst for justice and peace
and for fraternal charity in deeds and in truth.
Grant, O Lord,
peace in our days,
peace to souls,
peace to families,
peace to our country,
and peace among nations. Amen.

(Prayer for Justice and Peace, Pope Pius XII)

@ **Visit www.weliveourfaith.com to find appropriate music and songs.**

The BiG QuEStion:

What does it mean to be human?

Discover whether you can identify some characteristics of living creatures. Circle the name of the living thing that best completes each statement.

1 No two _____ have exactly the same pattern of stripes.

    humans   zebras   clownfish

2 _____ communicate with whistles and use individual "names" to identify one another.

    Penguins   Giraffes   Dolphins

3 An adult _____ is covered with about 5 million hairs—the same as an adult gorilla.

    elephant   human   mole rat

4 A _____ can reach speeds of 60 to 70 miles an hour when covering short distances.

    black bear   cheetah   tiger

5 Young _____ stay with their mothers for eleven to twelve years.

    lions   seals   orangutans

6 _____ have seven vertebrae, the same number of vertebrae found in the neck of a giraffe.

    Humans   Lemurs   Iguanas

7 Only _____ naturally sleep on their backs.

    cats   humans   sloths

Answers:

1. zebras 2. Dolphins 3. human 4. cheetah 5. orangutans 6. Humans 7. humans

What are some special characteristics that are specific to only humans?

In this chapter we learn that the Church continues the mission of Christ on earth. Through this chapter, we hope

 to understand the concept of human dignity and the importance of Catholic social teachings

 to respect each member of the human family, especially those who are poor or in need

to work for the common good of the whole human family, both now and in the future.

As humans we share many of the same basic needs and instincts with other living creatures. Yet we also possess a spiritual soul and therefore have special characteristics that set us apart from other species. These special characteristics are the qualities that make us distinctly human. Among these qualities are our human dignity—the value that each of us has because we are made in God's image—and our unique capacity for compassion—our ability to consider the feelings of others and to sympathize with them. Living in a truly human way, then, means recognizing one another's dignity and using our compassion to interact respectfully and responsibly with one another.

However, from the beginning of time, human beings have not always lived up to this standard. There have been times when a lack of compassion and respect has led human beings to inflict terrible injustices on one another. People have acted in ways that are not marked by compassion, sympathy, or consideration. They have disregarded others' rights and their own capacity for compassion. Because such injustices go against human nature, we often call these *inhumane* forms of treatment. Examples of inhumane treatment include slavery, persecution, torture, and racism.

Activity Even today there are places in our world where people are treated inhumanely. What are some examples?

What opportunities are there for you to use your compassion to prevent these forms of injustice? to foster respect? to recognize the human dignity of all people?

> "A human being is a part of the whole called by us *universe*. . . . Our task must be to free ourselves . . . by widening our circle of compassion to embrace all living creatures and the whole of nature in its beauty," said renowned scientist and genius Albert Einstein (1879–1955).

A sacramental view of life

God created the world to show his glory. All creation is his gift to us. Everything that comes from God—every person he has made, every living thing he has created—can be viewed as a sign of God's love and care. This is a sacramental view of life. The gifts of God's created world can remind us, in our daily lives, to honor and respect other human beings and the life all around us. We can respect and care for each person as being made in God's image. We can respect and care for all created things—animals and plants, rocks and mountains, lakes, rivers, and oceans. We can make efforts to reuse what we have and recycle what we no longer need. And we can also take better care of what we already have.

The Catholic Church uses the gifts of the created world—such as bread, wine, water, and oil—in her sacraments. And through the power of the Holy Spirit, these sacraments are effective signs through which God's grace enters our lives.

Discuss some things your group might do to show that you recognize all creation as a gift from God.

CATHOLIC IDENTITY

The risen Christ shares his life and mission with the Church.

All love comes from God, who, out of his great love, created us. And even after the first human beings sinned, God still loved all people. He loved us so much that he sent his only Son, Jesus Christ, to redeem us—to save us from sin and give us the hope of eternal life. Each of us could spend a lifetime listing the wondrous events of Jesus' life, his teaching, and all that he did for humankind out of love. Yet we can summarize it all in one phrase: the Paschal Mystery. Salvation was offered to the whole human family by means of the Paschal Mystery: Christ's suffering, death, Resurrection, and Ascension. Through the Paschal Mystery, the Father was made known to all of us in Christ, by the power of the Holy Spirit. As the *Catechism* explains, "It is Christ who is seen, the visible image of the invisible God, but it is the Spirit who reveals him" (689).

The Holy Spirit was at work with the Father and the Son from the beginning of the plan for our salvation to its completion. And on the day that would become known to us as Pentecost, the risen Christ poured out the Gift of the Holy Spirit upon his first disciples. The Holy Spirit would be their helper, giving them the strength to share God's love and spread the good news of Jesus Christ.

The risen Christ shared his life with his disciples by the power of the Holy Spirit. And Christ continues to do the same today. Pentecost was the completion of Christ's Passover, and the coming of the Holy Spirit was, and is today, the completion of the Paschal Mystery. From that moment onward "the mission of Christ and the Spirit becomes the mission of the Church" (*CCC*, 730).

Activity As a member of the Church you have been given a mission. Working in teams, read about this mission below. Brainstorm ways that your team can accept this mission and make it your "Mission Possible" this week.

Your mission is to:

- share the good news of Christ
- spread the Kingdom of God, the power of God's love active in our lives and in the world
- live a life of holiness through prayer, good works, and everyday living.

The Church must continue the work of Christ on earth.

The Church, "in the course of history, unfolds the mission of Christ, who was sent to evangelize the poor; so the Church, urged on by the Spirit of Christ, must walk the road Christ himself walked, a way of poverty and obedience, of service and self-sacrifice" (*CCC*, 852). As disciples of Christ and members of the Church, we must walk this road. We must follow Jesus' example and live out our faith.

Jesus stood up for those treated unjustly because they were ill or poor; protected people who could not protect themselves; and offered the peace and freedom that come from God's love and forgiveness. He called upon everyone to respect the human dignity of each person. And by his healings and miracles, Jesus showed people that life is a precious gift.

To follow Jesus' example, one of the things we must do today is to live according to the Church's social teachings. Catholic social teachings present the truths about: human dignity, the principles of justice and peace, and human **solidarity**—a virtue calling us to recognize that we are all one human family and that our decisions have consequences that reach

Faith Word

solidarity

around the world. Catholic social teachings also present the truths regarding moral judgments about economic and social matters and the requirements that those truths demand of us in light of justice and peace. The social teachings of the Catholic Church are founded on Jesus' life and teaching, and they call all of us to work for justice and peace as Jesus did.

> **"The Church, urged on by the Spirit of Christ, must walk the road Christ himself walked."**
> (*CCC*, 852)

When we live out the Church's social teachings, we are accepting our responsibility to care for others. We are showing our love of God through love for our neighbor.

Activity What might be the negative consequences of each of these decisions?

- to idolize celebrities
- to use foul language
- to cheat
- to tear other people down
- to obtain copyrighted songs or movies without paying for them (piracy)
- to shoplift

Name some decisions you can make that have positive consequences on society.

Social responsibility

As citizens we must all help to build up society in a spirit of justice and peace. This can be an especially demanding requirement for Catholic citizens when our political leaders or the laws they have instituted support what we know to be morally wrong. Yet, as Catholics, we are obligated to do what is right and work for justice.

As the *Catechism* explains, "The citizen is obliged in conscience not to follow the directives of civil authorities when they are contrary to the demands of the moral order, to the fundamental rights of persons or the teachings of the Gospel" (2242).

Similarly, the Church is obligated to share the light of the Gospel with society whenever society is dealing with questions, situations, and decisions that will influence human life and

affect whether people are treated justly. The Church has a responsibility "to pass moral judgments, even on matters touching the political order, whenever basic personal rights or the salvation of souls make such judgments necessary" (*Pastoral Constitution on the Church in the Modern World*, 76).

Name some recent events in which the Church has exercised this responsibility.

209

BELIEVING...

Catholic social teachings guide the Church in continuing Jesus' work.

What people are working for justice in today's world?

We are members of one human family who all share the same human dignity, since we are created in God's image. From the time of the creation of humanity, "the inner harmony of the human person, the harmony between man and woman, and finally the harmony between the first couple and all creation, comprised the state called 'original justice'" (*CCC*, 376). Justice is based on the simple fact that all people have human dignity.

Jesus' example of reaching out to those in society who were neglected or ignored gives us our best understanding of God the Father's call to justice. As Jesus' disciples, we follow his example of faith in God the Father and of living justly. And as members of the Church, together we take on the serious responsibility of continuing Jesus' work of social justice. One way that we can do this is by following the social teachings of the Church.

Activity In the second column below, add names of those you know who live out these teachings.

THEMES OF CATHOLIC SOCIAL TEACHING	THOSE WE HAVE STUDIED ABOUT WHO HAVE LIVED OUT THESE TEACHINGS
Life and Dignity of the Human Person Human life is sacred because it is a gift from God. We are all God's children and share the same human dignity from the moment of conception to natural death. Our dignity—our worth and value—comes from being made in the image and likeness of God. This dignity makes us equal. As Christians we respect all people, even those we do not know.	The Sisters of Life
Call to Family, Community, and Participation As Christians we are involved in our family life and community. We are called to be active participants in social, economic, and political life, using the values of our faith to shape our decisions and actions.	Sister Thea Bowman
Rights and Responsibilities of the Human Person Every person has a fundamental right to life. This includes the things we need to have a decent life: faith and family, work and education, health care and housing. We also have a responsibility to others and to society. We work to make sure the rights of all people are being protected.	Thomas Merton, Charles Carroll, Pope John Paul II
Option for the Poor and Vulnerable We have a special obligation to help those who are poor and in need. This includes those who cannot protect themselves because of their age or their health. At different times in our lives we are all poor in some way and in need of assistance.	Blessed Pier Giorgio Frassati, Saint Francis of Assisi, Dorothy Day
Dignity of Work and the Rights of Workers Our work is a sign of our participation in God's work. People have the right to decent work, just wages, and safe working conditions and to participate in decisions about their work. There is value in all work. Our work in school and at home is a way to participate in God's work of creation. It is a way to use our talents and abilities to thank God for his gifts.	Lech Walesa, Pope Leo XIII
Solidarity of the Human Family Solidarity is a feeling of unity. It binds members of a group together. Each of us is a member of the one human family, equal by our common human dignity. The human family includes people of all racial, cultural, and religious backgrounds. We all suffer when one part of the human family suffers, whether they live near us or far away from us.	Pope John XXIII
Care for God's Creation God created us to be stewards, or caretakers, of his creation. We must care for and respect the environment. We have to protect it for future generations. When we care for creation, we show respect for God the Creator.	Saint Francis of Assisi

The Church lives out the demands of justice and peace.

As Jesus' disciples and members of the Church, we are called to follow his example in word and deed. So, just as Jesus worked among the people, teaching them about the love of God his Father and encouraging them to turn to God, we are called to work among the people. Both individually and communally, we are called to bring the good news of Jesus Christ into society—to work for change in policies and laws so that the dignity and freedom of every person is respected.

There are many saints and holy people who have attested to the permanent value of the Church's teaching and to the true meaning of her Tradition, which is always alive and active. These saints and holy people have proclaimed the Gospel and witnessed to Jesus Christ. In unity with God and with one another, they have championed the dignity of their vocation, working for the common good of the whole human family. They have lived out "the demands of justice and peace in conformity with divine wisdom" (*CCC*, 2419).

Activity In the second column below, write what you can do to live out each teaching.

QUESTIONS TO CONSIDER	WAYS TO LIVE OUT THE CATHOLIC SOCIAL TEACHING
What are some ways the dignity of students or teachers is not respected during class? Why do you think this happens? What are some conflicts in your school that have been resolved in a way that recognizes the dignity of those involved?	
What are some virtues that individuals practice? that families practice? that neighbors practice? How does the practice of these virtues influence society as a whole?	
What is the difference between needing something and wanting something?	
What are some ways people might be poor? What are some ways people are vulnerable?	
How might different kinds of work make people feel? How can we help people to feel respected and valued for whatever work they do?	
What are some problems or challenges that we face in our country? How are they similar to those of other countries? How are they different?	
What are some examples in society of the environment not being protected? How can these situations be changed?	

"We are called to bring the good news of Jesus Christ into society."

RESPONDING...

Recognizing Our Faith

Recall the question at the beginning of this chapter: *What does it mean to be human?* Try to answer this question now from the perspective of:

• one of the people named in the chart on page 210

• yourself, having completed this chapter.

Living Our Faith

Choose one theme of Catholic social teaching, and, this week, be observant of situations in which this teaching needs to be lived out. Think of a way to help improve one such situation.

Partners in FAITH

Saint María de Jesús Sacramentado

María Navidad Venegas de la Torre was born in Mexico on September 8, 1868. When she realized that she wanted to spend her life serving people who were poor or ill, she decided to become a religious sister. Later she founded the Daughters of the Sacred Heart of Jesus. In the late 1890s Sister María, known as Sister María de Jesús Sacramentado, and the Daughters of the Sacred Heart of Jesus moved from Mexico to the western part of Texas because Catholics in Mexico were being persecuted for their faith. From that time forward they served the people of west Texas. They helped countless families leave Mexico, start new lives, and celebrate their faith without fear of persecution or death. Their many other works of kindness and service to those who are poor and sick still touch the residents of El Paso, Texas, and the surrounding region today.

Sister María de Jesús Sacramentado was named a saint on May 21, 2000—the first woman from Mexico to be canonized.

Sister María lived out the demands of justice and peace by helping others. What can you do to live out these demands?

For additional ideas and activities, visit www.weliveourfaith.com.

Putting Faith to Work

Talk about what you have learned in this chapter:

 We understand the concept of human dignity and the importance of Catholic social teachings.

 We respect each member of the human family, especially those who are poor or in need.

 We work for the common good of the whole human family, both now and in the future.

Decide on ways to live out what you have learned.

✝ ENCOUNTERING GOD'S WORD

" If you remove from your midst oppression,
false accusation and malicious speech;
If you bestow your bread on the hungry
and satisfy the afflicted;
Then light shall rise for you in the darkness. "

(Isaiah 58:9–10)

➡ **READ** the quotation from Scripture.

➡ **REFLECT** on the following question:
What can you do to follow the advice of this Scripture passage?

➡ **SHARE** your reflections with a partner.

➡ **DECIDE** on one way to respond to this passage this week.

Circle the letter of the correct answer.

1. _____ is a virtue calling us to recognize that we are one human family and that our decisions have worldwide consequences.

   a. Humanity   **b.** Justice   **c.** Solidarity   **d.** Dignity

2. Salvation was offered to the whole human family by means of _____.

   a. creation   **b.** Pentecost   **c.** the Paschal Mystery   **d.** social responsibility

3. The social teachings of the Catholic Church are founded on _____.

   a. Jesus' miracles   **b.** Jesus' healing   **c.** Jesus' life and teachings   **d.** Jesus' disciples

4. _____ is based on the fact that all people have human dignity.

   a. Inner harmony   **b.** Solidarity   **c.** Justice   **d.** Social responsibility

Short Answers

5. Describe one theme of Catholic social teaching. _____

6. Describe one way that Jesus worked for justice and peace. _____

7. In what ways can members of the Church bring the good news of Jesus Christ into society?

   _____

8. Identify a member of the Church who provides a good example of living out Catholic social teaching.

   _____

9–10. ESSAY: What does the term *original justice* mean? What might the world be like today if we all returned to the state of original justice?

RESPONDING...

Sharing Faith with Your Family

Discuss the following with your family:

- The risen Christ shares his life and mission with the Church.
- The Church must continue the work of Christ on earth.
- Catholic social teachings guide the Church in continuing Jesus' work.
- The Church lives out the demands of justice and peace.

Using the chart of Catholic social teachings on pages 210–211, make a poster or display of Catholic social teachings to share with your family or to post at home. Leave space for writing next to each teaching. Invite family members to work on living out the teachings and then to record their names and what they did in the appropriate space next to each teaching.

The Worship Connection

Both the prayer of the faithful and the sign of peace at Mass remind us of the needs of the Church and the world, especially of the need for peace. Make an effort to share peace throughout the week.

More to Explore

For more information explore the Catholic social teaching Web site belonging to the Archdiocese of St. Paul and Minneapolis Office for Social Justice.

Catholic Social Teaching ☑ Checklist

Theme of Catholic Social Teaching:
Choose a theme found in this chapter:

_____

How it relates to Chapter 19: Think of ways this theme relates to Chapter 19.

Describe how you can live out this teaching:

☐ At home:

_____

☐ At school/work:

_____

☐ In the parish:

_____

☐ In the community:

_____

Check off each action after it has been completed.

GATHERING...

> **"We are the temple of the living God."**
>
> (2 Corinthians 6:16)

✝ **Leader:** We, as members of the Church, are together on a journey toward God. Let us rejoice in this as we pray:

Group 1: "I rejoiced when they said to me, 'Let us go to the house of the LORD.' And now our feet are standing within your gates, Jerusalem."

(Psalm 122:1–2)

Group 2: "Jerusalem, built as a city, walled round about. Here the tribes have come, the tribes of the LORD."

(Psalm 122:3–4)

All: "I rejoiced when they said to me, 'Let us go to the house of the LORD.'"

(Psalm 122:1)

Group 1: "My home is by your altars, LORD of hosts, my king and my God! Happy are those who dwell in your house! They never cease to praise you."

(Psalm 84:4–5)

Group 2: "For family and friends I say, 'May peace be yours.' For the house of the LORD, our God, I pray, 'May blessings be yours.'"

(Psalm 122:8–9)

All: "I rejoiced when they said to me, 'Let us go to the house of the LORD.'"

(Psalm 122:1)

Amen.

 Visit www.weliveourfaith.com to find appropriate music and songs.

215

The BiG QuEStion:

What helps me to achieve my goals?

Discover some things that may help you to reach your goals. Using the gameboard below, design a board game that involves reaching a goal.

First, fill in a goal for yourself as a student or perhaps as a member of a team, your family, or the Church. Then, mark some spaces with things that would help you to reach your goal, plus rewards, such as "Move forward three spaces." Next, mark the remaining spaces with obstacles to reaching your goal, plus penalties, such as "Go back three spaces" or "Return to start." Then, use a die to play your game with a partner.

GOAL:

START

In what ways can looking ahead to the obstacles and the helps you will encounter in trying to achieve a goal assist you in making that goal a reality?

In this chapter we learn that the Church has both visible and invisible elements and is the beginning of the Kingdom of God on earth. Through this chapter, we hope

to recognize the role of the Church, and of ourselves as her members, in bringing about the Kingdom of God

to appreciate the Church's mission of spreading God's Kingdom through the power of the Holy Spirit

to choose to follow Christ as members of the Church and to look forward to the fullness of the Kingdom when Christ will come again at the end of time.

Father James Keller, a Maryknoll priest, wholeheartedly believed that when people help one another they can achieve their goals and truly make a difference in the world. In 1945 he founded The Christophers, a nonprofit group, to share the message that each of us has a personal responsibility to serve God and *all* of God's people. The name *Christopher* means "Christ-bearer." We become "Christ-bearers" when we share our God-given gifts with others.

Through books, videos, newspaper columns, radio programs, pamphlets, television programs, and now Web sites, The Christophers have faithfully pursued their goal of encouraging people to use their God-given talents to make a positive difference in the world. The Christophers' work continues today. They offer service programs and lectures. They also continue to share their message through pamphlets, which are often used as inserts in weekly parish bulletins. The Christophers' motto is "It's better to light one candle than to curse the darkness." And many candles, working together, can make one great light!

Activity What does The Christophers' motto mean to you? In small groups design an insert to be placed in your parish bulletin to encourage people to work together to achieve a goal that will make a difference in others' lives. Use the space below to make a plan for it.

Christopher CLOSEUP

Father James Keller

"It's better to light one candle than to curse the darkness," motto of The Christophers.

Jesus encourages us to put God at the center of our lives.

At the heart of Jesus' teaching was his love for God, his Father, and for the fulfillment of the Father's plan for all creation. Jesus told his disciples that they could trust in God because he cared about them and had a plan for their salvation. Jesus said, "Do not worry about your life, what you will eat [or drink], or about your body, what you will wear. . . . But seek first the kingdom [of God] and his righteousness, and all these things will be given you besides" (Matthew 6:25, 33).

The idea of God as king was understandable to the people of Jesus' time. It was a theme found in the Old Testament. A good king was to be like the father of his nation—caring for his people, protecting them from danger, and guaranteeing justice throughout his kingdom, especially for those who were weak and oppressed. The *Kingdom of God* was an image that reminded everyone that God is the Lord of the universe who cares for his people, brings them salvation, and expects them to return his love and follow his law. And, for those who belonged to the Kingdom, God would take a central place in their lives.

Jesus encouraged his disciples to put God at the center of their lives. He encouraged them to depend on God's **providence**, his plan for and protection of all creation. Jesus wanted

his disciples to know that God loves and protects each one of us personally. He wanted them to know that God leads his creation toward the perfection for which it was made. And, in his teachings about the Kingdom of God Jesus gave his disciples further insight into the providence of God.

Jesus would often teach about the Kingdom by using a **parable**, a short story with a message. Jesus' parables about the Kingdom of God can be found in the synoptic Gospels of Matthew, Mark, and Luke. In these parables Jesus used examples from farming, feasts, and everyday work to describe the Kingdom of God.

Faith Words

providence
parable

Activity Read these parables about the Kingdom of God listed in the chart. Then write a parable of your own about making God the center of your life. Share your parables.

PARABLE	MATTHEW	MARK	LUKE
The sower	13:1–23	4:1–20	8:4–15
The weeds among the wheat	13:24–30		
The mustard seed	13:31–32	4:30–32	13:18–19
The buried treasure and the pearls	13:44–46		
The net	13:47–50		
The unforgiving servant	18:23–35		
The great feast			14:15–24
The Pharisee and the tax collector			18:9–14
The workers in the vineyard	20:1–16		
The tenants	21:33–46	12:1–12	20:9–19
The wedding feast	22:1–14		
The ten virgins	25:1–13		

The Church is **"on earth the seed and beginning of that kingdom"** (*CCC*, 541).

As the Church we are the seed and the beginning of God's Kingdom on earth.

The parables also reminded Jesus' disciples to be alert to the presence of God's Kingdom and to be ready to accept his invitation to be part of it. Sometimes the words or details differ slightly from one Gospel writer to another. For example, Matthew refers to God's Kingdom as the *kingdom of heaven*. But the message is always the same: The Kingdom of God is the power of God's love active in our lives and in our world. And through the words, works, and presence of Jesus Christ, "the Father's plan of salvation in the fullness of time" would be accomplished (*CCC*, 763). The kingdom of heaven would be established on earth.

Jesus said, "Behold, the kingdom of God is among you" (Luke 17:21). Jesus let his disciples know that they would find the Kingdom of God in him. Jesus also told his disciples, "My kingdom does not belong to this world" (John 18:36), explaining that the Kingdom of God is not a physical place. It is God's rule and reign over people's lives.

God's Kingdom is present to all of Christ's disciples here on earth through the life and love of Jesus Christ—God with us. And, carrying out the will of God his Father, Christ gathered his disciples around him. They became the Church, "on earth the seed and beginning of that kingdom" (*CCC*, 541). As disciples of Jesus and members of the Church we are called to respond through our lives, both individually and communally, to God's invitation to eternal salvation in the fullness of his Kingdom.

As Jesus' disciples, we need to take an active part in spreading God's Kingdom. So, we pray, "Thy kingdom come" (Lord's Prayer). Though the Kingdom of God is present and can be entered into here and now, the fullness of God's Kingdom awaits us in heaven. And in Jesus Christ, through the power of the Holy Spirit, God's grace is active in us, empowering us to live as disciples, doing God's will "on earth, as it is in heaven" (Lord's Prayer).

Activity Reflect for a moment on the words *Thy kingdom come*. In what ways would the events in your life or in the world be changed if everyone worked together to spread God's Kingdom?

The Catholic Church

In the New Testament we read about the Church that grew out of the community of Jesus' first disciples. Where do we find this Church referred to in the New Testament? The bishops at the Second Vatican Council addressed this question when they wrote:

"This is the unique Church of Christ which in the Creed we avow as one, holy, catholic, and apostolic.... This Church, constituted and organized in the world as a society, subsists in the Catholic Church, which is governed by the successor of Peter and by the bishops in union with that successor, although many elements of sanctification and of truth can be found outside of her visible structure." (*Dogmatic Constitution on the Church*, 8)

This teaching states that in the Catholic Church, the Church of Christ is truly present in her essential completeness, although elements of goodness and truth are found outside of her.

What can you do today to show that you are a member of the Church?

CATHOLIC IDENTITY

BELIEVING...

Through the power of the Holy Spirit, Christ helps the Church to live out her mission.

In what ways does your membership in the Church help you to follow Christ?

As disciples of Christ and members of the Church, we believe that "the kingdom of God is at hand" and that we must "repent, and believe in the gospel" (Mark 1:15). Even today when we hear the parables, we are reminded of the conditions for entrance into the Kingdom of God. For example, in the parable of the wedding feast (Matthew 22:1–14) we are reminded that repentance and conversion of heart must be lived out in a life of good works.

Our conversion begins when we are baptized in the name of the Blessed Trinity. We take on the common mission of sharing the good news of Jesus Christ and of working together to spread God's Kingdom. Saint Paul tells us that the Kingdom of God is a kingdom of "righteousness, peace, and joy in the holy Spirit" (Romans 14:17). And ever since the Pentecost event, all of Christ's disciples have been guided by the Spirit to serve God and one another through lives of love and service in the Church.

In a special way, through the Church, in the Sacraments of Baptism and Confirmation, the Holy Spirit has been poured out upon each of her members. And, for each of us, the life of our faith comes to us through the Church. She is the mother of our new birth and our teacher in the faith. Throughout her long history, the Church has seen both moments of jubilation and moments of suffering. The Church has rejoiced in the goodness of her members and has suffered with them in their weaknesses. Yet Jesus Christ, through the power of the Holy Spirit, gives to the Church the help she needs to remain forever.

The Church, human and divine

When we were baptized into the Church, we received grace, a share in God's divine life. The whole Church shares in this divine life. The Church is a spiritual community—the Temple of the Holy Spirit, full of heavenly graces and blessings. The Church thus is human—having human members, including the pope, bishops, priests, religious, and laity—and yet she is also divine—filled with grace, living as the Body of Christ, cared for by the Father, and inspired by the Holy Spirit.

These two components of the Church—human and divine—are united with each other in the closest way. The divine component of the Church empowers the human component. The Church also includes the faithful people who are now happy with God in heaven. So, the Church both exists here on earth and in heaven. At the end of time, Christ will return and gather up the entire Church with him, both human and divine, "so that God may be all in all" (1 Corinthians 15:28).

How would you explain the human and divine components of the Church to your family or friends?

Activity Design a logo with a slogan that tells the world that the life of our faith comes to us through the Church.

Christ's lasting presence in the Church is revealed in many ways.

Through the Holy Spirit the Church was founded upon Christ and the Apostles. Today we continue to look to their successors, the pope and the bishops, for guidance. These men exercise their authority and ministry within the Church—teaching, governing, and sanctifying in Christ's name. As Catholics we look to the writings and teachings of the pope and bishops to gain understanding about the Catholic Church and guidance in living our faith.

After much reflection and discussion, the pope and the bishops who gathered from every part of the world for the Second Vatican Council taught that the Church, founded upon Christ and the Apostles, is made up of elements that are essential to the Church—to her life and faith. The Church's *visible elements* allow her to be readily seen and recognized by all as a community of people with leaders, beliefs, laws, and practices. Some of the visible elements of the Church are:

> **"The kingdom of God is at hand."**
>
> **(Mark 1:15)**

- Scripture, the Church's written record of God's Revelation. Because it is a permanent document, Scripture cannot be changed or ignored. (For a more detailed look at Scripture, see "Bible Basics" on pages 310–311.)

- Baptism, along with the other sacraments of the Church. Through Baptism we become members of the Church.

- the Eucharist, the Sacrament of the Body and Blood of Christ. The Eucharist is the source and high point of the Church's life.

- doctrines of faith. These are the teachings that come down to us from the time of the Apostles.

- episcopacy, or the office of bishop. This includes the pope, the bishop of Rome, and links the Church through the Apostles to Christ himself.

- devotion to Mary, the Mother of God. Mary's spiritual motherhood extends to all the members of the Church.

The *invisible elements* have to do with the Church's inner life—shown by the way the Church's members live. Some of the invisible elements of the Church are:

- the life of grace, a participation in the very life of God.

- the theological virtues of faith, hope, and love, which are gifts from God. These virtues enable us to act as children of God.

- the gifts of the Holy Spirit, who is continually sanctifying the Church.

Jesus' first disciples, through their closeness to Jesus himself, were privileged to know "the mysteries of the kingdom of heaven" (Matthew 13:11). Yet, even today, we, as disciples of Christ and members of the Church, can look to each of the visible and invisible elements of the Church as signs of Christ's lasting closeness to us. Through the Father, made known to all of us in Christ by the power of the Holy Spirit, we can find the strength to work together within God's Kingdom—always looking toward its fullness at Jesus' second coming at the end of time.

Activity With your group take a survey of the ways that your parish reflects these visible and invisible elements of the Church.

The NEW AMERICAN BIBLE

Recognizing Our Faith

Recall the question at the beginning of this chapter: *What helps me to achieve my goals?* What is the Church's goal or mission? What is your part in this mission? What can help you to achieve it? Over the next several weeks work with your group to gather images or photos that help to answer these questions. Make a collage to display in your parish titled "The Church at Work in the World." Below list some possible items to include.

Living Our Faith

Name one thing that you will do this week to put God at the center of your life.

Partners in FAITH

Danny Thomas

Danny Thomas was born in 1912 in Michigan to Lebanese Catholic immigrant parents. One of ten children, he helped to support his family during his youth. As an adult he held various jobs while trying to break into show business—his dream career. After getting married, he faced a difficult decision: Should he continue to struggle to pursue his goal, or choose a more secure profession to support his growing family? He prayed to Saint Jude, the patron saint of hopeless cases, to intercede for him with God. His prayer, "Show me my way in life and I will build you a shrine," was answered in time. He became one of America's best-loved entertainers and starred in a successful television show based upon his experiences as a father and an entertainer.

Keeping his promise to Saint Jude, Thomas decided that his "shrine" would be a charitable hospital for children—St. Jude Children's Research Hospital—which opened in 1962 in Tennessee. Danny Thomas died in 1991, but the hospital he founded continues to help children in need.

Think of a goal that you have for your life and ask God for help in following it.

@ For additional ideas and activities, visit www.weliveourfaith.com.

Putting Faith to Work

Talk about what you have learned in this chapter:

 We recognize the role of the Church, and of ourselves as her members, in bringing about the Kingdom of God.

We appreciate the Church's mission of spreading God's Kingdom through the power of the Holy Spirit.

We choose to follow Christ as members of the Church and to look forward to the fullness of the Kingdom when Christ will come again at the end of time.

Decide on ways to live out what you have learned.

✝ ENCOUNTERING GOD'S WORD

❝ Neither the one who plants nor the one who waters is anything, but only God, who causes the growth. . . . For we are God's co-workers; you are God's field, God's building. ❞

(1 Corinthians 3:7, 9)

➡ **READ** the quotation from Scripture.

➡ **REFLECT** on the following:
Saint Paul wrote these words to the Church community at Corinth, Greece. What are some of the possible meanings that these words have for the Church today?

➡ **SHARE** your reflections with a partner.

➡ **DECIDE** on a way to be "God's co-worker" this week.

Write *True* or *False* next to the following sentences. On a separate sheet of paper, change the false statements to make them true.

1. _____ Jesus encouraged his disciples to put the Church at the center of their lives.

2. _____ When Jesus taught about the Kingdom of God he often used *providence*, a short story with a message.

3. _____ Through the power of the Holy Spirit, Christ helps the Church to live out her mission.

4. _____ Jesus encouraged his disciples to depend on God's parables, his plan for and protection of all creation.

Complete the following.

5. The Kingdom of God is the power of God's love _____.

6. As Catholics we are baptized in the name of the Blessed Trinity and take on the common mission of

_____.

7. Some visible elements of the Church are _____.

8. Some invisible elements of the Church are _____.

9–10. **ESSAY:** Using the information in this chapter, explain the following Scripture passage: "Behold, the kingdom of God is among you" (Luke 17:21).

Sharing Faith with Your Family

Discuss the following with your family:

- Jesus encourages us to put God at the center of our lives.
- As the Church we are the seed and the beginning of God's Kingdom on earth.
- Through the power of the Holy Spirit, Christ helps the Church to live out her mission.
- Christ's lasting presence in the Church is revealed in many ways.

With your family find a way to participate in one of your parish's ministries so that together you can further the mission of the Church.

The Worship Connection

At every Mass, in the Lord's Prayer, we pray, "Thy kingdom come." When you pray these words, reflect on ways you can be more open to the Kingdom of God in your life.

More to Explore

Explore the Web sites of The Christophers and of St. Jude Children's Research Hospital to see how each group attains its goals and furthers the mission of the Church.

Catholic Social Teaching ☑ Checklist

Theme of Catholic Social Teaching:
Solidarity of the Human Family

How it relates to Chapter 20: In this chapter we have seen how as members of one human family, we are called to love and support all people.

How can you do this?

☐ At home:

_____

☐ At school/work:

_____

☐ In the parish:

_____

☐ In the community:

_____

Check off each action after it has been completed.

GATHERING...

Living As the Body of Christ

> "As a body is one though it has many parts, and all the parts of the body, though many, are one body, so also Christ."
>
> (1 Corinthians 12:12)

Reader 1: "Now you are Christ's body, and individually parts of it. Some people God has designated in the church to be, first, apostles; second, prophets; third, teachers; then, mighty deeds; then gifts of healing, assistance, administration, and varieties of tongues. Are all apostles? Are all prophets? Are all teachers? Do all work mighty deeds? Do all have gifts of healing? Do all speak in tongues? Do all interpret? Strive eagerly for the greatest spiritual gifts."

(1 Corinthians 12:27–31)

Leader: The greatest spiritual gift, says Saint Paul, is love:

Reader 2: "Love never fails. If there are prophecies, they will be brought to nothing; if tongues, they will cease; if knowledge, it will be brought to nothing. . . . So faith, hope, love remain, these three; but the greatest of these is love."

(1 Corinthians 13:8, 13)

All: Lord God of power and might,
nothing is good which is against your will,
and all is of value which comes from
    your hand.
Place in our hearts a desire to please you
and fill our minds with insight into love,
so that every thought may grow in
    wisdom
and all our efforts may be filled with
    your peace.

We ask this through Christ our Lord.
Amen.

(alternative collect, Twenty-Second Sunday in Ordinary Time)

Visit www.weliveourfaith.com to find appropriate music and songs.

The BiG QueStion:

What are my roles in life?

Discover some roles that people must take on in a specific setting: a baseball field. See if you can match each role with its description.

center fielder

left fielder   right fielder

shortstop   second base player

third base player   pitcher   first base player

catcher

1 fields ground balls on right side of diamond and receives throws on steal attempts

2 (applies to three roles) chases down and catches deep pop flies and throws balls to bases

3 tries to throw balls past batters and also catches short ground or bunted balls

4 protects the left field line and fields ground balls

5 fields ground balls on the left side of the diamond and catches shallow pop flies

6 catches or blocks pitches, covers home plate, and tries to throw out base stealers

7 protects right field line, and holds runners on base

Answers:
1. second base player; 2. left, center, and right fielders; 3. pitcher; 4. third base player; 5. shortstop; 6. catcher; 7. first base player

What are some other settings or situations in which people need to fulfill certain roles? Have you ever played a role in such a situation? Explain your answer.

In this chapter
we learn more about the many spiritual gifts of the Church that come through Christ, her head. Through this chapter, we hope

 to recognize
the Church as the Body of Christ, the Temple of the Holy Spirit, and the People of God

to love
the Church as Christ does

to work
to support and build up the Church in her four marks, or characteristics: one, holy, catholic, and apostolic.

Long ago, there were three blind men who lived in a village. They loved to listen to stories about the world because they could not see it for themselves. Among their favorite stories were those about elephants. The three men listened with awe to tales about the elephants' great strength in trampling forests and helping to build roads. They heard for themselves the elephants' powerful trumpeting. And they were told that mighty kings rode on elephants as they traveled to and from their kingdoms.

One day, a villager brought an elephant into the town, and the three blind men heard its trumpeting. The men approached the animal to find out once and for all what an elephant was like.

The first man reached out his hand and touched the elephant's side. "The elephant is strong and solid, like a wall!" he announced.

The second man then reached out and touched the elephant's trunk. "The elephant is agile like a snake," he claimed.

> "It's easy to get the players; it's getting them to play together that's the tough part," said Charles Dillon "Casey" Stengel (1890–1975), famous baseball player and team manager.

The third man took hold of the elephant's tail. "Why, an elephant is nothing but a fraying rope," he laughed.

The men argued all through the day.

"Wall!" the first cried.

"Snake!" the second cried.

"Rope!" the third cried.

When the villager returned, he demanded that the men stop shouting.

"Each of you touched only a part of the elephant," he said. "Put those parts together and you will see the truth."

The men stopped shouting and considered the villager's advice. Each one imagined the parts together—the elephant's wall-like side, its snakelike trunk, its ropelike tail—and finally had a picture of the whole animal for what it was.

Activity Discuss the following: What lesson did the three men learn? How can you apply this lesson to the way that various people's roles work together in a situation to make it "whole"? Then think about what you have discussed and how this might relate to the Church.

The Church is the Body of Christ and the Temple of the Holy Spirit.

During his earthly ministry Jesus taught his followers how to live as his disciples. He explained the meaning of the Ten Commandments and gave his disciples the Beatitudes as a model for living and working toward the happiness of God's Kingdom. Jesus called his disciples to love God, to love themselves, and to love one another as he loved them. And by the way he lived, Jesus showed his disciples the way to live out that love.

Yet it was only when Jesus' disciples received the Holy Spirit on the day of Pentecost that they were given a fuller understanding of Jesus' teachings and courage to live out all that Jesus taught. They were then able to give witness to Jesus Christ, God's only Son, still alive and present with them through the Holy Spirit. That is why the Pentecost event marks the beginning of the Church. As it is explained in the *Catechism*, "The mission of Christ and the Holy Spirit is brought to completion in the Church, which is the Body of Christ and the Temple of the Holy Spirit" (737).

The image of the Body of Christ was used by Saint Paul to describe the Church. He said, "Now you are Christ's body, and individually parts of it" (1 Corinthians 12:27), with Christ who "is the head of the body, the church" (Colossians 1:18). What a wonderful image! Christ is the head of the body, the Church, and we, the Church, are the Body of Christ.

The Church is also called the Temple of the Holy Spirit. Saint Augustine tells us that the Holy Spirit is to the Body of Christ what the soul is to the human body. This means that the Holy Spirit is "the principle of every vital and truly saving action in each part of the Body" (Pope Pius XII, *On the Mystical Body of Christ*, as quoted in the *CCC*, 798). Therefore, the Holy Spirit is the source of the Church's life, unity, and gifts.

Many other images, or descriptions, of the Church can be found in the New Testament and in other writings of the Church. In one way or another, they all point to the intimate relationship between Christ and the members of the Church.

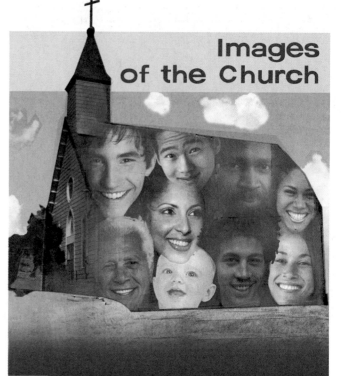

Images of the Church

The writers of the New Testament used poetic language and imagery to describe the Church. Their images of the Church express the intimate relationship between Christ and the members of the Church. You may wish to locate such images in Scripture, as follows:

- vine and branches (John 15:1–5)
- Bride of Christ (2 Corinthians 11:2)
- salt of the earth (Matthew 5:13)
- one loaf (1 Corinthians 10:17)
- God's building (1 Corinthians 3:9)
- household of God (Ephesians 2:19)
- light of the world (Matthew 5:14)
- Temple of the Holy Spirit (1 Corinthians 3:16)
- sheepfold (John 10:1–15)

All of these images are important. They help us to understand that the Church is the Body of Christ. As members of Christ's Body, we receive our life from Christ himself.

Work in groups to think of another image of the Church.

Activity In your group choose one of the images of the Church from the New Testament. Work together to make a mural of this image of the Church. Present the murals to your parish.

The Church is the People of God.

As members of the Church, we have been *chosen by God* to be his adopted children—chosen by God and invited to respond to him. Through our Baptism we became members of the Church. We received the Holy Spirit and were initiated into a life of **sanctifying grace**, the grace that we receive in the sacraments. We became part of "a chosen race, a royal priesthood, a holy nation, a people of his own" (1 Peter 2:9). God's choice and our Baptism brought us into a community, the People of God. And as God's people we have been chosen to live as sons and daughters of our heavenly Father.

From the time of the first Christian communities, the Church, as God's people, has been called to live according to Christ's command to love one another as he loved us. We have been called to love and serve all people as Christ did. And it is the Holy Spirit who guides the Church and strengthens us in this calling.

The Holy Spirit is constantly active in each of our lives through actual graces. **Actual graces** are interventions of God in our daily lives—the urgings or promptings from the Holy Spirit that help us to do good and to deepen our relationship with Christ. Through the Holy Spirit we receive the guidance that we need to live as Christ lived and to nourish God's Kingdom by our witness to Christ's presence in the world.

We must be the "salt of the earth" (Matthew 5:13) and the "light of the world" (Matthew 5:14). We are to work for peace and justice and proclaim the good news of Jesus Christ. We are witnesses to God's will for all people. Thus, the Church, the People of God, is also called the seed and beginning of God's Kingdom. And with the help of the Holy Spirit, the Church can fulfill her mission—that in Christ all people "may form one family and one People of God" (*AG*, 1).

> We are part of "a chosen race, a royal priesthood, a holy nation, a people of his own"
> (1 Peter 2:9).

Faith Words

sanctifying grace
actual graces

Activity Reflect on the events of your week so far. Identify and list some signs that the Holy Spirit has been active in your life as well as some examples of actual graces that you have received.

The Church is one and holy.

How are you united with other members of the Church?

As members of the Catholic Church, we are one in Christ, joined with the Father and with one another by the power of the Holy Spirit. We are united by our belief in Christ, and we celebrate our faith as a community. Together we form Christ's Body, the Church. And at each Eucharist, during the Nicene Creed, we state our belief in four special characteristics of the Church—the **marks of the Church**—praying, "We believe in one holy catholic and apostolic Church."

> **Faith Word**
>
> **marks of the Church**

The first mark of the Church is *one*. The Church is one because all its members believe in the one Lord, Jesus Christ. The Church is one because we all share the same Baptism and together are the one Body of Christ. As we read in the New Testament, there is "one body and one Spirit . . . one Lord, one faith, one baptism; one God and Father of all" (Ephesians 4:4, 5–6). And the Church is one because we are guided and united by the Holy Spirit under the leadership of the pope and bishops; we are one in the sacraments we celebrate and in the laws that help us to live as disciples of Christ and faithful members of the Church. The unity of the Church is a gift from God. We are called to foster that gift of unity and to nourish it until all Christians are one.

The second mark of the Church is *holy*. God alone is good and holy. But God shared his holiness with all people by sending his Son to us. And Christ shares his holiness with us today through the Church, where we are first made holy in Baptism. Then, throughout our lives, we are called to holiness by God and by the Church—a holiness that stems from the gift of grace that we receive in the sacraments, from the gifts of the Holy Spirit, and from the practice of the virtues.

Our holiness grows as we follow Jesus' example of praying, respecting all people, living fairly, and working for justice and peace. In doing these things we respond to God's love in our lives and live as Christ's disciples and members of the Church.

Activity Draw each of the following in one of the sections of the cross:

- a symbol for the *one* mark of the Church
- a symbol for the *holy* mark of the Church.

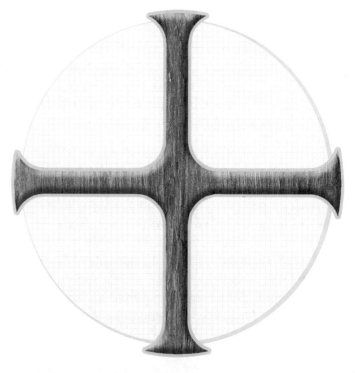

The Church is catholic and apostolic.

The third mark of the Church is *catholic*. The word *catholic* means "universal"—worldwide and open to all people everywhere. The Church has been universal since her beginning. Jesus commissioned his Apostles, saying, "Go, therefore, and make disciples of all nations, baptizing them in the name of the Father, and of the Son, and of the holy Spirit" (Matthew 28:19). Thus, the Apostles traveled wherever they could to preach the Gospel message. They baptized believers and established local Church communities. The Church continued to grow, and today there are Catholics all across the world.

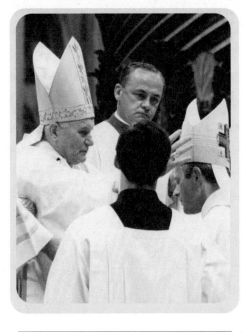

> "Go, therefore, and make disciples of all nations."
> (Matthew 28:19)

Since the Church is truly catholic, or universal, her members bring different customs and practices to the life of the Church, adding beauty and wonder to the Church. Yet even where there are differences, as Catholics we are the Church, the Body of Christ and the People of God. We are still one, united by our faith in Jesus and by our membership in the Church. We are joined by the celebration of the seven sacraments and by the leadership of our Holy Father, the pope, and all the bishops. We are united by our love for Christ and by our common call to holiness. We are strengthened to love as Jesus loved and to continue his work for justice and peace, welcoming all people as he did and telling everyone about his saving love and about the Church.

The fourth mark of the Church is *apostolic*, or built on the faith of the Apostles. Jesus chose the Apostles to care for and lead the community of believers. He gave them the mission of spreading the good news and baptizing new members of the Church. We read about the ministry of the Apostles and their work in the early Church in the New Testament. And in the Apostles' Creed, we profess our faith, remembering our beliefs about Jesus, his teachings, and the teachings of the Apostles.

The Church is apostolic today because the life and leadership of the Church is based on that of the Apostles. The pope—the bishop of Rome—and all the bishops, the successors of the Apostles, continue this ministry of the Apostles today. The pope and the bishops carry out the Apostles' mission, given to them by Jesus. As baptized Catholics, disciples of Jesus, and members of the Church, we too are encouraged to join in this work of sharing the good news of Christ and spreading the Kingdom of God.

Activity Complete the sections of the cross on page 230. Draw a symbol for the *catholic* mark of the Church and for the *apostolic* mark of the Church.

The Church, a sacrament

The *Catechism* states, "The seven sacraments are the signs and instruments by which the Holy Spirit spreads the grace of Christ the head throughout the Church which is his Body" (774). So, through the sacraments, grace, and the workings of the Holy Spirit, the Church is intimately united to Christ. The Church is an organized community unlike any other: Christ truly lives in her.

The light of Christ is the light that the Church works to share with the world. In this way the Church is like a sacrament: it makes Christ visible to the world. "By her relationship with Christ, the Church is a kind of sacrament or sign of intimate union with God, and of the unity of all mankind. She is also an instrument for the achievement of such union and unity." (*Dogmatic Constitution on the Church*, 1)

All this reminds us that the Church is necessary for our salvation, for it is in the Church that we are baptized and meet Christ our Savior.

Think of a role in the Church that you could take on to make Christ more visible to the world.

CATHOLIC IDENTITY

Recognizing Our Faith

Recall the question at the beginning of this chapter: *What are my roles in life?* Make a list of the roles that you named for yourself at the beginning of this chapter and a list of the roles that you now identify for yourself as a member of the Church. How do these roles differ? How do they complement each other?

Living Our Faith

This week think of a way to show that you (a) are a member of the Body of Christ, (b) are part of the Temple of the Holy Spirit, and (c) belong to the People of God.

Saint Alberto Hurtado Cruchaga

Partners in FAITH

Alberto Hurtado Cruchaga was born in Chile in 1901. His childhood was difficult. His father died, and his family became homeless. To help support his mother and younger brother, he had to take on many roles that were demanding for someone his age. But his faith was always the center of his life. He also had a desire to help others who were poor and he had an interest in learning. He earned a scholarship at a Jesuit school and later was ordained a Jesuit priest.

As an adult he took on many more roles to help others. As a priest he was a teacher and became involved in youth ministry. He reached out to Chile's poor and neglected youth. He opened shelters for the homeless and helped to rescue abandoned children. He founded an organization to promote Catholic social teaching principles in the workplace. He also wrote about Church teaching. Unfortunately, his life was cut short by pancreatic cancer in 1952. Father Alberto Hurtado Cruchaga was canonized by Pope Benedict XVI in 2005. He is Chile's second canonized saint.

Reflect on the roles that you now fulfill to help others. How can you add to these roles?

@✱ **For additional ideas and activities, visit www.weliveourfaith.com.**

Putting Faith to Work

Talk about what you have learned in this chapter:

We recognize the Church as the Body of Christ, the Temple of the Holy Spirit, and the People of God.

We love the Church as Christ does.

We work to support and build up the Church in her four marks, or characteristics: one, holy, catholic, and apostolic.

Decide on ways to live out what you have learned.

✝ ENCOUNTERING GOD'S WORD

❝Living the truth in love, we should grow in every way into him who is the head, Christ, from whom the whole body . . . brings about the body's growth and builds itself up in love.❞

(Ephesians 4:15–16)

➡ **READ** the quotation from Scripture.

➡ **REFLECT** on these questions:
In what ways could you grow more fully as a member of Christ's Body? How can you build up the Body of Christ, the Church?

➡ **SHARE** your reflections with a partner.

➡ **DECIDE** to contribute to the Church's growth by praying for the Church throughout the world and showing love by doing a good deed this week.

Define each mark of the Church.

1. *one*: _____.

2. *holy*: _____.

3. *catholic*: _____.

4. *apostolic*: _____.

Circle the letter of the correct answer.

5. On the day of _____, Jesus' disciples received courage to live out all that Jesus taught; this day marks the beginning of the Church.

   a. Jesus' death   **b.** Jesus' Resurrection   **c.** Pentecost   **d.** Jesus' Ascension

6. To describe the Church, one of the images used by Saint Paul was the _____ of Christ.

   a. People   **b.** Temple   **c.** Spirit   **d.** Body

7. The grace that we receive in the sacraments is called _____.

   a. actual grace   **b.** marks of the Church   **c.** sanctifying grace   **d.** images of the Church

8. The urgings or promptings from the Holy Spirit that help us to do good and to deepen our relationship with Christ are called _____.

   a. actual graces   **b.** images of the Church   **c.** beliefs   **d.** marks of the Church

9–10. **ESSAY:** Why is the Church considered the Body of Christ, the Temple of the Holy Spirit, and the People of God?

RESPONDING...

Sharing Faith with Your Family

Discuss the following with your family:

- The Church is the Body of Christ and the Temple of the Holy Spirit.
- The Church is the People of God.
- The Church is one and holy.
- The Church is catholic and apostolic.

The *Catechism* states, "The Christian home is the place where children receive the first proclamation of the faith. For this reason the family home is rightly called 'the domestic church,' a community of grace and prayer, a school of human virtues and of Christian charity" (1666). Together discuss what it means to be a family that is a "domestic church."

The Worship Connection

This Sunday, remember that when you celebrate the Eucharist, you are not celebrating just as an individual or even just as part of a parish. You are celebrating as part of the one, holy, catholic, and apostolic Church in union with your local bishop, who is your parish's link to the entire universal Church.

More to Explore

Find examples of the Church living out her roles as the Body of Christ, the Temple of the Holy Spirit, and the People of God.

Catholic Social Teaching ☑ Checklist

Theme of Catholic Social Teaching:
Rights and Responsibilities of the Human Person

How it relates to Chapter 21: As members of the Church, we are intimately united to Christ and called to share his love with the world. Thus, we have a special responsibility to care for others and ensure that their rights are upheld.

How can you do this?

☐ At home:

☐ At school/work:

☐ In the parish:

☐ In the community:

Check off each action after it has been completed.

22

Witnessing to Our Relationship with Christ

"Let the word of Christ dwell in you richly."

(Colossians 3:16)

Leader: Christ is present in our hearts and our lives in many ways. We are called to nurture our relationship with him. Let us keep this in mind as we pray some words from "Jesus in Everyday Life," a prayer by a student.

Reader 1: I see you Jesus
no longer just in my prayer,
no longer just in my Bible,
but in the breaking of the bread
of everyday life.

Reader 2: I see you Jesus
when you help me get done what's
got to get done:
my homework, my finals, my
everyday living.

Reader 3: Where do I see you?
More and more in the people
around me:
my friends, the people at the
dinner table,
my Mom and Dad, my sister,
the guy on the bus home.

Reader 4: You have become flesh in them;
you are not just the Spirit in the
sky any longer,
but you are right here in them to
love me,
for me to love.

Reader 5: Thanks for entering everyday
life . . . .
All I have to do is listen right here
and now
and I'll find you coming through,
gently, subtly touching my heart
with your love and wisdom.

All: I'm happy you love me just the
way I am,
helping me develop all the
potential that's in me,
all the potential that's in the world,
your precious gifts of every day.
Amen.

(Dan McGraw, from *Day by Day:
The Notre Dame Prayerbook for Students*)

Visit www.weliveourfaith.com to find appropriate music and songs.

The BiG QuEStion:

How do I nurture my relationships?

Discover ways to nurture your relationships. Read the following list of actions that can either build up or break down a relationship. Write a plus sign (+) next to the actions that you think can help to build up a relationship and a minus sign (-) next to the actions that would probably cause it to break down.

+ / **–** _____ being honest about your feelings

– / **+** _____ substituting a hard truth with a white lie

+ / **–** _____ being available to listen anytime

– / **+** _____ breaking plans for something more fun

+ / **–** _____ revealing a secret told in confidence

– / **+** _____ asking for help

+ / **–** _____ avoiding a difficult issue

– / **+** _____ discussing tough topics

+ / **–** _____ recognizing differences in the relationship

– / **+** _____ bailing when there's trouble

Results:
After you've completed this exercise, allow the list to become a topic of discussion, remembering that there are no right or wrong answers.

Think of your relationships with family, friends and others. Have any of the items in the list affected your relationships? for better or worse?

In this chapter
we learn that Jesus Christ is present with us always: in the sacraments, in the liturgy, and in our own relationship with him in prayer. Through this chapter, we hope

 to understand the various ways Christ is present with us, the Church

 to nurture our relationship with Christ in our own lives in every way possible

to witness to our relationship with Christ.

Since the earliest times, people from various cultures have tried to give expression to what they experience as their relationship with God. One way they have done this is through prayer—speaking and listening to God and trying to nurture their relationship with him.

The prayers below are based on the traditional prayers of different cultures. How are they like the prayers you pray? How are they different?

Activity Discuss with your group times when you experienced prayer from other cultures or traditions. Describe such experiences and how the prayers were similar to or different from your own.

As I walk, as I walk,
the universe is walking with me.
In beauty it walks before me.
In beauty it walks behind me.
In beauty it walks below me.
In beauty it walks above me.
Beauty is on every side.
As I walk, I walk with beauty.

(traditional Navajo prayer)

Blessed be the LORD,
who has shown me wondrous love,
and been for me a city most secure.

(Psalm 31:22, an example of a *berakah*,
a traditional Hebrew blessing)

May thy light be fair to me!
May thy course be smooth to me!
If good to me is thy beginning,
Seven times better be thine end,
Thou fair moon of the seasons,
Thou great lamp of grace!
He Who created thee
Created me likewise;
He Who gave thee weight and light
Gave to me life and death,
And the joy of the seven satisfactions,
Thou great lamp of grace,
Thou fair moon of the seasons.

(ancient Celtic prayer)

"What seem our worst prayers may really be, in God's eyes, our best. . . . God sometimes seems to speak to us most intimately when he catches us, as it were, off our guard," said C.S. Lewis (1898–1953), author of *The Chronicles of Narnia*.

BELIEVING...

The risen Christ is always present.

Jesus' first disciples experienced the presence of God's love because they could actually *see* Jesus. He was part of their lives. Even after he died and rose from the dead, Jesus appeared to his disciples and promised them, "I am with you always, until the end of the age" (Matthew 28:20). This promise to the disciples assured them that God would always be with them and that, through the Holy Spirit, Jesus' presence would continue in their lives.

As Jesus' disciples and members of the Church, we too have received this same promise. The risen Christ is always present with us. And we experience his presence in a special way in the seven sacraments. These seven sacraments are: Baptism, Confirmation, Eucharist, Penance and Reconciliation, the Anointing of the Sick, Holy Orders, and Matrimony.

In the New Testament writings, we find symbolic actions, or *rituals,* that the Church gradually recognized as powerful signs of the risen Christ made present in the community through the power of the Holy Spirit.

Christ Appearing to the Apostles by Duccio di Buoninsegna (1260–1319)

These signs became the foundation of the seven sacraments instituted by Christ. We find these signs and the effects they have in each of the sacraments of the Church:

- the pouring of water in Baptism brings about our new life in Christ through the Holy Spirit

- the laying on of hands and anointing with oil in Confirmation seals the baptized with the Gift of the Holy Spirit

- in the Eucharist the bread and the wine become the Body and Blood of Christ by the power of the Holy Spirit and through the words and actions of the priest. Jesus Christ becomes truly and fully present to us.

- the absolution by the priest, in Jesus' name, brings God's forgiveness of sin in Penance and Reconciliation

- the anointing with oil imparts strength, peace, and courage to those who are suffering or ill in the Anointing of the Sick

- the laying on of hands and anointing with oil confers on those receiving Holy Orders the authority to serve the Church in Jesus' name

- the vows exchanged by the couple in Matrimony make them gifts to each other and to the Church and unite them as one in Christ.

Each sacrament is celebrated by the whole Church. The celebrant and the other members of the Church who participate in the celebration of each sacrament represent the whole Church. Through the sacraments, by the power of the Holy Spirit, the Church continues Jesus' ministry of welcoming, healing, forgiving, feeding, and serving others.

Activity Look back at the signs and effects of the sacraments. Choose one sacrament and brainstorm with your group how its effects might be seen in a person's daily life.

238

In the sacraments the risen Christ shares God's life with the Church.

Belief in the seven sacraments, through which the risen Christ shares God's life with the Church, is unique to us as Catholics. Each **sacrament** is an effective sign given to us by Jesus Christ through which we share in God's life. The gift of sharing in God's life that we receive in the sacraments is sanctifying grace. It is especially through the seven sacraments that grace is given to us and that we are able to respond to the presence of God in our lives.

Yet God's relationship with us is a covenant. So, though God's grace prepares us to receive the sacraments, we must also respond to God's grace. To respond to God's grace we must have the proper *disposition,* or resolve, to accept the grace of each of the sacraments that we receive. God's grace, through the power of the Holy Spirit, then enables us to live what we have celebrated in the sacraments.

As the *Catechism* explains, the sacraments "bear fruit in those who receive them with the required dispositions" (1131). Bearing fruit as disciples of Christ, both as individuals and as the Church, requires reflection on the ways we live out our sacramental commitments. Each day we can ask ourselves:

• Does my daily life give evidence of my Catholic identity?

• Do I receive the Eucharist frequently and find in it the nourishment to serve others?

• Do I continually turn to God and away from sin, and embrace Jesus' mission of reconciliation?

• Do I attend to the inspiration of the Holy Spirit in my daily life and recognize the Spirit's presence in others?

> The sacraments "bear fruit in those who receive them with the required dispositions"
> (CCC, 1131).

Through the grace of the sacraments we also receive the strength to encourage others to live out their sacramental commitments. We can pray for all of our brothers and sisters—those in the laity, in the consecrated life, and in the ordained ministry—that they may be strengthened to live out their commitments. We can express our gratitude and support to all those who serve their families, their communities, and the Church. We can reach out to those who are ill and suffering to comfort them.

The sacraments enable us to live out the life that Jesus calls us to live. As members of the Church, we can help one another to live as sacramental people.

Faith Word
sacrament

Activity What are some practical ways that you can live out the sacraments? Role-play your responses with your group.

The seven sacraments

Sacraments of Christian Initiation—Our initiation into the Church takes places through three sacraments:

• **Baptism** is the sacrament in which we are freed from original and personal sin, become children of God, and are welcomed into the Church.

• **Confirmation** is the sacrament in which we are sealed with the Gift of the Holy Spirit.

• **The Eucharist** is the sacrament of the Body and Blood of Christ in which Jesus is truly present under the appearances of bread and wine.

Sacraments of Healing—Two sacraments are known as Sacraments of Healing:

• **Penance and Reconciliation** is the sacrament by which our relationship with God and the Church is restored and our sins are forgiven.

• **The Anointing of the Sick** is the sacrament by which God's grace and comfort are given to those who are suffering because of their old age or because of serious illnesses.

Sacraments at the Service of Communion—Church members who receive these sacraments are strengthened to serve God and the Church through one of two particular vocations:

• **Holy Orders** is the sacrament in which baptized men are ordained to serve the Church as deacons, priests, and bishops.

• **Matrimony** is the sacrament in which a baptized man and woman promise to be faithful to each other for the rest of their lives and serve their family and the Church.

Reflect on some ways that the strength and grace received through the sacraments can help support you in your relationship with God.

Prayer and the liturgy nourish our relationship with God.

How do we keep in touch with those we love?

Prayer is our covenant relationship with God in Christ through the Holy Spirit; prayer nourishes our union with Christ and with the Church. And each day God—Father, Son, and Holy Spirit—calls us to deepen our relationship with the Blessed Trinity through prayer, whether private or public. The official public prayer of the Church is the liturgy—which includes the celebration of the Eucharist and the other sacraments, as well as the Liturgy of the Hours.

Prayer is the raising of our minds and hearts to God. It is like a conversation: God calls to us in prayer, and we respond to his constant love for us. We listen and put our trust in God. We share our thoughts, dreams, and needs with him. We tell him what is happening in our lives and we know that he is listening. We can pray in the silence of our hearts, or we can pray aloud. We can pray alone or with others. We can even sing our prayer. Sometimes we do not use words to pray, but sit quietly, trying to focus only on God. But however we pray, we turn to God with hope and faith in his love for us. We rely on him for guidance and direction. We ask him to help us to follow his will. And we trust that he will help us to know his will for us. As members of the Church, we live "in a vital and personal relationship with the living and true God. This relationship is prayer" (*CCC*, 2558). Through prayer, both public and private, we can draw everything in our lives into Christ's love.

Faith Word

prayer

Jesus taught us to pray with patience and with complete trust in God. He taught us to pray by showing us how he prayed. Jesus prayed in many circumstances and in many ways. Jesus praised God and thanked him for his blessings. Jesus asked God to be with him and to act on his behalf. Jesus prayed for the needs of others. Jesus forgave sinners in the name of his Father. Even as he was dying, Jesus prayed, "Father, forgive them, they know not what they do" (Luke 23:34).

From the example and words of Jesus, and most especially from the Lord's Prayer, we learn to pray. Whenever we pray, we show God our love—through our thoughts, our words, our actions, and even our feelings and senses.

Urged by the Holy Spirit, we pray these five basic forms of prayer:

Blessing

"The LORD bless you and keep you! The LORD let his face shine upon you." (Numbers 6:24–25)

To *bless* is to dedicate someone or something to God or to make something holy in God's name. God continually blesses us with many gifts. Because God first blessed us, we too can pray for his blessings on people and things.

Petition

"My Father, if it is possible, let this cup pass from me; yet, not as I will, but as you will." (Matthew 26:39)

Prayers of *petition* are prayers in which we ask something of God. Asking for forgiveness is the most important type of petition.

Intercession

"I pray not only for them, but also for those who will believe in me through their word, so that they may all be one." (John 17:20–21)

Intercession is a type of petition. When we pray a prayer of *intercession*, we are asking for something on behalf of another person or a group of people.

Thanksgiving

"I thank you for you answered me; you have been my savior." (Psalm 118:21)

Prayers of *thanksgiving* show our gratitude to God for all he has given us. We especially give thanks for the life, death, and Resurrection of Jesus. We do this when we pray the greatest prayer of the Church, the Eucharist.

Praise

"I give praise to you, Father, Lord of heaven and earth." (Matthew 11:25)

Prayers of *praise* give glory to God for being God. Prayers of praise do not involve our needs or our gratitude. We praise God simply because he is God.

Activity With your group, compose prayers in each of these five forms of prayer.

The Church witnesses to Christ by praying at all times.

The Church is continually at prayer. Every day at every moment, the liturgy is being celebrated. Somewhere Church members are celebrating the Eucharist—often called "the *Holy and Divine Liturgy*, because the Church's whole liturgy finds its center and most intense expression in the celebration of this sacrament" (*CCC*, 1330). And Jesus, present in the Eucharist, is continually being praised by members of the Church praying before the Most Blessed Sacrament reserved in the tabernacle. This prayer is called Eucharistic adoration.

> We live "in a vital and personal relationship with the living and true God. This relationship is prayer"
> (*CCC*, 2558).

Millions of Catholics all over the world also gather daily for other forms of community prayer. Most important among these forms of community prayer is the Liturgy of the Hours. This liturgical prayer of the Church is most often prayed in monasteries, but many parishes gather for Morning Prayer, Midday Prayer, or Evening Prayer. Priests, religious, and laypeople gather for this prayer or pray parts of it privately—although the Liturgy of the Hours is never purely "private prayer." It is the prayer of the entire Church, even when prayed by one person.

There are also other prayers, which are forms of piety and popular devotion which members of the Church pray together. These forms of piety and popular devotion extend the liturgy of the Church. They express ways that people of many different cultures may pray and are a rich and diverse heritage that has been handed down to us through the centuries.

As individuals and as Church, we usually express our prayer through vocal prayer, meditation, or contemplative prayer. In vocal prayer we pray aloud, often with others. The prayers we pray at Mass and during the Liturgy of the Hours are vocal prayer, as is the rosary. Our vocal prayer can lead to meditation and contemplation. In meditation we can pray certain words or verses, often from Scripture, over and over until they become part of us, and our thoughts become a prayer. Or, we can use the passage as a "mirror" in which we can "see" into our own situation. The passage can help us to find God's way amid the choices we face each day. Meditation can also lead to contemplation which is wordless prayer. Contemplation is an awareness of God's presence that can last half a minute, half an hour, half a day, or a whole lifetime. It is a gift from God that can come to anyone who seeks God and is open to God's love.

No matter when we pray or what expression of prayer we use, whether we pray privately or through the liturgy, through prayer we can witness to Christ.

Activity Practice meditation now by reading your favorite Scripture passage and reflecting on certain words or verses within it or the ways that it relates to your own life.

Witnesses in prayer

Guided by the Holy Spirit, the Church prays in many different ways. The very first "school of prayer" is one's family. At home, through the example of parents and grandparents, we can learn to pray, perhaps praying the rosary, mealtime blessings, or bedtime prayers.

As we grow, we may find ourselves drawn to other schools of prayer, or *spiritualities*, that exist in the Church.

Spiritualities refer to certain ways of praying and nurturing one's relationship with God that, most often, were handed down to us by great saints in the Church—men and women who were true witnesses to Christ. For example, Saint Benedict handed down his Benedictine spirituality of "prayer and work." Saint Teresa of Ávila handed down her spirituality of meditation and contemplation. Saint Francis of Assisi left us with his Franciscan spirituality of living the Gospels through poverty and care for creation. And Saint Ignatius of Loyola passed along his Ignatian spirituality of "finding God in all things." The various spiritualities found in the Church enrich her liturgies and her life of prayer.

In your own life, who are some witnesses in prayer?

Recognizing Our Faith

Recall the question at the beginning of this chapter: *How do I nurture my relationships?* Complete the first column below by listing some of the responses that you had to the question when you began this chapter. Then, in the second column, list some ways of nurturing your relationship with God.

MY RELATIONSHIPS WITH OTHERS	MY RELATIONSHIP WITH GOD

Living Our Faith

Reflect on the ways you can live out your sacramental commitment by spending some time reflecting on the questions listed on page 239.

Blessed Teresa of Calcutta

"Everything starts from prayer," said Blessed Teresa of Calcutta. As a child growing up in Yugoslavia, she was interested in stories about missionary life and service to God. At the age of eighteen she began to think about serving God as a nun. She entered the Sisters of Loreto, a teaching order based in Ireland and known for its missionary work. After taking her vows, she took the name "Teresa" and began to serve in Calcutta, India, as a teacher. After many years of teaching, through prayer and reflection she recognized a call to serve the poorest among the poor on the streets of Calcutta. She left her order and founded the Missionaries of Charity in Calcutta in 1950. Through this order she worked to bring hope and dignity to those who were sick and dying, to educate those who were poor, and to share Christ's love with those who were neglected.

Prayer was a source of support and strength for Teresa. She died in 1997. She was beatified by Pope John Paul II on October 19, 2003.

Pray for the help to deepen your relationship with God through service to others.

@ For additional ideas and activities, visit www.weliveourfaith.com.

Putting Faith to Work

Talk about what you have learned in this chapter:

 We understand the various ways Christ is present with us, the Church.

 We nurture our relationship with Christ in our own lives in every way possible.

 We witness to our relationship with Christ.

Decide on ways to live out what you have learned.

✞ ENCOUNTERING GOD'S WORD

❝But when the Son of Man comes, will he find faith on earth?❞
(Luke 18:8)

➡ **READ** the quotation from Scripture.

➡ **REFLECT** on the following:
Jesus asks this question at the end of the Parable of the Persistent Widow—a parable about "praying always." You may want to read it in Luke 18:1–8. Then consider your answer to Jesus' question.

➡ **SHARE** your reflections with a partner.

➡ **DECIDE** on ways you can show that you have faith in God.

Write *True* or *False* next to the following sentences. On a separate sheet of paper, change the false statements to make them true.

1. _____ Through the grace of the sacraments we also receive the strength to encourage others to live out their sacramental commitments.

2. _____ The Church is continually at prayer.

3. _____ The Liturgy of the Hours is an important private prayer.

4. _____ The basic forms of prayer are blessing, petition, intercession, confession, and praise.

Complete the following.

5. A _____ is an effective sign given to us by Jesus Christ through which we share in God's life.

6. It is especially through the seven sacraments that _____ is given to us and that we are able to respond to the presence of God in our lives.

7. _____ is the raising of our minds and hearts to God.

8. The _____ is the official public prayer of the Church.

9–10. **ESSAY:** How is prayer a way to witness to our relationship with Christ? Use the terms *vocal prayer, meditation,* and *contemplative prayer* in your response.

Sharing Faith with Your Family

Discuss the following with your family:

- The risen Christ is always present.
- In the sacraments the risen Christ shares God's life with the Church.
- Prayer and the liturgy nourish our relationship with God.
- The Church witnesses to Christ by praying at all times.

With your family write a prayer that you can pray together at mealtimes or at other times when you are gathered together.

The Worship Connection

Listen closely to the prayers at Mass to identify among them the five basic forms of prayer: blessing, petition, intercession, thanksgiving, and praise.

More to Explore

Search through this book, a Catholic prayer book, the Internet, or other resources to find a prayer that has special meaning for you, and make it part of your daily prayers.

Catholic Social Teaching ☑Checklist

Theme of Catholic Social Teaching:
Care for God's Creation

How it relates to Chapter 22: This chapter listed the signs of the sacraments which include bread, wine, water, and oil. These are gifts of God's creation. As Catholics we are called to nurture, protect, and respect all of God's creation.

How can you do this?

☐ At home:
_____

☐ At school/work:
_____

☐ In the parish:
_____

☐ In the community:
_____

Check off each action after it has been completed.

23

Growing in Faith Together

> "And he gave some as apostles, others as prophets, others as evangelists, others as pastors and teachers, to equip the holy ones for the work of ministry, for building up the body of Christ."
>
> (Ephesians 4:11–12)

✝ Leader: Let us listen to a message from Saint Paul to the early Christian community at Ephesus, recognizing that his words are also meant for us and for all parish communities in the Church today.

Reader 1: A reading from the letter of Saint Paul to the Ephesians, and also to the parish(es) of (name parish or parishes to which you belong)

"I . . . urge you to live in a manner worthy of the call you have received, with all humility and gentleness, with patience, bearing with one another through love, striving to preserve the unity of the spirit through the bond of peace: one body and one Spirit, as you were also called to the one hope of your call; one Lord, one faith, one baptism; one God and Father of all, who is over all and through all and in all." (Ephesians 4:1–6)

The word of the Lord.

All: Thanks be to God.

Reader 2: For our parish(es) and for members of every parish and diocese in the Church, that we may live in a manner worthy of our call from Christ, we pray to the Lord.

All: Lord, hear our prayer.

Reader 3: For (name your diocese or archdiocese), that under the leadership of (name your bishop or archbishop), we may live with humility, gentleness, and patience, bearing with one another through love, we pray to the Lord.

All: Lord, hear our prayer.

Reader 4: For the Church in the United States, that we may strive to preserve our unity in the Holy Spirit and strengthen our bond of peace, we pray to the Lord.

All: Lord, hear our prayer.

Reader 5: For the Church throughout the world, that our unity may continue to grow, in one Body, one Spirit, one Lord, one faith, one Baptism, and with one God and Father of us all, we pray to the Lord.

All: Lord, hear our prayer. Amen.

@ **Visit www.weliveourfaith.com to find appropriate music and songs.**

The BiG QuEStion:

Where am I going in life?

D **iscover** some things you can do to give your life direction. First think about the person you hope to be at age twenty-five. Then complete the following contract with yourself, pledging to do things that might help you to become that person. Include things that you consider important to accomplish—for example, goals relating to education, a family, a career, athletics, health and well-being, and so on. Then sign and date your contract.

My Contract

I pledge to:

_____

_____

_____

_____

_____

_____

signature _____ date _____

Results:

If completing this contract was: **you:**

easy   have thought a lot about your goals. Keep working toward them.

somewhat challenging   have given some thought to your goals. Start reflecting even more about your hopes for your future and how you can fulfill them.

difficult   may not have given your direction in life much thought. You don't need to have it all figured out yet. You can, however, start thinking about your future and some goals you want to reach.

With your group discuss where the contributions and help of other people aid you in accomplishing your goals for the future.

In this chapter we learn that all authority and ministry in the Church comes from Christ and that the Church shares a common vocation of holiness and evangelization. Through this chapter, we hope

 to identify the various levels of authority and ministry in the Church

 to grow in faith together with all members of the Church, using our gifts and talents to fulfill our own particular vocation

 to respond to Christ by sharing his love and care with others each day.

Two roads diverged in a yellow wood,
  And sorry I could not travel both
  And be one traveler, long I stood
And looked down one as far as I could
To where it bent in the undergrowth;

Then took the other, as just as fair,
And having perhaps the better claim,
Because it was grassy and wanted wear;
Though as for that the passing there
Had worn them really about the same,

And both that morning equally lay
In leaves no step had trodden black.
Oh, I kept the first for another day!
Yet knowing how way leads on to way,
I doubted if I should ever come back.

I shall be telling this with a sigh
Somewhere ages and ages hence:
Two roads diverged in a wood, and I—
I took the one less traveled by,
And that has made all the difference.

("The Road Not Taken," Robert Frost (1874–1963))

Activity Reread the poem silently. Reflect on these questions. You may wish to share your reflections with a partner.

1. What are some possible meanings of this poem for you personally?

2. How does this poem relate to where you might go in life?

3. Can you relate the meaning of this poem to the role that other people can play in the direction your life is headed? If so, how? If not, why not?

"You have brains in your head. You have feet in your shoes. You can steer yourself in any direction you choose," wrote Theodor Geisel (1904–1991), better known as Doctor Seuss, in his book *Oh, the Places You'll Go!*

What is a parish?

A parish is a community of believers, usually made up of Catholics from the same town or region. Every parish is part of a diocese, a local area of the Church that is led by a bishop. A pastor is the priest who leads the parish in worship, prayer, and teaching. His most important work is to lead the parish in the celebration of the Eucharist. Other priests may work with the pastor and lead the parish in the celebration of the sacraments and in parish activities. A deacon, who has received the Sacrament of Holy Orders but is not a priest, may also serve the parish through works of charity and by preaching, baptizing, and assisting the priests. Some parishes may have a pastoral administrator, who can lead the parish when there is no resident pastor. However, only priests are the celebrants of the Mass and responsible for the other sacraments at the parish.

How do the members of your parish work together to meet the needs of the parish and all within it?

CATHOLIC IDENTITY

247

BELIEVING...

Jesus chose the Apostles to lead the Church.

Jesus Christ is the source of all authority and ministry in the Church. And Jesus shared his mission and authority with his Apostles. He sent them out after instructing them for their mission, saying, "As you go, make this proclamation: 'The kingdom of heaven is at hand.' Cure the sick, raise the dead, cleanse lepers, drive out demons" (Matthew 10:7–8). The Apostles were sent to bring peace to all those to whom they ministered, to speak as the Holy Spirit guided them to speak (see Matthew 10:20), to endure any hatred or persecution caused by their faith in Jesus Christ, and to courageously proclaim the coming of God's Kingdom. Jesus told them, "Whoever receives you receives me, and whoever receives me receives the one who sent me" (Matthew 10:40). Thus, the roots of Church leadership extend back to Jesus and the Apostles.

In Jesus' life and ministry the Apostles recognized that God's Kingdom was present. One day Simon Peter, speaking out for all of his fellow Apostles, said to Jesus, "You are the Messiah, the Son of the living God" (Matthew 16:16). After this great expression of faith, which was revealed to Simon Peter by the Father, Jesus said, "You are Peter, and upon this rock I will build my church, and the gates of the netherworld shall not prevail against it. I will give you the keys to the kingdom of heaven" (Matthew 16:18–19). In giving Peter "the keys," Jesus was giving him a place of authority in the Church. As the *Catechism* states, "Because of the faith he confessed Peter will remain the unshakeable rock of the Church. His mission will be to keep this faith from every lapse and to strengthen his brothers in it" (552).

Christ's mission was shared by Peter and by all of the Apostles. They received their mission together, were united to one another, forming a single, permanent assembly that is known today as the college of bishops. They were led by Peter, whose ministry continues today through the pope, the supreme head of the Church in Rome. Together the Apostles were the foundation of the Church—with Jesus Christ as the cornerstone. They would work together, as would their successors, to teach, govern, and sanctify people in Jesus' name.

Through the Apostles, God's will would continue to be accomplished: Believers in Jesus Christ would gather around him as the Church to share in the divine life of God—Father, Son, and Holy Spirit.

Activity Peter's mission was to "keep the faith" and to strengthen others in it. Make a list of the ways that others help you to keep your faith in a world where this is sometimes difficult. Which of these can you use to help others in keeping their faith?

The pope and the bishops are the successors of the Apostles.

After the Ascension of Jesus and the coming of the Holy Spirit, the Apostles courageously followed God's plan for salvation. As leaders of the whole Church, they traveled to every part of the world they knew of and established local Church communities. Once a local Church became established, the Apostles moved on. But they first selected local Church officers, or presbyters, whom they had ordained by the laying on of hands. Assisted by deacons, these local Church officers presided under the authority of the Apostles. Then, to ensure that the mission entrusted to them would continue after their death, the Apostles consecrated those who would succeed them in their ministry.

Eventually, the threefold ministry of bishop, presbyter (priest), and deacon was established throughout the Church. The title of bishop was reserved for the successors of the Apostles, the title of presbyter was used for the other local officers, and the title of deacon was kept for those who assisted the bishops and presbyters. Even today, through the laying on of hands by a bishop in the Sacrament of Holy Orders, we have the same threefold ministry. Bishops and priests exercise their degree, or order, of priestly participation, and deacons exercise their degree, or order, of service.

Bishops, the successors of the Apostles, teach, govern, and sanctify the members of the Church in the name of Christ. And they entrust this mission to those who succeed them as ordained bishops. They are the chief teachers of the Church and are charged with the sacred duty of handing on the complete and authentic teaching of Jesus Christ and the Church. Guided by the Holy Spirit, they are to transmit and make clear what has been revealed to us by God; they are entrusted by God to safeguard the **deposit of faith**, all the truth contained in Scripture and Tradition that Christ revealed and entrusted to the Apostles and thus to their successors, the bishops, and to the entire Church. This

> Jesus told his Apostles,
> **"Whoever receives you receives me"**
> (Matthew 10:40).

work of the bishops is done as a service to the other members of the Church so that our faith rests on a strong and secure foundation.

The bishops are the chief authorities and pastors, or shepherds, in the Church. In each diocese the bishop directs the life of the Church. He is the visible sign of the Church's unity. He coordinates her work, helps her to stay focused on her true mission of building God's Kingdom, and brings people of different backgrounds together in harmony. Like Christ the Good Shepherd, the bishops are to watch over all those under their care, especially those who are weak and oppressed or poor and in need. The bishop of Rome—the pope—is the successor of the Apostle Peter and has the special responsibility of caring for the whole Church. With the pope as their head on earth, the bishops are called to lead and guide the Church.

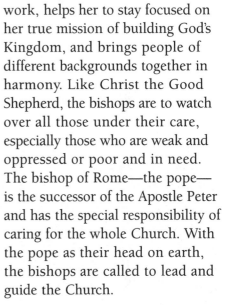

Bishop Dale J. Melczek of Gary, Indiana helps volunteers break ground for a Habitat for Humanity house.

A bishop receives the fullness of the Sacrament of Holy Orders. "The bishops . . . exercise their own authority for the good of their own faithful, and indeed of the whole Church" (*Dogmatic Constitution on the Church*, 22). A bishop is the chief priest of the presbyters, whom he ordains and who are his co-workers. With them he sanctifies the Church through prayer and work, and through ministry of both the word and the sacraments—especially the Sacrament of the Eucharist, which, in every parish and diocese, is "the center of the life of the particular Church" (*CCC*, 893).

> **Faith Word**
>
> deposit of faith

Activity With your group compose and pray a short prayer for our bishops, priests, and deacons.

BELIEVING...

Within the Church there are many ways of serving.

How can we serve in the Church?

As the People of God, the Church is a union of people under the guidance of the Holy Spirit and the direction of her leaders. As the Body of Christ worshiping together, the Church is more than an ordinary group of people; she is a people intimately united with Christ and with one another. We can say that the Church combines what is human and divine, what is earthly and heavenly, and what is found in time and in eternity.

All members of the Church share in the priesthood of the faithful and have a **common vocation**, our call from God to holiness and to evangelization. Yet, as the *Catechism* explains, "The ministerial or hierarchical priesthood of bishops and priests, and the common priesthood of all the faithful participate, 'each in its own proper way, in the one priesthood of Christ'" (1547). Thus, each member of the Church has unique gifts and talents and is called by God to fulfill a unique role in the Church—living out his or her common vocation through a particular vocation.

> ### Faith Word
> common vocation

We live out our common vocation in a particular way:

Laity: The laity are also called laypeople or the Christian faithful. They are the baptized members of the Church who share in the mission to bring the good news of Christ to the world. All Catholics begin their lives as members of the laity. Most remain members of the laity for their entire lives, following God's call either in the single life or in marriage.

Consecrated life: Some laity and some ordained ministers also live the consecrated life. They are men and women who profess, or promise God, that they will practice poverty, chastity through celibacy, and obedience to the Church and to their religious communities. Poverty, chastity, and obedience are called the evangelical counsels.

Ordained ministry: Some baptized Catholic men respond to God's call through this particular vocation. Through the Sacrament of Holy Orders, they are consecrated to the ministerial priesthood as priests and bishops or to service in the Church as permanent deacons.

Together, the laity, ordained ministers, and those in the consecrated life make up the Church and have a part in her mission. No one group is more important or special than another. Each works to proclaim the risen Christ and is able to do so in ways that others cannot. Each is also able to do for people what others cannot. Together they complete one another—united in Christ for the common good of everyone they meet. As Saint Paul wrote, "There are different forms of service but the same Lord" (1 Corinthians 12:5).

Activity Where do you think your call to holiness and evangelization will lead you? What particular vocation do you think you will live? Hold a "vocation day" to explore these questions together.

PEOPLE AT WORK
The value of work

Every member of the Church is important, as is the daily work that each member does. When we use the gifts and talents that God has given us, the work we do can honor God, our creator.

Work is not always easy, of course. But when we consider the example of Jesus, whose work among the people brought about the salvation of humanity, we can realize that work builds upon our human dignity and enables us to contribute to the world in a spirit of loving service. As disciples of Christ, our work contributes to the salvation of the world.

On the other hand, we must always remember that "work is for man, not man for work" (CCC, 2428). Once in a while, people may need to consider whether work is overwhelming their lives and placing unfair demands on their relationships.

How does the work you do now contribute to the world? What can you do to enhance that contribution?

<blockquote>
"There are different forms of service but the same Lord."

(1 Corinthians 12:5)
</blockquote>

apostolic succession, that is, the pope and other bishops, together with priests and deacons.

This is the Church that we experience in our local parishes and dioceses. This is the Church that we experience when we gather as an assembly around the Lord's table to celebrate the Eucharist. This is the Church that receives from Christ our Savior "the fullness of the means of salvation" (*Decree on Ecumenism*, 3). Together we are the members of the Body of Christ answering Jesus' call to discipleship as members of his Church.

Within our parishes we continue Jesus' mission.

The Catholic Church is the family of God and our family. We enter this family through the Sacrament of Baptism, becoming children of God. And in our parishes, our local faith communities, we live out our membership in the family of God. As members of the Church, like the members of any family, we are all different. Yet we share a common life through the Sacraments of Christian Initiation—as well as the other sacraments celebrated in our parishes. Within our parishes we are a community of believers:

- professing belief in Jesus Christ, the Son of God and risen Lord

- publicly affirming our belief in Christ through Baptism

- celebrating our faith through the Eucharist and other sacraments

- accepting the teachings of Christ that have come down from the time of the Apostles

- living the sacramental life and mission of the Church, under the leadership of those ordained in

Together all the members of the Church continue Jesus' mission of sharing God's life with all people. Here are just a few of the roles through which ordained ministers, lay ecclesial ministers, or the laity can do this within their parishes:

pastor, parish priest, director of religious education (or parish catechetical leader), Catholic school principal, deacon, religious sister and brother, pastoral administrator, extraordinary minister of Holy Communion, catechist, lector, teacher, altar server, director of music, usher, and member of parish organizations.

As Christ's disciples, each of us is called to bring the message of Christ everywhere. Each of us is called to live as Christ asked us to and to show forth his presence. And it is in our parish community that we, as Jesus' disciples, first come to experience Christ and the Church in our liturgy and worship. In our parishes our faith in God—Father, Son, and Holy Spirit—is guided and strengthened by the one, holy, catholic, and apostolic Church.

Activity Work together on, and then perform, a role-play that demonstrates the ways that, as disciples of Jesus, you might proclaim Christ's message.

RESPONDING...

Recognizing Our Faith

Recall the question at the beginning of this chapter: *Where am I going in life*? How have your thoughts on this question changed since beginning this chapter? In what ways can your personal goals for your life be connected to service in the Church?

Living Our Faith

Decide on one thing you can do today to be of service to your parish.

Saint Charles Lwanga

Charles Lwanga was born in the country of Uganda, in Africa, in 1865. He was athletic, strong, and compassionate. And he took his call to holiness and evangelization seriously, devoting his life to serving others and continuing Jesus' mission.

Partners in FAITH

Serving in the household of a ruthless tribal king, Charles witnessed abuse and brutality. But Charles, a leader among the workers in the royal household, protected others from abuse. He also was a catechist who taught about God's love and forgiveness. Evangelization was not popular with the king, however. He condemned prayer and the Catholic faith. Charles became a target of the king's wrath and was ordered to renounce his Catholic faith. Because Charles would not, he was sentenced to death. In 1887 Charles and twenty-one others serving in the royal household became martyrs for their faith. Charles was canonized in 1964 by Pope Paul VI. He is known as the patron saint of young African men. The Church remembers him and his fellow martyrs on June 3.

Think of one way to show that you take your call to holiness and evangelization seriously.

Talk about what you have learned in this chapter:

 We identify the various levels of authority and ministry in the Church.

 We grow in faith together with all members of the Church, using our gifts and talents to fulfill our own particular vocation.

 We respond to Christ by sharing his love and care with others each day.

Decide on ways to live out what you have learned.

✝ ENCOUNTERING GOD'S WORD

" Go, therefore, and make disciples of all nations, . . . teaching them to observe all that I have commanded you. And behold, I am with you always, until the end of the age."
(Matthew 28:19–20)

➡ **READ** the quotation from Scripture.

➡ **REFLECT** on the following:
"Making disciples of all nations" might sound like a daunting task. What are one or two practical things that you can do among your friends that might have the effect of leading them into discipleship to Christ?

➡ **SHARE** your reflections with a partner.

➡ **DECIDE** to do one of the practical things that you have thought of this week.

Complete the following.

1. Each member of the Church can live out his or her common vocation through one of these particular

   vocations: _____, _____, or _____.

2. The evangelical counsels are _____.

3. _____, the bishop of Rome, is the successor of Apostle Peter and has the special responsibility of caring for the whole Church.

4. The deposit of faith is all the truth contained in Scripture and Tradition that Christ _____

   _____.

Short Answers

5. Describe the roles of bishops, priests, and deacons. _____
   _____

6. Who are those who live the consecrated life, and how do they follow God's call? _____
   _____

7. Who are the laity, and how do they follow God's call? _____
   _____

8. Describe and explain the ministry of the bishops of the Catholic Church. _____
   _____

9–10. ESSAY: How can Catholics live out their common call to holiness and evangelization?

Sharing Faith with Your Family

Discuss the following with your family:

- Jesus chose the Apostles to lead the Church.
- The pope and the bishops are the successors of the Apostles.
- Within the Church there are many ways of serving.
- Within our parishes we continue Jesus' mission.

Interview some family members about the goals they had for their lives when they were your age. Ask them to describe how their lives today reflect these goals. Then together discuss ways your family can meet the goal of living out your common call to holiness and evangelization.

The Worship Connection

One dismissal you might hear at the end of Mass is, "Go in peace to love and serve the Lord." The next time you hear this, think of one way you can serve the Lord by sharing peace and love that very day.

More to Explore

Visit your parish or diocesan Web site and look for a listing or description of the various service opportunities available. Find one in which you can become involved.

Catholic Social Teaching ☑ Checklist

Theme of Catholic Social Teaching:
Call to Family, Community, and Participation

How it relates to Chapter 23: We can live out our call to holiness and evangelization by participating in service efforts within our families and communities, working for peace and justice, and sharing our Christian faith through what we do.

How can you do this?

☐ At home:

_____

☐ At school/work:

_____

☐ In the parish:

_____

☐ In the community:

_____

Check off each action after it has been completed.

GATHERING...

"*Since we are surrounded by so great a cloud of witnesses, let us . . . persevere . . . while keeping our eyes fixed on Jesus.*"

(Hebrews 12:1–2)

✚ **Leader:** As we strive to live our faith, let us pray a litany of saints, asking for the help of Mary, the saints, and all great witnesses to Jesus in the Church.

Group 1:	**Group 2:**
Lord, have mercy.	Lord, have mercy.
Christ, have mercy.	Christ, have mercy.
Lord, have mercy.	Lord, have mercy.
Holy Mary, Mother of God,	pray for us.
Saint Michael,	pray for us.
Holy angels of God,	pray for us.
Saint Peter and Saint Paul,	pray for us.
Saint John,	pray for us.
Saint Stephen,	pray for us.
Saint Perpetua and Saint Felicity,	pray for us.
Saint Prisca,	pray for us.
Saint Gregory,	pray for us.
Saint Augustine,	pray for us.
Saint Basil,	pray for us.
Saint Benedict,	pray for us.
Saint Francis and Saint Dominic,	pray for us.
Saint Catherine,	pray for us.
Saint Teresa,	pray for us.
(Add other saints as desired.)	
All holy men and women,	pray for us.

All: God of our ancestors . . . .
We are surrounded by these witnesses . . . .
In their midst we make every prayer
through Christ who is our Lord for ever and ever.
Amen.

(adapted from *Catholic Household Blessings and Prayers*)

@ Visit www.weliveourfaith.com to find appropriate music and songs.

The BiG QuEstion:

In what ways do I live my Catholic faith?

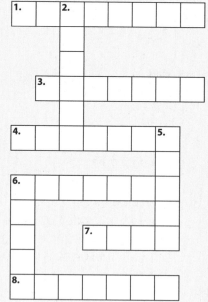

Discover some Catholics who truly lived their faith. The clues below describe some of the "Partners in Faith" you have studied this year. Use the clues to solve the crossword puzzle.

Across

1. "Everything starts with prayer" are the words of Blessed Teresa of _____.

3. To combat heresy and preach the Gospel, Saint _____ de Guzman founded the Order of Preachers.

4. Saint _____ of Assisi founded an order of mendicant friars called the Order of Friars Minor.

6. As Bishop of Milan, Saint _____ defended the truth of Christ's divinity against the Arian heresy.

7. Sister _____ Bowman shared God's message of love through song, story, poetry, and prayer.

8. Saint _____ Hurtado Cruchaga worked for the rights of workers, the homeless, and the poor in Chile.

Down

2. The Society of Jesus was founded by Saint Ignatius of _____, who also developed a method of prayer known as the Spiritual Exercises.

5. Saint Catherine of _____ used her wisdom to help others, including the pope, to make right decisions.

6. The daughter of a noble Spanish family, Saint Teresa of _____ was a brilliant spiritual writer.

Answers:

Across:
1. Calcutta
3. Dominic
4. Francis
6. Ambrose
7. Thea
8. Alberto
Down:
2. Loyola
5. Siena
6. Avila

Who was your favorite "Partner in Faith" discussed in this book? Make a list of clues about that person and have a partner guess who you are describing.

In this chapter
we learn that, as members of the Church, the Body of Christ, we belong to the communion of saints. Through this chapter, we hope

to understand that together we are called to become living examples of God's love

to await the day on which we will share in life everlasting with Mary and the entire communion of saints

to live our faith as the Pilgrim People of God, loving one another and giving witness to Jesus and our faith in him.

By completing this book you have hopefully learned much about what it means to live your faith as a member of the Church. You have read about the Church and her history, which has included times of great turmoil and times of incredible joy.

Each of us is a part of the Church's rich heritage. As disciples of Jesus, we are members of a community that has grown throughout the ages. We are closely connected to those in history who came before us. We are equally connected to those who will come after us.

Throughout this book you've been asked big questions. You've explored what you know and how you feel. You've met people whose courage and steadfastness have encouraged you in large or small ways. You have set goals for yourself and have been challenged to learn more about your faith and define who you are—a young Catholic with a rich heritage and a promising future.

Reflect on the heritage of the Church. How are *you* an important part of this rich heritage? of the Church's future?

Activity Think about who you are, especially in light of your belonging to the Church. How would you describe yourself to a younger person learning about ways to live his or her faith? Write this description below.

WHERE? am i going in life?

WHAT DO I DO TO TAKE CHARGE OF MY LIFE?

how do i respond in times of crisis?

How do I make decisions?

Does my VOICE? count

Do I welcome change or do I fear it?

What helps me to achieve my goals

"The foregoing generations beheld God and nature face to face; we, through their eyes," wrote Ralph Waldo Emerson (1803–1882), U.S. essayist, poet, and philosopher.

why do I need to follow laws?

Jesus Christ calls all of us into communion with his Father.

Jesus taught his disciples about many things. He taught them about God his Father and about his relationship to the Father and to them. He said, "I am the true vine, and my Father is the vine grower. . . . you are the branches. Whoever remains in me and I in him will bear much fruit" (John 15:1, 5). Jesus called his disciples to be joined to him—in union with him—as branches are joined to a vine. He wanted his disciples to share in the love and care of the Father, the vine grower. Jesus wanted his disciples to be in communion—in a deep relationship of love and unity—with God and with one another.

At the Last Supper Jesus prayed to his Father for his disciples, saying, "I pray not only for them, but also for those who will believe in me through their word, so that they may all be one, as you, Father, are in me and I in you" (John 17:20–21). Jesus' prayer was for all of his disciples through the ages—that they might be one, united in the faith that is passed on through the Apostles. Jesus asked his Father to bring all who would come to know him and believe in him into a deep relationship of love and unity with God and one another. Jesus asked that they would grow "in communion."

On the day now known as Pentecost, the Holy Spirit strengthened the faith and unity of Jesus' disciples. The Holy Spirit brought the world into "the time of the Church" (CCC, 732). Filled with the Holy Spirit, the disciples recognized the Eucharist as the reality of Christ's presence in the breaking of the bread. They understood that "all who eat the one broken bread, Christ, enter into communion with him and form but one body in him" (CCC, 1329). They shared a communion:

- in the faith
- of the sacraments
- of *charisms*, or special graces
- of possessions
- in charity.

As a community of disciples, the members of the early Church "devoted themselves to the teaching of the apostles and to the communal life, to the breaking of the bread and to the prayers. . . . And every day the Lord added to their number those who were being saved" (Acts of the Apostles 2:42, 47).

Activity What are some ways your life can show that you are part of a community of disciples who live in communion with God? As a group, role-play these ways.

Together all faithful members of the Church are joined in the communion of saints.

In Baptism we are saved—freed from sin—and born into the Church, the family of God. We are joined to Jesus Christ and filled with the Holy Spirit. We become part of the Body of Christ, the Church, and are united with all those who have been baptized in Christ. The Holy Spirit works in each of us, members of Christ's Body,

> **"All who eat the one broken bread, Christ, enter into communion with him and form but one body in him."**
> (CCC, 1329)

- preparing us through his grace to move toward Christ

- manifesting to us the meaning of Christ's death and Resurrection

- making present the mystery of Christ, especially in the Eucharist

- bringing us into communion with God, to reconcile us and ready us to live with him forever.

As disciples of Christ and faithful members of the Church, we, like the first disciples, are called to the mission of sharing the good news of Christ and spreading the Kingdom of God. We are called to live as the image of God in which we were created—giving witness to God's presence in the world. We are called to become living examples of God's love to everyone we meet. And to do this we need the help of other disciples. We need their example, their solidarity with us, their prayers on our behalf, and their encouragement to support us. We need the Church—the communion of all of those who have been baptized and who believe in and follow Jesus Christ.

As members of the Church, together we proclaim our beliefs. In the Apostles' Creed, after we state our belief in "the holy catholic Church," we acknowledge that we believe in "the communion of saints." The Church is the *communion of saints*. This communion is a union "in holy things," especially the Eucharist. It is also a communion "among holy persons," the faithful united in Christ.

The *Catechism* explains the communion of saints as "the communion of all the faithful of Christ, those who are pilgrims on earth, the dead who are attaining their purification, and the blessed in heaven, all together forming one Church" (*CCC*, 962, quoting *Credo of the People of God*, 30). All the members of the Church, from her very beginning until the present, are joined in the communion of saints, all praying for one another and helping one another to spread God's Kingdom here on earth while looking toward the fullness of the Kingdom in heaven.

Activity Reread this page and highlight the statements that you think are most important. Then prepare an announcement sharing this good news.

Popular devotions

Members of the Church can give worship to God and honor the saints through *popular devotions*. Although liturgical worship is our official way of praying, a popular devotion is a way of prayer that has grown up "among the people." Some examples of popular devotions, or "popular piety," are "the veneration of relics, visits to sanctuaries, pilgrimages, processions, the stations of the cross, religious dances, the rosary, medals, etc." (*CCC*, 1674). These devotions enrich, but may not replace, the Mass and the liturgical life of the Church. Popular devotions may be encouraged and supported in parish and diocesan life, but bishops have a responsibility to ensure that popular devotions lead to a deeper living of the Gospel of Christ. And popular devotions should never encourage an attitude of superstition or "magical thinking" about the way God gives us his blessings.

What devotions are popular in your family, parish, or diocese?

CATHOLIC IDENTITY

Mary is our greatest saint and the perfect example of discipleship.

How can we help one another to grow in holiness?

From the beginning of the Church, some members of the communion of saints have been remembered in a special way. We honor martyrs, who died heroically for their faith in Jesus Christ, and all other saints who lived lives of holiness on earth and now share in the joy of eternal life with God. Because the saints are closely united to Christ, they pray for us constantly. They help the Church to grow in holiness. Their love for the Church is great. Other holy men and women were also friends and servants of God. The lives of all these people are examples for us.

Yet in this communion of saints, the Church, we consider the Blessed Virgin Mary to be our greatest example of holiness. Her role is inseparable from her union with Christ and flows directly from it. Mary is the mother of the Son of God, the second Person of the Blessed Trinity, Jesus Christ. She was in union with Christ from the very moment that he was conceived within her. And Mary's faithfulness to God, her openness to his loving and saving plan, and her love and care for Jesus throughout his life and throughout his suffering and death truly show that she was Jesus' first and most faithful disciple.

Dying on the cross, Jesus said to his disciple John, "Behold, your mother" (John 19:27). Through these words Jesus gave us—those who believe in and follow him—his mother Mary as our mother and the Mother of the Church. And even after Jesus' death and Resurrection, as the disciples waited in prayer and with hope for the coming of the Holy Spirit, Mary, their mother, waited with them.

Looking forward to the glory that we will someday share with God—the Father, Son, and Holy Spirit—we, members of the communion of saints, look to Mary for our example of faithful discipleship. Like Mary we are called to live in openness to God's loving and saving plan for us. And we await the day on which we will share in life everlasting with Mary and all the other holy men and women in the Church.

Activity Meditate on the phrase *Behold, your mother.* Think of Mary. Reflect on her as the Mother of God and our role model for discipleship. Ask Mary to bring your prayers and concerns to her son.

Our Lady by Laura James

Mysteries of Mary's life

The Immaculate Conception: From the moment of Mary's conception, God preserved her from all sin, even from original sin, which affects every other human being born into this world. God preserved Mary from sin because he had chosen her to be the mother of his only Son, Jesus Christ.

The Annunciation: Mary's vocation as the Mother of God did not mean that she had no responsibility for her choices. At the Annunciation, when the angel Gabriel announced to the Virgin Mary that she was to be the mother of God's Son, she chose to reply in faithfulness and trust, "Behold, I am the handmaid of the Lord. May it be done to me according to your word" (Luke 1:38).

The Assumption: At the end of her life on earth, God blessed Mary in an extraordinary way: He brought her, body and soul, to live forever with the risen Jesus. This event, known as the Assumption of Mary, is an important feast in the Church, and is a holy day of obligation in many countries. As the *Catechism* states, "The Assumption of the Blessed Virgin is a singular participation in her Son's Resurrection and an anticipation of the resurrection of other Christians" (966).

Pray the Hail Mary, asking Mary to pray to God that you too will be Jesus' faithful disciple.

We are the Pilgrim People of God.

As Jesus' disciples and members of the Church, we look to Mary as the mother of Jesus and as our Mother, knowing that, "in the bodily and spiritual glory which she possesses in heaven, the Mother of Jesus continues in this present world as the image and first flowering of the Church as she is to be perfected in the world to come" (*Dogmatic Constitution on the Church*, 68).

> **"We await the day on which we will share in life everlasting with Mary and all the other holy men and women in the Church."**

We are the Pilgrim People of God. We are on an earthly pilgrimage toward the fulfillment of God's Kingdom. On this journey we are joined with all those members of the Church before us who have lived their faith in Jesus Christ. We are filled with the Holy Spirit, who dwells in and is shown forth through the Church's Tradition, Scripture, Magisterium, liturgy, prayer, charisms and ministries, signs of apostolic and missionary life, and witness of the saints. Through the inspiration of the Holy Spirit we, with all those who have preceded us and will follow us, are the People of God, the Body of Christ, the communion of saints, the seed of God's Kingdom on earth. And our mission is to proclaim the good news of Christ and to evangelize the world.

As disciples of Christ and members of the Church we await the fulfillment of God's Kingdom—when Christ will come again in glory at the end of time. *We live our faith*, acting justly, focusing on loving God and one another, and giving witness to Jesus and to our faith in him!

Activity Work together to write a mission statement for the Pilgrim People of God who live their faith each day. How will you put it into action in your own life?

261

RESPONDING...

Recognizing Our Faith

Recall the question at the beginning of this chapter: *In what ways do I live my Catholic faith?* Write down several ways that you can live your faith. In what way has what you have learned in this course affected your response?

Living Our Faith

Decide on one topic or saint from this book that you would want to learn more about or explore on your own.

The Seven Martyrs of Thailand

Partners in FAITH

In 1940 Thailand was at war with its neighboring countries. Foreign missionaries were banned from the country. Catholics living in Thailand were ordered to adopt Buddhism, the religion practiced by the Thai ruler. But many Catholics refused to give up their faith. Seven of these Catholics especially stand out. Among them was Philip Sipong, a father and catechist. He refused to stop teaching about Jesus and so was shot by police. The police then rounded up six other people, including two religious sisters and ordered them to give up their faith. But they also refused. On December 26, 1940, they were marched to the village cemetery and shot to death. The youngest of these martyrs was fourteen!

In 1989 Pope John Paul II beatified the seven martyrs of Thailand: Philip Sipong, Sister Agnes Phila, Sister Lucia Khambang, Agatha Phutta, Cecilia Butsi, Bibiana Khampai, and Maria Phon. Today a church stands at the place of their execution in Songkhon, Thailand.

What needs of the Church can we bring to these martyrs—these members of the communion of saints who pray to God on our behalf?

@ **For additional ideas and activities, visit www.weliveourfaith.com.**

Putting Faith to Work

Talk about what you have learned in this chapter:

 We understand that together we are called to become living examples of God's love.

 We await the day on which we will share in life everlasting with Mary and the entire communion of saints.

 We live our faith as the Pilgrim People of God, loving one another and giving witness to Jesus and our faith in him.

Decide on ways to live out what you have learned.

✝ ENCOUNTERING GOD'S WORD

Jesus said of his disciples,

❝ Here are my mother and my brothers. For whoever does the will of my heavenly Father is my brother, and sister, and mother ❞ (Matthew 12:49–50).

➡ **READ** the quotation from Scripture.

➡ **REFLECT** on the following:
Doing the will of God the Father makes us part of Jesus' family. How do you do the will of God? How can you show that Jesus is your brother and Mary is your mother?

➡ **SHARE** your reflections with a partner.

➡ **DECIDE** to ask Jesus and Mary for help in doing God's will.

Write *True* or *False* next to the following sentences. On a separate sheet of paper, change the false sentences to make them true.

1. _____ Jesus called his disciples to be joined to him as branches are joined to a vine.

2. _____ As disciples of Christ and faithful members of the Church, we are called to live as the image of God, giving witness to God's presence in the world.

3. _____ In the Lord's Prayer, after we state our belief in "the holy catholic Church," we acknowledge that we believe in "the communion of saints."

4. _____ Dying on the cross, Jesus said to his disciple Peter, "Behold, your mother," and so gave Mary to us as our mother and the Mother of the Church.

Underline the correct answer.

5. **(Charisms/Martyrs/Ministries)** died heroically for their faith in Christ.

6. On the day known as Pentecost, the **(Lord's Prayer/Holy Spirit/Magisterium)** strengthened the faith and unity of Jesus' disciples.

7. **(The Magisterium/The Apostles/The communion of saints)** includes all the members of the Church from its beginning until the present.

8. **(The Blessed Virgin Mary/Saint John/Saint Peter)** is Jesus' first and most faithful disciple and in the communion of saints is our greatest example of holiness.

9–10. **ESSAY:** What does it mean to speak of ourselves as the Pilgrim People of God?

Sharing Faith with Your Family

Discuss the following with your family:

- Jesus Christ calls all of us into communion with his Father.
- Together all faithful members of the Church are joined in the communion of saints.
- Mary is our greatest saint and the perfect example of discipleship.
- We are the Pilgrim People of God.

Ask your parents to reflect on the ways their parents or ancestors handed down the Catholic faith to them and their families. How will you hand down the faith to the next generations?

The Worship Connection

Some churches have bells that ring at 6 a.m., 12 noon, and 6 p.m. For centuries it was Catholic custom to stop and pray the Angelus (see page 308) upon hearing the bells.

More to Explore

Explore the Internet for more information on the topic or saint that you named in "Living Our Faith."

Catholic Social Teaching ☑ Checklist

Theme of Catholic Social Teaching:
Life and Dignity of the Human Person

How it relates to Chapter 24: As members of the Church we must live as the image of God in which we were created. We must also recognize God's image in all other human beings and treat all human life as sacred because it is a gift from God.

How can you do this?

☐ At home:
_____

☐ At school/work:
_____

☐ In the parish:
_____

☐ In the community:
_____

Check off each action after it has been completed.

Define the following.

1. common vocation _____
_____

2. sacrament _____
_____

3. sanctifying grace _____
_____

4. solidarity _____
_____

5. providence _____
_____

6. deposit of faith _____
_____

Fill in the circle beside the correct answer.

7. During the Nicene Creed, we state our belief in four special characteristics of the
   Church—the _____—praying, "We believe in one holy catholic and apostolic
   Church."

   ○ parables   ○ evangelical   ○ actual   ○ marks of the
                    counsels   graces   Church

8. Each member of the Church has unique gifts and talents and is called by God to
   fulfill a unique role in the Church—living out his or her _____ through one of
   the three particular vocations.

   ○ invisible   ○ actual   ○ visible   ○ common
     elements   graces   elements   vocation

9. The life of grace, the theological virtues of faith, hope, and charity, and the gifts of
   the Holy Spirit are all examples of the Church's _____, which have to do with the
   Church's inner life—shown by the way the Church's members live.

   ○ invisible   ○ actual   ○ visible   ○ common
     elements   graces   elements   vocation

10. Prayers of _____ are prayers in which we ask something of God. Asking for
    forgiveness is the most important type of this prayer.

    ○ blessing   ○ petition   ○ intercession   ○ thanksgiving

11. _____ is our greatest saint and the perfect example of discipleship.

    ○ Peter   ○ Paul   ○ Mary   ○ Catherine of Siena

12. _____ are interventions of God in our daily lives—the urgings or promptings from the Holy Spirit that help us to do good and to deepen our relationship with Christ.

    ○ Parables   ○ Evangelical counsels   ○ Actual graces   ○ Marks of the Church

Complete the following.

13. A _____ is a short story with a message.

14. _____ is the raising of our minds and hearts to God.

15. The five basic forms of prayer are _____,

_____, _____,

_____, and _____.

16. Each member of the Church can live out his or her common vocation through one of three particular vocations: _____,

_____, or _____.

17. The _____ includes all the members of the Church from her beginning until the present.

18. The _____ is the official public prayer of the Church.

Respond to the following.

19. Name and describe three characteristics of the Church—aside from the marks of the Church—that you learned about in this unit.

_____

_____

_____

_____

20. Use what you have learned in this unit to answer the question: _What does it mean to be Catholic?_

_____

_____

_____

_____

Imagine that you are a guest on a talk show panel to discuss the topic *Young Catholics Today*. Prepare a question and answer role-play describing what it means for young Catholics to live out their faith. Consider questions that a talk show host might ask on this topic. Use the material presented in Unit 4 to help you prepare your role-play.

With a partner, perform your role-play for the group.

Choose ten Faith Words from the box and write the definition for each.

reverence	conversion	eternal life	blasphemy	monastery
conclave	relativism	solidarity	deposit of faith	Decalogue
idolatry	covet	moral decision-making	social sin	holiness

1. _____

_____

2. _____

_____

3. _____

_____

4. _____

_____

5. _____

_____

6. _____

_____

7. _____

_____

8. _____

_____

9. _____

_____

10. _____

_____

Fill in the circle beside the correct answer.

11. Which of the following is *not* one of the Ten Commandments?

   ○ "I am the LORD your God: you shall not have strange gods before me."
   ○ "Honor your father and mother."
   ○ "Love one another. As I have loved you, so you also should love one another."
   ○ "Remember to keep holy the LORD's day."

12. Which of the following is *not* one of the five basic forms of prayer?

   ○ rosary   ○ thanksgiving   ○ intercession   ○ praise

13. Which of the following is *not* a theme of Catholic social teaching?

○ Care for God's Creation
○ Solidarity of the Human Family
○ Rights and Responsibilities of the Human Person
○ Liturgy of the Hours

14. Which of the following religious orders for women was *not* founded in the nineteenth century?

○ Ursulines
○ Sisters of Mercy
○ Missionaries of the Sacred Heart of Jesus
○ Sisters of the Blessed Sacrament

15. Which of the following is *not* a parable?

○ The Mustard Seed
○ The Workers in the Vineyard
○ The Kingdom of God
○ The Buried Treasure and the Pearls

16. Which of the following is *not* an example of the Church's visible elements?

○ Scripture   ○ Baptism   ○ devotion to Mary   ○ the life of grace

17. Which commandment calls us to always show reverence for God's name?

○ the third commandment
○ the second commandment
○ the fourth commandment
○ the fifth commandment

18. Who lived by the motto *Ora et labora*, or "Pray and work," and wrote a rule for monks and nuns which named seven specific times each day for community prayer?

○ Saint Basil the Great
○ Saint Scholastica
○ Saint Thomas Aquinas
○ Saint Benedict

19. Which of the following is not one of the four marks of the Church?

○ one   ○ invisible   ○ catholic   ○ apostolic

Complete the following.

21. Pope _____ wrote a number of encyclicals, two of which are considered the greatest social justice encyclicals in the history of the Church— *Mater et Magistra* and *Pacem in Terris*.

22. Pope _____ was involved in the development of the *Gregorian Sacramentary*, a book that would guide the celebration of Mass and the other sacraments for many centuries to come.

23. The _____ Council decreed that Catholics must receive Holy Communion at least once a year and the word *transubstantiation* would be used to describe the changing of the bread and wine into the Body and Blood of Christ that takes place during the consecration of the Mass, by the power of the Holy Spirit and through the words and actions of the priest.

24. In 1790 _____ became the first diocese of the Catholic Church in the United States.

25. The Catholic Bible consists of _____ books, divided into two parts called *testaments*.

26. Through the Sacrament of _____ we can be reconciled with God and with the Church.

Respond to the following.

27. Choose a saint or holy person discussed in this book and describe his or her contributions to the Church.

_____

_____

_____

_____

28. Choose two of the following topics and explain their impact on the Church: *Edict of Milan, Crusades, Black Death, Jesuits, Protestant Reformation, missionaries, monasteries, French Revolution, the Great Schism of the West,* or *Vatican II.*

_____

_____

_____

_____

29. Describe what a conscience is and what it means to have a well-formed one.

_____

_____

_____

_____

30. What have you learned this year that will help you to live out your Catholic faith?

_____

_____

_____

_____

Contents

In the liturgical year, the date of Easter Sunday, the celebration of our Lord's Resurrection, depends each year on the spring equinox and the rising of the full moon. Easter Sunday follows the full moon after the spring equinox. The spring equinox is the day on which the sun crosses the equator, making day and night of equal length everywhere. Thus, the timing of Easter Sunday reminds us that our Lord's Resurrection brings light to our darkness.

Astronomers can calculate the date of the spring equinox. Looking at their calculations we find that Easter Sunday is always between March 22 and April 25. Using the date for Easter Sunday, each year's unique liturgical calendar can be determined.

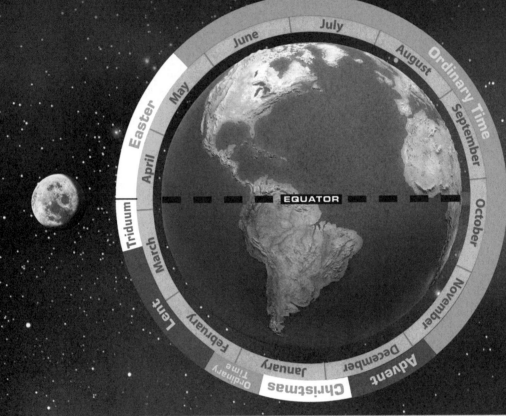

Activity As you complete each "Seasons and Celebrations" lesson, record below the dates when the Church celebrates each liturgical season this year. Then record what your group did to celebrate the season.

Advent   When: _____

What we did to celebrate: _____

_____

Christmas   When: _____

What we did to celebrate: _____

_____

Lent   When: _____

What we did to celebrate: _____

_____

Triduum   When: _____

What we did to celebrate: _____

_____

Easter   When: _____

What we did to celebrate: _____

_____

Ordinary Time   When: _____

What we did to celebrate: _____

_____

GATHERING...

♪ **Praise to Our God, Creation's Lord**

Praise to our God, creation's Lord,
Giver of gifts that fill our land,
All living things with us accord:
In love we know God's open hand.

Praise to our God for flow of time:
Journeys of sun and moon above,
Season to season joy sublime:
In these we mark our God's great love.

The Liturgical Year

The calendar followed in nearly every part of the world, which marks time from January to December each year, is known as the Gregorian calendar. It was named after Pope Gregory XIII, who, in the sixteenth century, appointed a group of astronomers to revise the calendar people followed at the time. In the new calendar, a year would be based on the actual length of time that it took the earth to complete one orbit around the sun. Most countries in Europe adopted this new calendar in 1582. England and its colonies in America adopted the calendar in 1752. Today the Gregorian calendar is a part of our everyday lives.

Think about the role that the calendar plays in your life. How essential is it? What does it help you to do with your time?

Activity There are many popular sayings about time: "Time waits for no one," "Time is money," "Time is of the essence," to name a few. Write a slogan that represents your attitude toward time.

In what way is time a gift from God?

The liturgical year celebrates that all time is a gift from God.

For Catholics, another calendar plays an important role in our lives. It is the *liturgical calendar*. The liturgical calendar charts the seasons of the Church year. The Church year, or the *liturgical year*, is the sequence of specific feasts and seasons that are celebrated over a year's time in the *liturgy*, the official public prayer of the Church. Examples of these seasons and feasts include Christmas, Lent, Easter, and Pentecost Sunday.

In every liturgical year we are actually celebrating the whole life of Jesus Christ. We celebrate his birth, his youth, his public ministry, and his Paschal Mystery—his suffering, death, Resurrection, and Ascension, through which he accomplished the work of salvation. We celebrate, too, his sending of the Holy Spirit. In every liturgy during the liturgical year, the Holy Spirit actually makes the salvation of Jesus Christ present and active in our lives. In this way, the liturgical year is a celebration of God's gift of salvation and his gift of all time.

The high point of the liturgical year is Easter, our celebration of Christ's rising from the dead. Everything in our lives revolves around this event in the life of Jesus. The "natural" year, or the year charted by the Gregorian calendar, revolves around the rising and the setting of the sun, the phases of the moon, the movement of the stars, and the ebb and flow of the tides. The liturgical year revolves around the rising of Jesus Christ, the Son of God. The Resurrection of Jesus is the key to our faith; it gives us the hope of our own resurrection and eternal life at the end of time. So, the celebration of Easter is the key to the liturgical year. Because we celebrate Easter, we can celebrate everything else—each day of the liturgical year, each season, each feast of Mary or the saints, and each event in our own personal lives, whether happy or sad—with faith and hope and joy.

In this way, the liturgical year reminds us that all time is sacred. All time is holy. All time is a gift from God. When the Church is celebrating the liturgy throughout the liturgical year, the Church is rejoicing in God's love and presence at all times.

Activity An entrance chant is a short verse that may be prayed or sung at the beginning of the liturgy. Shown below are entrance chants for different seasons of the liturgical year. Write these at the appropriate point on a calendar and pray them when the season arrives.

Advent: "Let the clouds rain down the Just One, and the earth bring forth a Savior." (See Isaiah 45:8.)

Christmas: "Let us all rejoice in the Lord, for our Savior is born to the world. True peace has descended from heaven."

Lent: "Lord, you are merciful to all, and hate nothing you have created. You overlook the sins of men and bring them to repentance. You are the Lord our God." (See Wisdom 11:24–25, 27.)

Triduum: "We should glory in the cross of our Lord Jesus Christ, for he is our salvation, our life and our resurrection; through him we are saved and made free." (See Galatians 6:14.)

Easter: "The Lord has indeed risen, alleluia. Glory and kingship be his for ever and ever." (See Luke 24:34 and Revelation 1:6.)

Ordinary Time: "I am the Savior of all people, says the Lord. Whatever their troubles, I will answer their cry, and I will always be their Lord." (Roman Missal)

We celebrate the life of Jesus Christ throughout the liturgical year.

The following seasons are included in the liturgical year. For each season, a specific color of church vestments and decorations is used.

Advent The liturgical year begins in late November or early December with the season of Advent. Advent is the time to prepare for the celebration of Jesus' birth. Every day we can celebrate that Jesus comes into our lives. But during Advent we await Christmas, the celebration of the coming of the Son of God, Jesus Christ, and we look forward to his second coming at the end of time. The color for Advent is purple, a sign of expectation.

Christmas The Christmas season begins on Christmas Day with the celebration of the birth of the Son of God. During this entire season we celebrate that God is with us always. The color for Christmas is white, a sign of joy.

Lent The season of Lent begins on Ash Wednesday. During Lent we remember that Jesus suffered, died, and rose to new life to save us from our sins and to give us new life in the Kingdom of God. During Lent we work to grow closer to Jesus and to one another through prayer, fasting, and almsgiving. We pray for and support all who are preparing for the Sacraments of Initiation. We prepare for the Easter Triduum. The color for Lent is purple, for penance.

Triduum The Easter Triduum is the Church's greatest and most important celebration. The word *triduum* means "three days." During the three days of the Easter Triduum—from Holy Thursday evening, through Good Friday and Holy Saturday, until Easter Sunday evening—we remember and celebrate in the liturgy, with many special traditions and rituals, the suffering, death, and Resurrection of Jesus Christ. The color for Good Friday is red, for Jesus' suffering. The color for the other days of the Triduum is white.

Easter The season of Easter begins on Easter Sunday evening and continues until Pentecost Sunday. During this season we rejoice in Jesus' Resurrection and in the new life we have in Jesus Christ. We also celebrate Christ's Ascension into heaven. The color for the Easter season is white, while Pentecost's color is red and signifies the descent of the Holy Spirit upon the Apostles.

Ordinary Time The season of Ordinary Time is celebrated in two parts. The first part is between Christmas and Lent, and the second part is between Easter and Advent. During this time we celebrate the life and teachings of Jesus Christ and learn what it means to live as his disciples. The color for Ordinary Time is green, a sign of life and hope.

Each Sunday of the liturgical year is a great celebration of the Church, or a solemnity. Beyond each Sunday, there are other solemnities in the liturgical year on which we are obliged to attend Mass to give special honor to Jesus Christ for the salvation he has given to us. These are called holy days of obligation. The following are the holy days of obligation in the United States:

Solemnity of Mary, Mother of God (January 1)
Ascension (when celebrated on Thursday during the Easter Season)*
Assumption of Mary (August 15)
All Saints' Day (November 1)
Immaculate Conception (December 8)
Christmas (December 25)

*(Some dioceses celebrate the Ascension on the following Sunday.)

Activity Make a personal liturgical calendar. List the seasons of the liturgical year. Under each season, list specific feast days, as well as days that are important to you and your family. You may include saints' days, family birthdays or anniversaries, the birthdays of friends, and so on. Display your calendar at home as a reminder to celebrate these times as holy times in the presence of Jesus Christ.

✛ Leader: Every season in the liturgical year is a season to praise God. Let us pray Psalm 148, a psalm that calls all creation to praise God.

Group 1: "Praise the LORD from the heavens;
give praise in the heights.
Praise him, all you angels;
give praise, all you hosts."

Group 2: "Praise him, sun and moon;
give praise, all shining stars.
Praise him, highest heavens,
you waters above the heavens."

Group 1: "Let them all praise the LORD's name;
for the LORD commanded and they
were created,
Assigned them duties forever,
gave them tasks that will never change."

Group 2: "You kings of the earth and all peoples,
princes and all who govern on earth;
Young men and women too,
old and young alike."

All: "Let them all praise the LORD's name,
for his name alone is exalted,
majestic above earth and heaven."

(Psalm 148:1–6, 11–13)

Leader: Father, as we celebrate each day of the liturgical year, may we use your gift of time in a way that gives you praise. And may you grant us the gifts of hope, eagerness, faith, kindness, gentleness, and peace.

All: Glory to the Father, and to the Son, and to the Holy Spirit:
as it was in the beginning, is now, and
will be for ever. Amen.

@⁎ Visit www.weliveourfaith.com for additional prayers and activities.

"Prepare the way of the LORD!
Make straight in the wasteland a highway for our God!"

(Isaiah 40:3)

♪ **Prepare the Way**

Refrain:
Prepare the way for the coming of God.
Make a straight path for the coming of God.

Verse:
Crooked pathways: make them straight.
All the roughland: make it smooth.
Crooked pathways: make them straight.
All the roughland: make it smooth. (Refrain)

Advent

It's always good to be prepared. Preparing for events that we know are going to happen can help these events to go more smoothly. For example, sports teams prepare for a big game by practicing so that they have a better chance of winning. Students prepare for tests by studying so that they can get better grades. What other kinds of things do people prepare for? Why?

Activity Work with a partner to complete the chart below.

	What do we prepare for?	Why?	How do we prepare?
At school			
At home			
In afterschool clubs, teams, or activities			
In my parish			

Advent is a season of preparation for Christ's coming.

The word *Advent* comes from the Latin word *advenire*, which means "to come." The season of Advent—the four weeks before Christmas, and also the beginning of the liturgical year—is a season of preparation for the coming of Jesus Christ. By praying, listening to God's word, examining our thoughts and our actions, and making an effort to turn back to God, we prepare to celebrate Jesus Christ's presence among us, to welcome him into our hearts when he comes at:

- *Christmas.* During Christmas we will celebrate Jesus' birth and rejoice in the Incarnation. We will celebrate that, in Jesus Christ, God became human like us in all ways except sin. Jesus Christ saves us from sin and shares God's life with us. Advent is a time to become spiritually ready to celebrate these wonderful truths.

- *his second coming.* At the end of time Jesus Christ will come again in glory to fully establish the Kingdom of God. He will judge all people and invite those who have lived holy lives to enjoy happiness with him in the Kingdom forever. During Advent we focus on how ready we are for the second coming of Christ and for sharing this everlasting life with him.

- *all times.* Every day of our lives, we encounter Christ. We meet him in the Eucharist, in prayer, in the love that we share with one another, and in the everyday events of our lives. Advent gives us an opportunity to examine our lives and see how well prepared we are to respond to Jesus Christ's presence each day.

In the Gospels we read that John the Baptist called people to prepare for Jesus' coming. John preached that, to prepare for Jesus and for the Kingdom he would establish, people needed to change their lives. "In those days John the Baptist appeared, preaching in the desert of Judea [and] saying, 'Repent, for the kingdom of heaven is at hand!' It was of him that the prophet Isaiah had spoken when he said:

'A voice of one crying out in the desert,
    "Prepare the way of the LORD,
        make straight his paths"'" (Matthew 3:1–3).

Saint John the Baptist

This Gospel passage is among the readings that we hear in the liturgy during Advent. John's call to repent, to "make straight" our lives for Christ, reminds us that, though Advent is a hopeful season, it is also a *penitential* season, a time to prepare for Christ's coming through penance. This means thinking about our behavior and whether we have lived out our faith. It means examining our conscience, expressing sorrow for our sins, praying for forgiveness, receiving the Sacrament of Penance, and practicing acts of kindness and love to show our desire to change our lives. It also involves giving what we can to others, especially those in need, and being willing to make sacrifices to follow Christ.

Activity Ask yourself: How prepared am I for Christ's coming at Christmas, for his second coming, and for his presence in my daily life? What are some of the ways that I can celebrate Advent as a penitential season?

Advent is a season of both hope and penance.

As a penitential season, Advent is similar to the season of Lent. In fact, in the Church's earliest centuries, Advent was considered "the Lent before Christmas." Like Lent, it actually lasted for forty days and involved fasting and abstaining from meat. Though these practices are no longer associated with Advent, the way the Church celebrates the liturgy during Advent points to the season's penitential nature. For example, the liturgical color for Advent is purple, which is also the liturgical color for the penitential season of Lent. In Masses during Advent, the Gloria, a hymn of great joy and praise for the glory of God, is omitted. And any flowers that would normally surround the altar in church are removed during Advent.

It is only on the Third Sunday of Advent, or *Gaudete Sunday*, that the Church suspends penitential practices for Advent. *Gaudete* means "rejoice," and on Gaudete Sunday we are reminded that Christ's coming is near and that we should be filled with joy. The liturgical color for this day is rose, a joyful color.

Naturally, we may want to celebrate *the whole season* of Advent as a joyful time, a time of anticipation for Christmas—not a time of penance, sorrow, and sacrifice—for, indeed, Advent is a time of great hope. What can be more joyful than expecting the coming of our Savior, Jesus Christ? Yet, in the weeks before Christmas, there is often so much holiday enthusiasm, hype, and commercialism in our world that we forget Advent's true purpose: to deepen our relationship with Christ. So, in a world that is preparing for Christmas by emphasizing parties, gifts, and material things, Advent's emphasis on prayer, penance, and spiritual things can help to bring us closer to Christ, making us "ready to greet him when he comes again" (Eucharistic Prayer III, Roman Missal).

We may wonder why the beginning of the liturgical year is a season of preparation and penance. Why don't we begin the Church year with the celebration of the Incarnation, the birth of Jesus Christ? Well, first, we must be prepared to welcome Jesus Christ. Then we can begin to celebrate his presence at Christmas and throughout the year. The penance and preparation of Advent help us to become more open to Jesus Christ as the Savior born in Bethlehem on Christmas Day, more responsive to his call to discipleship each day, and more ready to share eternal happiness with him when he comes again at the end of time.

And so, the Church devotes the four weeks of Advent to preparing us to celebrate the life of Jesus beginning with his nativity on December 25. Throughout Advent we are called to pay special attention to how we are living out our discipleship to Jesus Christ—for, by living out our discipleship to him, we will be ready for his judgment when he comes again at the end of time.

Activity Use the grid to make an Advent calendar showing some of the things that you and your family might do to prepare for Christ's coming this Advent season.

ADVENT CALENDAR

1st week							
2nd week							
3rd week							
4th week							Dec. 25

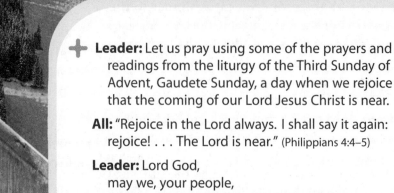

RESPONDING...

✝ **Leader:** Let us pray using some of the prayers and readings from the liturgy of the Third Sunday of Advent, Gaudete Sunday, a day when we rejoice that the coming of our Lord Jesus Christ is near.

All: "Rejoice in the Lord always. I shall say it again: rejoice! . . . The Lord is near." (Philippians 4:4–5)

Leader: Lord God,
may we, your people,
who look forward to the birthday of Christ
experience the joy of salvation
and celebrate that feast with love
        and thanksgiving.
We ask this through our Lord Jesus Christ,
        your Son,
who lives and reigns with you
        and the Holy Spirit,
one God, for ever and ever.
Amen.

(collect, Third Sunday of Advent)

Reader: A reading from the Letter of Saint James

"Be patient, therefore, brothers, until the coming of the Lord. See how the farmer waits for the precious fruit of the earth, being patient with it until it receives the early and the late rains. You too must be patient. Make your hearts firm, because the coming of the Lord is at hand. Do not complain, brothers, about one another, that you may not be judged. Behold, the Judge is standing before the gates. Take as an example of hardship and patience, brothers, the prophets who spoke in the name of the Lord." (James 5:7–10)

Leader: God of mercy, . . .
free us from our sins,
and prepare us for the birthday of our Savior,
who is Lord for ever and ever.

All: Amen.

(prayer after Communion, Third Sunday of Advent)

> @ ✳ **Visit www.weliveourfaith.com for additional prayers and activities.**

GATHERING...

> **"They were overjoyed at seeing the star, and . . . they saw the child with Mary his mother."**
>
> (Matthew 2:10–11)

♪ **We Three Kings**

Refrain:
O star of wonder, star of night,
Star with royal beauty bright,
Westward leading, still proceeding,
Guide us to thy perfect light.

Verse:
We three kings of Orient are;
Bearing gifts we traverse afar
Field and fountain,
Moor and mountain,
Following yonder star. (Refrain)

Christmas

Each of us is on a journey, though we may not *physically* move from one location to another. We are on a journey through life. Sometimes we have an easy time on this journey. Sometimes we meet hardships along the way. And sometimes we find that we have changed and grown in ways we might have never predicted.

Activity Write a letter to yourself that describes your journey through life. Your letter might explore these questions: How would I describe the current stage of my journey through life? Where was I last year at this time? How have I changed since then? Where do I think I will be next year at this time? What words of wisdom might I have for my future self?

When you are finished writing your letter, fold and seal it. Label it "Letter to myself. Open next Christmas." Keep it in a safe place. When you read it next year, see where your journey has led you so far.

During the Christmas season we celebrate the manifestation of the Savior to all people.

Christmas is the season of the liturgical year in which we celebrate the birth of Jesus Christ, the Son of God. We celebrate the Incarnation, the truth that the Son of God, the second Person of the Blessed Trinity, became man and lived among us. The Christmas season begins on December 25, Christmas Day—known in the liturgical year as the Solemnity of the Nativity of the Lord. A *solemnity* is an important day in the Church's liturgical calendar. Solemnities celebrate events in the life of Christ, Mary, and the saints that are of particular importance to the whole Church.

Before the Christmas season ends in January with the Feast of the Baptism of the Lord, the Church celebrates a special solemnity known as the Solemnity of the Epiphany of the Lord. This solemnity is celebrated on the Sunday between January 2 and January 8. It recalls a specific event in the Gospels: the visit of the Magi—or the "three kings" or "wise men"—to the infant Jesus. Their encounter with Jesus is described in the Gospel of Matthew. (See Matthew 2:1–12.) Matthew's Gospel explains that the Magi journeyed to the infant Jesus in Bethlehem by following a star. The Magi were probably astrologers who studied the stars to find signs of important events. When they found Jesus, they "did him homage. Then they opened their treasures and offered him gifts of gold, frankincense, and myrrh" (Matthew 2:11).

Epiphany comes from a Greek word that means "manifestation." To *manifest* is to "show" or

The Three Kings by Paul Hey (1867–1952)

"reveal." Christians see in the Gospel story of the Magi the manifestation, or the revealing, of Jesus Christ as Savior to all the nations. The Magi were Gentiles, or non-Jews. They were pagans, people who worshiped many gods. So, they did not know the Scriptures, the Ten Commandments, or the prophets, all of which God had given to the Jews. And they did not know the one, true God. Yet the Messiah, Jesus Christ, was still revealed to them. They gave him gifts and were the first Gentiles to worship him. So, the story of the Magi helps us to recognize that the Messiah came to save not only the Jews, but all people.

The gifts that the Magi gave to the infant Jesus also have special meaning for us. They are signs of the humanity and divinity of Christ. Gold is the most precious metal in the world and something that, at that time, only kings would own. It symbolizes Christ's kingship. Frankincense is used in the worship of God. It symbolizes Christ's divinity. And myrrh was a spice used in anointing the bodies of the dead. It symbolizes Christ's death as a human being. Along with these precious gifts, the Magi also brought themselves to Jesus, in reverence and love. The Solemnity of the Epiphany of Our Lord reminds us to do the same.

Activity Because the Magi followed a star, the liturgy for the Epiphany is filled with references to the light of Christ. Design a Christmas card that uses the theme of light to proclaim the birth of Jesus Christ. You might include the following Scripture quote from the Epiphany liturgy:

"Rise up in splendor! Your light has come, the glory of the Lord shines upon you."
(Isaiah 60:1)

Epiphany celebration, New York

Epiphany is an important part of celebrating Christmas.

The Church originally celebrated the Epiphany on January 6. And, for three centuries, this celebration was the early Church's only celebration of the birth of Jesus Christ. It was a day on which the Church actually celebrated four important events that revealed Jesus as the Son of God:

• the birth of Jesus, when God the Son took flesh and became visible

• the visit of the Magi, when Jesus was first manifested to the Gentile nations

• the baptism of Jesus, when Jesus was manifested as the Son of God—when "a voice came from the heavens, saying, 'This is my beloved Son, with whom I am well pleased'" (Matthew 3:17)

• the miracle at Cana, when Jesus worked his first miracle "and so revealed his glory" (John 2:11).

In time, the Western Church established December 25 as the day to celebrate the birth of Christ, or Christmas. This new date coincided with a Roman pagan feast, the "Feast of Lights," and so encouraged people to turn from the pagan festival toward the true Light of the World, Jesus Christ. Although the celebration of the birth of Christ was thus separated from the celebration of the Epiphany, the

other three "manifestations of Jesus" continued to be celebrated on the Epiphany. Later, two of them, the Baptism of Jesus and the miracle at Cana, were established as celebrations in their own right on separate Sundays following the Epiphany. But the Epiphany continued to be celebrated on January 6.

After the bishops met at the Second Vatican Council in 1962–1965, the bishops of some countries, including our own, agreed that celebrating the Epiphany on a weekday was difficult for people. So, they moved the celebration of the Epiphany from January 6 to the Sunday between January 2 and January 8. Moving the celebration to a Sunday allowed Catholics to hear the story of the Magi, fully celebrate the Epiphany, and renew their own journey of finding and following Jesus in their everyday lives.

Activity As a sign of the important connection between Christmas and the Epiphany, when Eastern Catholic Churches celebrate Christmas Day, they proclaim the Gospel story of the Magi and sing:

"Your Nativity, O Christ our God, has shown to the world the light of wisdom! For by it, those who worshiped the stars were taught by a star to adore you."

Work with your group to write verses that you can pray together this Christmas season to celebrate that Jesus Christ has been manifested as the Savior of the whole world.

✛ Leader: On the feast of the Epiphany some families practice a custom of praying for God's blessing on their homes. Let us now pray for God's blessing on the place where we gather together here.

Reader 1: O God, we remember the Magi, who, guided by a star, journeyed to the place in Bethlehem where the infant Jesus was born. Bringing their gifts to that holy place, they were blessed. Today we ask our Lord, Jesus Christ, to bless this place and to dwell with us here.

Reader 2: A reading from the holy Gospel according to Saint John

"In the beginning was the Word,
and the Word was with God,
and the Word was God.
He was in the beginning with God.
   All things came to be through him,
   and without him nothing came to be. . . ."

"And the Word became flesh
and made his dwelling among us,
and we saw his glory,
the glory as of the Father's only Son,
full of grace and truth." (John 1:1–3, 14)

Leader: Father,
   you revealed your Son to the nations
   by the guidance of a star.
   Lead us to glory in heaven
   by the light of faith.
   (collect, Solemnity of the Epiphany of the Lord)

All: Bless this place, and bless all of us. May your Word made flesh make his dwelling among us. Amen.

Visit www.weliveourfaith.com for additional prayers and activities.

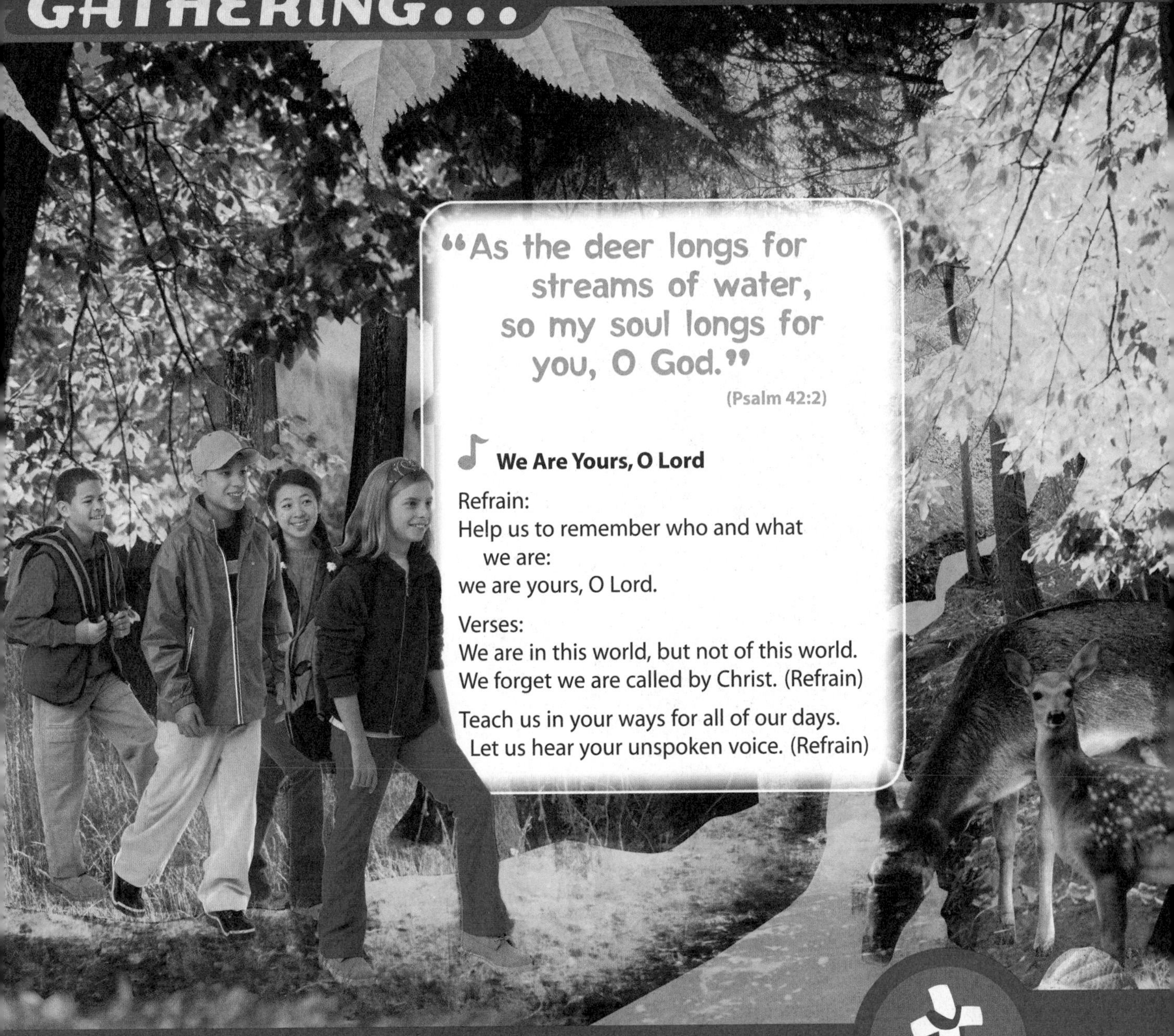

> "As the deer longs for
> streams of water,
> so my soul longs for
> you, O God."
>
> (Psalm 42:2)

♪ **We Are Yours, O Lord**

Refrain:
Help us to remember who and what
   we are:
we are yours, O Lord.

Verses:
We are in this world, but not of this world.
We forget we are called by Christ. (Refrain)

Teach us in your ways for all of our days.
   Let us hear your unspoken voice. (Refrain)

Lent

ife can be pretty demanding at times. One obligation or responsibility follows another. All of us need to be able to "take time out," to slow down, to get a break from the hustle and bustle of living. Sometimes we need time out for other reasons, too. We might need time out to prepare ourselves for a significant event or change in our lives. Or, if something's not going right, we need time out to shift our focus and make a plan. For example, coaches sometimes call a timeout in the middle of a game so that players can focus on what they need to change about their strategy. What other kinds of timeouts do people take, and why?

Activity Take time out right now. Think back over your day. Recall the things that were good about your day. Recall the things that were not so good. What can you learn from both types of experiences? What are some things you wish you could remember when life gets too hectic or things don't go so well?

Christ in the Desert by Ivan Kramskoi (1837–1887)

During Lent we take time to prepare for the celebration of Christ's death and Resurrection.

Lent is a season that allows us to take time to prepare for the celebration of Christ's death and Resurrection at Easter. This season of preparation lasts forty days, beginning on Ash Wednesday and concluding on the evening of Holy Thursday, the beginning of the Easter Triduum. The number 40 is a symbolic number in Scripture. It often marks a period of time that was taken to prepare for a significant event or change:

- In Scripture we read of the great flood, which lasted *forty* days. When it ended God made a covenant with Noah and with the whole human race. This was a time of new life for humankind.

- The Israelites, God's chosen people, wandered for *forty* years in the desert, guided by the one, true God, on a journey to reach the land that God had promised to make their own. Reaching this promised land marked the beginning of a new life for them.

- And Jesus Christ, the Son of God, prayed and fasted for *forty* days and *forty* nights in the desert to prepare himself for his public ministry as Messiah. Jesus' time in the desert prepared him not only for his ministry but eventually for the giving of his life for our salvation.

And Lent reflects the significance of each of these events:

- The great flood is symbolic of the waters of Baptism. In Baptism Christians die and then rise again to new life. Lent is a time when we as a Church prepare to renew, at Easter, the promises that we made at Baptism to live as Jesus' disciples. It is also a time when catechumens, people preparing for membership in the Catholic Church, get ready to receive the Sacraments of Christian Initiation during the liturgy of the Easter Vigil.

- Lent is our "time in the desert" when we listen to God, pray, fast, do penance, and share what we have.

- Lent is a time when we prepare to celebrate Jesus Christ's death and Resurrection, his giving of himself for our salvation.

During the forty days of Lent, the Church encourages us to take the time to change anything about our lives that is leading us away from Christ. Without taking this "time out" to renew our lives, we cannot be ready to enter fully into the joy of Christ's Resurrection. So, during Lent, we take time to pray, to give to those in need, to fast, to do some form of penance, to carefully examine our lives, to celebrate the Sacrament of Penance and Reconciliation, and to take a step back from the distractions that can keep us from fully living out our faith.

Activity Renewing our baptismal promises at Easter consists of answering "I do" to a series of questions. These questions are shown on page 288. As a Lenten exercise, take time to reflect on and respond silently to each question.

Lent is a time of prayer, fasting, and almsgiving.

One of the ways that we take time to renew our lives during Lent is by participating in the Lenten practices of prayer, fasting, and almsgiving.

Prayer: Our Lenten prayers are focused on asking for the strength to become better disciples of Jesus. We ask for help to live as he did, and we thank him for dying and rising so that we too can rise to new life. During Lent parishes provide special times of prayer throughout the week. These include times for celebrating the Sacrament of Reconciliation, for praying the Stations of the Cross (found on page 307), or for *retreats*, special times set aside for careful reflection and prayer. During Lent we may also pray by reading and reflecting on Scripture. Taking time to read Scripture each day is an important way to renew our lives during Lent. In Scripture we find the word of God for our lives.

Fasting: Fasting is a way to cleanse our bodies of harmful things and our hearts and minds of things that keep us from loving God and others. Fasting is also a form of penance. Doing penance helps us to turn to God and focus on the things that are important to our lives as Christians. Doing penance is a way to show that we are sorry for our sins.

All Catholics eighteen years of age or older and in good health are obliged, through their fifty-ninth birthday, to fast on Ash Wednesday and Good Friday. Fasting on these days means eating only one full meal, plus two additional small meals as long as they do not, together, equal another full meal. Eating between meals is not allowed. Every Catholic fourteen years of age and older is also obliged to give up meat on these days and on all the Fridays during Lent. Another way to fast during Lent is to voluntarily give up things we enjoy, like a favorite food or activity. Doing so, we can unite ourselves to the sacrifice of Christ, who gave his life for us.

Almsgiving: Almsgiving, or giving alms, is the practice of giving money or other resources to help people in need. The money that we save

Eighth graders sell pumpkin pies to raise money to help people in need.

during Lent by fasting or by denying ourselves in other ways can be shared with those who are less fortunate than we are.

These Lenten practices are a way to turn our hearts and our lives back to God during Lent. Then we can celebrate the Resurrection knowing that it is a promise of our own resurrection and eternal life with Jesus Christ at the end of time.

Activity How will prayer, fasting, and almsgiving be part of your Lenten practices this year? You may want to make almsgiving a group effort. Write your ideas here.

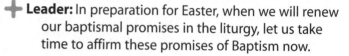

✚ Leader: In preparation for Easter, when we will renew our baptismal promises in the liturgy, let us take time to affirm these promises of Baptism now.

Leader: Do you reject Satan?

All: I do.

Leader: And all his works?

All: I do.

Leader: And all his empty promises?

All: I do.

Leader: Do you believe in God, the Father almighty, creator of heaven and earth?

All: I do.

Leader: Do you believe in Jesus Christ, his only Son, our Lord,
who was born of the Virgin Mary,
was crucified, died, and was buried,
rose from the dead,
and is seated at the right hand of the Father?

All: I do.

Leader: Do you believe in the Holy Spirit,
the holy catholic Church, the communion of saints,
the forgiveness of sins, the resurrection of the body,
and the life everlasting?

All: I do.

(Rite of Baptism)

Leader: Father,
through our observance of Lent,
help us to understand the meaning
of your Son's death and resurrection,
and teach us to reflect it in our lives.
Grant this through our Lord Jesus Christ, your Son,
who lives and reigns with you and the Holy Spirit,
one God, for ever and ever.

All: Amen.

(collect, First Sunday of Lent)

@ **Visit www.weliveourfaith.com for additional prayers and activities.**

**"Father,
we share in the light
of your glory
through your Son, the
light of the world."**

(Blessing of the Fire and Lighting of the
Easter Candle, Easter Vigil)

♪ **Christ, Be Our Light**

Refrain:
Christ, be our light!
Shine in our hearts.
Shine through the darkness.

Christ, be our light!
Shine in your church, gathered today.

Verse:
This is the night when Christ our redeemer
rose from the grave triumphant and free,
leaving the tomb of evil and darkness,
empty for all to see.

Triduum

Darkness and light have always had powerful effects on human beings. As children some of us go through a stage when we're afraid of the dark. When we're older some of us feel gloomy in the season when sunlight shines for fewer hours each day, and happier when sunlight shines brightly for most of the day. And even if we're no longer "afraid of the dark," we may still be cautious or uneasy when it's dark outside.

With all their effects in our lives, darkness and light have become powerful religious symbols. Since ancient times, light has been used as a symbol for wisdom, joy, truth, goodness, and grace. And darkness has been used as a symbol for ignorance, sadness, untruth, evil, and sin.

Activity What are some of the good things that light brings about or represents?

The Triduum reminds us that Christ is the Light of the World.

"In the beginning, when God created the heavens and the earth, the earth was a formless wasteland, and darkness covered the abyss. . . .

". . . God said, 'Let there be light,' and there was light. God saw how good the light was. God then separated the light from the darkness." (Genesis 1:1–4)

In these first words of the Bible, darkness and light are elements that have great meaning for us as people of faith: Light is God's first gift. Created directly by him, it does away with the darkness of chaos. Throughout the Bible light and darkness continue to be powerful images. We read that the light of God, in a pillar of fire by night, led the people of Israel, our ancestors in faith, through the desert to the promised land. And we read the words of the prophets who, in telling the people about the promised Messiah, compared him to light:

"The people who walked in darkness
   have seen a great light" (Isaiah 9:1).

Jesus Christ is this great light. Jesus taught, "I am the light of the world" (John 9:5). Following Jesus, we can rise out of the darkness of sin, hatred, and evil and journey to the light of everlasting life in heaven. We are able to see the right path to follow in life, the path that leads us to God. We can see through false values in our world and find love and peace, honesty and integrity, shining before us. And we need not be afraid.

The Easter Triduum is a time in the liturgical year that reminds us that Christ is our Light. It leads us to and encompasses the Easter celebration, when we rejoice that Christ, in rising from the dead, has overcome the darkness of death and sin. The Triduum celebrates Christ's passing from death to the light of new life.

The word *triduum* means "three days." During the Easter Triduum we follow a practice for counting days that comes from our Jewish ancestors in faith: counting the period from one sunset to the next as one day. The Triduum begins on the evening of Holy Thursday, when we recall Christ's giving of

The Light of the World by William Holman Hunt (1827–1910)

his Body and Blood at the Last Supper. It continues through Good Friday, when we remember that Jesus Christ, the Son of God, suffered and died for humankind. He descended into the realm of the dead and opened the gates of heaven. And it extends through Holy Saturday, when we reflect and pray about his death and then celebrate the Easter Vigil. At the Easter Vigil, through special prayers and rituals, we celebrate Christ as our Light. Then the Triduum concludes on Easter Sunday evening with the liturgy of evening prayer.

Thus, beginning on Holy Thursday evening and ending on Easter Sunday evening, the Triduum is a total of three consecutive days from sunset to sunset. Each liturgical celebration on these three days form one connected liturgy that heightens our awareness of Jesus Christ as the Light of the World. These three days are the most important three days of the liturgical year.

Activity With your group arrange a prayer service with Scripture readings, songs, and prayers that celebrate Christ as the Light of the World.

The Triduum celebrates the light of Christ.

The liturgical celebrations of the Easter Triduum recall the events through which Jesus Christ offers us the light of himself.

The whole Triduum reminds us to rejoice because:

"the light shines in the darkness,
and the darkness has not overcome it"
(John 1:5).

The Triduum concludes with Evening Prayer on Easter Sunday, when we celebrate the day that Christ rose from the dead.

On **Holy Thursday**, we celebrate the Evening Mass of the Lord's Supper. This liturgy recalls Jesus' last meal with his Apostles before his death. At the Last Supper Jesus gave an example of love and service: He washed his disciples' feet as a sign of his love for them. Then while they were gathered together to celebrate Passover, Jesus shared the bread and wine with them, saying, "This is my body, which will be given for you" and "This cup is the new covenant in my blood, which will be shed for you" (Luke 22:19, 20). Through his words and actions that night, Jesus gave us himself in the Eucharist.

In the Mass on Holy Thursday evening, a reenactment of Jesus' washing of his Apostles' feet takes place. And we celebrate in a special way Christ's giving of his Body and Blood, which he shared then and still shares with us today in the Eucharist. Through the Eucharist, Jesus continues to be with us always, conquering the darkness in our lives.

On **Good Friday**, we celebrate the Lord's Passion. This liturgy often takes place around three o'clock in the afternoon, in keeping with Gospel accounts of Jesus' death: "At noon darkness came over the whole land until three in the afternoon. And at three o'clock Jesus cried out in a loud voice, ... and breathed his last" (Mark 15:33–34, 37). This liturgy has three parts: the Liturgy of the Word, the veneration of the cross, and Holy Communion. In the Liturgy of the Word, we hear a reading from the Gospel of John telling of the passion of Christ. The Liturgy of the Word concludes with a special prayer of the faithful in which ten prayers are prayed. In one we ask God "that the light of the Holy Spirit" may show those who do not believe in Christ "the way to salvation" (Roman Missal).

Then the veneration of the cross takes place. It is a ritual in which we show reverence, or honor and respect, for the cross, because upon it hung the Savior of the world. The Liturgy of the Eucharist is not celebrated, so a short communion service takes place. Then all depart in silence.

On **Holy Saturday**, we gather in the evening with our parish for the celebration of the Easter Vigil. In the Church, a vigil is a liturgy that celebrates Sunday or a very important feast day but takes place the night before. The Easter Vigil begins after sunset on Holy Saturday, the night before Easter Sunday. It is the most important vigil of the year, the high point of the Easter Triduum. It celebrates the new life Jesus has gained for us by his death and Resurrection.

The first part of the Easter Vigil liturgy is the Service of Light. With the celebrant we assemble in front of a fire that has been made outside of or in the back of the church. This fire is blessed, and the Easter, or Paschal, candle is lit from it. The lighted Paschal candle represents the risen Christ among us and our own passing with him from death to life, from darkness to light. The candle is carried with great reverence into the darkened church. We may light small candles from it. Then, the deacon, priest, or a parish member chants the *Exsultet*, or Easter Proclamation. The *Exsultet* announces that this is the most beautiful and exciting night of the year.

The second part of the Easter Vigil is the Liturgy of the Word. The Scripture readings encourage us to meditate on the wonderful things God has done for his people from the beginning. The third part of the Easter Vigil is the Liturgy of Baptism. New members of the Church are baptized and confirmed. And they will also partake of the Eucharist for the first time. All present also receive a candle lit from the Paschal candle, renew their baptismal promises, and are sprinkled with the baptismal water, a sign of their new life in Christ. The fourth part of the Easter Vigil liturgy is the Liturgy of the Eucharist. The whole Church is called to the table that the Lord prepared for his people by his death and Resurrection.

Activity When you participate in the liturgical celebrations of the Triduum this year, pay special attention to the ways that light and darkness are highlighted in these celebrations.

RESPONDING...

Leader: Let us now pray using a ritual from the Easter Vigil liturgy in which the Paschal candle is prepared for use in that liturgy and other liturgies throughout the year. The ritual begins with the priest carving the vertical arm of a cross into the Paschal candle and praying, "Christ yesterday and today."

All: Risen Lord, you are with us now and always.

Leader: The priest then carves the horizontal arm of the cross into the candle and prays, "the beginning and the end."

All: Risen Lord, we begin and end in you.

Leader: The priest carves the first letter of the Greek alphabet, or *alpha*, into the candle and prays, "Alpha." Then, carving the last letter of the Greek alphabet, or *omega*, into the candle, he prays, "and Omega."

All: Risen Lord, you are first and last and always.

Leader: The priest carves the first numeral of the current year above the upper left corner of the carved-in cross and prays, "All time belongs to him." Then he carves the second numeral of the year in the upper right corner and prays, "and all the ages."

All: Risen Lord, we offer you our time, our days, and this entire year.

Leader: The priest carves the third numeral of the year in the lower left corner and prays, "to him be glory and power." Then he carves the fourth numeral of the year in the lower right corner and prays, "through every age for ever. Amen."

All: Amen.

Leader: Then the priest may insert five grains of incense into the shape of the cross on the candle. As he does this, he prays, "By his holy and glorious wounds may Christ our Lord guard us and keep us. Amen."

All: Amen.

Leader: The priest then lights the candle from the fire and prays: "May the light of Christ, rising in glory, dispel the darkness of our hearts and minds." Then the priest or a deacon lifts the candle high and sings, "Christ our light."

All: Thanks be to God.

Visit www.weliveourfaith.com for additional prayers and activities.

> **"For the Lamb . . .**
> **will shepherd them**
> **and lead them to springs**
> **of life-giving water."**
>
> (Revelation 7:17)

♪ **Come to the Water**

O let all who thirst, let them come to
 the water.
And let all who have nothing, let them
 come to the Lord:
without money, without price.
Why should you pay the price, except
 for the Lord?

And let all who seek, let them come to
 the water.
And let all who have nothing, let them
 come to the Lord:
without money, without strife.
Why should you spend your life, except
 for the Lord?

Easter

About seventy percent of the earth is covered by water. Water is a basic necessity of life. Living things need it to survive. In fact, a person can survive only eight to ten days without it. It helps our bodies to digest the foods we eat, absorb the nutrients we need, remove the elements we don't need, maintain the health of muscles and tissues, and generally function properly. The human body itself is actually sixty-five percent water!

Water also has the power to cleanse, refresh, and renew. With all of water's amazing properties, there's no denying that it is a powerful sign of life.

Activity List some of the ways that water is an essential part of things that you do each day.

293

the waters of Baptism original sin was washed away, we received grace, or God's life in us, and we became part of Christ, who lives forever. After we renew our baptismal promises, the priest sprinkles us with the blessed baptismal water after praying:

"God, the all-powerful Father of our Lord Jesus Christ,
has given us a new birth by water and the Holy Spirit and forgiven all our sins.
May he also keep us faithful to our Lord Jesus Christ for ever and ever."
(Roman Missal)

At Easter, then, we are celebrating that Jesus Christ gave his life for us. By his Resurrection and through the grace that he gives us, he frees us from the power of sin and death. Because we have become part of his Body in the Sacrament of Baptism, we too can share everlasting life with Christ—we too can rise from the dead and have endless glory with the Lord.

The Easter season highlights the waters of Baptism as a sign of new life.

The Church sets aside an entire season, from Easter Sunday to Pentecost Sunday, to celebrate in a special way the Resurrection of Christ. During this season, the Easter season, water takes on added significance in the Church.

During Easter the waters of Baptism become an especially important sign for the whole Church of the new life that Christ gives us by his Resurrection. Throughout the Easter season, many parishes draw special attention to the baptismal font or pool. This acts as a reminder that, through our Baptism, we too have died and risen with Christ and that our Easter celebration truly begins in the waters of Baptism. At the Easter Vigil, new members of the Church are baptized; the baptismal water is a sign of their new life as children of God. They have died to sin and risen up from the water into life with Christ.

At the Easter Vigil and on Easter Sunday, we also renew our baptismal promises. In doing so, we recall the grace of our own Baptism, the sacrament through which we entered the Body of Christ. In

Activity If you and your group were going to make a display for your parish titled *Our Easter Began in the Waters of Baptism,* what would it consist of? How might this display help the members of your parish?

The Easter season celebrates the new life that Christ gives us.

When we celebrate Easter, we celebrate Christ's Resurrection and rejoice in the new life that we have because of him. Christ's Resurrection is a promise of our own resurrection, reminding us that sin and death are not permanent conditions. Throughout our lives we can overcome the tendency to sin through the grace that Christ shares with us. When we do sin, our sins will be forgiven if we are truly sorry, ask for forgiveness, and firmly intend not to sin again. Thanks to the life-giving Resurrection of Jesus Christ, we are freed from the control of sin.

When we realize that we, with Jesus, are victorious over death and sin, what other response could there be but one of pure joy? Our joy is expressed in many ways throughout the Easter season—in the white vestments and altar coverings of the season; in the flowers and banners used to decorate the church; and in this season's readings from the Acts of the Apostles heard at the first reading in the liturgy. The Acts of the Apostles recounts the earliest days of the Church, when Christian life was new. Now that we have once again risen with Christ, the Christian life is again new for us, too.

Our joy during Easter is also expressed by singing the "Alleluia" before the Gospel reading. The days of the Easter season "above all others are the days for the singing of the *Alleluia*" (*General Norms for the Liturgical Year and the Calendar*, 22). *Alleluia* means "Praise God!" During Lent, instead of singing the "Alleluia" before the Gospel reading, we sing or say, "Glory and praise to you, Lord Jesus Christ" or other similar words of praise. But at Easter the "Alleluia" returns to the liturgy and we joyfully sing it over and over again. We rejoice in the new life we have because of Christ.

Activity Share the joy of Easter by writing an "Alleluia Song." Use a melody familiar to you. Write verses about Easter and Christ's Resurrection, and use the word *Alleluia* as a main verse that repeats throughout your song. Or do artwork expressive of an Alleluia theme.

RESPONDING...

✚ **Reader 1:** A reading from the holy Gospel according to Matthew

"After the sabbath, as the first day of the week was dawning, Mary Magdalene and the other Mary came to see the tomb. And behold, there was a great earthquake; for an angel of the Lord descended from heaven, approached, rolled back the stone, and sat upon it. His appearance was like lightning and his clothing was white as snow. The guards were shaken with fear of him and became like dead men. Then the angel said to the women in reply, 'Do not be afraid! I know that you are seeking Jesus the crucified. He is not here, for he has been raised just as he said.'" (Matthew 28:1–6)

All: Christ is risen. Alleluia, Alleluia!

Reader 2: The angel said, "Go quickly and tell his disciples, 'He has been raised from the dead, and he is going before you to Galilee; there you will see him.' Behold, I have told you" (Matthew 28:7).

All: Christ is risen. Alleluia, Alleluia!

Reader 3: "Then they went away quickly from the tomb, fearful yet overjoyed, and ran to announce this to his disciples. And behold, Jesus met them on their way and greeted them. They approached, embraced his feet, and did him homage. Then Jesus said to them, 'Do not be afraid. Go tell my brothers to go to Galilee, and there they will see me.'" (Matthew 28:8–10)

All: Christ is risen. Alleluia, Alleluia!

Leader: God our Father,
by raising Christ your Son
you conquered the power of death
and opened for us the way to eternal life.
Let our celebration today
raise us up and renew our lives
by the Spirit that is within us.
Grant this through our Lord Jesus Christ,
your Son,
who lives and reigns with you
and the Holy Spirit,
one God, for ever and ever.

All: Amen. Alleluia, Alleluia!

(collect, Easter Sunday)

@✦ **Visit www.weliveourfaith.com for additional prayers and activities.**

"The Spirit of the Lord is upon me."

(Luke 4:18)

♪ **Holy Spirit**

Refrain:
Holy Spirit, come into our lives.
Holy Spirit, make us truly wise.

Verses:
Give us a spirit of wisdom,
    an understanding heart.
Give us a spirit of knowledge,
    and lead us to the truth. (Refrain)

Give us a spirit of courage,
    and judgment that is wise.
Give us a spirit of rev'rence,
    of wonder and of awe. (Refrain)

Pentecost

Sometimes we wish we could stop time and hold on to all the joyful and meaningful moments in our lives. But each of our moments, times, and days are unique. We can't repeat them or go back to them. However, we can remember them with good feelings in our hearts. And we can honor these experiences and the people who were part of them by learning from them, thanking God for them, and keeping them with us always in our memories.

Activity List some joyful and meaningful times and places, or faith-filled experiences that you would have liked to hold on to forever. How did these affect you? What did you learn from them? How can you continue to keep them with you?

BELIEVING...

Descent of the Holy Ghost by Pieter Coecke van Aelst (1502–1550)

On Pentecost we celebrate the coming of the Holy Spirit to Jesus' first disciples.

For three years, Jesus was with his disciples as their leader and their teacher. They witnessed his powerful love, his forgiveness of sins, and his miracles. He gradually showed them who he was, revealing his humanity and divinity. Then, after his death and Resurrection, he appeared to them, risen and glorified. And forty days after his Resurrection, Jesus Christ ascended to his Father in heaven. No doubt, the disciples wished they could hold on to all their moments with Jesus forever! But they didn't need to worry because, just before he ascended into heaven, Christ had assured them that he would be with them always—not physically, and not just in their memories of him, but *through the Holy Spirit*. Christ said that the Holy Spirit would teach them everything they needed to know to continue his work on earth. He told them to return to Jerusalem to await the Holy Spirit.

So, the first disciples of Jesus Christ, together with his mother, Mary, went to an upper room in Jerusalem, fearful and unsure of what to do next. Yet the Holy Spirit came upon them as Christ had promised. The Holy Spirit created them anew so that they could build up the community of disciples and renew the earth in God's love. Immediately they began to proclaim the good news of Christ to all the people gathered in Jerusalem. Even though these people did not all speak the same language, they all understood the good news. And, that very day, about 3,000 people were baptized.

Who was this Holy Spirit that enabled the disciples to do such things? The Holy Spirit is the third Person of the *Blessed Trinity*, the one God in three Persons—Father, Son, and Holy Spirit. The third Person of the one God, the Holy Spirit has been present throughout time, with the Father and the Son. It was through the power of the Holy Spirit that Jesus Christ, the Son of God, shared the life of God with all people and saved them from sin. It was also through the power of the Holy Spirit that Jesus taught, healed, and worked miracles. Everything that Jesus Christ said and did, he said and did with the strength and guidance of the Holy Spirit. The Holy Spirit is our helper and guide, who inspires faith within us and gives us the power to live by it. The Holy Spirit helps us to become holy by making the truth clear to us, reminding us of Jesus' teachings, helping us to understand God's word, and helping us to do good works and avoid sin.

On Pentecost Sunday—the last and final Sunday of the Easter season—the Church celebrates, with great joy, the Gift of the Holy Spirit. We celebrate the coming of the Holy Spirit to the first disciples. We also celebrate the beginning of the Church, and we rejoice because the Holy Spirit fills our hearts today.

Activity Find the prayer to the Holy Spirit on page 305. Make a poster that includes this prayer, or lines from it, as its focal point. Use the liturgical color for Pentecost (see page 299) in your poster. Decorate and display your poster, in the parish church or center, if possible, in preparation for Pentecost Sunday.

On Pentecost we celebrate the Holy Spirit's presence in the Church today.

The fiftieth day after Passover was a harvest festival for the Jewish people. It was called Pentecost since the word *Pentecost* comes from a Greek word meaning "fiftieth." And today Pentecost Sunday is celebrated fifty days after Easter, for it was during this feast that the Holy Spirit came to Jesus' first disciples.

The liturgical color for Pentecost is red, recalling that the Holy Spirit came to the first disciples in the form of "tongues as of fire, which parted and came to rest on each one of them" (Acts of the Apostles 2:3). Red also represents the love that the Holy Spirit spreads throughout the world through the prayers and actions of Jesus' followers.

In the liturgy of Pentecost Sunday we sing or recite the sequence for Pentecost. A *sequence* is a special hymn that is used in the liturgy of an important celebration. There are four days on which we sing a sequence: Easter Sunday, Pentecost Sunday, the Solemnity of the Most Holy Body and Blood of Christ, and the memorial of Our Lady of Sorrows. The words of each sequence express joy over the events that are celebrated on that day. The sequence is sung, or may be read, immediately after the second reading in the Liturgy of the Word.

The sequence for Pentecost Sunday is *Veni, Sancte Spiritus*, which is Latin for "Come, Holy Spirit." The verses of this sequence contain many different titles for the Holy Spirit. Each title can give us insights about the presence and the action of the Holy Spirit in our lives. Below are a few of the sequence's titles for the Holy Spirit.

- Father of the poor
- Source of all our store (all that we have)
- Of comforters the best
- Soul's most welcome guest
- In our labor, rest most sweet
- Grateful coolness in the heat (in difficult times)
- Solace in the midst of woe (distress)
- Most blessed Light divine
- Sweet refreshment

The Holy Spirit is all of these and more. The Holy Spirit is sent to us as the great gift of the Father and the Son. In the Holy Spirit, we know that Christ and the Father are truly with us, here and now, right where we are. So, Pentecost is not simply a historical event that we commemorate every year. When we celebrate Pentecost, we are celebrating the coming of the Holy Spirit to the Church *today*. We celebrate the Holy Spirit's coming to each one of us as baptized members of the Church.

Activity How would you explain the Holy Spirit to someone who is learning about the Catholic faith?

RESPONDING...

✚ **Leader:** That the Holy Spirit, Father of the poor, will come to the aid of all those in need, let us pray:

All: Come, Holy Spirit, come!

Leader: That the Holy Spirit, Source of all our store, will fill us with wisdom and all the gifts we need to follow Christ more faithfully, let us pray:

All: Come, Holy Spirit, come!

Leader: That the Holy Spirit, Solace in the midst of woe, will strengthen us in sadness or sorrow, let us pray:

All: Come, Holy Spirit, come!

Leader: That the Holy Spirit, most blessed Light divine, will reconcile divisions in the world and lead us in the ways of justice and peace, let us pray:

All: Come, Holy Spirit, come!

Leader: Father in heaven,
fifty days have celebrated the fullness
of the mystery of your revealed love.
See your people gathered in prayer,
open to receive the Spirit's flame.
May it come to rest in our hearts
and disperse the divisions of word and tongue.

With one voice and one song
may we praise your name in joy and
thanksgiving.
Grant this through
Christ our Lord.

(alternate collect, Vigil Mass for Pentecost)

All: Come, Holy Spirit, come! Amen.

@✴ Visit www.weliveourfaith.com for additional prayers and activities.

Come, Holy Spirit

GATHERING...

"Help us to cherish the gifts that surround us, to share your blessings with our brothers and sisters, and to experience the joy of life in your presence."

(alternate collect, Seventeenth Sunday in Ordinary Time)

♪ **Psalm 98: All the Ends of the Earth**

Refrain:
All the ends of the earth have seen
the saving pow'r of God.
All the ends of the earth have seen
the saving power of God.

Verse:
The LORD has made his salvation known:
in the sight of the nations
he has revealed his justice.
He has remembered his kindness
and his faithfulness
toward the house of Israel. (Refrain)

Ordinary Time

We do not usually think of everyday life as something to be celebrated. But, if we pay attention, there is something to be celebrated, or at least to be thankful for, at each moment of our day. Upon waking, we can be thankful for our time of rest. Upon our first meal of the day, we can be joyful for having a healthy start. Upon beginning the schoolday, we can be grateful for the opportunity to learn. And upon doing our homework, we can celebrate that it will soon be finished!

In any case, no matter what the everyday event, we have an opportunity to recognize the blessings that we have been given.

Activity Write down your daily routine, and write a short prayer of thanksgiving that applies to each part of your day.

During Ordinary Time we celebrate every aspect of the life of Christ.

The Church sets aside a whole liturgical season to celebrate every aspect of the life of Christ, and thus the everyday life of each member of his Body, the Church. This season of celebrating everyday life—the season of Ordinary Time—is also the longest season of the Church year. The season of Ordinary Time has two parts. The first part is the time between the seasons of Christmas and Lent. The second part is the time between the seasons of Easter and Advent. All together, the season of Ordinary Time lasts almost half a year. This is a long time! Think of all that can happen in this time frame—both big events, such as weddings, funerals, vacations, or family reunions, and more commonplace events, such as time spent with friends, meals shared with family, or assemblies at school. What Ordinary Time allows us to do is to celebrate Jesus' love and presence not only in the big events, but in the everyday ones, too.

The days of Ordinary Time, especially its Sundays, "are devoted to the mystery of Christ in all its aspects" (*General Norms for the Liturgical Year and the Calendar*, 43). As we celebrate every aspect of the life of Christ—his conversations with his disciples, his teachings, his healings, his times of prayer, his joys and sorrows—we realize that we can find new hope in celebrating our own lives. We can find in Jesus' teachings words of wisdom for our lives each day. We can recognize that Jesus is with us today just as he was with his disciples when he walked from town to town with them. During Ordinary Time, we realize that we do not live our everyday lives alone, but with Jesus—every minute of every day.

The purpose of Ordinary Time is to celebrate Christ in every way: his life, his teachings, his parables, his miracles. Sunday after Sunday, and each weekday too, we listen carefully to Scripture and learn from Jesus Christ and his teachings. We receive Christ's Body and Blood in the Eucharist and are strengthened to share his life with others in word and action.

Activity With your group make a projected timeline of the events, big and small, that may happen in your lives during the upcoming period of Ordinary Time. Together write a prayer to Jesus Christ asking him to help you and to share his love with you through all these events.

The celebration of Ordinary Time revolves around Sunday.

It is important to remember that the celebration of Ordinary Time revolves around Sunday, the day of Christ's Resurrection. The Sunday celebration has always been important in the life of the Church. Until the Resurrection, Saturday was considered to be the Sabbath day, or the Lord's Day, a day of rest set apart in honor of God. Sunday was considered to be the last day of the week, the seventh day. After Jesus' Resurrection, Sunday became the Lord's Day for Christians. Christians began counting it as "the first day" because Sunday recalled the beginning of the new creation in the risen Christ.

The third commandment, *Remember to keep holy the Lord's Day*, obliges us to take time out of our busy lives on Sunday to honor God with our community of faith. So, on Sunday, we rest from labor as best we can, spend time in leisure with our families and friends, and avoid making demands on others that would prevent them from observing the Lord's Day themselves. And we come together to celebrate the Paschal Mystery of Christ—his suffering, death, Resurrection, and Ascension—at Mass every Sunday (or at the Saturday night vigil Mass for Sunday).

This Sunday celebration of the Eucharist is the key element of Ordinary Time. Every week on the Sundays during Ordinary Time, we are celebrating the saving love of God expressed within our everyday lives, as we celebrate the death and Resurrection of Jesus and his continued presence under the appearances of bread and wine. Jesus gives us his own Body and Blood in the Eucharist. The risen Christ unites us to himself and one another. We come together as one family to rejoice in the great gift of life and the salvation that God has given us in Jesus Christ. Our Sunday celebration enables us to begin our week nourished by the presence of Christ, the Bread of Life. Everything else in our lives flows from the strength of that reality and that presence.

Activity Using a missalette or another liturgical resource, find the Scripture readings for this coming Sunday. As a group take turns reading them aloud. Ask for the Holy Spirit's help in understanding what you hear. Then discuss each reading. Recall this discussion when you listen to the readings and the homily at Sunday Mass. Be attentive for insights into the readings that you gain at Mass.

✝ **Leader:** Let us pray that we will be centered in the Lord during two of the everyday events in our lives: going out and coming home.

Reader 1: A Prayer for Going Out from Home Each Day:

Blessed are you, Lord, God of all creation:
you guide my footsteps.

Blessed are you, Lord, God of all creation:
you spread out the earth upon the waters.

Direct our steps to yourself, O God,
and show us how to walk in charity and peace.

All: Amen.

Reader 2: A Prayer for Coming Home Each Day:

Hear us, Lord,
and send your angel from heaven
to visit and protect,
to comfort and defend
all who live in this house.

Reader 3: May the Lord of peace give us peace
all the time and in every way.
The Lord be with us.

(Catholic Household Blessings and Prayers)

Leader: "The LORD will guard your coming and going both now and forever." (Psalm 121:8)

All: Amen.

@ **Visit www.weliveourfaith.com for additional prayers and activities.**

Glory to the Father

Glory to the Father, and to the Son,
   and to the Holy Spirit:
as it was in the beginning,
   is now, and will be for ever. Amen.

Our Father

Our Father, who art in heaven,
hallowed be thy name;
thy kingdom come;
thy will be done on earth
   as it is in heaven.
Give us this day our daily bread;
and forgive us our trespasses
as we forgive those
   who trespass against us;
and lead us not into temptation,
but deliver us from evil. Amen.

Hail Mary

Hail Mary, full of grace,
the Lord is with you;
blessed are you among women,
and blessed is the fruit
   of your womb, Jesus.
Holy Mary, Mother of God,
pray for us sinners,
now, and at the hour of our death.
Amen.

Prayer to Saint Joseph

Father,
you entrusted our Savior to the
   care of Saint Joseph.
By the help of his prayers
may your Church continue to serve
   its Lord, Jesus Christ,

who lives and reigns with you and
   the Holy Spirit,
one God, for ever and ever.
Amen.

Apostles' Creed

I believe in God, the Father Almighty,
   creator of heaven and earth.
I believe in Jesus Christ,
    his only Son, our Lord.
   He was conceived by the power
    of the Holy Spirit
    and born of the Virgin Mary.
He suffered under Pontius Pilate,
   was crucified, died, and was buried.
He descended to the dead.
On the third day he rose again.
He ascended into heaven,
   and is seated at the right hand
    of the Father.

He will come again to judge
   the living and the dead.

I believe in the Holy Spirit,
   the holy catholic Church,
   the communion of saints,
   the forgiveness of sins,
   the resurrection of the body,
   and the life everlasting. Amen.

Prayer to the Holy Spirit

Come, Holy Spirit, fill the hearts
   of your faithful.
And kindle in them the fire
   of your love.

Send forth your Spirit and they
   shall be created.
And you will renew the face
   of the earth.

Nicene Creed

We believe in one God,
   the Father, the Almighty,
   maker of heaven and earth,
   of all that is, seen and unseen.

We believe in one Lord, Jesus Christ,
   the only Son of God
   eternally begotten of the Father,
   God from God, Light from Light,
   true God from true God,
   begotten, not made, one in Being
      with the Father.
   Through him all things were made.
   For us men and for our salvation
      he came down from heaven:
   by the power of the Holy Spirit
      he was born of the Virgin Mary,
         and became man.

For our sake he was crucified
      under Pontius Pilate;
   he suffered, died, and was buried.
   On the third day he rose again
      in fulfillment of the Scriptures;
   he ascended into heaven
      and is seated at the right hand
         of the Father.
   He will come again in glory to judge
         the living and the dead,
      and his kingdom will have no end.

We believe in the Holy Spirit, the Lord,
      the giver of life,
   who proceeds from the Father
      and the Son.
   With the Father and the Son he is
      worshiped and glorified.
   He has spoken through the Prophets.

We believe in one holy catholic
      and apostolic Church.
   We acknowledge one baptism
      for the forgiveness of sins.
   We look for the resurrection
      of the dead,
         and the life of the
            world to come.
         Amen.

Act of Contrition

My God,
I am sorry for my sins with all my heart.
In choosing to do wrong
and failing to do good,
I have sinned against you
whom I should love above all things.
I firmly intend, with your help,
to do penance,
to sin no more,
and to avoid whatever leads me to sin.
Our Savior Jesus Christ
suffered and died for us.
In his name, my God, have mercy. Amen.

The Divine Praises

Blessed be God.
Blessed be his holy name.
Blessed be Jesus Christ, true God and true man.
Blessed be the name of Jesus.
Blessed be his most sacred heart.
Blessed be his most precious blood.
Blessed be Jesus in the most holy sacrament of
   the altar.
Blessed be the Holy Spirit, the Paraclete.
Blessed be the great mother of God, Mary most
   holy.
Blessed be her most holy and immaculate
   conception.
Blessed be her glorious assumption.
Blessed be the name of Mary, virgin and mother.
Blessed be Saint Joseph, her most chaste spouse.
Blessed be God in his angels and in his saints.

The Precepts of the Church
(from *CCC*, 2041–2043)

1. You shall attend Mass on Sundays and holy days of obligation and rest from servile labor.
2. You shall confess your sins at least once a year.
3. You shall receive the sacrament of the Eucharist at least during the Easter season.
4. You shall observe the days of fasting and abstinence established by the Church.
5. You shall help provide for the needs of the Church.

The Rosary

A rosary is made up of groups of beads arranged in a circle. It begins with a cross followed by one large bead and three small ones. The next large bead (just before the medal) begins the first "decade." Each decade consists of one large bead followed by ten smaller beads.

Begin the rosary with the Sign of the Cross. Recite the Apostles' Creed. Then pray one Our Father, three Hail Marys, and one Glory to the Father.

To pray each decade, say an Our Father on the large bead and a Hail Mary on each of the ten smaller beads. Close each decade by praying the Glory to the Father. Pray the Hail, Holy Queen as the last prayer of the rosary.

The mysteries of the rosary are special events in the lives of Jesus and Mary. As you pray each decade, think of the appropriate Joyful Mystery, Sorrowful Mystery, Glorious Mystery, or Mystery of Light.

The Five Joyful Mysteries

1. The Annunciation
2. The Visitation
3. The Birth of Jesus
4. The Presentation of Jesus in the Temple
5. The Finding of Jesus in the Temple

The Five Sorrowful Mysteries

1. The Agony in the Garden
2. The Scourging at the Pillar
3. The Crowning with Thorns
4. The Carrying of the Cross
5. The Crucifixion and Death of Jesus

The Five Glorious Mysteries

1. The Resurrection
2. The Ascension
3. The Descent of the Holy Spirit upon the Apostles
4. The Assumption of Mary into Heaven
5. The Coronation of Mary as Queen of Heaven

The Five Mysteries of Light

1. Jesus' Baptism in the Jordan
2. The Miracle at the Wedding at Cana
3. Jesus Announces the Kingdom of God
4. The Transfiguration
5. The Institution of the Eucharist

Stations of the Cross

From the earliest days of the Church, Christians remembered Jesus' life and death by visiting and praying at the places where Jesus lived, suffered, died, and rose from the dead.

As the Church spread to other countries, not everyone could travel to the Holy Land. So local churches began inviting people to "follow in the footsteps of Jesus" without leaving home. "Stations," or places to stop and pray, were made so that stay-at-home pilgrims could "walk the way of the cross" in their own parish churches. We do the same today, especially during Lent.

There are fourteen "stations," or stops. At each one, we pause and think about what is happening at the station.

1. Jesus is condemned to die.
2. Jesus takes up his cross.
3. Jesus falls the first time.
4. Jesus meets his mother.
5. Simon helps Jesus to carry his cross.
6. Veronica wipes the face of Jesus.
7. Jesus falls the second time.
8. Jesus meets the women of Jerusalem.
9. Jesus falls the third time.
10. Jesus is stripped of his garments.
11. Jesus is nailed to the cross.
12. Jesus dies on the cross.
13. Jesus is taken down from the cross.
14. Jesus is laid in the tomb.

The Canticle of Mary, the Magnificat

"My soul proclaims the greatness of the Lord;
    my spirit rejoices in God my savior.
For he has looked upon his handmaid's lowliness;
    behold, from now on all ages will call me
      blessed.
The Mighty One has done great things for me,
    and holy is his name.
His mercy is from age to age
    to those who fear him.
He has shown might with his arm,
    dispersed the arrogant of mind and heart.
He has thrown down the rulers from their thrones
    but lifted up the lowly.
The hungry he has filled with good things;
    the rich he has sent away empty.
He has helped Israel his servant,
    remembering his mercy,
according to his promise to our fathers,
    to Abraham and to his descendants forever."

(Luke 1:46–55)

The Angelus

The angel spoke God's message to Mary,
and she conceived of the Holy Spirit.
Hail Mary …

"I am the lowly servant of the Lord:
let it be done to me according to your word."
Hail Mary …

And the Word became flesh
and lived among us.
Hail Mary …

Pray for us, holy Mother of God,
that we may become worthy of the
    promises of Christ.

Let us pray.
Lord,
fill our hearts with your grace:
once, through the message of an angel
you revealed to us the Incarnation of your Son;
now, through his suffering and death
lead us to the glory of his resurrection.
We ask this through Christ our Lord.
Amen.

Act of Faith

O God, we believe in all that Jesus has taught
    us about you.
We place all our trust in you
    because of your great love for us.

Act of Hope

O God, we never give up on your love.
We have hope and will work for your kingdom
    to come and for a life that lasts forever
      with you in heaven.

Act of Love

O God, we love you above all
things. Help us to love
ourselves and one another as
Jesus taught us to do.

Prayer Before Communion

Jesus,
you are God-with-us,
especially in this Sacrament
of the Eucharist.
You love me as I am
and help me to grow.

Come and be with me
in all my joys and sorrows.
Help me share your peace and love
with everyone I meet.

The Mass

Introductory Rites

Entrance Chant: Altar servers, readers, the deacon, and the priest celebrant process forward to the altar. The assembly sings as this takes place. The priest and deacon kiss the altar and bow out of reverence.

Greeting: The priest and assembly make the sign of the cross, and the priest reminds us that we are in the presence of Jesus.

Act of Penitence: Gathered in God's presence the assembly sees its sinfulness and proclaims the mystery of God's love. We ask for God's mercy in our lives.

Gloria: On some Sundays we sing or say this ancient hymn.

Collect: This prayer expresses the theme of the celebration and the needs and hopes of the assembly.

Liturgy of the Word

First Reading: This reading is usually from the Old Testament. We hear of God's love and mercy for his people before the time of Christ. We hear stories of hope and courage, wonder and might. We learn of God's covenant with his people and of the ways they lived his law.

Responsorial Psalm: After reflecting in silence as God's word enters our hearts, we thank God for the word we just heard.

Second Reading: This reading is usually from the New Testament letters, the Acts of the Apostles, or the Book of Revelation. We hear about the first disciples, the teachings of the Apostles, and the beginning of the Church.

Alleluia or Gospel Acclamation: We stand to sing the Alleluia or other words of praise. This shows we are ready to hear the good news of Jesus Christ.

Gospel: The deacon or priest proclaims a reading from the Gospel of Matthew, Mark, Luke, or John. This reading is about the mission and ministry of Jesus. Jesus' words and actions speak to us today and help us to know how to live as his disciples.

Homily: The priest or deacon talks to us about the readings. His words help us understand what God's word means to us today. We learn what it means to believe and be members of the Church. We grow closer to God and one another.

Profession of Faith: The whole assembly prays together the Nicene Creed (p. 306) or the Apostles' Creed (p. 305). We are stating aloud what we believe as members of the Church.

Prayer of the Faithful: We pray for the needs of all God's people.

Liturgy of the Eucharist

Preparation of the Gifts: The altar is prepared by the deacon and the altar servers. We offer gifts. These gifts include the bread and wine and the collection for the Church and for those in need. As members of the assembly carry the bread and wine in a procession to the altar, we sing. The bread and wine are placed on the altar.

Prayer Over the Offerings: The priest asks God to bless and accept our gifts. We respond, "Blessed be God for ever."

Eucharistic Prayer: This is the most important prayer of the Church. It is our greatest prayer of praise and thanksgiving. It joins us to Christ and to one another. The beginning of this prayer, the **Preface**, consists of offering God thanksgiving and praise. We sing together the hymn "Holy, Holy, Holy." The rest of the prayer consists of: calling on the Holy Spirit to bless the gifts of bread and wine; the consecration of the bread and wine, recalling Jesus' words and actions at the Last Supper; recalling Jesus' passion, death, Resurrection, and Ascension; remembering that the Eucharist is offered by the Church in heaven and on earth; praising God and praying a great "Amen" in love of God: Father, Son, and Holy Spirit.

Communion Rite: This is the third part of the Liturgy of the Eucharist. It includes the:

Lord's Prayer: Jesus gave us this prayer that we pray aloud or sing to the Father.

Rite of Peace: We pray that Christ's peace be with us always. We offer one another a sign of peace to show that we are united in Christ.

Breaking of the Bread: We say aloud or sing the Lamb of God, asking Jesus for his mercy, forgiveness, and peace. The priest breaks apart the Host, and we are invited to share in the Eucharist.

Holy Communion: We are shown the Host and hear "The Body of Christ." We are shown the cup and hear "The Blood of Christ." Each person responds "Amen" and receives Holy Communion. While people are receiving Holy Communion, we sing as one. After this we silently reflect on the gift of Jesus and God's presence with us. The priest then prays that the gift of Jesus will help us live as Jesus' disciples.

Concluding Rites

Greeting: The priest offers the final prayer. His words serve as a farewell promise that Jesus will be with us all.

Blessing: The priest blesses us in the name of the Father, Son, and Holy Spirit. We make the sign of the cross as he blesses us.

Dismissal: The deacon or priest sends us out to love and serve God and one another. The priest and deacon kiss the altar. They, along with others serving at the Mass, bow to the altar, and process out as we sing the closing song.

Introducing . . . the Bible

The Bible is a collection of seventy-three books written under the inspiration of the Holy Spirit. The Bible is divided into two parts: the Old Testament and the New Testament. In the forty-six books of the Old Testament, we learn about the story of God's relationship with the people of Israel. In the twenty-seven books of the New Testament, we learn about the story of Jesus Christ, the Son of God, and of his followers.

The word *Bible* comes from the Greek word *biblia*, which means "books." Most of the books of the Old Testament were originally written in Hebrew, the New Testament in Greek. In the fifth century, a priest and scholar named Saint Jerome translated the books of the Bible into Latin, the common language of the Church at the time. Saint Jerome also helped to establish the *canon*, or the Church's official list, of the books of the Bible. Many centuries later, in 1384, the first translation of the Bible into English was completed.

The chart below lists the sections and books of the Bible. It also shows abbreviations commonly given for the names of the books in the Bible.

OLD TESTAMENT

Pentateuch ("Five Scrolls")

These books tell about the formation of the covenant and describe basic laws and beliefs of the Israelites.

Genesis (Gn)
Exodus (Ex)
Leviticus (Lv)
Numbers (Nm)
Deuteronomy (Dt)

Historical Books

These books deal with the history of Israel.

Joshua (Jos)
Judges (Jgs)
Ruth (Ru)
1 Samuel (1 Sm)
2 Samuel (2 Sm)
1 Kings (1 Kgs)
2 Kings (2 Kgs)
1 Chronicles (1 Chr)
2 Chronicles (2 Chr)
Ezra (Ezr)
Nehemiah (Neh)
Tobit (Tb)
Judith (Jdt)
Esther (Est)
1 Maccabees (1 Mc)
2 Maccabees (2 Mc)

Wisdom Books

These books explain God's role in everyday life.

Job (Jb)
Psalms (Ps)
Proverbs (Prv)
Ecclesiastes (Eccl)
Song of Songs (Song)
Wisdom (Wis)
Sirach (Sir)

Prophetic Books

These books contain writings of the great prophets who spoke God's word to the people of Israel.

Isaiah (Is)
Jeremiah (Jer)
Lamentations (Lam)
Baruch (Bar)
Ezekiel (Ez)
Daniel (Dn)
Hosea (Hos)
Joel (Jl)
Amos (Am)
Obadiah (Ob)
Jonah (Jon)
Micah (Mi)
Nahum (Na)
Habakkuk (Hb)
Zephaniah (Zep)
Haggai (Hg)
Zechariah (Zec)
Malachi (Mal)

NEW TESTAMENT

The Gospels

These books contain the message and key events in the life of Jesus Christ. Because of this, the Gospels hold a central place in the New Testament.

Matthew (Mt)
Mark (Mk)
Luke (Lk)
John (Jn)

Letters

These books contain letters written by Saint Paul and other leaders to individual Christians or to early Christian communities.

Romans (Rom)
1 Corinthians (1 Cor)
2 Corinthians (2 Cor)
Galatians (Gal)
Ephesians (Eph)
Philippians (Phil)
Colossians (Col)
1 Thessalonians (1 Thes)
2 Thessalonians (2 Thes)
1 Timothy (1 Tim)
2 Timothy (2 Tim)
Titus (Ti)
Philemon (Phlm)
Hebrews (Heb)
James (Jas)
1 Peter (1 Pt)
2 Peter (2 Pt)
1 John (1 Jn)
2 John (2 Jn)
3 John (3 Jn)
Jude (Jude)

Other Writings

Acts of the Apostles (Acts)
Revelation (Rv)

Finding Your Way Through the Bible

The Bible is divided into books, which are divided into chapters, which are divided into verses. Below is a page of the Bible with these parts labeled.

Book

Chapter

Verse

Matthew, 13   28

The Demand for a Sign 38 *r* *Then some of the scribes and Pharisees said to him, "Teacher, we wish to see a sign from you." 39 *He said to them in reply, "An evil and unfaithful generation seeks a sign, but no sign will be given it except the sign of Jonah the prophet. 40 *Just as Jonah was in the belly of the whale three days and three nights, so will the Son of Man be in the heart of the earth three days and three nights. 41 *At the judgment, the men of Nineveh will arise with this generation and condemn it, because they repented at the preaching of Jonah; and there is something greater than Jonah here. 42 *s* At the judgment the queen of the south will arise with this generation and condemn it, because she came from the ends of the earth to hear the wisdom of Solomon; and there is something greater than Solomon here.

The Return of the Unclean Spirit 43 *t* *"When an unclean spirit goes out of a person it roams through arid regions searching for rest but finds none. 44 Then it says, 'I will return to my home from which I came.' But upon returning, it finds it empty, swept clean, and put in order. 45 Then it goes and brings back with itself seven other spirits more evil than itself, and they move in and dwell there; and the last condition of that person is worse than the first. Thus it will be with this evil generation."

The True Family of Jesus 46 *u* *While he was still speaking to the crowds, his mother and his brothers appeared outside, wishing to speak with him. [47 *Someone told him, "Your mother and your brothers are standing outside, asking to speak with you."] 48 But he said in reply to the one who told him, "Who is my mother? Who are my brothers?" 49 And stretching out his hand toward his disciples, he said, "Here are my mother and my brothers. 50 For whoever does the will of my heavenly Father is my brother, and sister, and mother."

CHAPTER 13

The Parable of the Sower 1 *v* *On that day, Jesus went out of the house and sat down by the sea. 2 Such large crowds gathered around him that he got into a boat and sat down, and the whole crowd stood along the shore. 3 *And he

Passage title
Titles are sometimes added to show the themes of the chapters, but these titles are not part of the actual words of the Bible.

Passage
A passage is a section of a chapter made up of a number of verses.

This passage shows Matthew 12:46–50, which means: the Gospel of Matthew, chapter twelve, verses forty-six to fifty.

Chapter number

When you are given a Scripture passage to read, here are five easy steps that will help you to find it! Follow these steps to look up the passage given in the example below.

Example: Lk 10:21–22

1 **Find the book.** When the Scripture passage that you're looking up contains an abbreviation, find the name of the book for which this abbreviation stands. You can find this information in the chart at left or on the contents pages at the beginning of your Bible.

2 **Find the page.** Your Bible's contents pages will also indicate the page on which the book begins. Turn to that page within your Bible.

3 **Find the chapter.** Once you arrive at the page where the book begins, keep turning the pages forward until you find the right chapter. The image above shows you how a chapter number is usually displayed on a typical Bible page.

4 **Find the verses.** Once you find the right chapter, locate the verse or verses you need within the chapter. The image above also shows you how verse numbers will look on a typical Bible page.

5 **Start reading!**

absolute monarchs (p. 145) the kings and queens of Europe in the 1600s–1700s who had complete, or absolute, power over all aspects of the lives of their people, even the religion the people were to practice

actual graces (p. 229) the urgings or promptings from the Holy Spirit that help us to do good and to deepen our relationship with Christ

adultery (p. 57) infidelity in marriage, unfaithfulness to one's husband or wife

antipope (p. 120) not the true pope

atheism (p. 45) a sin against the first commandment in which one rejects or denies God's existence

blasphemy (p. 46) a thought, word, or act that makes fun of or shows contempt or hatred for God, the Church and the saints, or sacred objects

chastity (p. 57) the virtue by which we use our human sexuality in a responsible and faithful way

Church (p. 15) the community of people who believe in Jesus Christ, have been baptized in him, and follow his teachings

Christendom (p. 110) the cultural and political atmosphere that came into existence during the High Middle Ages in Europe when nearly everyone was Catholic and Catholicism influenced every aspect of people's lives

common vocation (p. 250) our call from God to holiness and to evangelization

conclave (p. 184) the secret meeting in which the cardinals elect a new pope

conscience (p. 14) the ability to know the difference between good and evil, right and wrong

conversion (p. 35) turning back to God with all one's heart

Counter-Reformation (p. 131) the period in history in which the Church began a substantial program of reform which answered, or countered, the crisis begun by the Protestant Reformation

covet (p. 66) to wrongly desire someone or something

cursing (p. 46) calling on God to do harm to someone

Decalogue (p. 44) the Ten Commandments

deposit of faith (p. 249) all the truth contained in Scripture and Tradition that Christ revealed and entrusted to the Apostles and thus to their successors, the bishops, and to the entire Church

ecclesial (p. 99) of or relating to the Church

envy (p. 67) a feeling of sadness when someone else has the things we want for ourselves

eternal life (p. 15) a life of happiness with God forever

evangelical counsels (p. 98) poverty, chastity, and obedience

evangelize (p. 144) to proclaim the good news of Christ to people everywhere

excommunication (p. 109) a severe penalty imposed by the Church for serious sins against the Catholic religion; it brings exclusion from participation in the sacramental life of the Church

free will (p. 14) God's gift to human beings of the freedom and ability to choose what to do

Gentile (p. 80) non-Jewish

grace (p. 15) a participation, or a sharing, in God's life and friendship

Great Commandment (p. 44) "You shall love the Lord, your God, with all your heart, with all your soul, and with all your mind. This is the greatest and the first commandment. The second is like it: You shall love your neighbor as yourself." (Matthew 22:37–39)

Great Schism of the West (p. 120) a split in the Catholic Church that developed in the late 1300s when competing cardinals elected two new popes, each one claiming to be the real pope

greed (p. 67) an excessive desire to have or own things

holiness (p. 16) a participation in God's goodness and a response to God's love by the way that we live

human dignity (p. 14) the value and worth that we share because God created us in his image and likeness

humanism (p. 121) a Renaissance philosophy that placed an increased emphasis on the importance of the person

human sexuality (p. 57) the gift of being able to feel, think, choose, love, and act as the male or female person God created us to be

idolatry (p. 45) giving worship to a creature or thing instead of God

indulgence (p. 129) the remission of the temporal punishment due to sins already forgiven by God. Indulgences can be obtained from the Church for ourselves or for the souls in purgatory through certain good works and prayers.

justice (p. 64) respecting the rights of others and giving them what is rightfully theirs

Kingdom of God (p. 17) the power of God's love active in our lives and in our world

lay investiture (p. 109) illicit practice by secular leaders to invest, or empower, a Church leader with authority

lie (p. 65) to speak or act falsely with the intention of deceiving others

marks of the Church (p. 230) the four characteristics of the Church: one, holy, catholic, and apostolic

modesty (p. 66) the virtue by which we think, speak, act, and dress in ways that show respect for ourselves and others

monastery (p. 98) a place where monks or nuns live

monastic life (p. 98) a life dedicated to prayer, work, study, and the needs of society

moral decision-making (p. 24) the process by which we make choices between right and wrong, good and evil, eternal life and sin

natural law (p. 14) the law of God within us, which is known by human reason

New Commandment (p. 37) Jesus' teaching that we are to love one another as he loves us

original sin (p. 14) the first sin committed by the first human beings

papal infallibility (p. 164) the divine guarantee that the pope's official statements of doctrine regarding faith and morals are free from error

Papal States (p. 157) a section of central Italy governed by the pope

parable (p. 218) a short story with a message

Paschal Mystery (p. 47) the suffering, death, Resurrection, and Ascension of Jesus Christ

perjury (p. 46) the act of making a false oath

pilgrimage (p. 108) a journey to a shrine or other holy place for spiritual and devotional reasons

plenary council (p. 174) a council to be attended by all the bishops of a specific country or region

poor in spirit (p. 67) depending on God and making God more important than anyone or anything else

prayer (p. 240) the raising of our minds and hearts to God

providence (p. 218) God's plan for and protection of all creation

pure of heart (p. 66) living in the love of God, our Father, just as his Son, Jesus Christ, calls us to do, and allowing the Holy Spirit to fill us with goodness and love

relativism (p. 186) the viewpoint that concepts such as right and wrong, good and evil, or truth and falsehood are not absolute but change from culture to culture and situation to situation

Renaissance (p. 121) a period marking the end of the Middle Ages and beginning of the Modern Age, characterized by a rediscovery of the cultures of ancient Greece and Rome and a revival of European culture

reverence (p. 46) honor, love, and respect

Sabbath (p. 47) a day set apart to rest and honor God

sacrament (p. 239) an effective sign given to us by Jesus Christ through which we share in God's life

sacred (p. 46) holy

sanctifying grace (p. 229) the grace that we receive in the sacraments

scribes (p. 44) scholars of the law during the time of Jesus

Shema (p. 44) a prayer from the Book of Deuteronomy reminding the Jewish people to love God with all their heart, soul, and strength

simony (p. 109) the buying and selling of spiritual things, spiritual services, or Church offices

social sin (p. 27) unjust situations and conditions that negatively impact society and its institutions

solidarity (p. 209) a virtue calling us to recognize that we are all one human family and that our decisions have consequences that reach around the world

stealing (p. 64) any action that unjustly takes away the property or rights of others

temperance (p. 66) a cardinal virtue that moderates the attraction of pleasures and helps us to bring our desires into balance

Temple (p. 44) the holy place in Jerusalem where Jewish people gathered to worship God

temptation (p. 66) an attraction to choose sin

Torah (p. 80) the sacred law of faith given by God to Moses

transubstantiation (p. 110) the term used to describe the changing of the bread and wine into the Body and Blood of Christ that takes place during the consecration of the Mass, by the power of the Holy Spirit through the words and actions of the priest

well-formed conscience (p. 25) a conscience that is educated so that it is able to recognize what is good and then direct us to act on that good

The following is a list of topics that appear in the pupil's text. Boldface indicates an entire chapter or section.

Photo Credits

Illustrator Credits